OS/2® Batch Files To Go

Ronny Richardson

Windcrest®/McGraw-Hill

New York San Francisco Washington, D.C. Auckland Bogotá
Caracas Lisbon London Madrid Mexico City Milan
Montreal New Delhi San Juan Singapore
Sydney Tokyo Toronto

FIRST EDITION
FIRST PRINTING

Published by Windcrest, an imprint of McGraw-Hill, Inc.
The name "Windcrest" is a registered trademark of McGraw-Hill, Inc.

Library of Congress Cataloging-in-Publication Data

Richardson, Ronny.
OS/2 batch files to go / by Ronny Richardson.
p. cm.
Includes index.
ISBN 0-07-052370-3 (paper) ISBN 0-07-052369-X (hard)
1. OS/2 (Computer file) 2. Electronic data processing—Batch processing. I. Title.
QA76.76.063R5435 1994
005.4'469—dc20 93-31286
CIP

Editorial team: Brad Schepp, Acquisitions Editor
Kellie Hagan, Book Editor
Production team: Katherine G. Brown, Director
Patsy D. Harne, Layout
Ollie Harmon, Typesetting
Bonnie Marie Paulson, Typesetting
Cindi Bell, Proofreading
Jodi L. Tyler, Indexing
Design team: Jaclyn J. Boone, Designer
Brian Allison, Associate Designer
Paperbound cover design: Margaret Karczewski, Vienna, Va 4516
Textured paper background: Douglas M. Parks, Blue Ridge Summit, Pa. WP1

Contents

PART 2

SIMPLE BATCH FILE TOPICS

PART 3

INTERMEDIATE BATCH FILE TOPICS

PART 5

BATCH FILE APPLICATIONS AND UTILITIES

APPENDICES

Acknowledgments

Personally, I want to thank my wife Cicinda, my son Tevin, and my daughter Dawna for their support and patience. Because I have only a limited amount of time, some of the time I spent writing this book had to come from the time I would have spent with my family. They were all very understanding and supportive.

I got a lot of answers to my questions in the different OS/2 forums on CompuServe. Without the help I received from those forums, this book would have been more difficult to write and less complete than it now is. While I would hate to miss anyone, I want to especially thank Ron Beauchemin, George Fulk, Michael H. Galpin, Bill Hinkle, D. MacArthur, Peter G. Magid, Gary Murphy, Steven Obarowski, Srinivas Paruchuri, and Anthony Thomas. The local IBM people and OS/2 users group were also very helpful. I especially want to thank Raymond A. Greenfield.

If you haven't dealt with IBM lately, you might want to check them out. I've seen a very helpful and positive attitude in every IBM employee I've worked with on this book. If they keep it up, they'll teach Microsoft a thing or two.

Introduction

Your local bookstore has many books intended to introduce you to PC-compatible computers and the OS/2 operating system. All of these books spend a lot of time explaining OS/2. Then they usually spend about one chapter explaining the basics of batch file programs—if that much. One chapter is enough to convince you that batch files are powerful tools, but it isn't enough to teach you how to use batch files effectively, much less how to write really useful batch files.

Who this book is for

This book will help you learn to use the power of batch files. In writing this book, I'm assuming you have a general understanding of OS/2. You don't have to be a computer whiz, but you should know how to boot the computer, format a disk, how to erase and rename files, and generally how to use the graphical user interface. You should also know how to make, delete, and change directories on your hard disk. Finally, you should know how to access the OS/2 command line and enter some simple commands. In general, you should feel comfortable performing simple tasks using the OS/2 operating system. If this isn't the case, you should start with a general book first.

How this book is structured

This book covers one topic per chapter. Sometimes the topic involves one command, and other times it involves several commands. Most chapters include one or more example batch files.

The first time you read this book, you'll get much more from it if you're in front of a computer. As you read about each new topic, you should either enter and run the batch file or run the batch file from the disk that comes with this book. This is also an excellent time to experiment; you'll retain the information much longer if you try to modify it to your own needs. As you read about the various batch files, try to modify them to better suit your needs or perform some similar task that interests you. This is the best way to learn new material.

Special notes

The book has a number of brief portions of text that are marked with icons. These items are very important. Even if you're only skimming a chapter, you should read these. You'll find the following different types of messages:

- Note--this is a general point of interest.
- Remember this--it's an important point that can cause minor problems if you forget it.
- Hint--this is a quick item that can save you time.
- Notice--this is important information on how batch files work.
- Warning! This is an important point that can cause you significant problems or loss of data if you aren't careful.

Hardware and software

Writing a computer book is difficult. I never know what type of hardware and software you have; I don't even know what version of the operating system you're using. In writing about batch files, I'm more fortunate than many writers. Most batch files will run on any hardware configuration that supports OS/2. While I wrote this book using a beta version of OS/2 2.1, most of the batch files should run under OS/2 2.*x* and many of them will run under even earlier versions of OS/2. For most of the examples in this book, I assume that the files supporting external commands like FORMAT and BACKUP are either in the current subdirectory or in the path when an example batch file requires one of these programs.

Writing the book

I wrote this book using a Gateway 2000 486/66 and printed everything on an HP Laserjet III. The word processor I used for everything except the batch files and tables was Microsoft Word 5.5. I modified the batch files and other ASCII files with the Enhanced Editor that's built into OS/2. Finally, I created all the tables using QuarkXPress for the Macintosh running the Tableworks extension. The screen shots were captured using the OS/2 Presentation Manager screen-capture program by Jürg Von Känel.

Conventions

Keep the following few important pieces of information in mind when reading this book:

- The numbered function keys on the keyboard are shown as F1 through F12. Most older keyboards have ten function keys on the left side of the keyboard, labeled from F1 to F10. Newer keyboards have twelve function keys, F1 to F12, generally along the top of the keyboard.
- Enter stands for the Enter or Return key, which can also be represented on the keyboard as Rtrn or a bent arrow. Most other named keys, like Del or Tab, are also referred to by their name. The directional keys are simply up, down, right, and left arrow.
- Information you type into the computer and pieces of programs broken out from the regular text is in an `alternate, monospaced typeface`. The names of keys you hit, like F6 or Enter, and explanatory text is in regular type.
- The caret symbol, ^, generally means that you hold down the Control, or Ctrl, key and then tap the following key. So ^Z means hold down the Ctrl key and press the Z key. This type of key combination is shown as both Ctrl–Z or ^Z.
- Any command inside brackets, [], is optional. Brackets are generally used when I'm giving the syntax for a command. In the following, for example:

  ```
  DIR [/P]
  ```

  the /P switch is optional. It causes the listing to pause each time the screen is full. Pressing any key restarts the listing.
- Variable information in a command, such as the drive letter or filename, will be shown in *italic*. If it's contained in a section of typed-in information, it will be in the *italic alternate typeface.*
- Most of the commands in this book in uppercase when shown on a command line. For the most part, OS/2 doesn't care. Entering DIR, dir, or DiR on the command line are all the same to OS/2. About the only time it matters is when you're using the equal sign to compare two strings.

Last notes

If this book causes you to develop a nice batch hint or raises a batch-related question not currently answered in the book, write to me in care of Windcrest and let me know. While I can't always respond to individual letters, your hint or question just might show up in the next edition of this book. The address is:

Ronny Richardson
c/o Windcrest/McGraw-Hill
Blue Ridge Summit, PA 17294-0850

Your letters will get to me much quicker if you make sure to include my name on the outside of the envelope and my name and the name of the book on the letter. If you're active in the on-line community, you can also reach me on CompuServe, where my address is 70322,3100.

I tested all the batch files in this book under a beta version of OS/2 2.1. Windcrest and I have done everything possible to ensure that the programs and batch files included with this book and on the disk do exactly what we claim they will do. Neither they nor I make any warranty of any type, expressed or implied, regarding the programs, batch files, and documentation included in this book and on the included disk. In addition, we aren't liable for incidental or consequential damages in connection with, or arising from, the performance of these programs and batch files.

PART 1
Batch file introduction

Before you learn to write batch files, these first chapters will help you understand more global issues relating to batch files.

Chapter 1: Writing OS/2 batch files Batch files are programs, so they need to be written as ASCII files. That's often difficult to do with a word processor, but OS/2's Enhanced Editor makes short work of writing batch files. This chapter explains how to use the OS/2 Enhanced Editor. It also explains how you can use your word processor to write batch files.

Chapter 2: Starting a batch file Under DOS, the only way to start a batch file is to enter its name on the command line. This works under OS/2, but as a graphical user interface OS/2 offers a second way—you can install the batch file as an icon and just click on that icon to run the batch file. This chapter explains how to use both methods to run a batch file.

Chapter 3: Using batch files Batch files have four major uses: keystroke reduction, new command construction, consistency, and safety. OS/2 can run three different types of batch files: DOS batch files, OS/2 batch files, and OS/2 REXX programs. This chapter explains these concepts in more detail.

Chapter 4: Batch file construction This chapter explains naming conventions and layout considerations you need to understand when you begin to write batch files.

When you finish these four chapters, you'll be able to consolidate one or more commands you would normally enter from the command-line prompt into a batch file.

1

Writing OS/2 batch files

Before you can begin to write batch files, you need a tool with which to do your writing. OS/2 comes with the perfect tool, its Enhanced Editor in the Productivity folder. This chapter presents a brief tutorial on starting and using the OS/2 Enhanced Editor. It concentrates on those features most useful for writing batch files. For more information on all its features, see your OS/2 documentation.

Before I cover the OS/2 Enhanced Editor, let me say a few words about alternatives. Almost any word processor or editor—no matter how simple or advanced it is—can be used to write batch files. Many batch files have been written under DOS with Edlin, one of the weakest and most difficult editors ever written. By the same token, I've written a number of batch files using Microsoft Word, one of the most powerful word processors available.

Batch files must be saved as unformatted text. Any editor or word processor that can save unformatted text (also called ASCII or plain text) can write batch files. If you aren't sure about your editor, try creating a small batch file with it and saving it as ASCII text. Then try to run that batch file. If it runs alright, then your editor is fine for writing batch files.

The Enhanced Editor is fairly powerful for an editor. It offers features like search and replace, move, word wrap, and multiple-file editing. In fact, if your needs are simple, you could use the Enhanced Editor for all your word processing. This chapter provides a tutorial for using the Enhanced Editor. If you're experienced with editors in general you might want to skip the first few sections in this chapter. If you plan on writing your batch files with your word processor or another editor, you might want to skip this chapter altogether.

It's ASCII

To help you understand the file format used by the Enhanced Editor, let's try an experiment first. Create a small file (say one or two paragraphs) with the word processor you normally use. Be sure to format all the text like you normally would. When you've finished, save the file and exit your word processor. Now drop out to the OS/2 command prompt and change to the subdirectory containing your file. Once you've done that, issue the command TYPE *myfile.txt*, substituting the name you used to save your file for *myfile.txt*.

This command will cause OS/2 to display the contents of your short file to the screen. You should see most of the text you entered in the file, but you should also see a lot of characters you didn't type. These characters contain the formatting information your word processor adds to the file. Some word processors, like Microsoft Word, add file-summary information to files, and you'll see these characters as well.

While this information is useful to your word processor and helps make your file look attractive when it's printed, it's poison to a batch file. Batch files must be saved containing the text you enter and nothing else. This format is called ASCII, which stands for American Standard Code for Information Interchange. ASCII files are sometimes called unformatted files. The Enhanced Editor creates ASCII files automatically. To see this, create a small file with the Enhanced Editor, save it, and then exit to the OS/2 command prompt and type that file to the screen with the command TYPE *myfile.txt*. This time, you won't see any extra characters.

Formatting commands are poison to a batch file.

Because of the Enhanced Editor's limited formatting abilities, it's not the best choice for serious word processing. However, the Enhanced Editor is one program where it's safe to format your batch files for printing because it stores all formatting information in the Extended Attributes file. In addition to writing batch files, it's great for editing system files like your CONFIG.SYS file, keeping simple to-do lists if the OS/2 ToDo program isn't to your liking, and for writing brief memos or notes to yourself. It's also a good way to view the documentation files that come with shareware packages, even if you have no intentions of making any modifications to these files.

Starting the Enhanced Editor

The Enhanced Editor is stored in the Productivity folder, which is stored inside the OS/2 System folder. The steps and illustrations in this and following sections assume that you've left the Enhanced Editor in that location. If you've moved it, you'll have to alter these steps. Figure 1-1 shows a typical OS/2 desktop. Move the mouse cursor to inside the OS/2 System icon (on the left near the top) and press the left mouse button twice very quickly. (Pressing the left mouse button twice very quickly is called *double clicking*.) This will open the OS/2 System folder. Your system should look something like the one shown in FIG. 1-2.

Next, move the mouse cursor over the Productivity folder and again double click the left mouse button. This will open the Productivity folder. Your system should look something like the one shown in FIG. 1-3. Move the mouse cursor over the Enhanced Editor icon and once again double click. This will open the editor with a blank file ready to accept characters. Figure 1-4 shows this.

I use the Enhanced Editor a lot so I created a shadow icon on the desktop itself to speed up starting the Enhanced Editor. To do this, click on the Enhanced Editor icon using the right mouse button and select Create shadow from the menu. When it asks you for a location, select the desktop.

➠ Make the Enhanced Editor a shadow on the desktop to quickly create and edit batch files.

Notice in FIG. 1-4 that there's a line =====Top of File===== at the top, and =====Bottom of File===== at the bottom. These are markers. You cannot

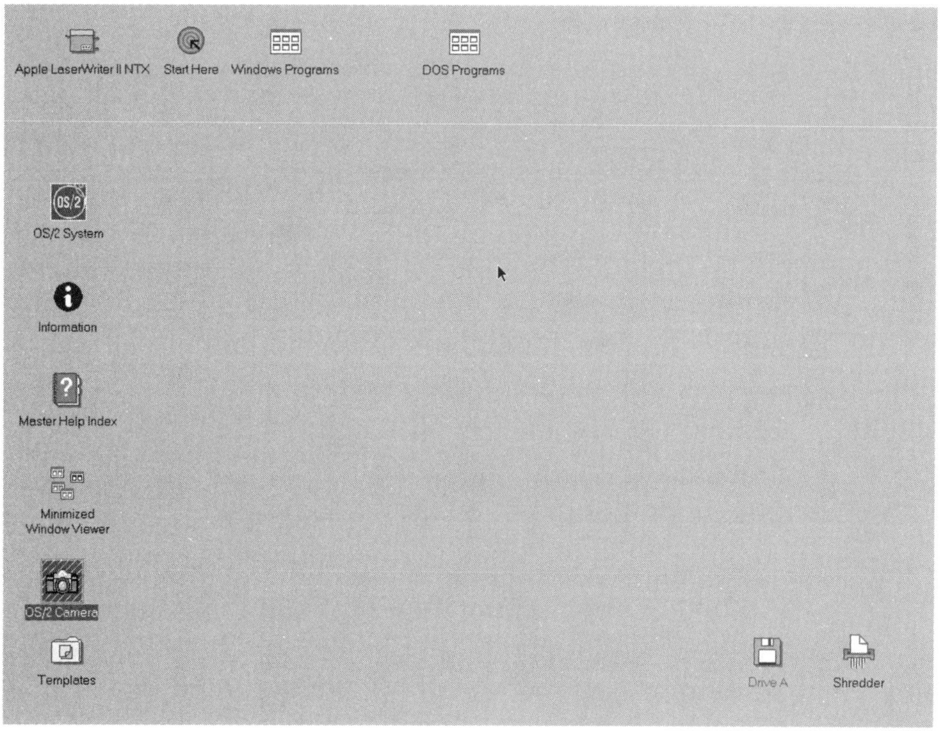

1-1 The opening OS/2 desktop.

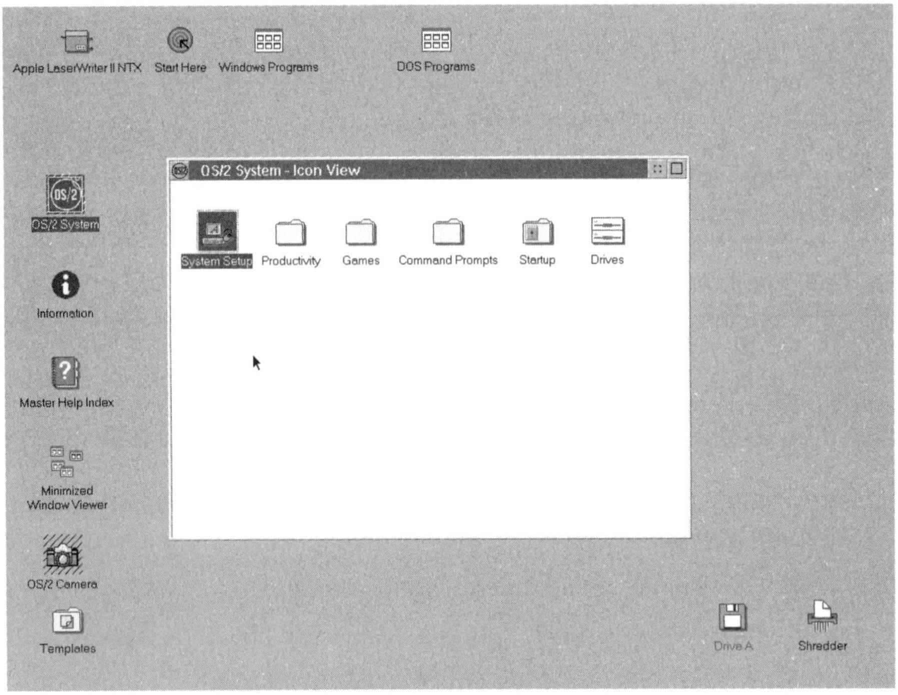

1-2 Opening the OS/2 System folder.

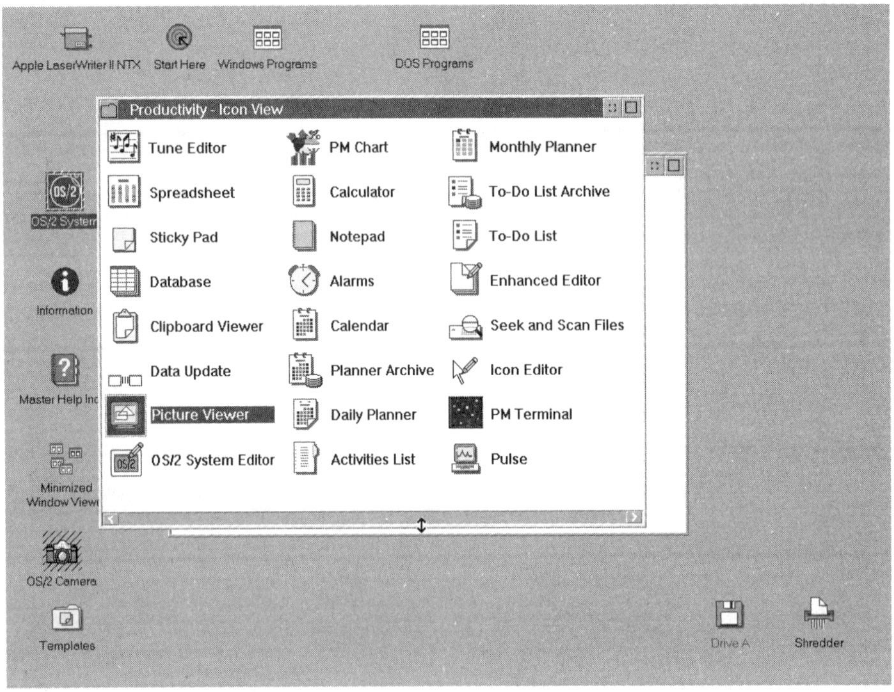

1-3 Opening the Productivity folder.

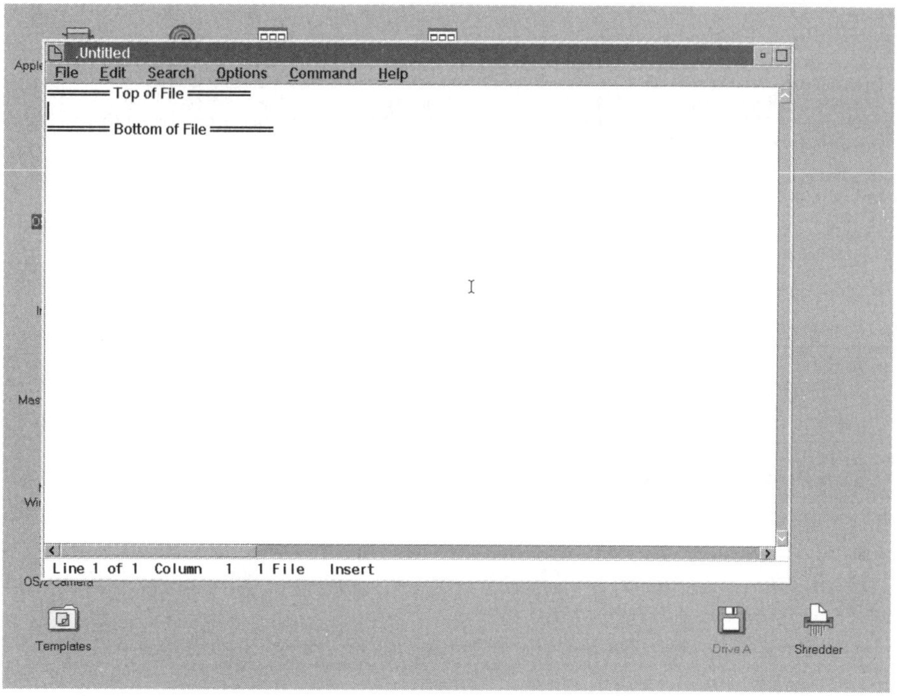

1-4 Opening a new file in the Enhanced Editor.

delete them and they aren't saved as part of the file you're creating. Also notice in FIG. 1-4 that the Enhanced Editor has a status line at the bottom of the screen, a menu along the top of the screen, and a title bar above the menu screen.

We'll explore the menu bar later but let's take a minute to review the status line at the bottom of the screen and the title at the top. Figure 1-5 shows the Enhanced Editor being used to edit an early draft of this chapter. At the time I captured this screen, I was editing line 67 of 67, so the file had 67 lines in it and I had the cursor on the last line of the file. The cursor was near the right side of the screen in column 110. I had only this one file loaded into memory so the status bar specified 1 File. I had the Enhanced Editor in insert mode so if I moved the cursor to the middle of the file and started typing, the new characters would be inserted rather than overwriting existing characters. Finally, the file had been modified since the last time I saved it, so the status line displayed Modified. From the top of the screen, you can see that the name of the file I was editing was D:\BOOK11\EDITOR.DOC.

Basic editing

If you haven't yet done so, start the editor so you can follow along with this example. Notice that there's a flashing vertical black line on the screen.

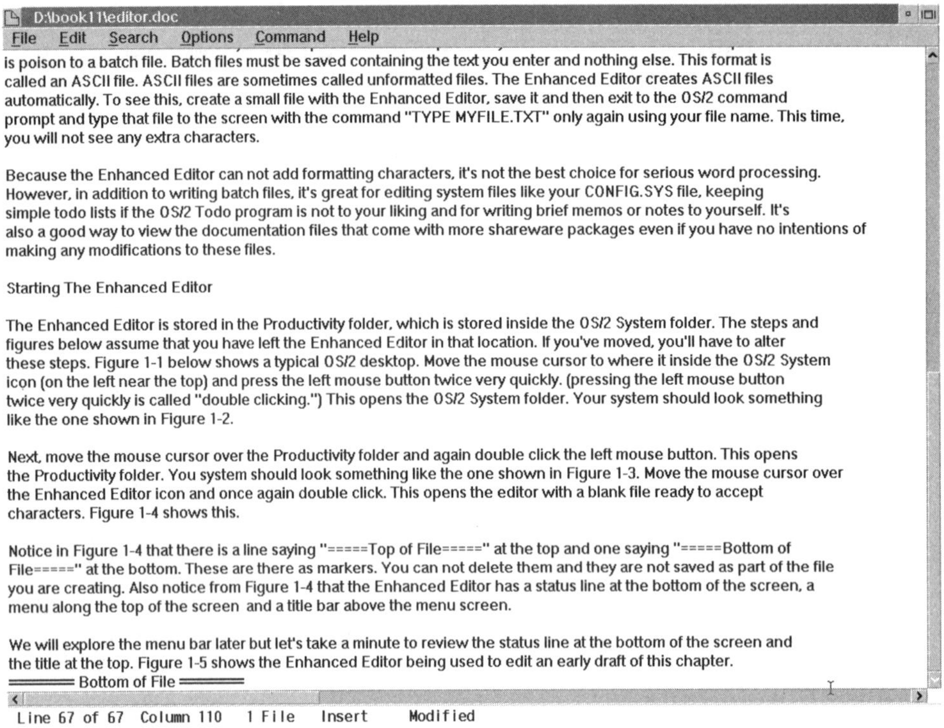

1-5 Editing a file with the Enhanced Editor.

This is the cursor. It's always located on the space where the next character will be inserted into the file. The line and column numbers on the status line refer to the position of this cursor.

One of your most common editing activities will be to move this cursor around to different locations in order to insert or delete text. The up, down, left, and right arrow keys move the cursor one space in the appropriate direction. The Control–left and Control–right cursor-key combinations moves the cursor one word in the appropriate direction. PgUp and PgDn move the file one page up or down. Ctrl–PgUp moves the cursor to the top of the current page and Ctrl–PgDn moves it to the bottom of the current page. Home moves the cursor to the beginning of the current line and End moves it to the end of the current line. Ctrl–Home moves the cursor to the beginning of the file and Ctrl–End moves it to the end of the file. Table 1-1 summarizes this information.

Moving the cursor around with these keys can be cumbersome when you need to move the cursor up twelve lines and over eight words. Fortunately, the Enhanced Editor has a speedier way. In addition to the text cursor, you should also see a mouse cursor. It looks like a large capital I with the top bars bent up and the bottom bars bent down. If you move it outside the editing area, it will change to an arrow. To move the text cursor quickly to any point on the screen, move the mouse cursor there and click once.

Table 1-1 The OS/2 Enhanced Editor cursor-movement keystrokes.

Keystroke	Action
End	Moves the cursor to the end of the line.
Home	Moves the cursor to the start of the line.
PgDn	Moves the cursor down one page.
PgUp	Moves the cursor up one page.
Down arrow	Moves the cursor down one line.
Up arrow	Moves the cursor up one line.
Left arrow	Moves the cursor to the left one character.
Right arrow	Moves the cursor to the right one character.
Ctrl–End	Moves the cursor to the end of the file.
Ctrl–Home	Moves the cursor to the beginning of the file.
Ctrl–PgDn	Moves the cursor to the bottom of the current page.
Ctrl–PgUp	Moves the cursor to the top of the current page.
Ctrl–left arrow	Moves the cursor to the left one word.
Ctrl–right arrow	Moves the cursor to the right one word.

You can also use the mouse cursor to easily scroll around the file. The small gray bar along the right side of the screen is called a *mouse elevator.* A smaller gray bar inside the mouse elevator indicates the current position in the file. Clicking above this bar works just like pressing PgUp while clicking below it is just like pressing PgDn. Notice that there's also a mouse elevator above the status bar for moving the file to the left or right when it's too wide to fit on a single screen.

Go ahead and create a four-line batch file by entering the following text using the Enhanced Editor, exactly as it's shown below:

```
ECHO This Is A Simple Batch File Example
ECHO The Name Of This File Is SAMPLE.CMD
ECHO You'll Use SAMPLE.CMD To Illustrate
ECHO Using The Enhanced Editor
```

Save the file by pressing the F2 key and using the name SAMPLE.CMD. This is a simple OS/2 batch file. The ECHO command causes the text that follows to be displayed on the screen. I'll cover the batch file commands in a later chapter so don't worry about it now; this is just sample text.

To insert text, move the text cursor to the left of *Batch* on the first line. Check the status bar to make sure the Enhanced Editor is in insert mode (if you see *Replace*, then press the Ins key to toggle to insert mode). Now type in OS/2. See how the text to the right of the cursor moves over to make room for the new text. Now move the cursor to the *You* on the third line and press the Ins key to toggle to overstrike mode. Notice that the *Insert* at the bottom of the screen changes to a *Replace*, and the text cursor changes to a black box that covers one character. That covered character is the one you want to replace. Type We to replace *You* and press the Del key to delete the remaining *u*.

As mentioned previously, the Del key is one way to delete characters. In replace mode (also called overstrike mode) pressing the Del key deletes the character inside the cursor. In insert mode, it deletes the character to the right of the text cursor. In either replace or insert modes, pressing the Backspace key deletes the character to the left of the text cursor key.

There are two other ways to delete text that are generally used on larger blocks of text. With both of these approaches, you begin by highlighting the text to delete. To highlight with the mouse cursor, move the mouse cursor to the first character to delete, press and hold the right mouse button, and drag the cursor to the last character to delete. As you do this, everything you're highlighting will be shown inside a black box. To highlight text with the cursor key, move the text cursor to the first character and hold down the Shift key while using any of the cursor-movement keys to move the text cursor to the last character to delete. Using either method, once the text is highlighted, you can press the Del key to delete it or simply begin typing. The first letter you type will be placed in the file and all the highlighted text will be automatically erased.

I should mention that some keyboards have trouble selecting text using the keyboard method. My Gateway 2000 computer will do it only if I use the cursor arrow keys next to the letters. The cursor pad on the far right will enter just numbers when you press the Shift key. If you have trouble with your keyboard, you might want to experiment by using different cursor keys, turning on the NumLock, and trying both Shift keys.

Intermediate editing

Like most OS/2 programs, there are two ways to access the menus. If you're using a mouse, the first thing you want to do is move the mouse cursor to the desired menu and click once. Then point to the option you want from a menu and click on it to execute it. You can also use the keyboard. First, press the Alt key, which will cause the File menu to be highlighted. Use the arrow key to highlight the desired menu and press Enter to bring up that menu. Then move the highlight to the desired option and press Enter. Figure 1-6 shows an early draft of this chapter with the File menu pulled down.

To save a file, pull down the File menu and select the Save option. Notice that this option has an F2 shown beside it. That indicates that pressing the F2 function key is a "keyboard shortcut" that lets you save a file quickly without working through all the menus. Any keyboard shortcut will be listed next to the menu option, like that for the Save command. If you use the Enhanced Editor a lot, you'll want to learn a few of the more common keyboard shortcut keys, as pressing F2 is the fastest way available to save a file.

☑ Keyboard shortcuts make quick work of the more common menu options.

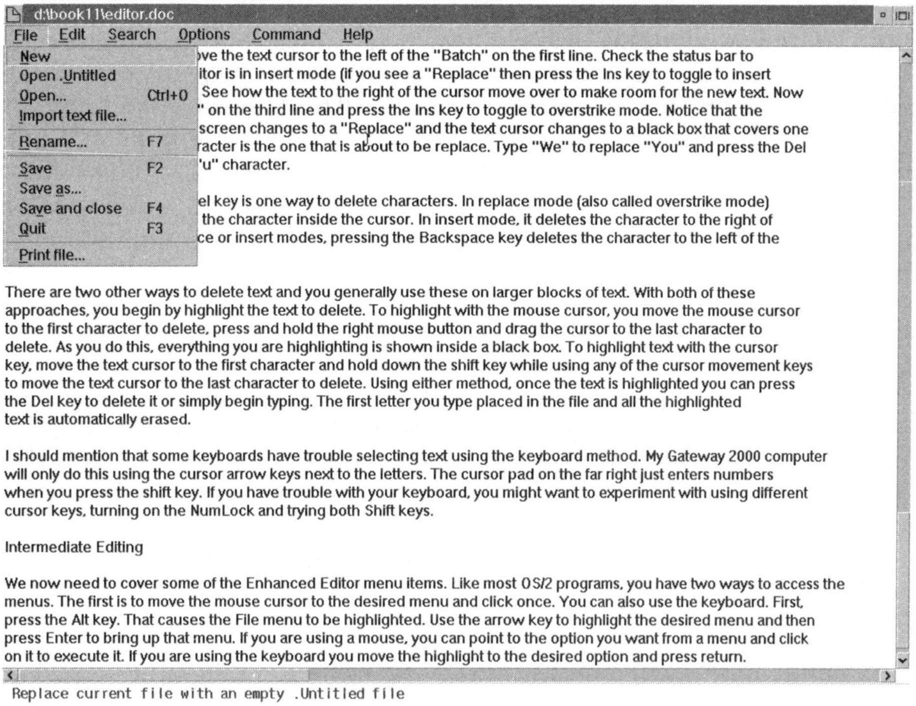

1-6 Using menus in the Enhanced Editor.

To open a file that already exists on the disk to either edit, print, or read, bring up the File menu and use the Open command. If you want to start a new file without having to exit the Enhanced Editor first, bring up the File menu and use the New command. The File menu offers the following additional commands:

New Removes the current file from memory before starting a new file.

Open.Untitled This command keeps the current file in memory and available for editing while starting a new file for you to work on.

Import text file This command inserts the contents of text file on disk into the current file at the cursor position. Think of it as a merge command.

Rename This lets you change the name of the file you are currently working on.

Save as This lets you save the current file to a new name on the disk.

Save and close This saves the current file and exits the Enhanced Editor.

Quit This exits the Enhanced Editor. If your file has been modified since the last time you saved it, the Enhanced Editor will warn you and give you the option of saving it first.

Print file This sends the current file to the printer.

The Edit menu is used primarily for working with blocks of text. Recall from the previous discussion that text can be selected using either the keyboard cursor keys or the mouse cursor. Once that block is selected, in addition to deleting it, you can use the Edit menu to operate on it. Selecting Copy from the Edit menu places a copy of the text in the paste buffer without disturbing the original text. The paste buffer is a special holding area for text. Only one block of text can exist in the paste buffer at a time so if there is already text in the paste buffer then selecting the Copy command replaces the text currently in the paste buffer with the highlighted text. If you select Cut rather than Copy, then the text is still placed in the paste buffer but it is also removed from the file.

Once there is text in the paste buffer, you can move the text cursor to any location you like and copy the text in the paste buffer to the file using the Paste command. Doing this does not disturb the text in paste buffer so you can make as many pastes of the same text as you like. Cutting and then pasting is how you move text around in the file. Copying and pasting is how you make copies of text in the file. The text remains in the paste buffer as you move between files (but not when you quit the Enhanced Editor) so this is an easy way to copy or transfer text between different files.

Another function of the Edit menu is to let you "undo" or reverse changes you have made. It offers two options for doing this, Undo line and Undo. The Undo line command lets you reverse any changes you have made to the current line. Once you move the cursor off the current line, the Undo line command no longer works. If you select the Undo line command by accident, you can select it again to reverse the undo operation.

The Undo command lets you undo commands even after you have moved off that line. When you select the Undo command, it brings up a dialog box with a mouse elevator. As you click on the mouse elevator, successive actions are reversed. You should be able to see the changes taking place on the screen underneath the dialog box. This box allows you to reverse multiple changes.

The Enhanced Editor offers search as well as search and replace. Go back to the original SAMPLE.CMD batch file and move the cursor to the top of the file with the Ctrl–Home command. Select the Search menu and then the Search command from that menu. This brings up a dialog box where you enter the text to search for and optionally, the text you want to replace it with. For practice, try searching for the text "name" without replacing it with anything. Once the Enhanced Editor locates the text, it draws a circle around it. Had you misspelled a command, you could have the Enhanced Editor go ahead and replace the misspelling with the proper spelling by entering it in the replace field. There are five option buttons for a search or search and replace:

Ignore cases This causes the Enhanced Editor to ignore capitalization so "Ronny" matches "RONNY" and "ronny."

Marked area If you highlighted text prior to entering the Search command, this causes the action you select to be confined to the highlighted area so text outside that area is unaffected.

Reverse search This causes it to search starting at the bottom of the file and going towards the top. The default is to start at the top.

Grep This is an advanced (and confusing) pattern matching option. If you're interested, check out the Help section.

Change all occurrences This makes all the changes for you without asking you about each one.

Once you have entered your search text and optionally your replace text, there are six different buttons at the bottom you can use to start the process:

Find This locates the next occurrence of the text you entered in the Search field.

Change This locates the next occurrence of the text you entered in the Search field and replaces it with the text you entered in the Replace field.

Change, then find This does exactly what the Change command does then it finds the next occurrence of the text you entered in the Search field.

Change, cancel This locates the next occurrence of the text you entered in the Search field and replaces it with the text you entered in the Replace field and then exits the Search dialog box.

Cancel This exits the Search dialog box without performing any action. Pressing Escape does the same thing.

Help This brings up the help menu. Pressing the F1 function key does the same thing.

While you have SAMPLE.CMD loaded, add the line "@ECHO OFF" to the top of the file and the line "PAUSE" as the last line in the file. These should be entered without the quotation marks. We will be using SAMPLE.CMD in the next chapter and these two changes will make it work better as an example. Their meaning will be explained later. The final batch file should look like this:

```
@ECHO OFF
ECHO This Is A Simple OS/2 Batch File Example
ECHO The Name Of This File Is SAMPLE.CMD
ECHO We'll Use SAMPLE.CMD To Illustrate
ECHO Using The Enhanced Editor
PAUSE
```

Advanced editing

Oftentimes, it's useful when writing a new batch file to have an existing batch file handy to look at to copy some of the syntax. The Enhanced Editor allows you to scroll between several different files. You can copy the commands you are interested in from the existing file and paste them into the new file. The Enhanced Editor also gives you several different ways that you can look at both files at once.

The first way is to put both files on the screen at once. To do that, first load the existing file into the Enhanced Editor. Move the mouse cursor to the very right of the screen. It will turn into a two-sided arrow. Press the left mouse button and drag the border to the middle of the screen. If you need to reposition the smaller screen, you can move the mouse cursor to the title bar and while holding down the left button, move the window to where you want it. Next, use the Open command to open the next file (or the New untitled command to start a new one) and use the same technique to size it and place it beside the original screen. Using this approach, you can look at both files at once. Use the mouse cursor to click on one or the other to make that screen the active screen for editing the file.

If you want to switch between different files for editing but don't need to see more than one at a time, then ring editing is a better approach since it lets you use the entire screen for one file. First, pull down the Options menu and move to the right of the Preferences menu. Move the cursor down to the Ring enabled menu and press return. Two buttons that look like rings will appear near the top right of the screen. Next, pull down the File menu. It will now have a new option, Add file. This lets you insert another file to edit into the ring of files. You use the Quit command from the File menu to remove the current file from the ring.

You have two different ways to switch between the various files in the ring. The first is to click on either of the two rings at the top of the screen. They move you in different directions through the ring. The second method is to use the List ring command from the Options menu. This lists the titles of all the files. To switch to one, highlight it and click on the Switch button.

Keeping it simple

If you find learning the Enhanced Editor too much just to create a few batch files and you are looking for something simpler, OS/2 has just the thing for you. It's called the System Editor. It's much like a stripped down Enhanced Editor. Under the File menu, you'll find New, Open, Save, Save as, and Autosave and nothing more. Under the Edit menu, you'll find an Undo button, the block commands of Cut, Copy and Paste, a Clear command to erase the highlighted block, and Find and Select all commands. The Option menu lets you set the color and font and turn word wrapping on and off. That's it, nice and simple.

Summary

This chapter has explained how to use many—but not all—of the features of the Enhanced Editor. Rather than trying to cover all of its features, I've concentrated on those you are most likely to use while creating and editing batch files. To learn about its remaining features, check on the on-line documentation for OS/2 or pick up a general-purpose OS/2 book.

2
Starting a batch file

OS/2 offers you two different ways to start your batch files. In this chapter, I'll show you both ways using the SAMPLE.CMD batch file created in chapter 1 as an example. If you didn't create SAMPLE.CMD while reading chapter 1, you'll find a copy of it on the disk included with this book. Just to refresh your memory, SAMPLE.CMD is shown below:

```
@ECHO OFF
ECHO This Is A Simple OS/2 Batch File Example
ECHO The Name Of This File Is SAMPLE.CMD
ECHO We'll Use SAMPLE.CMD To Illustrate
ECHO Using The Enhanced Editor
PAUSE
```

The function of these commands will be explained in detail later. Briefly, this batch file will display four lines of information and then wait until you press a key. At that point it will terminate.

Creating a subdirectory and modifying your path

You need to copy SAMPLE.CMD to a subdirectory that's in your path. As a general rule, it's a good idea to collect all your batch files together into a single subdirectory (I use \BAT on my system) and to include that subdirectory in your path.

To create a subdirectory in which to begin storing your batch files, open the OS/2 System folder and then the Command Prompts folder. Double click on the OS/2 Full Screen icon to get to the OS/2 command line. Move to the root directory with the CD\ command. Now create the subdirectory with the MD BAT command. You can change to this subdirectory with the CD\BAT command. Copy SAMPLE.CMD from its current location with the Copy command. Finally, enter EXIT to return to OS/2.

Now you need to add this subdirectory to your path command. Unlike DOS, OS/2 keeps its path command in its CONFIG.SYS file. This is stored in the root directory of the drive containing OS/2. Open this file with either the System Editor or the Enhanced Editor. You'll see a line for the path command. Append this new subdirectory by adding a ;C:\BAT to the end. Of course, you should use the drive and subdirectory appropriate to your system. This change will take effect the next time you start OS/2. You want to do this before going on to the next session.

Using a command line

The easiest way to run a batch file is to get to an OS/2 command prompt and just enter name of the batch file on the command line. If the subdirectory containing the batch file is in your path, you can run the batch file from any location on your hard disk. Figure 2-1 shows SAMPLE.CMD running in an OS/2 window.

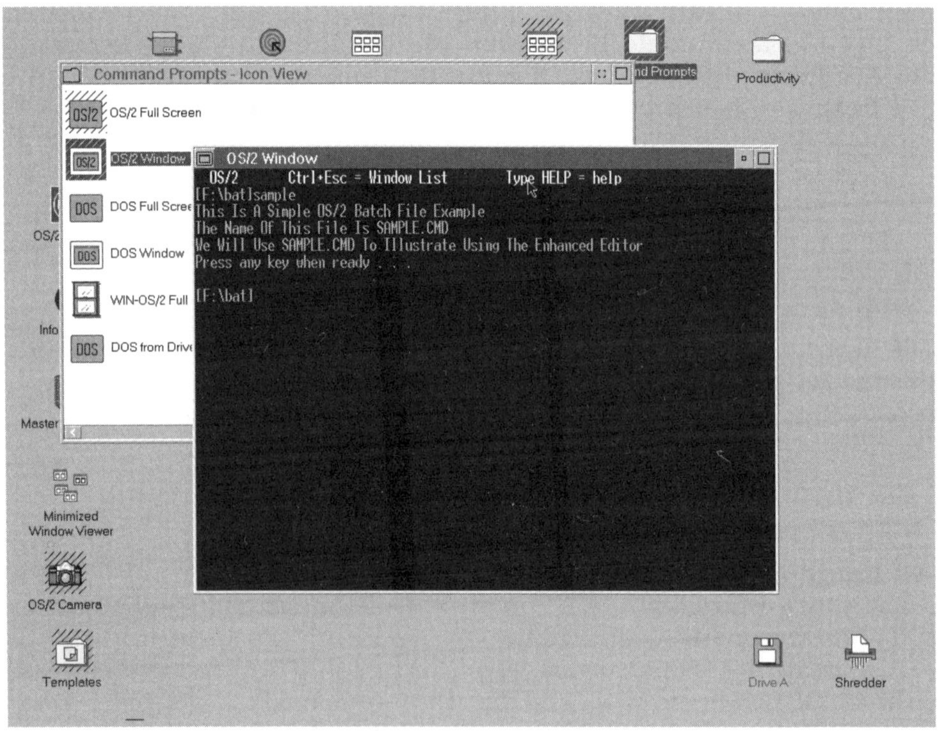

2-1 Running a batch file in a window.

Using an icon

OS/2 is a graphical user interface, so it seems backwards to go to a command line to run a batch file. Fortunately, OS/2 makes it easy for you to install a batch file as an icon either on your desktop or in a folder. That way, all you have to do is double click on the icon to run the batch file. The steps for installing SAMPLE.CMD as a desktop icon are described in this section.

The first step is to open the Template folder. OS/2 uses templates to install new items. Figure 2-2 shows a desktop with the Template folder open. As is the case with all these screen shots, your screen might look different depending on how you installed OS/2.

Next, move the mouse cursor over the Program icon and press and hold down the right mouse button. Drag the icon out of the folder and onto the desktop. With templates, this creates a new copy at the location to which you drag it. To position the batch file icon inside a folder, open that folder first and drag the Program icon to it. As soon as you release the right mouse button, OS/2 will bring up the first page of a dialog box you fill out on every new program and batch file. On this Program page, you want to

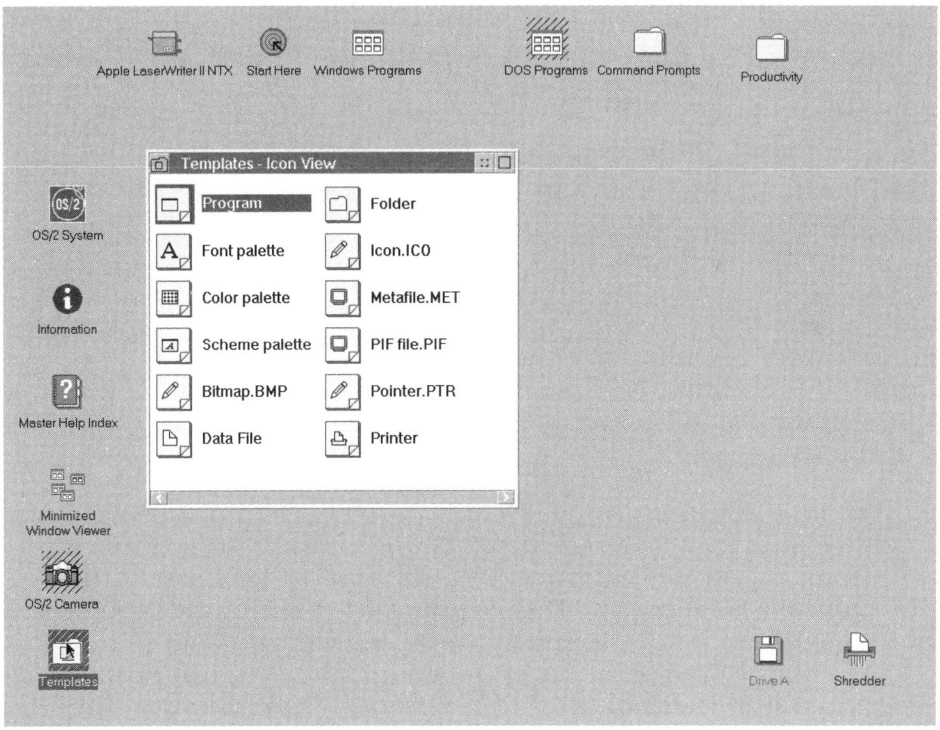

2-2 Opening the Template folder.

enter the path to, and name of, the batch file. Optionally, you can enter parameters to pass to the batch file and the subdirectory in which the batch file should start working. Figure 2-3 shows this.

The next page is the Sessions page, as shown in FIG. 2-4. Here you tell OS/2 what type of session to run and how to handle the window when the program terminates. Notice that some of the options are grayed out in FIG. 2-4. Since OS/2 knows from the extension that SAMPLE.CMD is an OS/2 batch file, it doesn't give you the option of running it in a DOS or Windows window. The next page is the Association page (FIG. 2-5), which is used to link data files to programs. This page is generally not used for batch files.

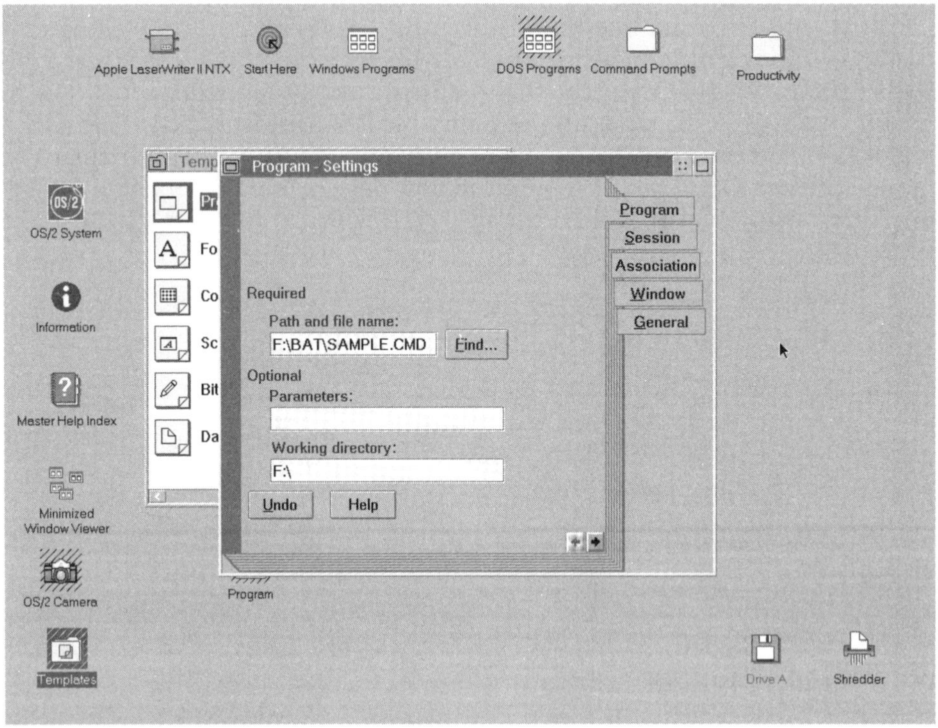

2-3 The Settings page.

The next page is the Window page, shown in FIG. 2-6. This window is used to control the behavior of the OS/2 window while the program is running. It too is generally not used for batch files. The final page is the General page, shown in FIG. 2-7. This page is used to enter a title for the icon and optionally redesign the icon to appear any way you want it to.

Once you've filled in the necessary information, you can close this dialog box, and the batch file icon is ready to use. Figure 2-8 shows an OS/2 desktop with an icon to run SAMPLE.CMD in the middle of it. To run the batch file, all you have to do is double click on its icon. From that point on, it will run just like it would if you had run it from an OS/2 command line.

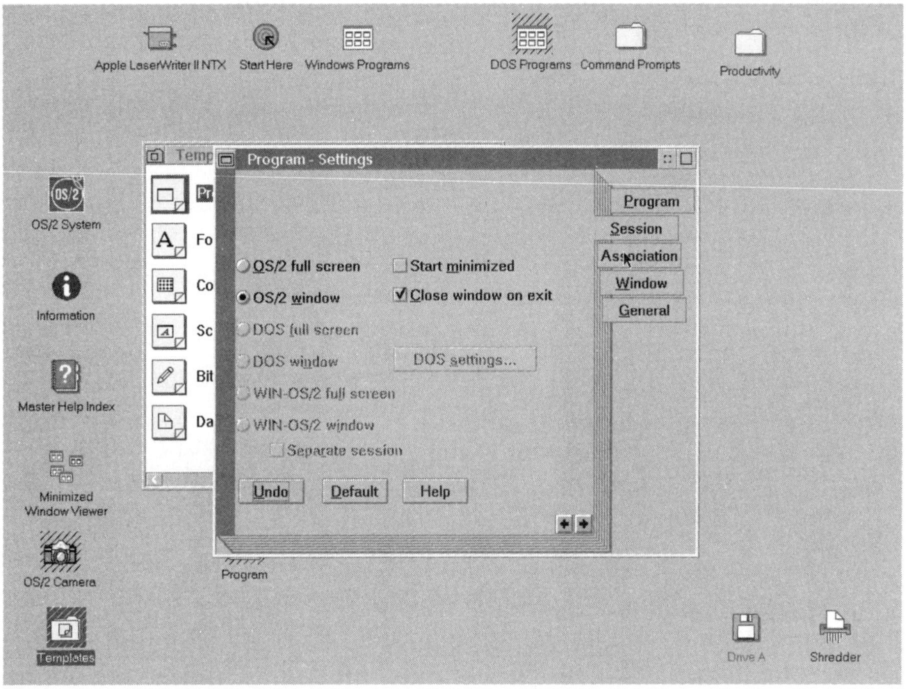

2-4 The Sessions page.

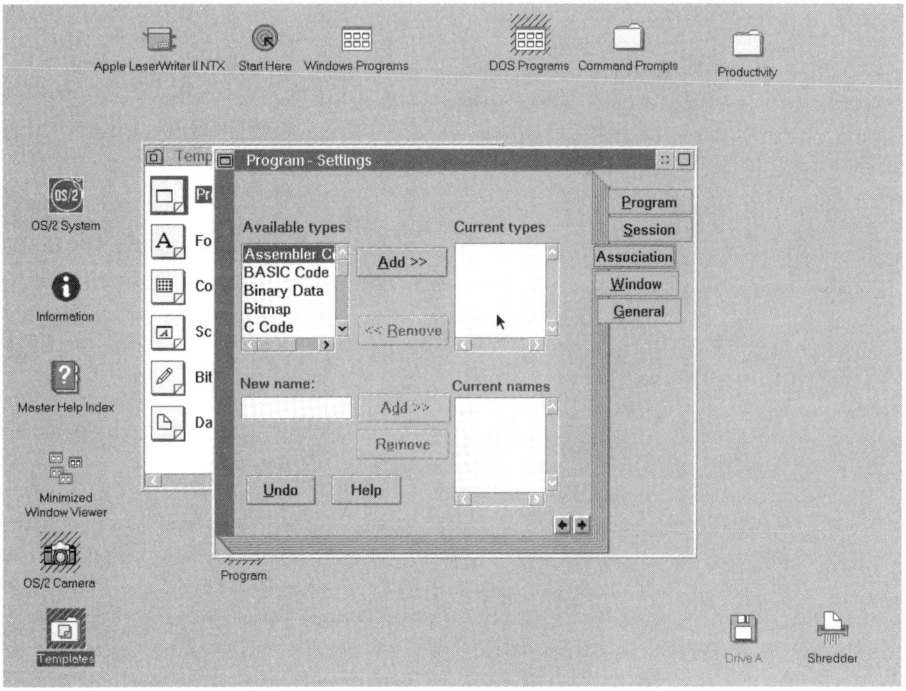

2-5 The Association page.

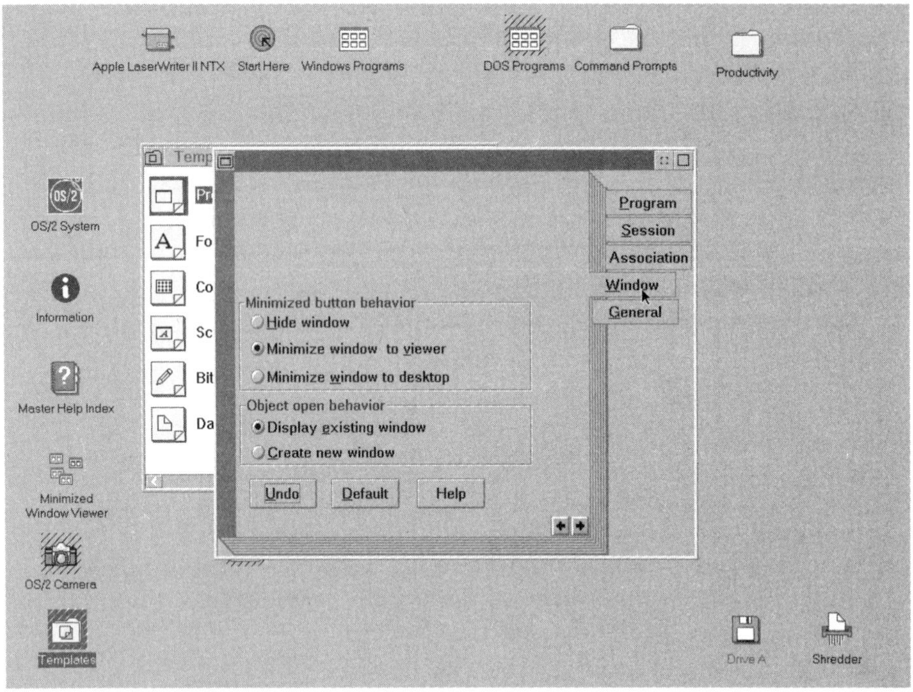

2-6 The Window page.

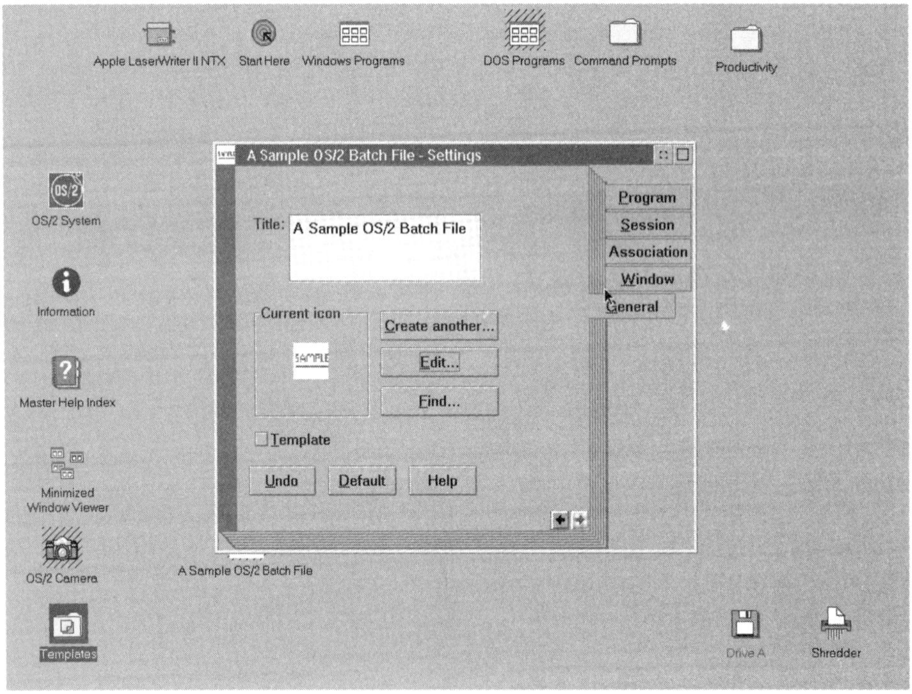

2-7 The General page.

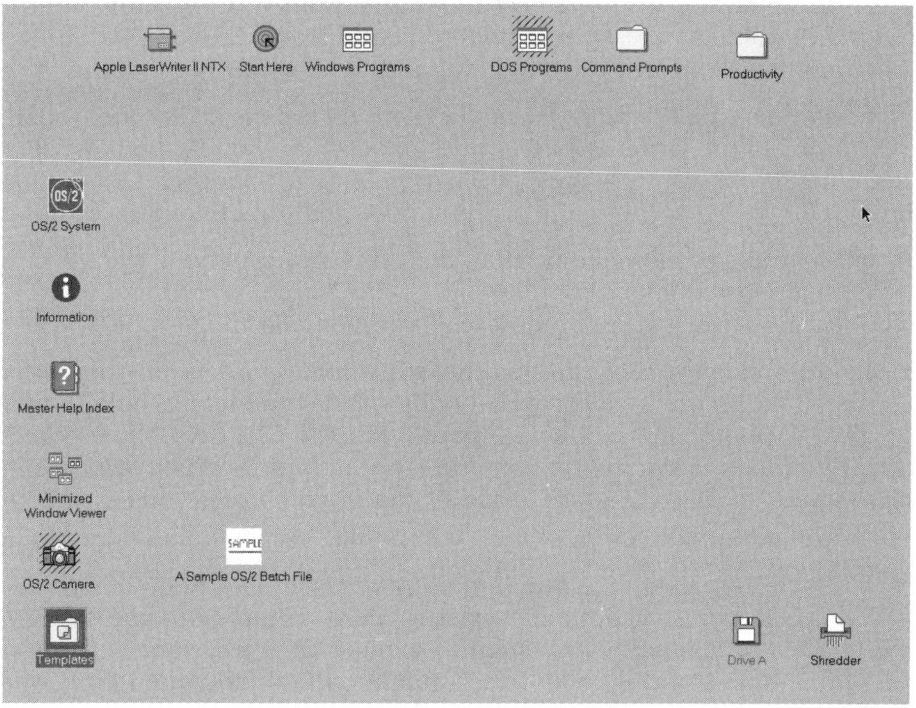

2-8 The OS/2 desktop with SAMPLE.CMD installed as an icon.

More on icons

Since OS/2 is a graphical user interface, each program and batch file you want to run by double clicking on it from the desktop needs an icon. Icons need to have three characteristics. They must be:

Distinctive If all your icons look the same, then you lose the main feature of a graphical user interface because you can't quickly identify the function of each icon. To see this problem in action, start up Windows and look at the main screen. Every folder looks the same. That forces you to either try and remember the location of specific folders or to read the titles below the folders. OS/2 folders initially have this same problem but, since you can alter the appearance of your folders under OS/2, you can eliminate this problem.

Attractive You don't want ugly icons on your screen, even if they're distinctive. Depending on your screen resolution, your icons are limited to at most 64×64 pixels, with each pixel limited to sixteen colors. One of the things you'll quickly find out is that this small size greatly limits your artistic abilities when creating icons.

Simple Your icons are limited to 64×64 pixels, but most of them are actually 32×32. They're generally shown on the screen very small, so you have to keep the artwork simple in order to be able to make it out on the screen.

While these three items seem very limiting at first, you'll quickly find that it's still possible to create some very artistic icons for your batch files. There are three different ways to develop icons for your batch files:

Load them from a file of existing icons I'm not very artistically inclined, so this is my favorite way. The disk for this book contains an icon file for most of the batch files. It also contains a collection of public-domain icons you can look through for your batch files and any programs you want to use under OS/2.

Draw them yourself If you're artistic, then drawing your own icons can be both fun and rewarding. If you have access to CompuServe or an OS/2 bulletin-board system, you might want to share your icon creations with others.

Modify existing icons Oftentimes, the easiest way to develop the perfect icon is to take an existing icon and modify it. I have an icon of a floppy disk I'm always modifying for other purposes. For the CHECK.CMD batch file icon, I just took it and added a check mark across the disk. With all the icons on the enclosed disk, you have a good many choices you can modify.

Icon Editor

To draw your own icons or modify existing icons, you need to use the OS/2 Icon Editor, so let's take a moment to explore this program. This isn't a complete tutorial on the Icon Editor, but it will tell you enough to work with batch file icons. For more detailed information, consult your OS/2 on-line documentation.

There are three ways to start the Icon Editor. The first is to double click on the program. It's stored in the Productivity folder. The other two first require you to select the Settings menu, select the General page, and then click on either Edit or Create another, beside the picture of the existing icon. Except for the fact that the Edit button loads the existing icon into the Icon Editor, all three methods take you to the same screen.

You might want to start the Icon Editor now to follow along with these instructions. Once you start the Icon Editor, your screen will look like the one in FIG. 2-9. Along the top of the Icon Editor, you'll see the main menu. Below that, you'll see several pieces of information:

Form Size This shows you the size of the icon. Typically, icons are 32×32. The numbers represent the number of pixels stored in the icon. The first number is the width of the icon in pixels and the second is the height of the icon in pixels. You can also use the Icon Editor to edit bitmapped files of different sizes. When you're using it to create a bitmapped file, the Icon Editor will first prompt you for the size.

Pen Location This is the current location of the "pen" used to edit the icon. As with Form Size, the first number represents the width coordinate and the second represents the height coordinate. The bottom left corner is 0,0; the top left corner is 0,31 (the numbers go 0–31, not 1–32); the top right is 31,31; and the bottom right is 31,0.

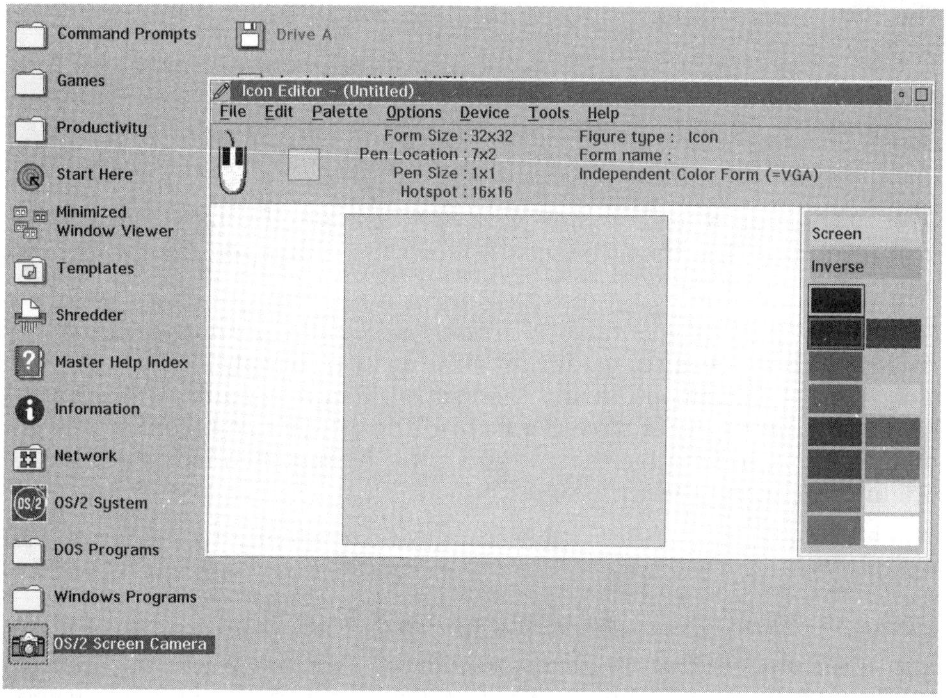

2-9 This is how the Icon Editor looks without an icon being edited.

Pen Size Normally, the pen alters a single pixel at a time, thus the 1×1. Using the Option menu, you can change the pen size to a 2×2, 3×3, and so on, up to 9×9.

Hotspot The "hotspot" is the portion of the icon that the mouse pointer must be touching when you double click.

Figure type The Icon Editor can edit icons, pointers, or bitmapped files. This tells you what type of file is being edited.

Form name Once an icon has been saved and named, it's shown here.

Independent Color Form (=VGA) This line shows the format being used to store the icons. All icons on the disk are stored in the Independent Color Form (=VGA) format at 32×32 pixels. Other available formats include:

- Independent BW Form (=1.1 format) at 32×32 pixels.
- Independent Form - (1.2 format) at 64×64 pixels.
- 8514 – 16 colors at 40×40 pixels.
- 8514 at 40×40 pixels.
- 8514 – (1.2 format) at 64×64 pixels.
- CGA at 32×16 pixels.
- EGA at 32×32 pixels.
- VGA – (1.2 format) at 32×32 pixels.

The File menu has four options that are particularly useful for editing batch file icons. They are:

New This lets you start a new icon with a clean slate.

Open This lets you open an existing icon and move it into the editor for manipulation.

Save This is used to save your work to a disk file. If you're saving a new icon file for the first time, the Icon Editor will prompt you for the name to use.

Save as... This lets you save an already saved file to another name. It's useful when you want to modify an existing icon. Simply load the existing icon using the Open option and then save it to a new name with the Save as... option. It's best to save the icon to the new name before you begin modifications so you don't forget and save the modified icon back to the original name and overwrite that icon.

The Edit menu has seven options that are particularly useful for editing batch file icons. They are:

Undo This reverses the last changes that were made.

Cut This removes the selected portion of the icon (or the entire icon) from the file and places it in the paste buffer. The removed portion of the icon is replaced with a screen-colored background.

Copy This copies the selected portion of the icon (or the entire icon) to the paste buffer without disturbing the icon.

Paste This copies the icon or portion of icon in the paste buffer to the icon you're working on. Icons or icon fragments loaded into the paste buffer remain there until they're replaced by new material or until the Icon Editor is removed from memory. The Icon Editor has its own paste buffer that it doesn't share with other programs, so using Cut, Copy, and Paste in other programs won't affect the Icon Editor.

Clear This erases the selected area and replaces it with a screen-colored background.

Select Selecting this menu option converts the mouse cursor from a pen to a selection tool. Use this tool to select an area to Cut or Copy to the paste buffer.

Select all This quickly selects the entire icon. You would generally use this to Copy the entire icon to the paste buffer.

Under the Tool menu, you'll find a Color Fill option. This replaces the pen cursor with a tiny paint can. Everywhere you click the cursor, the pixel you click on and every other pixel of the same color connected to that pixel will be changed to the currently selected color. This is a quick way to fill the interior of items in your icons.

Now that you've finished your tour of the Icon Editor screen and its more important menu items, let's draw an icon.

The Icon Editor lets you work with a palette of sixteen colors. You'll see these to the right of the work area. Additionally, you'll see a color labeled Screen and Inverse. The screen color always displays as the same color as the OS/2 desktop screen and makes your icons look professional by giving them a clear background. The inverse color is the color that contrasts best with the desktop color.

The Icon Editor allows two colors to be active at once. Move your mouse cursor to one color and press the left button. That is the color that will be painted while you hold down the left button. Now move the pointer to another color and press the right button. That is the color that will be painted while you hold down the right button. Normally, I set the left button up to be the color I'm working with at the time and the right button to be the background color for the area I'm working in. That way, if I click in the wrong spot using the left button, I can quickly erase my mistake by clicking in the same spot with the right button.

Now you're ready to edit. The best way to think of an icon is a matrix with 32×32 dots. All you're going to do is change the colors of some of the dots in this matrix. You can do this by moving the mouse cursor to a particular pixel and clicking either mouse button or by holding down either mouse button and dragging the mouse cursor across the screen.

By way of an example, let's draw an icon of a 5.25-inch floppy disk. A 5.25-inch floppy disk is mostly a black square with holes in it, so let's begin by drawing a black square. You'll see this in FIG. 2-10. There are two notches at the front of the disk (one pixel each) and one larger notch (four pixels) on one side of the disk. You'll see these added in FIG. 2-11. There's a large hole in the middle for the disk hub, a smaller hole near the front of the disk where the disk is read, and a tiny hole (one pixel) near the large center hole (see FIG. 2-12). Finally, the hole in the front is entirely filled with the gray center platter of the disk and some of that platter is visible in the large hole in the center. You will see these added in the final version of the icon in FIG. 2-13. Save the icon to a disk file and you're ready to use it.

Installing an icon

When you go to install an icon for a batch file, OS/2 gives you four different ways to create or install it. You can have a disk file ready, create a new icon from the General page of the Settings notebook, paste an existing icon from the paste buffer in the General page of the Settings notebook, or drop and drag. Let's look at each of these in more detail:

Have a disk file ready An icon file is a file created with the Icon Editor that contains one icon and has an .ICO extension. If an icon file exists in the same subdirectory as a batch file or program and has the same name, when you use a template to install that batch file or program to the desktop or to a folder, then OS/2 will automatically use that icon for the batch

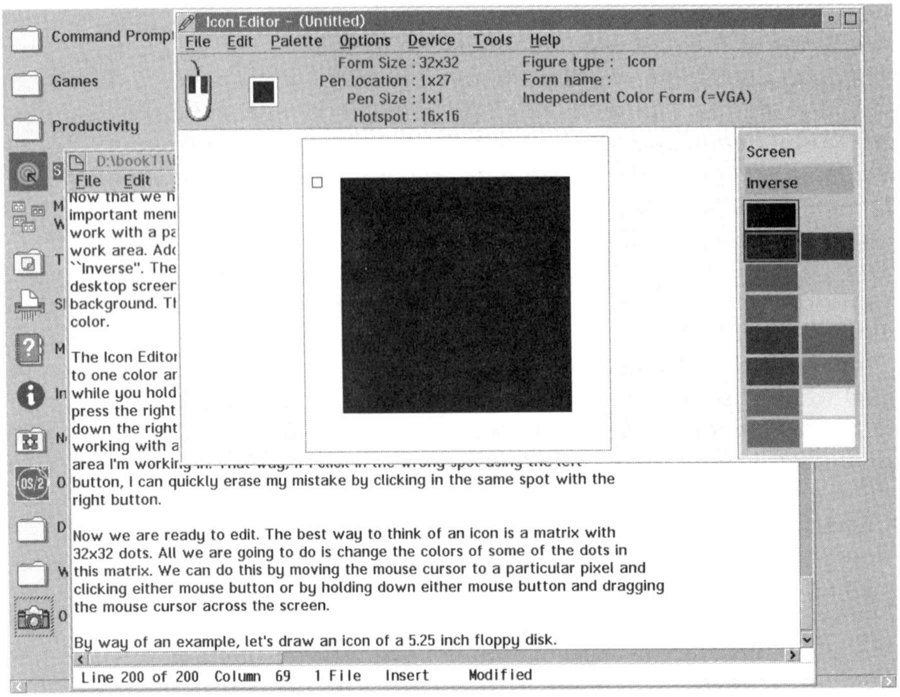

2-10 The start of a 5.25-inch floppy-disk icon. Right now, all you have is a black box that will form the bulk of the disk.

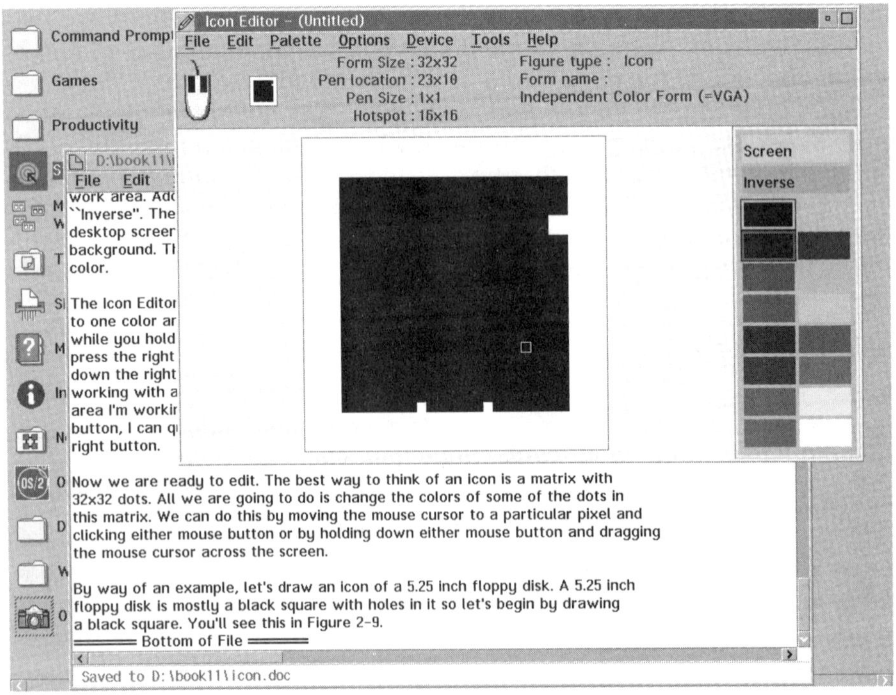

2-11 Three notches have been added to the disk's exterior.

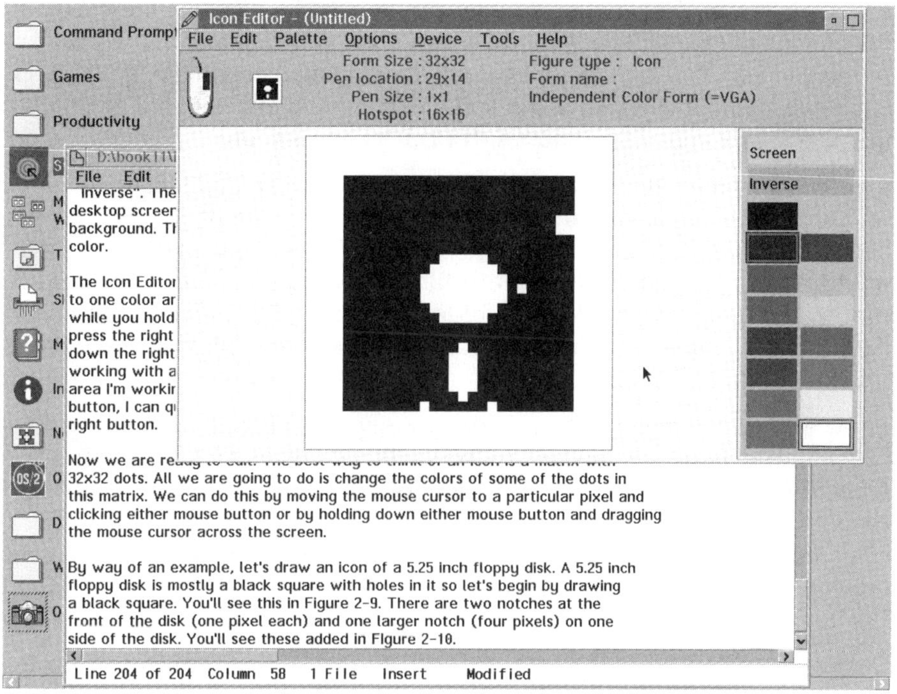

2-12 Now the floppy disk icon has the three holes found in its interior.

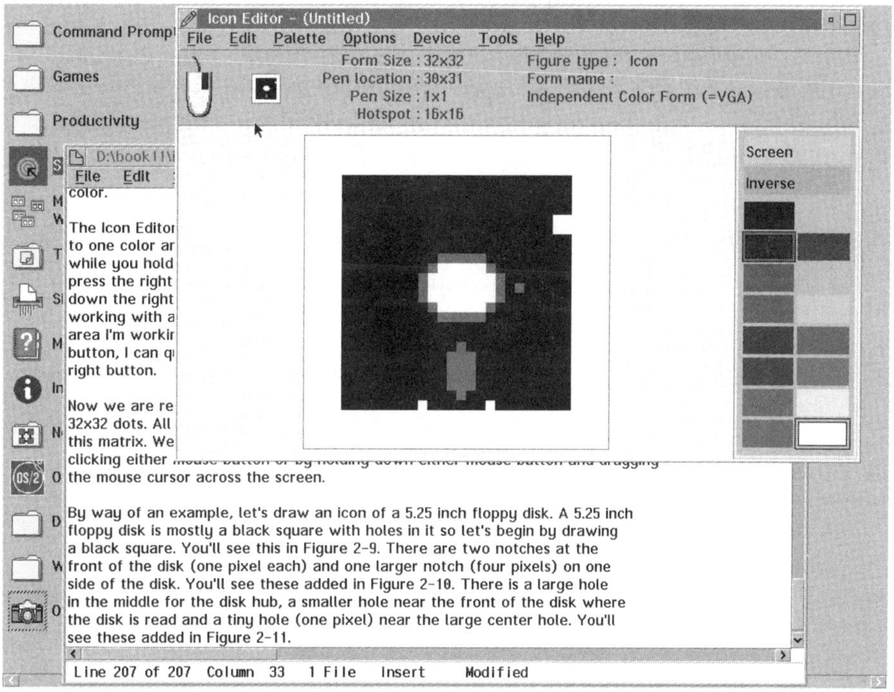

2-13 Finally, the floppy-disk icon shows the interior disk where it's visible through two of the holes. It is now finished.

file or program. For example, assume you have a batch file called SAMPLE.CMD in your C:\BAT subdirectory that you're planning to add to your batch file folder. Just use the Icon Editor first to create SAMPLE.ICO and save it to your C:\BAT subdirectory. Then when you install SAMPLE.CMD, OS/2 will automatically use SAMPLE.ICO as its icon.

Create a new icon If you don't have a previously created icon, you can click on the Create another button on the General page of the Settings notebook. This will take you to the Icon Editor and automatically have you working on the icon for the batch file or program you're installing. If you just want to modify the default folder icon used for folders or the box icon used for programs, click on the Edit button rather than on the Create another button.

Paste an existing icon If you've previously used the Icon Editor and have copied an existing or modified icon to the paste buffer, you can use that icon to replace the default icon for a batch file or program. Just click on the Create another button (the Edit button won't work for this) on the General page of the Settings notebook to go to the Icon Editor. Then select Paste from the Edit menu to paste the icon in the paste buffer into the Icon Editor.

Drop and drag an icon If another item on your desktop uses the same icon you want to assign to an item, then making that assignment is as easy as dragging the icon and dropping it in place. First, bring up the Settings notebook for the item to have its icon changed, and change to the General page. Then press the right mouse button with the cursor on the item that has the icon you want to use, hold the mouse button, drag the item to the General page, and then release the mouse button. The new icon will be dropped into place.

Summary

This chapter has showed you two different ways to run OS/2 batch files: from the command line and as an icon. It also showed you how to store your batch files in a common subdirectory and include that subdirectory in your path statement so the batch files will run from any subdirectory.

3
Using batch files

The basic idea of a batch file is really very ingenious. When you want the computer to perform a given task more than once, why not have it store the steps used to perform that task? A batch file contains those stored steps. When you tell the computer to execute a batch file, it reads and follows that batch file just like an actor reads and follows a script. In fact, the concept of the computer following a script is an excellent mental image of a batch file.

What are batch files good for?

Think of this section as a batch file "sales pitch" where I try to convince you that batch files are worth using! As you'll see, batch files have four major functions:

- Keystroke reduction
- New command construction
- Consistency
- Safety

Keystrokes reduction

When I sat down to begin writing this chapter, I was using the OS/2 command line in a full-screen window. Rather than changing back to the desktop to run my word processor, I decided to just run it from the command line. Before actually starting the word processor, I had to enter some other commands:

F: I had been doing some "house cleaning" on my D: drive. My word-processing software is on my F: drive, so the first thing I did was change to that drive.

CD\WORD My word processor is stored in the CD\WORD subdirectory, so I then changed to that subdirectory.

WORD I issued the command WORD to start my word processor.

Counting the Enter needed at the end of each line, I had to type 16 keystrokes to start my word processor. As you'll see, a computerized script (in other words, a batch file) can easily reduce this to as few as two keystrokes. So the first advantage of a batch file is keystroke reduction.

Batch files can save you a lot of keystrokes.

I'll offer an example to prove this and give you your first experience with batch files. The command to get a directory from the A: drive is:

```
DIR A:*.* /P
```

But you can shorten this command. Without worrying about what you're typing, enter the following command into a new file using the Enhanced Editor and then save the file to your batch subdirectory under the name A.CMD:

```
DIR A:*.* /P
```

Now put a disk in drive A:, type A, and hit the Enter key at the OS/2 command prompt. If everything goes well, you'll now see a directory of the A: drive. If you have a problem, make sure your batch subdirectory is in your path or just change to that subdirectory before issuing the command.

You might be thinking to yourself, "So what? I can simply type DIR A:*.* /P when I want a directory." The advantage of A.CMD is that you can get a directory with two keystrokes instead of 16. I used a similar batch file to start my word processor with two keystrokes rather than the 16 described.

New command construction

When I first started using computers and was still running DOS, I had a great deal of difficulty remembering the command to check a disk. Instead of trying to force myself to remember the command CHKDSK (CHecK DiSK), I wrote a batch file called CHECK.BAT, containing the single command CHKDSK. Typing CHECK instead of CHKDSK saves one keystroke, but that isn't the primary purpose of CHECK.BAT—I can remember the word *check* much easier than I can remember the nonword *chkdsk*.

Batch files allow you to create new commands or change the name of existing commands.

Of course, I could have renamed CHKDSK.COM to CHECK.COM and achieved the same thing, but then no one else would have been able to check a disk on my computer. Writing a batch file allowed me to use the name I wanted without interfering with normal operations.

In this simple example, *new command construction* is a very fancy name for making a command accessible under another name, much like calling a garbage collector a sanitation engineer or a salesman a purchase consultant. However, as you'll see later, a long series of commands can be connected to form fairly intelligent sets of commands.

Consistency

Now it's time for a simple one-question test. Put away your OS/2 manual, don't use the OS/2 on-line help, and don't look at the single-line command a couple of paragraphs from here. What's the solution to this problem? We all know how important it is to back up our hard disks. You should be making frequent full backups, say weekly or monthly, and daily incremental backups. So write down the proper syntax of a full backup using the OS/2 program BACKUP.COM to back up all the files from the C: drive to the A: drive, and format any floppy disks as a 1.2Mb disk.

A batch file can remember complex syntax for you.

Most of you probably didn't do well on this test. Computer software often uses complex commands that are difficult for the user to remember. Happily, you don't have to. Figure out the command syntax once and then put it into a batch file and forget it. That way, you'll never have to remember.

By the way, in case you still haven't figured it out, the syntax for that backup is:

```
BACKUP C:\*.* A: /S /F:1200
```

But you could easily store this command in a batch file called B.CMD, and have to remember just B—short for *backup*. If you can't remember that, you can pick another name. With batch files, you get to decide.

I can see you mentally waving a flag. You're asking, "Hey, isn't this just another example of new command construction?" The answer is both yes and no. True, you've created a new command called B that's easier to remember than the string of switches previously listed, just as Check is easier to remember than CHKDSK. That statement, however, can be made about almost every batch file you'll construct. The real purpose of this batch file is to always perform a backup consistently—without having to remember the syntax.

Most of the batch files you've looked at so far have one thing in common—they each do only one thing. But they don't need to be limited to one activity. OS/2 keeps track of its location in a batch file even while it's doing something else. Let's do away with that one-command constraint right now. Consider this simple two-line batch file:

```
CHKDSK
DIR
```

First it runs CHKDSK. While CHKDSK is running, OS/2 maintains its place in the batch file. Think of yourself putting your finger in a book so that you won't lose your place while answering the phone. After your phone conversation is over, you can pick up reading where you left off.

When CHKDSK finishes, OS/2 reads the next command in the batch file and runs DIR. Although CHKDSK takes only a few seconds to run, it could have been the command to start a word-processing program, which could run almost indefinitely. It doesn't matter. OS/2 remembers and picks up the batch file whenever the program finishes. If you want to experiment, you'll find this batch file on the disk under the name 2-THINGS.CMD.

☑ Batch files run programs consistently.

In this last example, the batch file established a standard script to be followed each time it's run. While this isn't important in this example, consider the next one:

```
C:
CD\WORD
WORD
```

This batch file automates loading my word processor, using the steps previously described. This way, I know my word processor always accesses the proper drive and proper subdirectory before it starts.

Safety

A final reason for using batch files is safety. Some commands are pretty dangerous. In fact, any operating system is inherently dangerous. Anything that gives you the power to format disks and erase files has the potential for accidents!

Typing FORMAT instead of FORMAT A: can destroy the data on your hard disk. Sure, the operating system has safeguards, but do you really want to even take the chance of a mishap? Using the command ERASE *.DOC instead of ERASE *.BAK can erase all your documents, and there are many other accidents out there waiting to happen.

If an accident causes you to erase files, you'll need the OS/2 undeleting program or a utility program and some luck to get your files back. If you don't notice the mistake right away, your chances of recovery are greatly reduced. Batch files can form a strong line of defense against the indiscriminate use of these powerful commands.

☑ Batch files make dangerous commands safer.

You can prevent accidental formatting of a hard disk by first renaming FORMAT.COM to XYZ.COM and then creating FORMAT.CMD, which contains the single command @XYZ A:. The @ sign will be examined later, but I'll reveal now that it keeps the XYZ from showing on the screen. If you saw the name, you might be tempted to bypass the batch file and just enter XYZ on the command line.

☑ Batch files are the easiest programming language to learn!

When most computer users think of programming, they think of spending months to learn languages such as Pascal or C. Like programs created with Pascal or C++, batch files are programs. Unlike other programming languages, however, batch file commands are made up of mostly OS/2 commands, which are already familiar to many of you. If you know how to use OS/2, you already know most of what you need to know in order to write effective batch files.

When you learn to program in most computer languages, you must learn a great deal before you're able to write even the simplest program. This isn't true with batch files. As you'll soon see, you can write some very powerful batch files with standard OS/2 commands and just a few special batch commands.

Although batch files are easy to write, this ease comes at a price: batch files are limited in what they can do. One of your most common thoughts as you study this book will be, "If only . . ." You'll see many situations where you could really automate things if only batch files could . . . The real drawback to batch files is that they're easy to learn and easy to write, but they always seem to stop just short of having enough power.

Three different types of batch files

While I haven't yet made the distinction, OS/2 can actually run three different types of batch file: DOS .BAT batch files, OS/2 .CMD batch files, and OS/2 .CMD REXX programs. DOS .BAT files and OS/2 .CMD files are very similar to one another. Since this is an OS/2 book, the older DOS batch files are not covered here. If you're interested in this topic, please see my *MS-DOS Batch File Programming* book, also from Windcrest. This book covers the OS/2 .CMD batch files in detail.

OS/2 also includes a second procedural language, called REXX. REXX was designed and first implemented between 1979 and 1982 by an IBM employee, Mike Cowlishaw. It first became commercially available in 1983 as a procedural language for the IBM VM/CMS operating system. In 1987 when IBM announced their Systems Application Architecture (SAA), they included REXX as the standard procedural language. They also announced that REXX would be available for all their operating systems. Thus, it's available under OS/2.

REXX programs are stored in .CMD files just like batch files, and REXX is a very batch-like language. However, batch commands and REXX commands cannot be intermixed, and REXX is really much more than a batch language. This book will introduce you to REXX. For more detailed coverage, please see my *Writing OS/2 REXX Programs*, from McGraw-Hill.

Summary

In summary, batch files have four major functions. They can:

- Reduce the number of keystrokes needed to execute a command.
- Allow you to combine one or more existing commands into your own specialized commands.
- Allow you to store the proper syntax of command sequence in a script file so you don't have to remember this information.
- Protect you from dangerous OS/2 commands.

Batch files are the easiest programs to write because they consist of mostly OS/2 commands with just a few special batch file commands thrown in.

OS/2 can run three different types of batch files: DOS batch files, OS/2 batch files, and REXX programs. This book ignores DOS batch files, covers OS/2 batch files in detail, and introduces REXX programs.

4
Batch file construction

So far you've been introduced to some good reasons to use batch files, and you've seen how to use the nice Enhanced Editor that's included with OS/2. Now it's time to begin writing your own batch files. But before that, let's spend a few minutes talking about how to structure them.

What is a batch file?

A batch file script is a special file containing one or more OS/2 commands and a few batch subcommands, with each command on a separate line. That's it—nothing more and nothing less. Consider the following:

```
first command
second command
third command
fourth command
fifth command
(and so on)
```

A batch file is a list of OS/2 commands for the computer to follow.

You run a batch file by entering its name at the command line or by clicking on its icon on the desktop. You can enter the .CMD extension, but you don't have to. For example, to run a batch file named FRED.CMD, you would enter:

```
FRED
```

Some batch files require additional information, which you must enter after the batch file name. This additional information is contained in *replaceable parameters*. The batch file name and each separate piece of information must be separated by either a space or a comma, for example:

```
FRED Yes,1,*.BAK No
```

When items are enclosed inside quotation marks, OS/2 treats them as one replaceable parameter. For example, with:

```
FRED "Yes,1,*.BAK No"
```

everything after FRED would be treated as the first replaceable parameter.

➠ Replaceable parameters are data you enter on the command line after the name of the batch file.

Batch file formatting

OS/2 doesn't require batch files to have any special kind of formatting. The computer doesn't care either; it will successfully execute any properly written batch file, as long as it's an ASCII file. The only reason to format batch files in any special way is for human readability.

What follows is the scheme I've developed for use with my batch files. It makes the batch files easily readable, while using the limited formatting that OS/2 allows in batch files. If you develop a different system that works better for you, feel free to use it.

Capitalization

In general, I use capitalization in the following fashion:

- I use all capital letters in both the batch files and the messages they display to draw attention to particularly important elements.
- I use all capital letters for OS/2 commands and program names in the batch files. They're also capitalized in this book.
- I capitalize the first letter of each word in most messages and remarks.
- When a message tells you what to enter on the command line, I capitalize the command line.

Spacing

In a long batch file, it can be difficult to see the different sections if you enter text on each line. To visually break the program up into different sections, I leave one or more blank lines between each section. These blank lines don't affect the operation of the batch file because OS/2 ignores them, but they do make it much easier to read.

While the batch files in this book have blank lines between the sections, I've left those blank lines out of the longer batch files contained in the figures. I've found that, while blank lines enhance the readability of programs, they don't work with the tabular format of the longer programs.

Indenting sections

I've also found that it can be useful to indent the lines of a section between the beginning and ending label of the section. If you do that, a batch file segment might look like this:

```
:HELP
  ECHO This Runs Your Backup Program
  ECHO You Must Start It With Either An F or I
  ECHO On The Command Line
  ECHO The F Is For A Full Backup
  ECHO The I Is For An Incremental Backup
GOTO END
```

As you can see, this clarifies which statements belong in this section, something that's especially useful in longer programs.

Message length

You'll notice that most of the messages in my programs have fairly short lines. For longer messages, I use multiple lines. It's been my experience that shorter lines are easier to read on the screen than longer ones. It's a lot like printing your documents in a multicolumn format, except the batch files use only the left column. Plus, if you run the batch file in an OS/2 window, not all of a long message will be visible.

Line-length limit

Commands entered from the command line are limited to 300 characters. Batch files are limited to about 400 characters. As a general rule, batch file line lengths will rarely exceed 50 characters.

As you'll see later in this book, OS/2 treats some lines in your batch file as being longer than their physical length. That can sometimes make it difficult to gauge the actual length of the line, but the line must still be 400 characters or less after OS/2 expands it to its final length.

Fortunately, you'll rarely encounter this problem. In fact, you'll rarely encounter this limitation in DOS where the batch file line limit is a paltry 127 characters. However, it's a good idea to keep the limit in the back of your mind in case you ever find yourself typing in a very long line.

Let's write a batch file

So far in this book, I haven't introduced a single batch file command. I'm not going to introduce any until the next chapter. But you can still write some useful batch files. You've already seen a couple of useful batch files:

B.CMD, which performs an incremental backup, and CHECK.CMD, which runs the CHKDSK program. Both of these are included on the disk that comes with this book. Now let's look at two more situations where batch files are useful.

The problem

A number of major software packages like Lotus, Word, WordPerfect, and WordStar let you shell out to perform some minor task. This is a holdover from DOS days when you could run only one program at a time. When you're shelled out this way, the original program stays in memory so only a small amount of free memory is available.

It's usually difficult to tell when you're shelled out of a program, so sometimes users are tempted to start another program from this command prompt. However, you either won't have enough memory to load another program or memory will be so scarce that the second program will run poorly.

The solution

You want to make it obvious when you're shelled out of Lotus, but Lotus won't do that by itself. If you start Lotus with a batch file, however, it's very easy to do so. Do the following in the batch file:

1. Change to the drive containing Lotus. This will be a command like C:.
2. Change to the subdirectory containing Lotus. This would be a command like CD\123 or CD\LOTUS, depending on how you have your hard disk structured.
3. Change the prompt from the usual prompt to a reminder that Lotus is running. This would be a command like PROMPT Type EXIT To Return To Lotus$_$P$G. You won't be able to see this prompt in Lotus, but if you shell out of Lotus you'll see the reminder.
4. Start Lotus. This would be a command like 123 to bypass the initial menu, or LOTUS to go through the initial menu.
5. Once Lotus terminates and the batch file has taken back over, reset the prompt. This would be a command like PROMPT $l[$P].

None of these steps requires a batch file command, so you already know enough to write this batch file. You might even want to put this book down and fire up the Enhanced Editor and give it a shot. Go ahead; I'll wait.

The resulting batch file requires five lines, one for each of the things you just listed:

```
C:
CD\LOTUS
```

```
PROMPT Type EXIT To Return To LOTUS$_$P$G
123
PROMPT $I[$P]
```

With the Type EXIT To Return To Lotus C:\> prompt showing, it will be hard for you to accidentally run a second copy of Lotus. Figure 4-1 shows this. I ran this batch file in an OS/2 window and then used the /System command in Lotus to shell out. If you want to experiment, this batch file is on the enclosed disk under the name LOTUS.CMD.

By the way, this solution isn't limited to Lotus. You can use it with any program you start with a batch file that offers a way to shell out.

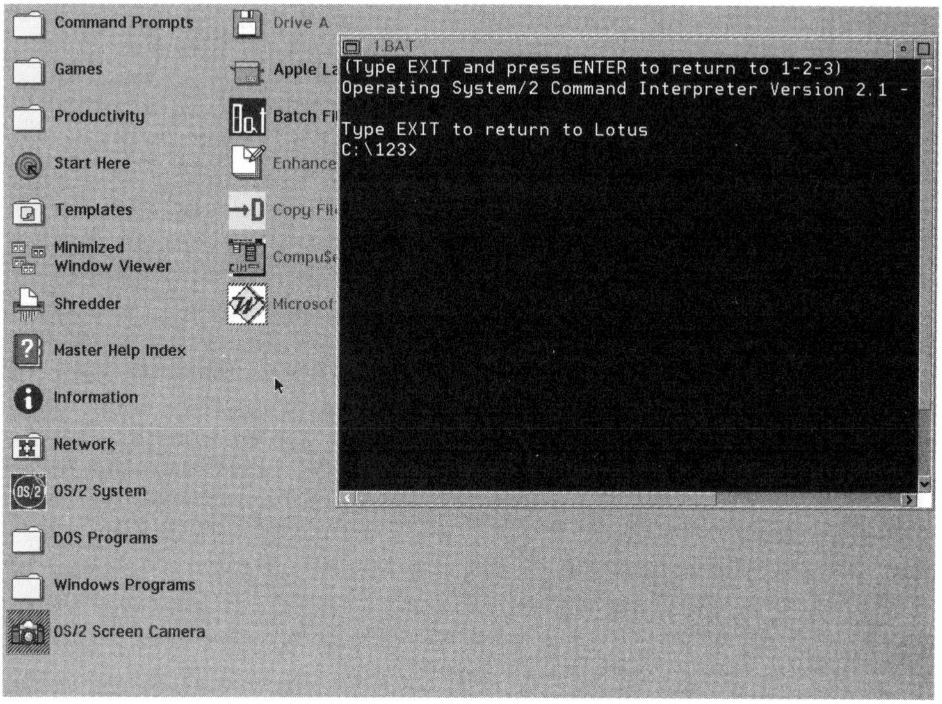

4-1 Shelling out of Lotus in an OS/2 window. Notice that the new prompt makes it clear you've shelled out of another program.

A second problem

I like to perform an incremental backup at the end of every day using the XCOPY command. However, there are certain files that get modified every day that I don't need to back up, including .BAK files (I'll have a backup of the original file so I don't need a backup of the backup file) and .OBJ files (compilers create these while compiling, but after linking they're no longer needed).

I need a backup batch file that first removes the archive setting for these files and then performs the incremental backup.

Another solution

The first step is to make sure the computer is in the root directory of the current drive. After that, it takes three lines to remove these archive settings. The operational segment of PREPARE.CMD, which does just this, is as follows:

```
CD\
ATTRIB *.BAK -A /S
ATTRIB *.OBJ -A /S
```

If you like, you could add one more line, XCOPY *.* A: /S /M, to perform the actual backup from the same batch file.

Once again, this batch file is nothing more than the same commands you would enter at the command line to perform this same task. However, once you've figured out how to do it once, you can forget about it because the batch file remembers everything for you. And entering the name of the batch file takes far fewer keystrokes than entering all those commands.

Summary

- Batch files can be nothing more than a series of OS/2 commands, identical to the commands you would enter on the command line.
- You can create batch files by writing down the commands you use at the command line prompt and then entering them into a batch file.
- Proper formatting can make batch files more readable without affecting the computer's ability to execute them. However, the formatting that OS/2 allows in a batch file is very limited.
- Consistent capitalization, blank lines between parts of the batch file, and indenting commands within a section all contribute to a readable batch file.
- You can write very useful batch files without using a single special batch command.

PART 2
Simple batch file topics

Now that you've seen how to name, write, structure, and install batch files to the desktop, it's time to look at some of the simpler batch subcommands. A batch subcommand is an OS/2 command designed to run inside a batch file. However, most of them will also work from the command line.

Chapter 5: Documentation, or "why in the world did I do that?" The batch language has only a few commands of its own but it can also run any program you own. As a result, some batch files tend to become very long. Using the REM command to document those longer batch files can make following their logic easier when you have to modify them in the future.

Chapter 6: Keeping it quiet The default mode of operation for a batch file is to have command-echoing on, which means that commands are displayed on the screen before they're executed. By turning command-echoing off, your screens will look much neater.

Chapter 7: Talking to the user Batch files frequently need to "talk" to the user to display information, ask questions, or provide warnings. The ECHO command provides the method for doing this. This chapter explains how to use the ECHO command effectively.

Chapter 8: Using high-ordered ASCII characters You can make your batch files much more attractive by using some of the high-ordered ASCII characters. This chapter explains how to use these characters.

Chapter 9: Hold that batch file! Sometimes you need a batch file to wait for the user to catch up. Maybe it has put a lot of information on the screen or the user needs a chance to press Ctrl–Break and halt the batch file. This chapter explains how to use the PAUSE command in a batch file to suspend its operation until a key is pressed.

Chapter 10: Review #1 Before moving on to the intermediate batch subcommands, you should understand the commands and concepts covered so far. This chapter is a quick test. Pass it, and you're ready to move on.

5

Documentation, or "why in the world did I do that?"

One of the worst possible feelings a programmer can have is going back to an old program and not understanding how it works. Basic programmers even have a name for the type of code most likely to cause this condition: "spaghetti code." It's called spaghetti code because it twists, turns, and winds around like cooked spaghetti.

In any programming language, it's important to document your work—both written documentation and documentation inside the program. If you look at the source code for any well-written program in any language, you'll see lots of documentation, shown as comments. Comments are lines of text inside the program that have nothing to do with the actual program. They're simply intended to help you understand the surrounding code, especially when you haven't seen the program before.

Internal documentation for a batch file consists of the remark line, started with the REM command. If you start a line with REM followed by a space, you can enter almost anything you want to. The only thing you can't use are the redirection (piping) characters. The computer will skip the remark lines, so the information on those lines are simply comments for anyone who has to go back to modify the code. Take a look at the following batch file:

```
:START
ERASE %1.BAK
COPY %1.DOC B:
COPY C:\WORD\NORMAL\%1.STY B:
ERASE C:\WORD\NORMAL\%1.BAK
COPY C:\WORD\%1.CMP B:
SHIFT
IF (%1)==() GOTO END
GOTO START
:END
```

This example includes some commands you haven't learned yet, but they're not the important part. The important thing is that %1 takes the place of a filename while the batch file is running. Given that, do you know what the file is doing? Probably not. Now consider the same batch file, properly documented:

```
REM YESDOC.CMD
REM Batch File To Copy New Files To Floppy Disk
REM :START Is Top Of Loop
:START
  REM Erase The .BAK Backup File
  ERASE %1.BAK
  REM Copy The Document File To Floppy
  COPY %1.DOC B:
  REM Copy The Associated Style Sheet To Floppy
  COPY C:\WORD\NORMAL\%1.STY B:
  REM Erase .BAK Backup Of Style Sheet
  ERASE C:\WORD\NORMAL\%1.BAK
  REM Copy Document Dictionary To Floppy
  COPY C:\WORD\%1.CMP B:
  REM Get Next Name
  SHIFT
  REM Test For Another Name, Exit If Not Found
  IF (%1)==() GOTO END
  REM Loop Through Next Name
GOTO START
:END
```

It's the same batch file; none of the working commands are any different. But now you can probably understand the batch file without my explaining the commands I haven't yet covered.

This isn't a made-up example, the first batch file is an actual working batch file. The author of the batch file could probably modify it, but it isn't likely that anyone else could. The point is that batch files aren't so simple that you can skip documentation. No one ever suffered from too much documentation.

Use the REM command inside your batch files to document their logic.

All the REM command does, therefore, is allow you to add comments to your batch file. In the next chapter, you'll see how to keep remark lines from showing when you run your batch files.

Written documentation

You can also use written documentation, one example of this being the tables in this book that list the batch files. The code is on the left, and a detailed explanation is on the right. Of course, you probably won't need to document your batch files in this level of detail, but you might find it adequate to simply print out a listing and write marginal notes.

☑ If other people use your batch files, written documentation can help them use those batch files more effectively.

A third form of documentation is a printed user's manual. In appendix B, you'll find a brief description of what each batch file that comes with this book does and what it needs as an input. If you use a lot of batch files on your system, you might find it useful to keep a similar listing of your own programs. You might also find it useful to keep this sort of documentation on the utility programs you add to your system.

Even more documentation

Over the course of the years, I've written six books for Windcrest/McGraw-Hill dealing with batch files. While working on all these books, I've written and debugged almost 1,000 batch files! In addition, I've looked at and debugged countless batch files written by others. Because of my diverse experience with batch files, I've developed some ideas on what they should look like.

Self documentation

OS/2 has a nifty feature for most of its commands. If you're not sure what they do or how to use them, you can start them with a /? switch and get a screen of helpful information. This makes it quick and easy for the user to find out what a program does or what inputs it needs.

Implementing this switch in a batch file is fairly easy. A section of code near the top of each of the batch files tests to see if the user entered a /?. If he did, the batch file will display a help screen and exit. I use the /? switch to be consistent with OS/2. Later in the book, after covering some advanced topics, you'll see the details of how to add this to batch files.

Special information at the top

Some information is important enough that every batch file should have it. The importance of this information suggests that you put it at the top of each program:

Name The first line of the program gives the name of the batch file. This isn't extremely crucial because you know the name from the filename. However, some very useful batch files in the interior of this book will use this information. These batch files will be much more useful if this line is included in each batch file.

Purpose The second line of the program gives the purpose of the batch file. In this book's sample programs, I've kept the purpose line fairly short and used multiple lines for a longer purpose in order to make the tables look good. For reasons you'll see later in the book, you should use as descriptive a purpose statement as possible, but still keep the entire line short enough to fit on one line. This isn't absolutely necessary, but some batch files shown later in the book use this information and work better with line lengths below 80. It's okay to use multiple lines for the purpose as long as each line begins with a REM PURPOSE:.

Version The first version of a program is 1.00. A tiny change would make it 1.01, a larger change would make it 1.10, and a major change would make it 2.00. Because programs tend to evolve over time, this line is a good indicator of how long a batch file has been in use.

You might notice that many of the batch files in this book are version 1.00. This isn't because I write perfect programs each time, but rather because my programs undergo extensive testing before I add them to my book. As is common with many software vendors, I begin numbering my test, or *beta*, copies at 0.00 and mark them as 1.00 only after I've finished testing them. As a result, they don't get a number higher than 1.00 unless I enhance them, fix a bug after beta testing, or go back and figure out a better way to do something.

Date This is the date of the last modification to the program. A program that hasn't been updated for a very long time is either very stable or not used very often. Following this scheme, the top of a typical batch file would look something like this:

```
REM NAME:     PREPARE.CMD
REM PURPOSE:  Prepare For An Incremental Backup
REM VERSION:  1.00
REM DATE:     April 15, 1993
```

Revision Recently, I've started adding a fifth line of documentation below the date. I call this the revision line. When I make a change to a batch file, I not only update the version and date, I add a note about the reason for the update. That makes it easier to follow the evolution of my batch files over time. This is a recent addition, so not all the batch files on the disk have this line (none of the version 1.00 would because they haven't been revised) and those that do might not have notes back to 1.00 when the changes were made before I started doing this. Following this modified scheme, the top of a typical batch file would look something like this:

```
REM NAME:     PREPARE.CMD
REM PURPOSE:  Prepare For An Incremental Backup
REM VERSION:  1.04
REM DATE:     May 25, 1993
```

```
REM REVISION: 1.01: Added *.OBJ To Ignored Files
REM REVISION: 1.02: Added *.INI To Ignored Files
REM REVISION: 1.03: Added Processing Messages To Batch File
```

☑ Adding the name, purpose, version number, date created/modified, and revision data to the top of each batch file is an excellent form of documentation.

If you study the sample programs that come with this book, you'll see that almost all of them follow this documentation scheme.

Bypassing the comments

The GOTO command and labels are detailed in chapter 12. The GOTO command causes the batch file to jump over lines to a line beginning with a colon and the label specified after the GOTO command. For example, GOTO START would cause a batch file to jump to the line containing :START. Because jumping over lines is quicker than processing those lines, a batch file segment like this:

```
GOTO START
REM Name:     BATCH.CMD
REM PURPOSE: Show Skipping Documentation
REM VERSION: 1.00
REM DATE:     May 28, 1992
:START
```

would run quicker than the same batch file segment without the GOTO command. In fact, because the remark lines are jumped over and never executed, the REM command isn't necessary, so this batch file could be written as:

```
GOTO START
Name:     BATCH.CMD
PURPOSE: Show Using Colon To Mark Documentation
VERSION: 1.00
DATE:     May 28, 1992
None Of These Lines Will Execute Or Show On The
Screen, So The Function Is Similar To REM
:START
```

Summary

- Remark lines starting with the REM command make your batch files much easier to understand and follow.
- Written documentation is important to both the users of your batch files and anyone who later wants to modify them.

- Batch files should be able to explain their purpose to a user who starts them, with a /? switch on the command line. How to do this is covered later in the book.
- Adding some standard information to the top of each batch file is a good way to begin documenting your batch files, and will allow batch files introduced later in this book to access that information in a useful fashion.
- A batch file will skip over documentation remarks quicker with a GOTO command than with REM.

6
Keeping it quiet

Let's take a moment to recreate the batch file called A.CMD, presented in an earlier chapter, that performed a directory of the A: drive. This time, you can use what you learned in the last chapter to include some documentation at the top of the batch file. Your resulting batch file might look like this:

```
REM NAME:     A.CMD
REM PURPOSE: Directory Of A: Drive
REM VERSION: 1.00
REM DATE:     May 8, 1992
DIR A:
```

Now run that batch file. Go ahead and do this now because the rest of the chapter will make more sense once you see this batch file run.

The file A.CMD on the disk has some additional commands added to it, which I won't go into now. However, there is a file on the disk called SHOW-A.CMD that looks exactly like the batch file above. In case running this batch file isn't convenient at the moment, FIG. 6-1 shows a screen shot of it in operation.

While the batch file runs properly and you get the information you want, the screen is very unattractive. As the batch file runs, every command in the batch file shows up on the screen—even when the user doesn't need or want this information.

Back in chapter 1, I introduced the concept of a batch file being a script that the computer follows. Well, the computer has a bad habit of reading everything in the script. Take the following text, for example:

Billy: Sally, you can't leave me. I need you.
Sally: I'm leaving you. [Opens door and walks out.]

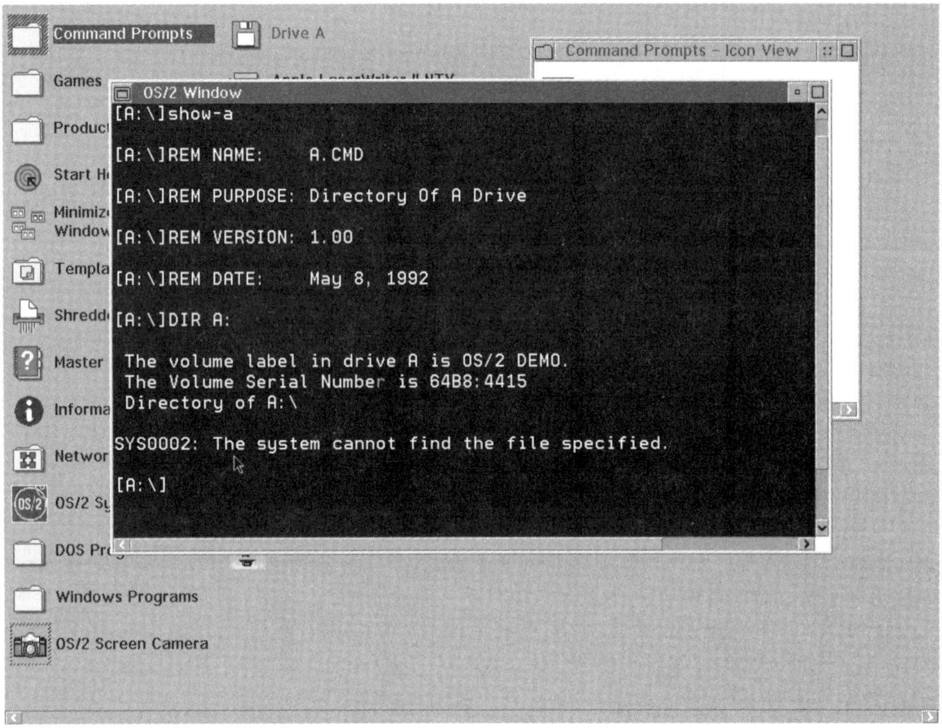

6-1 SHOW-A.CMD running. Notice that commands are echoed to the screen.

While the author expects Sally to open the door and walk out, he expects her to do it quietly. While running a tax program, you don't expect to see:

```
Line Input A$
SalesTax = Income * .04 - (State * 2.3)
```

When you use a word-processing or spreadsheet program, you never see the code running. Why should a batch file be any different?

Command echoing

The process of showing commands on the screen while they're being executed is called *echoing* or *command echoing*. When echoing is on, you see commands as they execute. When echoing is off, you don't see commands as they execute. Every batch file starts with echoing turned on.

You can turn echoing off in two different ways, and each method has its own uses. Normally, you can add an ECHO OFF command at the top of the batch file, which turns command echoing off for the entire batch file and any batch file this batch file runs (a process examined later in the book), although not for any other batch files that execute after the batch file terminates. So, as a general rule, you'll need an ECHO OFF command at the top of each batch file.

The ECHO OFF command turns off just command echoing; it doesn't turn off OS/2 messages. If you copy a file in a batch file, you'll see the OS/2 1 File(s) copied message. If you use a batch file to start a program, you'll still see that program on the screen. All ECHO OFF affects is the display of batch file commands while that specific batch file is running.

➡ The ECHO OFF command keeps the screens produced by your batch files cleaner.

The second way to turn off command echoing affects only a single line. When a line in a batch file is preceded by the at character (@), that single line will execute without being echoed to the screen, even if command echoing is on. Most users combine these two methods, adding the command @ECHO OFF as the first line of their batch files. (If you don't use the @, ECHO OFF will appear on the screen.) You can now modify A.CMD to present a much clearer screen:

```
@ECHO OFF
REM NAME:     A.CMD
REM PURPOSE: Directory Of A: Drive
REM VERSION: 1.00
REM DATE:     May 8, 1992
DIR A:
```

Only the first line has changed. Go ahead and modify your batch file and then run it. As you can see, with command echoing off, the screen is much clearer. In case you don't have the time to try this yourself, FIG. 6-2 shows A.CMD running with these modifications.

➡ Adding an @ in front of a command turns off command echoing for that command, even if command echoing is on for the entire batch file.

For almost all batch files, you can safely add an @ECHO OFF command to the top and forget about it. As you'll see in the next chapter, you can communicate with the user in spite of command echoing being off. And a few batch files need to have command echoing on. Once command echoing is turned off, you can turn it back on with the ECHO ON command.

Summary

- The normal state of batch files is to have command echoing on, where commands are displayed on the screen before being executed.
- ECHO OFF turns off command echoing for an entire batch file and any other batch files that it runs.
- Preceding a batch file command with an @ prevents command echoing for that command, regardless of the status of command echoing.

- Most users start each batch file with an @ECHO OFF command.
- On the rare occasion when you need command echoing on in a portion of a batch file, you can turn it back on with ECHO ON.

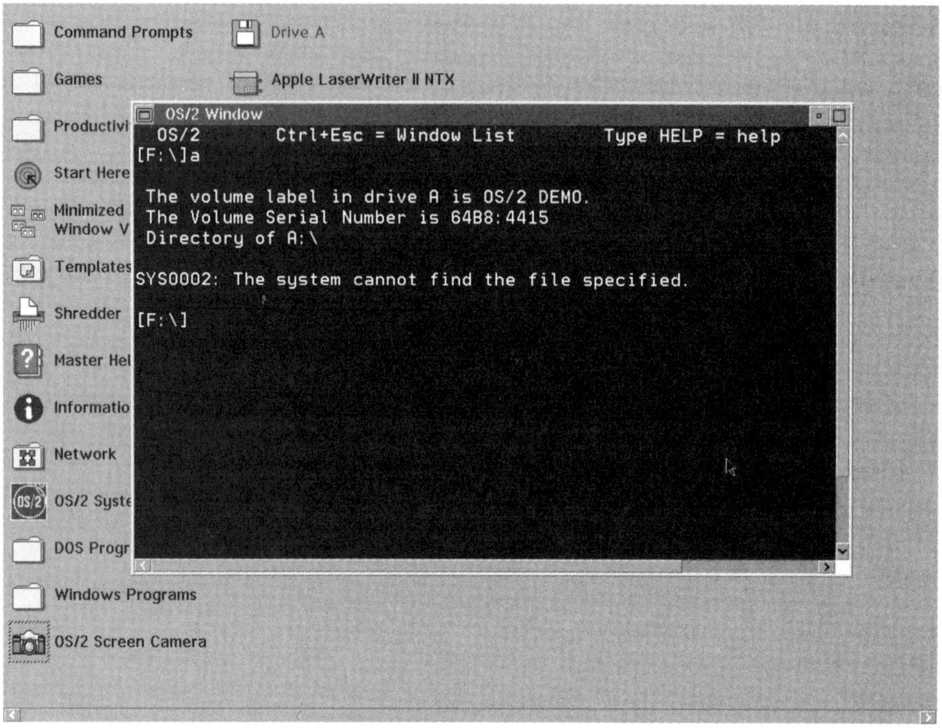

6-2 With the addition of the @ECHO OFF command at the top of the batch file, none of the commands are echoed to the screen, and you get only the information provided by the DIR command.

7
Talking to the user

Some commands are *multimodal*, meaning they perform different functions depending on how they're used. For example, the command SET by itself displays the contents of the environment, while the command:

```
SET VARIABLE=VALUE
```

stores a value to an environmental variable. (If the value is missing, it will delete the environment variable—meaning that it will store a nul value in it.)

While SET is bimodal, the PATH command is trimodal because it has three different functions. The PATH command by itself displays the contents of the path, a command like:

```
PATH=C:\;C:\WORD;C:\123
```

stores a value to the path, and the command PATH; resets the path to nul.

➡ Some commands perform several different functions depending on how they are used.

Like the PATH command, the ECHO command is trimodal. In the last chapter, you saw that when it's combined with an ON or OFF, the ECHO command can be used to change the status of command echoing. This is only one use for the ECHO command. When used by itself, the ECHO command displays the status of command echoing.

Displaying messages

While the ECHO command can turn command echoing on or off and display the status of command echoing, it has another even more important function: You can use it to communicate with the user. When ECHO is followed by a space and then a message, that message is displayed on the screen.

When command echoing is on, the message is actually displayed twice. It gets displayed once when the command is issued by the batch file (due to command echoing) and a second time when the command is carried out. When command echoing is off, the message is displayed only once.

Let's stop for a moment and look at a simple example. Type in this brief batch file segment and then run it:

```
@ECHO OFF
ECHO Hello World
ECHO I Am A Brand New Batch File!
```

When you run the batch file, two messages will be displayed, one per line. Figure 7-1 shows this batch file running in an OS/2 window. There are several good reasons to echo messages in a batch file, some of which are explained in the following sections.

Telling the user what's going on

Any time a batch file is doing something for the user, you should let him know what's going on—especially if the process takes a long time. Mes-

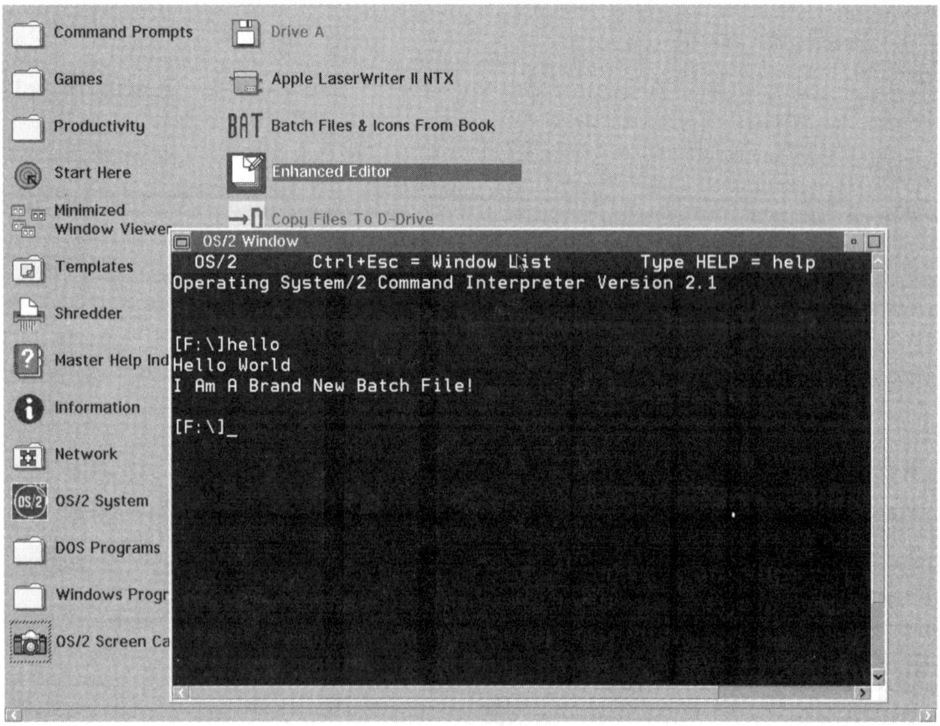

7-1 Using the ECHO command, a batch file can display messages to the screen even after an @ECHO OFF command has been used.

sages like "Defragmenting The Hard Disk: This Takes Two Hours" or "Backing Up To Tape Drive: This Takes Twenty Minutes" or even "Attempting To Log Onto Network: Please Wait" can go a long way to comfort the user when the computer doesn't immediately respond. After all, you don't want the user rebooting or shutting down a session because she thinks the computer has locked up.

Keeping the user informed

Not all commands take a very long time to run, but it's still nice to keep the user informed. To see this, let's take another look at the operational portion of PREPARE.CMD. My computer has a 1-gigabyte hard disk (1000Mb) and even though my 486/66 is very fast, it takes thirty seconds or more to run each of the ATTRIB commands in this batch file. Since the OS/2 ATTRIB command generates no screen display, without ECHO commands this batch file would cause nothing to be generated on the screen for over a minute. So adding the ECHO commands keeps the user informed of the progress of the batch files.

```
@ECHO OFF
CD\
ECHO Processing *.BAK Files
ATTRIB *.BAK /S -A
ECHO Processing *.OBJ Files
ATTRIB *.OBJ /S -A
ECHO Processing *.INI Files
ATTRIB *.INI /S -A
GOTO END
```

Giving the user instructions

Sometimes the computer needs for the user to either physically do something or provide some information. Messages displayed from within the batch file are an excellent way to provide the user with additional information on what to do.

The following batch file, called I.CMD, is an improved version of B.CMD. This batch file backs up only those files that have changed since the last backup, called an *incremental backup*. Rather than using the BACKUP program, it uses the XCOPY command.

```
@ECHO OFF
ECHO This Batch File Performs An Incremental Backup
ECHO Using The XCOPY Command
ECHO Insert A Freshly Formatted Disk In The A: Drive
ECHO And Then Press Any Key When Ready
ECHO Note: If The Disk Fills Up,
ECHO The XCOPY Command Will Abort
ECHO Without Finishing
ECHO If That Happens, Run The Batch File Over With
```

```
ECHO Another Freshly Formatted Disk To Copy The Files
ECHO That Were Missed The First Time
PAUSE
XCOPY C:\*.* /S /M A:
```

With the extra information provided by the ECHO commands, even someone who has never performed an incremental backup will know what to do.

☑ The ECHO command lets you display text on the screen to give instructions and keep the user informed.

Making your messages attractive

Probably the single most important aspect of writing attractive messages is to make sure the message you echo to the screen is no wider than the screen. When a message is too long for the screen, it goes to the end of the screen and then wraps to the next line without regard for words. If the break occurs in the middle of a word, then the line is broken in the middle of a word.

In addition to avoiding messages too wide for the screen, I also tend to avoid long messages in general. It has been my experience that messages of 40 or fewer characters across are much easier for the user to read than messages that go all the way across the screen. As an additional advantage, shorter messages avoid problems when the batch file is run in an OS/2 window rather than in full-screen mode.

You can center titles by putting additional spaces between ECHO and the message. When I have several screens of information, I tend to display a title first on each screen and center that title with a blank line under it.

Where appropriate, I also use subtitles. For these, I display a blank line above and below the subtitle, and I underline the subtitle by displaying a series of dashes equal in length to the subtitle. Both items help to draw attention to the subtitle, as well as breaking up the lines of text displayed on the screen.

Plan for OS/2 windows

DOS requires everything to run in full-screen mode. That means you can plan on your batch file having access to the entire screen and being the only thing on display. That isn't the case under OS/2. For that reason, OS/2 requires more planning.

Smaller screen

In full-screen mode, a batch file can display 80 characters across the screen and 24 lines of text. However, OS/2 can also run batch files in smaller windows. Since these windows can be resized, you never know for sure the size of the window in which a batch file runs.

Look back at FIG. 7-1. Here, a batch file was run in a smaller window.

This batch file has less than 80 characters across and 24 lines down to display its messages. OS/2 does provide "elevators" along the bottom and right of this window so you can scroll around the full 80×24 screen, but this is a very cumbersome method of reading larger batch file messages.

If you're installing the batch files, you can avoid display problems by installing them to run in a full screen. This is controlled by the Settings page on the Sessions notebook you fill in when you install a batch file. Look back to chapter 2 for more details on this.

If you're writing batch files that others will install and use, you can recommend that they install them to run in full-screen mode, but you can't enforce it. To avoid problems, design your messages to be as short as possible, even if it means more lines. Also, try to uses fewer lines of messages per page, even if it means more pages.

Background operation

When running in the foreground, it's easy for a batch file to display an error message or otherwise grab the user's attention with a message displayed with the ECHO command. You might need to use some of the techniques discussed in this book to make it more eye-catching, but those are fairly easy to include.

The problem is that OS/2 allows the user to minimize batch files and run them in the background where nothing they write to the screen is visible. Batch files can't force themselves to the foreground when there's a problem, so how can a batch file with a problem make the user aware of the problem?

As it turns out, the solution is again the lowly ECHO command. When a Ctrl–G character (written as ^G) is included in an ECHO message, the ^G beeps the bell once. The bell beeps even if the batch file is running in the background. So replacing the error message:

```
ECHO XCOPY Ran Out Of Floppy Disk Space
```

with the message:

```
ECHO XCOPY Ran Out Of Floppy Disk Space^G^G^G
```

means the user will always know the batch file ran into problems—even when it's running in the background.

The ^G character doesn't display on the screen when the ECHO command executes so you can place it anywhere in an existing message without changing the formatting. For my own readability, I generally place the ^Gs at the end of a message. The faster your machine, the quicker the beep, so the more ^Gs you'll need. Experiment to see what's best for your machine.

With the OS/2 Enhanced Editor, you enter a ^G into a file by holding down the Alt key and entering 007 from the keypad. You must use the keypad as the numbers along the top of the keyboard won't work.

If your editor or word processor doesn't allow you to enter a ^G into a file, there is a solution. Go to the command line, change to your batch subdirectory, and issue the following command:

```
ECHO ^G > BELL
```

(Make sure to hold down the Ctrl key and press G for the ^G.) This command will pipe the single ^G to the file call BELL. You can load this into your editor or word processor, highlight that single character (which looks like a dot on the screen), copy it into the paste buffer, and then paste it into your batch files where you need it.

☑ Sounding the bell is a good way for a batch file running in the background to call attention to itself.

Blank lines

As I just mentioned, I often times use blank lines in my screen messages to call attention to certain portions of the message or just to break up long messages. However, displaying a blank line is not as simple as it sounds. You might expect that putting an ECHO on a line by itself would skip a line, but as I said earlier, this displays the status of command echoing.

You can choose from three different ways to display a blank line, and the one you select will depend on several different factors:

Use an almost blank line The easiest way to display a blank line is to use commands like these:

```
ECHO !
ECHO .
```

Both of these commands display a printable character that is fairly inconspicuous. Most users will either not notice or else ignore the single inconspicuous character. This approach is the easiest but is also the least attractive.

Use an undocumented trick You can easily display a blank line using the command:

```
ECHO.
```

where there's no space between the ECHO and the period. This is quick and easy, but it relies on an undocumented quirk in ECHO that might not be supported in future versions. This is best reserved for quick-and-easy batch files that are not likely to be used for too long.

Use a high-ordered ASCII character High-ordered ASCII characters are special characters supported by the computer but not shown on the screen. I'll explain more about them later. However, one of them is perfect for displaying blank lines. The high-ordered ASCII character with a value of 255 looks like a space on the screen, even though it isn't, so it's treated like any other character. Thus, the command:

```
ECHO Alt-255
```

will display a blank line on the screen. Of course, you'll need to hold down the Alt key and type 255 on the keypad to get the high-ordered ASCII character. This is how you'd enter it in the Enhanced Editor as well. Note that using the numbers at the top of the keyboard won't work.

Some editors and word processors either do not accept high-ordered ASCII characters at all or make the process of entering them difficult. There's an easy solution to this problem. From the command line, enter the command:

```
COPY CON 255
```

hit Enter, and then type:

```
Alt-255^Z
```

to include an Alt–255 and nothing else in a file called 255. (Type F6—which produces the ^Z character—and then hit Enter to end and save the file.) Now import that into your word processor and paste it wherever you need it in the file.

What you can and can't echo

While the ECHO command is very flexible, there are a few things either you can't display using the ECHO command or that displaying is more difficult than displaying most characters.

Pipes

You can include the pipe symbols <, >>, >, or | in an ECHO statement. However, if you do, the text to be displayed by the ECHO command will be piped into a file or alternative device rather than displayed on the screen. To use these symbols as part of an ECHO message, you must precede them with a caret (^). So < must be entered as ^<, > must be entered as ^>, and | must be entered as ^|. The >> characters cannot be entered as ^>>, rather they must be entered as ^>^>. Piping is examined in more detail later in the book.

Take extreme care when including piping symbols in an ECHO command. The text is piped somewhere other than the screen.

Percent sign

You cannot directly include a percent sign in an ECHO statement because OS/2 tries to interpret a single percent sign as a variable. If you need a percent sign in your ECHO statement, include a double percent sign (%%). OS/2 will display this as a single percent sign.

☑ To display a single percent sign in an ECHO command, you must enter two percent signs.

On/Off

You can't echo any message that begins with an ON or OFF because OS/2 interprets this as an ECHO ON or ECHO OFF command. You can solve this in two ways. The easiest way is to rewrite the message so that the words ON or OFF aren't the first words in the message. If rewriting the message isn't possible, then begin the message with the Alt–255 character described earlier. Because the high-ordered Alt–255 is treated as an invisible character, the ON or OFF are no longer the first words in the message.

Summary

- Some commands have two or more functions, depending on how they're used.
- The ECHO command can turn command echoing on and off, display the status of command echoing, and display a message on the screen—all depending on how it's used.
- Displaying messages to the user via the ECHO command is useful for the following reasons: to tell the user either that the batch file is running a process that takes a very long time or what the batch file is doing, and to give the user additional instructions.
- Echo messages should be 80 characters or less to prevent unexpected wrapping on the screen.
- Shorter echo messages are easier to read than longer messages and are more likely to fit in an OS/2 window.
- The ECHO ^G command allows a batch file to signal attention even when running in the background.
- You can enter echo messages by adding additional spaces between ECHO and the message.
- You can display nearly blank lines by following ECHO with a single inconspicuous character.
- You can display a blank line with the undocumented command of placing a period directly after ECHO without a space in between.
- You can display a blank-looking line by echoing the high-ordered ASCII character Alt–255.
- Piping symbols cannot be displayed in an ECHO command unless they're preceded by a caret.
- In order to display a single percent sign, the ECHO command must have two percent signs, side by side.
- The words ON and OFF cannot be used as the first word of an ECHO message.

8
Using high-ordered ASCII characters

OS/2 can use 256 different characters, each one having an associated ASCII value that runs from 0 to 255. TABLE 8-1 is an ASCII chart listing each value. Most users concern themselves only with the values below 128 because these are the values they can enter by pressing a key on the keyboard. However, the values of 128 and higher offer some nice formatting tools for batch files.

Table 8-1 The 256 ASCII characters.

Dec	Hex	Character	Dec	Hex	Character
0	0		17	11	◄
1	1	☺	18	12	↕
2	2	☻	19	13	‼
3	3	♥	20	14	¶
4	4	♦	21	15	§
5	5	♣	22	16	▬
6	6	♠	23	17	↨
7	7	•	24	18	↑
8	8	◘	25	19	↓
9	9	○	26	1A	→
10	A	◙	27	1B	←
11	B	♂	28	1C	∟
12	C	♀	29	1D	↔
13	D	♪	30	1E	▲
14	E	♫	31	1F	▼
15	F	*	32	20	
16	10	►	33	21	!

Table 8-1 Continued.

Dec	Hex	Character	Dec	Hex	Character
34	22	"	82	52	R
35	23	#	83	53	S
36	24	$	84	54	T
37	25	%	85	55	U
38	26	&	86	56	V
39	27	'	87	57	W
40	28	(	88	58	X
41	29	)	90	5A	Z
42	2A	*	91	5B	[
43	2B	+	92	5C	\
44	2C	,	93	5D	]
45	2D	-	94	5E	^
46	2E	.	95	5F	_
47	2F	/	96	60	`
48	30	0	97	61	a
49	31	1	98	62	b
50	32	2	99	63	c
51	33	3	100	64	d
52	34	4	101	65	e
53	35	5	102	66	f
54	36	6	103	67	g
55	37	7	104	68	h
56	38	8	105	69	i
57	39	9	106	6A	j
58	3A	:	107	6B	k
59	3B	;	108	6C	l
60	3C	<	109	6D	m
61	3D	=	110	6E	n
62	3E	>	111	6F	o
63	3F	?	112	70	p
64	40	@	113	71	q
65	41	A	114	72	r
66	42	B	115	73	s
67	43	C	116	74	t
68	44	D	117	75	u
69	45	E	118	76	v
70	46	F	119	77	w
71	47	G	120	78	x
72	48	H	121	79	y
73	49	I	122	7A	z
74	4A	J	123	7B	{
75	4B	K	124	7C	|
76	4C	L	125	7D	}
77	4D	M	126	7E	~
78	4E	N	127	7F	⌂
79	4F	O	128	80	Ç
80	50	P	129	81	ü
81	51	Q	130	82	é

Dec	Hex	Character	Dec	Hex	Character
131	83	â	180	B4	┤
132	84	ä	181	B5	╡
133	85	à	182	B6	╢
134	86	å	183	B7	╖
135	87	ç	184	B8	╕
136	88	ê	185	B9	╣
137	89	ë	186	BA	║
138	8A	è	187	BB	╗
139	8B	ï	188	BC	╝
140	8C	î	189	BD	╜
141	8D	ì	190	BE	╛
142	8E	Ä	191	BF	┐
143	8F	Å	192	C0	└
144	90	É	193	C1	┴
145	91	æ	194	C2	┬
146	92	Æ	195	C3	├
147	93	ô	196	C4	─
148	94	ö	197	C5	┼
149	95	ò	198	C6	╞
150	96	û	199	C7	╟
151	97	ù	200	C8	╚
152	98	ÿ	201	C9	╔
153	99	Ö	202	CA	╩
154	9A	Ü	203	CB	╦
155	9B	¢	204	CC	╠
156	9C	£	205	CD	═
157	9D	¥	206	CE	╬
158	9E	₧	207	CF	╧
159	9F	ƒ	208	D0	╨
160	A0	á	209	D1	╤
161	A1	í	210	D2	╥
162	A2	ó	211	D3	╙
163	A3	ú	212	D4	╘
164	A4	ñ	213	D5	╒
165	A5	Ñ	214	D6	╓
166	A6	ª	215	D7	╫
167	A7	º	216	D8	╪
168	A8	¿	217	D9	┘
169	A9	⌐	218	DA	┌
170	AA	¬	219	DB	█
171	AB	½	220	DC	▄
172	AC	¼	221	DD	▌
173	AD	¡	222	DE	▐
174	AE	«	223	DF	▀
175	AF	»	224	E0	α
176	B0	░	225	E1	ß
177	B1	▒	226	E2	Γ
178	B2	▓	227	E3	π
179	B3	│	228	E4	Σ

Table 8-1 Continued

Dec	Hex	Character	Dec	Hex	Character
229	E5	σ	243	F3	≤
230	E6	μ	244	F4	⌠
231	E7	τ	245	F5	⌡
232	E8	Φ	246	F6	÷
233	EA	Θ	247	F7	≈
234	EB	Ω	248	F8	°
235	EC	δ	249	F9	•
236	ED	∞	250	FA	·
237	ED	φ	251	FB	√
238	EE	∈	252	FC	ⁿ
239	EF	∩	253	FD	²
240	F0	≡	254	FE	■
241	F1	±	255	FF	
242	F2	≥			

If you wanted to draw a box without using high-ordered ASCII characters, you would have to use colons or | pipes (which must be entered as ^|) for the vertical bars, plus sign for the corners, and the hyphen for the horizontal bars. However, with high-ordered ASCII characters, nice boxes are easy.

HI-ASCII.CMD illustrates this. The lines that appear to be an ECHO by itself also have an Alt–255 character to produce a blank line. When printed, the bottom set of boxes looks disarranged. This is due to the requirement that the vertical bar be preceded with a caret that doesn't show on the screen. When HI-ASCII.CMD is run, the boxes are displayed properly. A copy of HI-ASCII.CMD is on the disk, and is as follows:

```
@ECHO OFF
CLS
ECHO
ECHO ┌────────────────────────────────────────┐
ECHO │High-Order ASCII Character Demonstration│
ECHO └────────────────────────────────────────┘
ECHO
ECHO ┌────┬────┬────┬────┬────┬────┬────┬────┐
ECHO │    │    │    │    │    │    │    │    │
ECHO │    │    │    │    │    │    │    │    │
ECHO └────┴────┴────┴────┴────┴────┴────┴────┘
ECHO
ECHO ╔════╦════╦════╦════╦════╦════╦════╦════╗
ECHO ║    ║    ║    ║    ║    ║    ║    ║    ║
ECHO ║    ║    ║    ║    ║    ║    ║    ║    ║
ECHO ╚════╩════╩════╩════╩════╩════╩════╩════╝
ECHO
ECHO Now Doesn't That Look Better Than This
ECHO
ECHO +----+----+----+----+----+----+----+----+
ECHO ^|    ^|    ^|    ^|    ^|    ^|    ^|    ^|    ^|
ECHO ^|    ^|    ^|    ^|    ^|    ^|    ^|    ^|    ^|
ECHO +----+----+----+----+----+----+----+----+
PAUSE
```

Characters with an ASCII value of 128 or higher are called high-ordered ASCII characters. Figure 8-1 lists those high-ordered ASCII characters that are most useful in batch files.

If you ever need to quickly look up an ASCII value, you don't have to look for your copy of this book. Just copy ASCII.EXE from the enclosed disk to a subdirectory in your path, and then run ASCII to get a display of all the ASCII characters with values 30–255. (Values below 30 are mostly used for control functions, so most of them won't display on the screen anyway.) ASCII.EXE is a DOS program and so must be run in an OS/2 DOS session. In order to see the entire display, ASCII.EXE must also be run in full-screen mode.

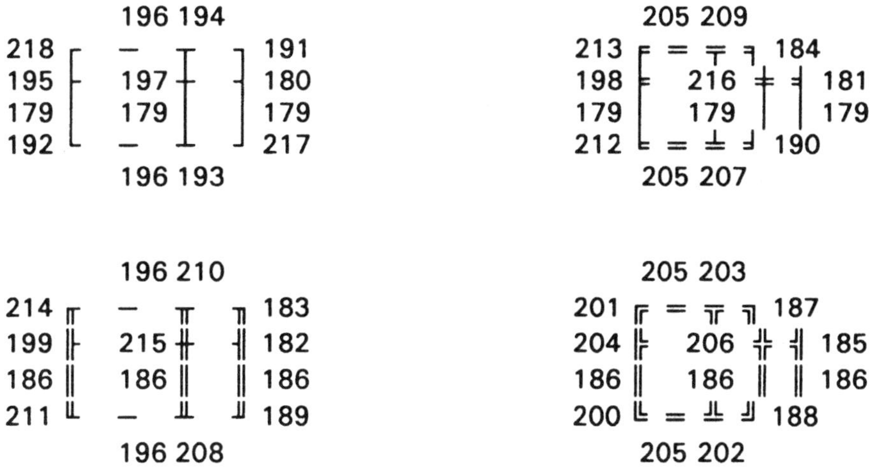

8-1 A few of the ASCII characters with codes above 128 are useful for drawing boxes and lines in batch files.

Entering high-ordered ASCII characters

If you're using the Enhanced Editor or the OS/2 System Editor to create your batch files, then entering high-ordered ASCII characters is easy:

1. Hold down the Alt key.
2. Type the three-digit code for the character using the number pad. (The numbers at the top of the keyboard won't work.)
3. Release the Alt key.
4. Repeat steps 1–3 for any additional characters you want to enter.

This method isn't limited to just high-ordered ASCII characters; you could use Alt–68 to enter a capital D, for example. However, using the keyboard for the low-ordered ASCII characters is much easier.

Some editors make it easy to enter the box-drawing characters. Microsoft Word, for example, has a line-drawing utility that draws using single or double lines as you move around the screen, and automatically inserts the proper joint when the lines cross.

Many word processors, however, make it difficult to enter high-ordered ASCII characters. In Microsoft Word, you use the Alt key to pull down menus so you sometimes have to enter the high-ordered ASCII character several times before Word figures out you're entering a character and not requesting a menu. Some versions of WordStar require you to enter a ^P and then the three-digit code rather than using the Alt-key combination. If the Alt-key combination doesn't work in your editor or word processor, check your manual to see what your program expects.

Entering high-ordered ASCII characters when your editor won't let you

A few editors and word processors make it impossible to enter high-ordered ASCII characters into your batch files. There's an easy solution, however, that works with almost every editor and word processor:

1. From the command-line prompt, enter the command COPY CON *file name*. I find it handy to create one file per character for each character I use a lot and to use the ASCII number as the filename.
2. Hold down the Alt key and type in the ASCII code for the high-ordered ASCII character to include in the file.
3. Press F6.
4. Press Enter.

At this point, the file exists and contains the character of interest. To get this character into your file, just import it into the file using the editor's or word processor's import command. If it doesn't have one, open the file first and copy the character to the paste buffer (the area where you store characters to paste into other files). If your editor or word processor can't import a file and doesn't have a paste buffer, you might want to consider finding another editor.

More on the Enhanced Editor

Using the Enhanced Editor to edit batch files has one minor drawback. Go ahead and load a copy of HI-ASCII.CMD into the Enhanced Editor. (There's a copy on the disk that comes with this book.) You'll see that the boxes in HI-ASCII.CMD don't line up the way they do in the display earlier in this chapter. Yet, if you run HI-ASCII.CMD, the boxes show properly on the screen.

The reason for this is the Enhanced Editor defaults to using a proportional font for characters. With a proportional font (like the text in this book), the space allowed for a character is proportional to the width of the character, so an M gets a lot of space while an i or a space character gets very little space. The result is that the characters don't line up on the screen. While this affects the display in the editor, information on the font is not stored in the batch file, so it displays using a monospaced font when the batch file is executed. With a monospaced font (like the program listings in this book), every character gets the same amount of space, so everything lines up on the screen.

The solution to this minor dilemma is to use the Style command under the Edit menu to reformat the characters in the batch file as a monospaced font such as Courier. This doesn't alter the batch file itself as the formatting information is stored in a file called EPM.INI in the \OS2 subdirectory, but it does cause it to be displayed properly by the Enhanced Editor. Figure 8-2 shows using the Style command to reformat HI-ASCII.CMD.

➠ In the Enhanced Editor, reformatting a batch file with a monospaced font makes everything line up properly.

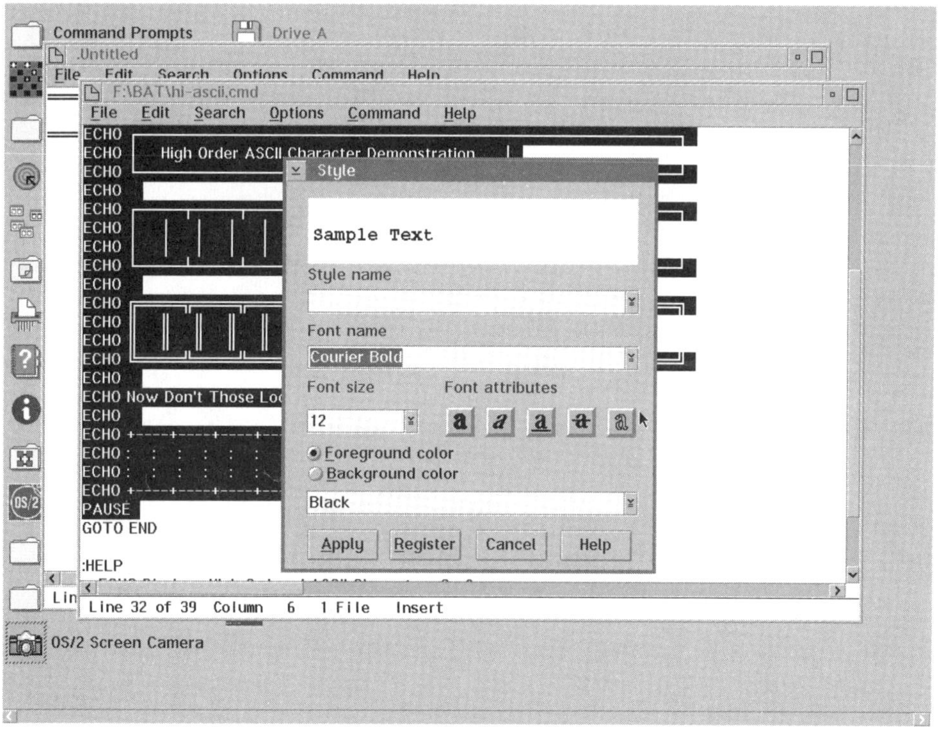

8-2 The Enhanced Editor can format text using a nonproportional font so that everything lines up on the screen. This display and print formatting does not alter the batch file itself since the formatting information is stored in Extended Attributes.

The OS/2 System Editor has the same problem and shares the same solution. Only in the OS/2 System Editor, you change the font using the Set font command on the Options menu.

Summary

- High-ordered ASCII characters allow you to draw attractive boxes inside a batch file.
- ASCII.EXE, on the enclosed disk, displays an ASCII chart of most characters on the screen.
- Many editors let you enter high-ordered ASCII characters by holding down the Alt key and entering the associated number from the number pad.
- If your editor or word processor won't let you enter high-ordered ASCII characters, you can pipe them to a file and then read that file into your editor or word processor.
- In order to display batch files using a monospaced font in the Enhanced Editor or the OS/2 System Editor, you must reformat the text using the Style command.

9
Hold that batch file!

Imagine you're running the following batch file segment:

```
@ECHO OFF
CLS
ECHO Warning: The Following Program Will Do Damage
ECHO          It Erases All Documents
ECHO          And .EXE Programs
ECHO          In This Subdirectory
ECHO          And It Removes The
ECHO          \BAT Subdirectory
RUNIT
```

This batch file presents a fairly stern warning to the user but doesn't give him the ability to do anything about it: by the time the user has read the warning, the program has already started running!

It's unlikely you would ever run such a damaging program—at least intentionally. However, the purpose of a warning is to give the user the time to read it and react to it.

Additionally, what if you had a lot of information to give to the user and that information was going to take 60 ECHO commands? Using the commands you've learned so far, all you could do is put one after another in a batch file. However, unless the computer was very slow, the messages would scroll by too fast to read.

Pausing a batch file

The PAUSE command is the solution to this dilemma. When a batch file comes to a PAUSE, it stops and displays a "Press any key when ready . . ."

message. The batch file then waits until the user presses any printable key. Keystrokes like Alt, Shift, Ctrl, and NumLock that don't produce a character on the screen won't cause a batch file to resume while waiting on a PAUSE command.

If the user presses Ctrl–Break, the batch file will immediately abort its execution and return the user to either the command line or desktop, depending on how the batch file was run. Using this, you can build an "escape clause" into your batch files. Let's reconsider the first batch file with a PAUSE command used as an escape clause:

```
@ECHO OFF
CLS
ECHO Warning: The Following Program Will Do Damage
ECHO          It Erases All Documents
ECHO          And .EXE Programs
ECHO          In This Subdirectory
ECHO          And It Removes The
ECHO          \BAT Subdirectory
ECHO
ECHO To Skip Running The Program,
ECHO Hold Down The Control Key
ECHO And Press The Break Key
PAUSE
RUNIT
```

The batch file now tells the user how to abort processing and has a PAUSE and that gives the user a chance to think about the messages on the screen and decide how to respond.

➡ The PAUSE command stops the computer while the user reads the screen or thinks about a response. It even gives the user a chance to stop the batch file by pressing Ctrl–Break.

PAUSE is useful even if the user doesn't need to press Ctrl–Break; it simply gives her time to read the messages and think about them before continuing. If you're going to display several different screens of information, then PAUSE followed on the next line by CLS is crucial in order to ensure that the user is able to read all the information.

Aborting a batch file

As mentioned previously, you can use Ctrl–Break to stop a batch file immediately and have control immediately return to OS/2. This makes it easy for the user to abort a batch file prior to running a dangerous command. Later on, you'll see a better way to give the user an escape clause.

Summary

- PAUSE stops a batch file until the user presses any printable keystroke.
- If the user presses Ctrl–Break at a PAUSE command—or any other point in the batch file—OS/2 will stop processing the batch file.

10
Review #1

It's time to stop and catch our breath. While it might not seem so at first, you've covered a tremendous amount of material. You now know how to use a brand-new editor, how to run OS/2 batch files from the command line, and how to install OS/2 batch files as desktop icons. You've also learned how to write simple batch files that contain a mixture of OS/2 commands and a few batch subcommands.

That's why you should now take a few moments and make sure that you're up to speed before continuing. What follows are three quick problems. Take a few moments and try to work them out. If you get stuck, glance back through the first few chapters. It's important that you have the skills necessary to solve these problems before you go on; otherwise, you'll find continuing difficult.

Problem 1

Write a batch file to format a floppy disk that's in the A: drive. Assume that FORMAT.COM has been renamed to XYZ.COM so the user won't be tempted to run the command without the batch file. Use plenty of ECHO statements to tell the user what to do, and be sure to turn command echoing off so the user won't see the XYZ command and be tempted to run the program directly.

Install this batch file to your desktop and give it the name FORMAT .CMD. You'll find an icon called FORMAT.ICO on the disk that comes with this book that you can use for this purpose.

Problem 2

Write a batch file to reset the path to include the following subdirectories:

```
C:\
C:\NORTON
C:\123
C:\WP
C:\UTILITY
C:\BAT
```

create the following environmental variables:

```
TEMP=C:\TEMP
DOSONLY=NO
LIB=D:\BLDLITE
OBJ=D:\BLDLITE
```

and run the program CONFIGPT.EXE to configure the printer. While order generally doesn't matter, remember that if the path doesn't point to a subdirectory, then you must change to that subdirectory before running a program contained in it.

Install this batch file to your desktop and give it the name PROBLEM2.CMD. You'll find an icon called PROBLEM2.ICO on the disk that comes with this book that you can use for this purpose.

Problem 3

Your system has three accounting programs—DAILY.EXE, WEEKLY.COM, and ANNUAL.EXE—that can be run only on your computer by authorized people. Write an informational batch file called ACCTHELP.CMD to give users information about these programs. That information should include:

- The names of the programs
- The people authorized to run the programs
- The fact that passwords are required
- The name of the person to contact for help with these programs

Finally, note how important it is to perform a backup after running one of these programs and to send a copy of the backup to the appropriate department at the corporate headquarters. For the names and numbers you need for this problem, make up any information that you don't have.

Install this batch file also to your desktop and give it the name ACCTHELP.CMD. Use the icon ACCTHELP.ICO on the included disk for this purpose.

Answers

There are a number of ways to tackle each of these problems. My solutions are shown in appendix A in the back of the book. It isn't important that you match my answers; if you develop a working solution to the problem, your solution might be as good as mine and maybe even better.

PART 3
Intermediate batch file topics

Now that you've seen simple batch file commands, it's time to take a look at some slightly more complex commands. As it turns out, the chapters in this section are the "meat" of the book. As you write your own batch files, you'll find that the vast majority of the batch file commands you use are either REM or ECHO or the commands covered in these chapters. Just to be sure, there's a chapter at the end of this section where you can test your knowledge.

Chapter 11: Replaceable parameters Unless you have a way to get information into a batch file, it's difficult to have the batch file perform differently each time it runs. Replaceable parameters are a method of adding additional information on the command line that the batch file then has access to. This information can be filenames, extensions, subdirectories, commands, or just about anything you use in a batch file.

Chapter 12: Using more than ten replaceable parameters When it first starts, the batch file has access to only its name and the first nine pieces of information you entered on the command line. This chapter shows you how to gain access to additional information.

Chapter 13: Looping and program flow This chapter shows you how to define different execution paths through the batch file and how to create loops within a batch file.

Chapter 14: The environment The environment is an important scratch pad for the operating system. It uses the environment to store information that all the programs need to access.

Chapter 15: The errorlevel The errorlevel is a one-byte portion of memory that programs can use to communicate to each other or with a batch file. While only a few programs use the errorlevel, batch file utilities use it to pass results back to the batch file that ran them. This chapter provides an overview of the errorlevel.

Chapter 16: Command-line punctuation Many of the batch files you've seen so far have used varying types of punctuation to help them perform their work. This chapter documents that punctuation as a resource to help you understand these batch files as well as write more powerful batch files of your own.

Chapter 17: Logic testing The different paths you learned to create are useless unless you have a method of selecting different paths at different times. Additionally, the loops you learned to create are endless unless you have a way to get out of them. In both cases, logic testing is the solution. This chapter shows you how to build logic testing into your batch files. Logic testing is what keeps a batch file from being just a dumb script the computer plays back, and makes it an intelligent program.

Chapter 18: Review #2 Before moving on to the advanced batch subcommands, you should understand the commands and concepts covered so far. This chapter is a quick test. Pass it, and you're ready to move on.

11
Replaceable parameters

Batch files would be useful if they did nothing more than what's been covered so far. However, one big limitation of the commands that you've looked at is that they're "written in stone." If you want to erase a file with a batch file that uses just these commands, you'll need to physically enter that filename in the batch file code. This is called *hardwiring*.

Sometimes you want to hardwire filenames. If you want to copy all your spreadsheet files to a floppy disk as backup, then hardwiring the:

```
COPY *.WK1 A:
```

command is appropriate. Other times, however, you want the batch file to be able to process different files. Replaceable parameters offer this kind of flexibility.

You need to know two things in order to use replaceable parameters: how to give the values for the replaceable parameters to the batch file, and how to code the replaceable parameters in the batch file.

Sending replaceable parameters to a batch file

Giving the values of the replaceable parameters to the batch file is easy if you run the batch file from the OS/2 command line. Replaceable parameters are entered after the batch file name, before you press Enter. For example, the command:

```
BATCH Par_1 Par_2 Par_3 Par_4
```

will run BATCH.CMD and pass it Par_1 through Par_4 as replaceable parameters.

Each parameter is separated by either a space, comma, or semicolon. How many replaceable parameters does the previous line have? The obvious (and wrong) answer is four. OS/2 counts the name of the batch file as a parameter, so there are five replaceable parameters on this line. Just to make things confusing, OS/2 names them %0, %1, %2, %3, and %4 and not the %1 through %5 you'd expect (see FIG. 11-1).

%0 = BATCH
%1 = *.BAK
%2 = *.DOC
%3 = *.TMP
%4 = *.WKS
%5 = *.WK1
%6 = *.TXT
%7 = *.DBF
%8 = *.PRG
%9 = *.IN

11-1 A sample command line and the replaceable parameters seen by BATCH.CMD when the command line is: BATCH *.BAK *.DOC *.TMP *.WKS *.WK1 *.TXT *.DBF *.PRG *.IN *.OLD.

When a series of replaceable parameters are enclosed in quotation marks, they're passed to the batch file as a single replaceable parameter. This is necessary so a single replaceable parameter can contain a filename with a space in it when you're using the High-Performance File System (HPFS). So if you enter the command:

```
BATCH "Letter To Mother"
```

Then the entire "Letter To Mother" string will be passed to the batch file as the first replaceable parameter, after the filename.

Everything on a command line inside quotation marks is passed to the batch file as a single replaceable parameter.

The notation OS/2 uses leaves me with a dilemma in writing this book. Do I refer to %1 as the first replaceable parameter or the second? It truly is the second, but that causes confusion for two reasons. First, most readers expect the second replaceable parameter to be %2. Second, %1 is actually the first piece of information you enter for the batch file to use, so it really is the first replaceable parameter. The name is entered only to run the batch file. So I've decided that, throughout this book, I will refer to %1 as the first replaceable parameter, %2 as the second, %3 as the third, and so on. When I need to talk about %0, I will refer to it by the name %0.

➠ When describing replaceable parameters, I will refer to %1 as the first replaceable parameter, and so on. I will refer to the %0 parameter by the name %0.

The general rule is that everything you enter on the command line prior to the space becomes %0, everything between the first and second spaces becomes %1, and so on. This means that the name of the batch file becomes %0. This is stored exactly as you enter it on the command line, so if you run BATCH.CMD with the command BATCH, %0 contains BATCH without the .CMD extension—just as you entered it.

There's one area where OS/2 batch files behave differently than DOS batch files—when the batch file name is immediately followed by a slash. Many programs expect command-line parameters to be entered with a slash, like the command:

```
DIR/W
```

OS/2 doesn't care if you place a space between the DIR and the /W because it knows that DIR is the command and the /W is a parameter. It treats batch files the same way. DR DOS also handles batch files this way. Under DR DOS, if you run BATCH.BAT with the command:

```
BATCH/?
```

then BATCH becomes %0 and /? becomes %1. However, MS-DOS works differently and treats everything until the first space as %0. OS/2 maintains this quirk if you run a DOS .BAT batch file in a compatibility box.

To summarize the issue of following a batch file name directly with a slash and a parameter, like BATCH/?: under OS/2 the slash and parameter are separated so the %0 variable becomes BATCH and the %1 variable becomes /?, under DR DOS exactly the same thing happens, and under DOS and the DOS compatibility of OS/2 the %0 variable becomes BATCH/? and the %1 variable isn't defined.

☠ OS/2 and DR DOS handle replaceable parameters differently when the name of a batch file is followed immediately by a slash and parameter than do MS-DOS and the OS/2 compatibility box. OS/2 and DR DOS makes the slash and everything that follows %1. The OS/2 compatibility box and MS-DOS treats everything before the first space as %0.

This can be quite confusing, so let's look at a couple of examples. For each of these examples, you'll need a batch file. SHOWREPL.CMD is as follows and handles the job nicely:

```
@ECHO OFF
ECHO %%0 = %0
ECHO %%1 = %1
ECHO %%2 = %2
ECHO %%3 = %3
ECHO %%4 = %4
ECHO %%5 = %5
ECHO %%6 = %6
ECHO %%7 = %7
ECHO %%8 = %8
ECHO %%9 = %9
```

Before running SHOWREPL.CMD, note that the ECHO command with a %%0 is used to display a %0. In order to display a percent sign using an ECHO command, OS/2 requires the ECHO to have two percentage signs.

SHOWREPL.CMD is expanded later, and that expanded version is included on the disk. However, the expanded version works fine for these examples, so you don't need to key in the batch file. If you run SHOWREPL.CMD with the command:

```
SHOWREPL/H/I/J One
```

then the replaceable parameters are:

%0	SHOWREPL
%1	/H/I/J
%2	One

Note that the three switches /H, /I, and /J are separated from SHOWREPL but not from each other. OS/2 does this consistently. When SHOWREPL.CMD is started with the command:

```
SHOWREPL /H /I /J One
```

then the replaceable parameters are:

%0	SHOWREPL
%1	/H
%2	/I
%3	/J
%4	One

If you're still confused, you might want to run SHOWREPL.CMD several times with different combinations of replaceable parameters to make sure you understand how OS/2 is translating your command lines into replaceable parameters. A copy of SHOWREPL.CMD is included on the enclosed disk for that purpose. If you want to see the differences in how MS-DOS treats replaceable parameters, simply rename SHOWREPL.CMD to SHOWREPL.BAT and experiment with it in a DOS compatibility box.

We'll revisit this issue when you begin to build on-line help into your batch files. For now, just realize that MS-DOS and the OS/2 compatibility box behave differently than either OS/2 or DR DOS.

Passing replaceable parameters when running a batch file from the desktop

With OS/2 being a graphical user interface and so many batch files being run from the desktop, it makes sense to ask how you can possibly incorporate replaceable parameters with clicking on an icon.

With OS/2, the process is very simple. In the Settings notebook on the program page, enter a pair of square brackets with a space between them ([ ]) in the Parameter field of the Optional section.

If you want the batch file to prompt the user for specific information, then place a prompt inside the square brackets. For example, [Enter The Filename To Erase]. Figure 11-2 shows doing this. Now, each time you click on the icon to run this batch file, OS/2 brings up a box and prompts you for replaceable parameters (see FIG. 11-3). You can press return to skip the replaceable parameters, or enter as many as the batch file expects.

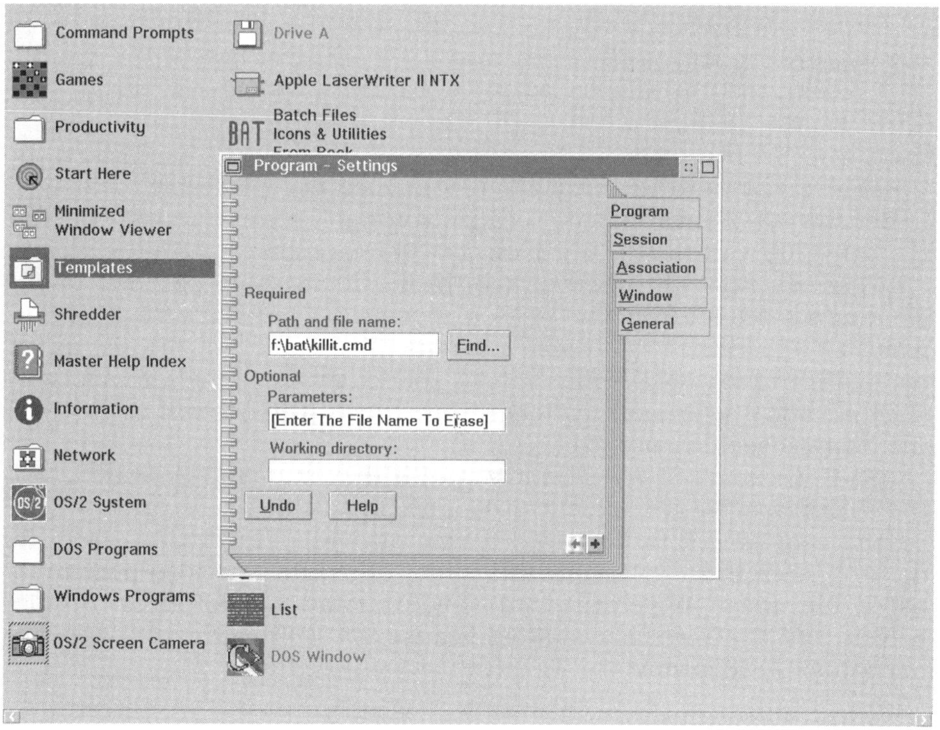

11-2 When you fill out the Settings notebook for a batch file, you can tell OS/2 to prompt you for one or more replaceable parameters, and you can supply the prompt.

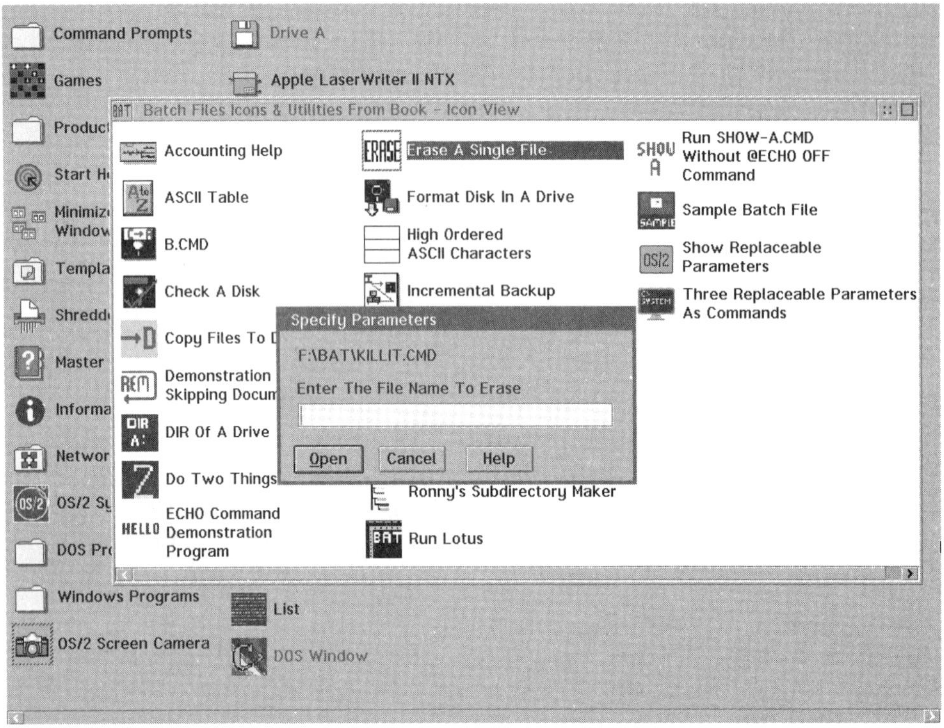

11-3 When configured to prompt for replaceable parameters, OS/2 pops up a dialog box for you to enter them in when you run the batch file by clicking on its icon.

This turns out to be a very handy way to enter replaceable parameters under the OS/2 environment because you don't have to remember what the batch file wants and enter it on the command line.

There is, however, one quirk involving replaceable parameters and running a batch file from the desktop. If you run a batch file from the command line, then the %0 variable contains the name of the file just as you entered it on the command line. But if you follow the name with a forward slash (/) and one or more switches, then those switches will be moved to the %1 replaceable parameter.

So if you start SHOWREPL.CMD with the command Showrepl, then the %0 replaceable parameter will contain Showrepl, just as you entered it on the command line. However, if you run SHOWREPL.CMD from the desktop, then the %0 variable will contain the fully specified path to the batch file, in all uppercase and inside quotation marks. So running SHOWREPL.CMD in this way would cause the %0 replaceable parameter to contain the following:

```
"F:\BAT\SHOWREPL.CMD"
```

Of course, the path would match the one on your system. The quotation marks are needed because an OS/2 fully qualified name needs the quotation marks around it in case of embedded blanks in the name under HPFS.

The %0 variable is treated differently when a batch file is run from the desktop than when it is run from the command line.

Most of the time having the full path in the %0 replaceable parameter won't cause the batch file to operate any differently, but if you're working with the %0 replaceable parameter you need to be aware of this quirk. Having quotation marks around the filename won't cause any problems at all because they're always allowed under HPFS, and OS/2 knows how to handle them.

Using replaceable parameters in batch files

Replaceable parameters are global variables and are therefore available to any command in the batch file. However, once the batch file terminates, the values of the replaceable parameters are terminated as well. When a batch file runs a second batch file, the replaceable parameters aren't available to that second batch file unless they're specifically passed to that second batch file by the command that runs it. This is covered in the chapter on subroutines. However, once the second batch file terminates and control returns to the original batch file, its replaceable parameters are once again available to it.

OS/2 uses replaceable parameters as if they don't exist. That sounds like an extreme statement, but the supporting logic is solid. Everywhere *you* see a replaceable parameter, *OS/2* sees the value of that parameter. That statement will make more sense if you look at an example.

First, we need a batch file. I've modified the SHOWREPL.CMD batch file shown earlier to include some REM commands at the bottom, and I've turned command echoing on just prior to the remarks. These new lines are as follows:

```
ECHO ON
REM Notice That You Do Not See
REM %%1 Or %%9 On The Next Line
REM Displays %1 Through %9
@ECHO OFF
```

Before running SHOWREPL.CMD, note that the next to last REM line has two replaceable parameters in it. Command echoing is on when the batch file reaches this point, so notice how OS/2 treats this line. Go ahead and run the batch file. Be sure to enter some replaceable parameters when you run it.

You can see the results of running SHOWREPL.CMD in FIG. 11-4. When a batch file executes with command echoing on—beginning in the middle of the batch file—each command in the batch file is preceded by the command-line prompt—in this case, [F:\]. In other words, OS/2 treats the commands in the batch file exactly like it would if you entered them from the command-line prompt. This is consistent with the idea of a batch file being a script the computer follows. Now notice the next-to-last REM line. In the batch file, it reads:

```
REM Displays %1 Through %9
```

When I ran this batch file, I ran it with the command:

```
showrepl one two three four five six seven eight nine
```

so showrepl became %0 and nine became %9. If you do the same, in the REM line on the screen, you can see that OS/2 has replaced this line with:

```
REM Displays one Through nine
```

With the single exception of a %%0, everywhere there's a %0 in the batch file OS/2 sees the value of the replaceable parameter. Except for %%1, everywhere there's a %1 in the batch file OS/2 sees the value of the replaceable parameter, and so on. In fact, they're called replaceable parameters

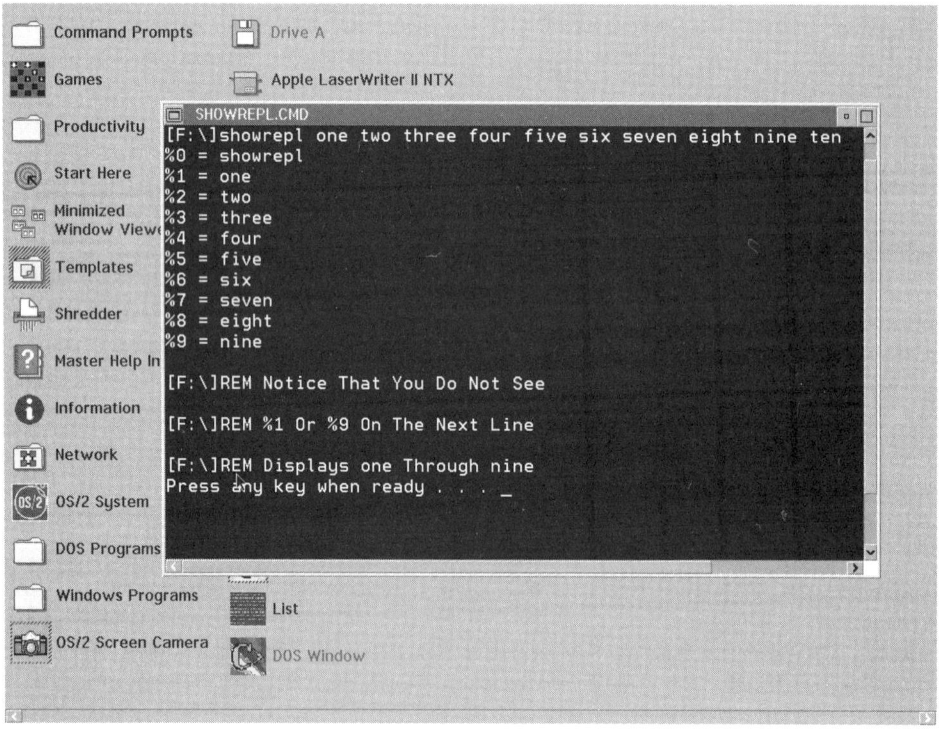

11-4 Running SHOWREPL.CMD with ten replaceable parameters. Notice how it replaces the %1 and %9 values in the last REM line.

for exactly that reason—the values come from the command line, so you can replace them with new values each time you run the batch file.

Limits to the number of replaceable parameters

OS/2 doesn't directly place a limit on the number of replaceable parameters you can specify on the command line. However, it does place an indirect limit. A command line is limited to 300 characters, and the name of the batch file and the first replaceable parameter—as well as each set of replaceable parameters—must be separated by a space, comma or semicolon. If you run a batch file with a single-character name, like A.CMD, and you give it only single-character replaceable parameters, like:

```
A1 2 3 4 5 6 7 8 9 0 A B C . . .
```

Then you'll have room for 149 replaceable parameters. However, only the replaceable parameters %0 through %9 are valid in your batch file. You'll see a way around this problem in the next chapter.

Some uses for replaceable parameters

Back in chapter 3, you looked at the following batch file segment to start Microsoft Word:

```
C:
CD\WORD
WORD
CD\
MENU
```

At the time it didn't have a name, so let's call it WP.CMD. Like many programs, Microsoft Word gives you the ability to immediately begin editing a file by specifying the name of that file on the command line. If you start Word with the command:

```
WORD CHAP-11
```

you not only start Word, you cause it to load CHAP-11.DOC so that you can begin to edit it. (If CHAP-11.DOC doesn't yet exist, Word will warn you and then create the document for you.) Using replaceable parameters and the commands you've learned since chapter 3, you can make this a much more useful batch file:

```
@ECHO OFF
C:
CD\WORD
WORD %1
CD\
```

Now when the user starts this batch file with the command:

```
WP CHAP-11
```

the batch file both starts Word and tells Word to load the CHAP-11.DOC document. (Note that Word doesn't require you to enter the extension; it automatically uses .DOC.)

You might wonder what happens when you start WP.CMD without a replaceable parameter. In that case, %1 has no value. OS/2 performs an exact replacement of the value of %1, so the batch file line WORD %1 is treated by OS/2 as WORD.

In other words, no replaceable parameter was entered, so OS/2 treats that line as though the %1 doesn't exist. That gives you the flexibility of using the same batch file both when you want to specify a filename and when you don't.

Replaceable parameters as commands

OS/2 is extremely literal in replacing replaceable parameters with their values and treating those values as though they were hardwired in the batch file. So literal, in fact, that replaceable parameters can be used even as commands. For example, this batch file:

```
@ECHO OFF
REM NAME:     COMMANDS.CMD
REM PURPOSE: Show Using Replaceable Parameters
REM          As Commands
REM VERSION: 1.00
REM DATE:    May 12, 1992
%1
%2
%3
```

would treat the first three replaceable parameters as commands. If you ran the batch file with the command:

```
COMMANDS DIR/W CHKDSK/F WORD
```

it would first perform a DIR/W, then run CHKDSK/F, and finally run the word-processing program.

Of course, just because this works doesn't mean it's a good idea. When you allow the user to enter the command, you lose the control the batch file was designed to provide. So, as a general rule, using replaceable parameters as commands isn't a good idea.

While OS/2 will let you use replaceable parameters as commands in a batch file, it isn't a good idea.

A couple of examples

Let's create a couple of example batch files using replaceable parameters. As I introduce additional commands for working with replaceable parameters as well as general batch file commands, you'll revisit these batch files to make improvements to them. They're on the disk that comes with this book, each in its own subdirectory branching off the \BAT subdirectory (for example, \BAT\A). In each of these subdirectories, you'll find chapter subdirectories. So, the version of A.CMD discussed here is in the \BAT\A\CHAP-11 subdirectory.

This first batch file—A.CMD—performs a directory of the A: drive. It uses a single replaceable parameter. When you run it without a replaceable parameter, it gives you all the files on the A: drive. You can enter a replaceable parameter like *.DOC to narrow the search.

```
@ECHO OFF
REM NAME:     A.CMD
REM PURPOSE: Directory Of A: Drive
REM VERSION: 1.00
REM DATE:     May 12, 1992

DIR A:%1 /P
```

The second batch file—RONNYMD.CMD, or Ronny's MD command—will create a subdirectory branching off the current subdirectory and then change to that subdirectory:

```
@ECHO OFF
REM NAME:     RONNYMD.CMD
REM PURPOSE: Make And Change To A Subdirectory
REM VERSION: 1.00
REM DATE:     May 12, 1992

MD %1
CD %1
```

A.CMD runs fine if you don't enter a replaceable parameter—you just get a listing of all the files. RONNYMD.CMD has a small problem. The MD %1 becomes MD when no replaceable parameter is entered—resulting in an OS/2 "The syntax of the command is incorrect" error message. Without a replaceable parameter, the CD command displays just the current subdirectory. One of the enhancements you'll be making to these batch files in the chapters that follow is error checking to avoid problems.

While A.CMD runs fine without a replaceable parameter, and RONNYMD.CMD has a problem with one line, this final batch file—TOA.CMD—has significant problems when used with the wrong number of replaceable parameters.

```
@ECHO OFF
REM NAME:     TOA.CMD
REM PURPOSE: Copy .CMP And .DOC Files To A: Drive
REM           While Deleting .BAK Files
REM VERSION: 1.00
REM DATE:     May 12, 1992

DEL %1.BAK
COPY %1.DOC A:
COPY %1.CMP A:
```

```
REM %2 - %8 Are Handled In A Similar Fashion
REM I've Removed Their Code From The Figure
REM For The Sake Of Space

DEL %9.BAK
COPY %9.DOC A:
COPY %9.CMP A:
```

TOA.CMD is designed to be run followed by exactly nine replaceable parameters. Each replaceable parameter designates a document to be copied to the A: drive and must be entered without the .DOC extension. The batch file performs three steps for each replaceable parameter:

1. Deletes the .BAK backup file.
2. Copies the .DOC document file to the A: drive.
3. Copies the .CMP user dictionary for that file to the A: drive.

As written, this batch file has several significant problems. In fact, I've included it because it has many of the problems associated with using replaceable parameters in batch files. The problems with this batch file are as follows:

- TOA.CMD doesn't check to make sure that nine replaceable parameters were entered. If only six were entered, then %7, %8, and %9 don't exist. For each of these, the commands DEL .BAK, COPY .DOC A:, and COPY .CMP A: will generate a "The system cannot find the files specified" error message. The filename is missing because the replaceable parameter is empty, and OS/2 treats the period before the extension as part of a path.
- TOA.CMD ignores any replaceable parameters beyond %9.
- TOA.CMD doesn't check to see if the .BAK file exists before it tries to delete it.
- TOA.CMD doesn't check to see if the .DOC and .CMP files exist before it tries to copy them.

In the chapters to come, you'll see how to avoid each of these problems.

Summary

- A replaceable parameter is information you enter on the command line after the name of a batch file when you run that batch file.
- Replaceable parameters must be separated by a space, comma, or semicolon on the command line.
- Replaceable parameters are global variables that are available anywhere in the batch file.
- In addition to being available anywhere in a batch file, replaceable parameters can be passed by one batch file to another batch file or by a batch file to a program.

- Replaceable parameters are used in a batch file using the terms %0 to %9. %0 is the name of the batch file, %1 is the first replaceable parameter, %2 is the second, and so on.
- When replaceable parameters are enclosed in quotation marks, they're treated as one long replaceable parameter.
- When a batch file name on the command line is followed by a slash and switches and there's no space between the name of the batch file and the slash, OS/2 and DR DOS separate the name of the batch file into %0 and the parameters into %1. MS-DOS and the OS/2 DOS compatibility box don't do this.
- Everywhere OS/2 sees a %1, it replaces that %1 with the value of the first replaceable parameter as entered on the command line.
- OS/2 places no limit on the number of replaceable parameters you can enter on the command line, other than the 300-character limit on the command line.
- OS/2 is flexible enough to allow you to use replaceable parameters as commands inside your batch files, but this isn't a good idea.
- A.CMD performs a directory of the A: drive. If a file specification is entered on the command line, it uses that as part of the DIR command.
- RONNYMD.CMD first creates a subdirectory branching off the current subdirectory and then changes to that subdirectory. RONNYMD.CMD expects the user to enter a valid subdirectory name and will have problems if no name is entered.
- TOA.CMD tries to copy nine .DOC and .CMP files matching the nine replaceable parameters it expects to the A: drive, as well as delete the nine associated .BAK files. This batch file has significant problems that will be the basis of future discussion.

12
Using more than ten replaceable parameters

As I mentioned in chapter 11, OS/2 doesn't directly place a limit on the number of replaceable parameters you can specify on the command line. However, it does place an indirect limit. A command line is limited to 300 characters, and the name of the batch file and the first replaceable parameter, as well as each set of replaceable parameters, must be separated by a space, comma, or semicolon. The upper limit for replaceable parameters is 149, but most batch files use far less.

No matter how many replaceable parameters you pass to a batch file, only the replaceable parameters %0 through %9 are valid in your batch file. While the particular set of ten replaceable parameters to which the batch file has access can be altered, a batch file is always limited to accessing only ten replaceable parameters at any one time.

☑ A batch file can access only ten replaceable parameters at once.

The SHIFT command

Because a batch file can "see" only ten replaceable parameters, OS/2 offers the SHIFT command. The SHIFT command discards the %0 parameter, moves the remaining parameters down one value, and brings in a new %9 value if one exists. So after a SHIFT, the value in %1 moves into %0, the value in %2 moves into %1, and so on. This is illustrated in FIG. 12-1. Figure 12-2 shows SHOWSHIF.CMD, which demonstrates the SHIFT command.

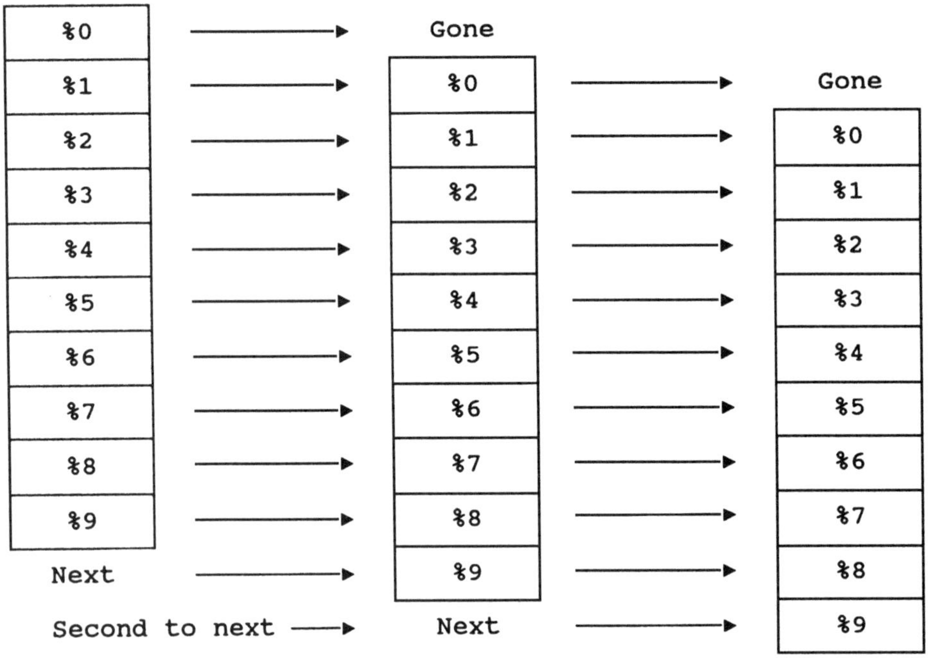

12-1 The action of the SHIFT command.

Batch File Line	**Explanation**
`@ECHO OFF`	Turn command-echoing off.

`REM NAME:     SHOWSHIFT.CMD`
`REM PURPOSE:  Show The Shift Command`
`REM VERSION:  1.00`
`REM DATE:     May 12, 1993`
	Documentation remarks.

`IF (%1)==(?)  GOTO HELP`
`IF (%1)==(/?) GOTO HELP`
`IF (%1)==(/h) GOTO HELP`
`IF (%1)==(/H) GOTO HELP`
	If the user requested help, jump to a special section to display help information.

`ECHO Before Shifting`
`ECHO ---------`
`ECHO %%0=%0 %%1=%1 %%2=%2 %%3=%3 %%4=%4`
`ECHO %%5=%5 %%6=%6 %%7=%7 %%8=%8 %%9=%9`
`ECHO`
	Show the replaceable parameters as entered on the command line.

`SHIFT`	Move all the replaceable parameters down one level.

12-2 The batch file SHOWSHIF.CMD illustrates the action of the SHIFT command.

Batch File Line	Explanation

`ECHO After First Shift`
`ECHO ----------`
`ECHO %%0=%0 %%1=%1 %%2=%2 %%3=%3 %%4=%4`
`ECHO %%5=%5 %%6=%6 %%7=%7 %%8=%8 %%9=%9`
`ECHO`
	Show the replaceable parameters after one SHIFT command.

`SHIFT`	Move all the replaceable parameters down one level.

`ECHO After Second Shift`
`ECHO ----------`
`ECHO %%0=%0 %%1=%1 %%2=%2 %%3=%3 %%4=%4`
`ECHO %%5=%5 %%6=%6 %%7=%7 %%8=%8 %%9=%9`
`ECHO`
	Show the replaceable parameters after two SHIFT commands.

`PAUSE`	Pause the program until the user presses a key.
`CLS`	Clear the screen.
`SHIFT`	Move the replaceable parameters down one level.

`ECHO After Third Shift`
`ECHO ----------`
`ECHO %%0=%0 %%1=%1 %%2=%2 %%3=%3 %%4=%4`
`ECHO %%5=%5 %%6=%6 %%7=%7 %%8=%8 %%9=%9`
`ECHO`
	Show the replaceable parameters after three SHIFT commands.

`SHIFT`	Move the replaceable parameters down one level.

`ECHO After Fourth Shift`
`ECHO ----------`
`ECHO %%0=%0 %%1=%1 %%2=%2 %%3=%3 %%4=%4`
`ECHO %%5=%5 %%6=%6 %%7=%7 %%8=%8 %%9=%9`
`ECHO`
	Show the replaceable parameters after four SHIFT commands.

`SHIFT`	Move the replaceable parameters down one level.

`ECHO After Fifth Shift`
`ECHO ----------`
`ECHO %%0=%0 %%1=%1 %%2=%2 %%3=%3 %%4=%4`
`ECHO %%5=%5 %%6=%6 %%7=%7 %%8=%8 %%9=%9`
`ECHO`
	Show the replaceable parameters after five SHIFT commands.

`PAUSE`	Pause the program until the user presses a key.

12-2 Continued.

Batch File Line	Explanation
`GOTO END`	Exit the batch file.

`:HELP`
`  ECHO Show SHIFT Command`
`GOTO END`
	Display a help screen and exit the batch file when the user requests help.

`:END`	Label marking the end of the batch file.

Batch file tables

As you've seen in the first 11 chapters of this book, I've presented short batch files in the text. That is a neat way to show batch files that need only a little explanation, and I'll continue to use this approach where appropriate.

However, as you move through this book, many of your batch files will start to become longer and more complex, which is why I've developed the concept of this table. The batch file code is listed on the left side of the table. For each single line or group of very similar lines, the right side of the table has a detailed explanation.

I've varied the width of the left side of the tables to avoid—to the extent possible—having to use word wrap on the batch file commands. I've also slightly altered the messages that are part of the ECHO and REM commands. No functional commands have been altered. When it proved to be necessary to use word wrap, I've indented every line except the first one.

If you have any doubts regarding the contents of a batch file, load the original batch file on the disk that comes with this book into the Enhanced Editor.

What SHIFT can do

Take a moment and run SHOWSHIF.CMD with a command like:

```
showshif 1 2 3 4 5 6 7 8 9 10 11 12 13 14 15
```

The result of this is shown in FIG. 12-3. As you can see, each time the batch file issues a SHIFT, the replaceable parameters move down one level with another replaceable parameter becoming available as %9.

The one thing you can't see is what happens to the value contained in %0 after the SHIFT command. When SHOWSHIF.CMD is first run with just the command line shown, the value in %0 is showshif. When the first SHIFT is issued, the showshif is removed to make room for moving the contents of %1 into %0. That value is unrecoverable. There is no UNSHIFT command. Once you've shifted a value away, there's no way to access it, so use SHIFT with care.

There is no UNSHIFT command, so use the SHIFT command with care.

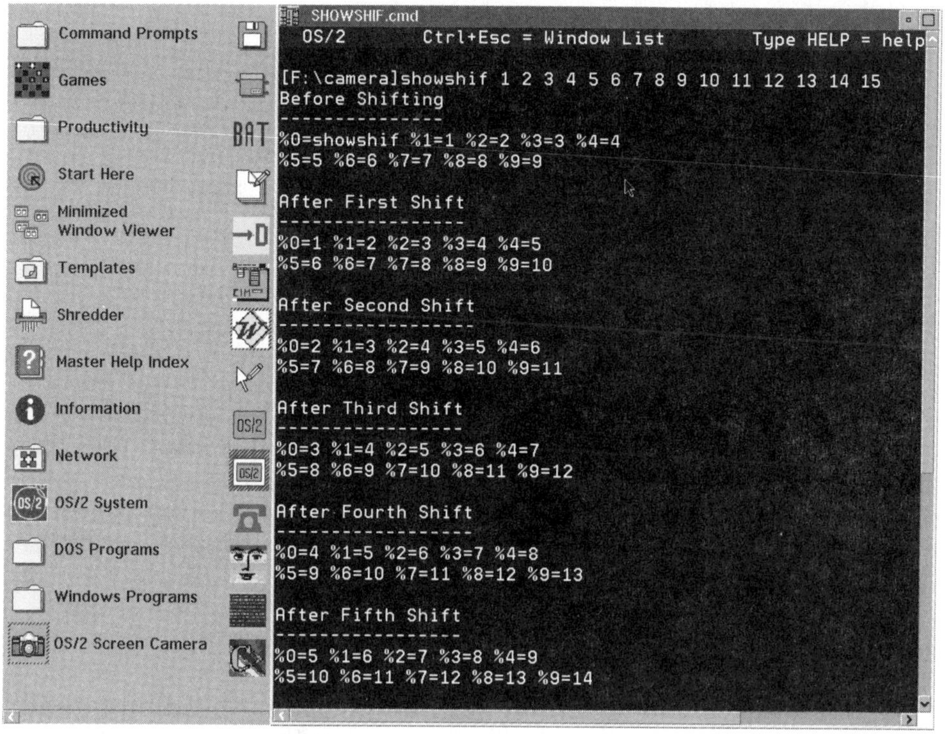

12-3 Running SHOWSHIF.CMD in an OS/2 window.

Using the SHIFT command

The SHIFT command has two major purposes. First, by moving the replaceable parameters into lower positions, you can use a single replaceable parameter for all coding by forcing the program to loop through the code. This makes it much easier to update the code when necessary. (I describe looping starting in chapter 13.) Second, it allows the batch file to handle more than ten replaceable parameters. Just keep in mind that the total number of replaceable parameters is constrained by the 300-character command-line limitation and the requirement to separate each replaceable parameter on the command line.

Of the three sample batch files introduced in chapter 10, only TOA.CMD can benefit from the SHIFT command. First, take a quick look back at the original version of TOA.CMD in chapter 11. Now compare that to the modified version shown here:

```
@ECHO OFF
REM NAME:     TOA.CMD
REM PURPOSE:  Copy .CMP And .DOC Files To A: Drive
REM           While Deleting .BAK Files
REM VERSION:  2.00
```

```
REM DATE:  May 12, 1992

DEL %1.BAK
COPY %1.DOC A:
COPY %1.CMP A:
SHIFT

Note: The Above Four Lines Are Repeated Eight More Times
```

With this new version, the SHIFT command is used repeatedly so that TOA.CMD is always dealing with the same small section of code:

```
DEL %1.BAK
COPY %1.DOC A:
COPY %1.CMP A:
SHIFT
```

which it uses nine times. If there was a way to reuse that code, TOA.CMD would be much shorter. As it turns out, there are two approaches to reusing this section of code: looping and subroutines. Looping is covered in the next chapter, and subroutines are covered in chapter 23. We'll revisit TOA.CMD in both chapters.

Summary

- OS/2 places no limit on the number of replaceable parameters you can enter on the command line, other than the 300-character limit on the command line.
- The SHIFT command discards %0, moves %1 to %0, %2 to %1, and so on. It also brings another replaceable parameter into the %9 slot.
- The SHIFT command is not reversible.
- When combined with looping or subroutines, SHIFT allows one section of a batch file to work with all the replaceable parameters.

13
Looping and program flow

So far, the simple batch files you've created have done what I recommend my students do with term papers—start out at the beginning and end at the ending. While that results in some very useful batch files, it doesn't give the batch file any decision-making abilities. The batch file must start at the top and progress downwards even if the conditions that exist at the time of execution are different than when the batch file was designed.

The process of designing batch files to react differently to different circumstances will span several different chapters. This chapter begins by examining several ways to alter the normal top-down progression of a batch file. By doing this, you create several alternative paths the batch file can take depending on circumstances.

Later, you'll build on this concept by introducing decision-making tools to the batch file so it can choose from these different paths through the batch file depending on conditions. So, this chapter shows how to define multiple paths through your batch file, while a later chapter shows how to have the batch file pick a path.

Pseudocode

If you program in a general-purpose computer language—like C or Pascal—you'll generally follow these steps:

1. Start with an idea.
2. Translate your idea into code you can understand, called *pseudocode*. (Most computer tutorials recommend you draw a flowchart first, but no one ever does that!)

3. Run a compiler that converts the code you wrote into a program the computer can understand. You might have to debug it several times before the compiler can successfully convert the code into a program.
4. Begin running and testing it.

Batch files don't need to be compiled because the operating system reads each line and interprets it as it executes, rather than creating a program file of executable code.

Pseudocode is computer code written for a human to understand.

Pseudocode is computer code written in English for later conversion into a programming language. Consider the following pseudocode example of a loop:

```
Mark the top of a loop
Do something
If some test is met, jump out of this loop
Go to top of loop
```

This program goes around in a continuous loop until a certain condition forces it to jump out of the loop. However, the real point of this example is that you understand it without knowing any programming commands!

In addition, pseudocode is language-independent. If I were to flesh out this example with a few actions and specify the condition for when to jump out of the loop, a REXX, Basic, or C programmer could write a program to perform the same task in their respective languages.

Pseudocode is not new. I originally learned pseudocode while learning to program in dBASE II on an Apple II with a CP/M card in 1983. I will be using pseudocode occasionally in this book to explain the flow of longer batch files because it makes the logic easier to follow.

Naming program lines

The first thing that the previous section of pseudocode requires is that you "mark the top of a loop." In a batch file, there's no specific marking for the boundary of a loop. Instead, you can give any line a name so the batch file can then jump to that line. To name a line, start with a colon and then type in a name with the following characteristics:

- The line name must follow the colon with no spaces between the colon and name. While not required, it's a good idea to left-justify the colon and name.
- The name should have eight characters or less. Actually, the name can be longer than eight characters; OS/2 just ignores everything after the eighth character. This can cause problems if you have labels like GOTOTHIS1 and GOTOTHIS2, because they're identical

through the first eight characters. As a result, both GOTO GOTOTHIS1 and GOTO GOTOTHIS2 will cause OS/2 to jump to the label that appears first in the batch file.
- There can be nothing after the name.
- Capitalization doesn't matter. The labels :END and :End work equally well.
- There can be no spaces in the name.
- While you don't have to, it's a good idea to make the name mean something, like *top* or *end*.

These rules are quickly summarized as follows:

- Begin the line to name with a colon in the left-most position.
- Immediately follow the colon with a line name of eight or fewer characters.
- Do not enter anything after the name.
- Capitalization does not matter.
- Do not use spaces in the name.
- Try to have the label name mean something.

✍ Unless you have a good reason to do otherwise, you should left-justify your labels.

The next two lines in the pseudocode example are "do something" and "if some test is met, jump out of this loop." The "do something" line represents typical commands in a batch file. For example, a segment of the TOA.CMD batch file we've examined over the last two chapters might look like this:

```
:MAINPART
DEL %1.BAK
COPY %1.DOC A:
COPY %1.CMP A:
SHIFT
```

The first line is the label, and the next four lines are what this section is discussing. The "if some test is met, jump out of this loop" line represents logic testing. This topic is covered in detail in the next chapter.

The GOTO command

The last line in the pseudocode is "go to top of loop." In a batch file, you jump to another section of the batch file by jumping to a line with a name. Because the line containing the name doesn't perform any action, the batch file behaves as though it jumps to the line following the name.

The command used to jump to another line is the GOTO command. The GOTO must be followed by the name of the label to jump to without the colon that precedes the label.

GOTO has two specific uses. You can use it to repeat a series of commands more than once (in other words, looping), and transfer control to another section of the batch file. We'll look at both uses.

You can jump to a new line with the GOTO command.

Looping

One important use of GOTO is to loop through a section of code more than once. You can see this with a couple of simple examples, the first one being ENDLESS.CMD:

```
@ECHO OFF
REM NAME:     ENDLESS.CMD
REM PURPOSE: Demonstrate GOTO Command
REM VERSION: 1.00
REM DATE:     May 13, 1993
:TOP
ECHO Before A GOTO Command
GOTO TOP
ECHO After A GOTO Command
```

There is a copy of ENDLESS.CMD on the disk that comes with this book. If you run ENDLESS.CMD, you'll see a series of Before A GOTO Command messages scrolling up the screen. Press Ctrl–Break or Ctrl–C to stop ENDLESS.CMD.

Let's review the operation of this batch file and you'll see how it works. The steps in the batch file are as follows:

1. Process the @ECHO OFF command.
2. Skip over the REM commands.
3. Skip over the :TOP label. (Labels are completely ignored except when the batch file is trying to figure out where to jump to after a GOTO command.)
4. Run the ECHO Before A GOTO Command line, displaying its message.
5. The GOTO TOP line is executed, causing the batch file to jump back up to step 3.

Because it jumps back to the :TOP label each time it reaches the GOTO command, this batch file will continue looping until you force it to stop. This is called an endless loop because, if left alone, it would continue without ending.

In the next chapter, you'll see how to add logic testing to batch files so the batch file itself can figure out if it needs to jump out of a loop rather than depending on the user pressing Ctrl–Break. This "stopping logic" is almost always needed when using the GOTO command to construct a loop.

The steps between the :TOP label and the GOTO command in ENDLESS.CMD form a multiline loop. It's standard programming practice to indent everything inside a loop—everything except the top (the label) and the bottom (usually the GOTO command). This helps you visualize the loop as you look at the code, and it actually forms documentation of sorts. OS/2 doesn't require that the commands be indented; in fact, the indentation slows down the batch file a little. It does, however, make the batch file easier to understand.

Using this information, you can modify the TOA.CMD batch file you saw in the last two chapters. Look back to chapter 12. In that version, it performed the same few steps nine times. The new version uses a loop to consolidate those few steps inside a single loop. It looks like this:

```
@ECHO OFF
REM NAME:    TOA.CMD
REM PURPOSE: Copy .CMP And .DOC Files To A: Drive
REM          While Deleting .BAK Files
REM VERSION: 3.00
REM DATE:    May 12, 1993

:TOP
  DEL %1.BAK
  COPY %1.DOC A:
  COPY %1.CMP A:
  SHIFT
GOTO TOP
```

The first two versions of TOA.CMD had problems if fewer than nine replaceable parameters were entered because it was designed to handle exactly nine. This third version has a different problem. Because there's nothing in the batch file to cause it to stop, it will continue running forever. Of course, it will run out of replaceable parameters, and you must press Ctrl–Break to stop it. You'll see how to avoid this in chapter 17.

Transferring control

While it makes little sense, the following batch file is completely legal:

```
@ECHO OFF
GOTO END
ECHO This Message Never Seen
ECHO This Message Skipped Too
:END
```

When the batch file processes the second line, control is immediately transferred to the last line of the batch file and it terminates. While the unconditional jumping shown in this example makes little sense, it often makes good sense for a batch file to jump to different locations depending on conditions. Let's look as the pseudocode for the version of TOA.CMD you'll be producing in a later chapter:

```
Top Of Loop
  Test For Another Replaceable Parameter Pending
   If No Then Jump To End Of Batch File
   If Yes Then Continue
  Erase The *.BAK File
  Copy The .DOC File To A: Drive
  Copy The .CMP File To A: Drive
  Shift Replaceable Parameters Down One Level
Go Through Loop Again
```

I haven't yet covered logic testing so you can't yet produce this batch file as written, but you can see how the ability to jump out of that loop when the batch file runs out of replaceable parameters is useful.

You can use this unconditional transfer of control to jump to different sections of the batch file, depending on the conditions the batch file finds when it begins operation. Of course, that means you must write different sections of the batch file to deal with these different conditions.

Quick exit

Many of the batch files in this book will have one or more GOTO END commands to exit the batch file quickly without processing the remainder of the batch file. When this command is executed to terminate a batch file and not a batch file functioning as a subroutine, there's actually a quicker way. In your batch file subdirectory, enter the command:

```
TYPE NOFILE > QUIT.CMD
```

where NOFILE is the name of a nonexistent file. Make sure you don't already have a QUIT.CMD because this command would erase it. This line creates a zero-length file called QUIT.CMD. Now replace the GOTO END commands with the QUIT command. Running QUIT.CMD without CALL keeps control from returning to the original batch file, and because QUIT.CMD has no commands the batch file immediately terminates.

There isn't a copy of QUIT.CMD on the disk that comes with this book because neither OS/2 nor DOS will copy a zero-length file.

A handy formatting option

When I mentioned looping earlier, I said that you should indent everything between the top and bottom of the loop as a visual aid in debugging and maintaining the batch file. If you do that, the loop from TOA.CMD would look like this:

```
:TOP
  DEL %1.BAK
  COPY %1.DOC A:
  COPY %1.CMP A:
  SHIFT
GOTO TOP
```

As you begin developing longer batch files, you'll find these to be very compartmentalized. In many cases, the batch files will have many different sections for handling specific tasks. For example, a full-blown version of TOA.CMD might have sections to perform the following:

- Display help when the user starts the batch file with a /? switch.
- Display an error message when the user fails to enter a replaceable parameter.
- Display an error message when the user specifies a filename as a replaceable parameter and the .DOC version of that file doesn't exist. (Not all files have associated .CMP and .BAK files, so don't give an error message if one of those is missing.)
- Display an error message when the target disk is full or if other copying problems occur.
- Perform the actual copying.

Clearly, you need a method to keep these sections separate, both in execution and visually.

Code separation

Making sure the batch file executes only the correct section of code is fairly easy. Jump into the appropriate section of code using the GOTO command as the result of a logic testing statement. At the end of the section, the batch file will jump to the next section of the batch file. You can see the TOA.CMD segment reproduced earlier. It doesn't need to jump into the loop because it reaches it sequentially, but it jumps at the end of the loop.

Visual separation

One way to visually separate sections is to place blank lines between the different sections. If the section is a loop, then you have the visual clue of the indenting used inside the loop. I tend to use the same form of indenting with sections that aren't loops. For example, a section of TOA.CMD to display an error message when the user fails to enter a replaceable parameter might look like this:

```
:NOTHERE
  ECHO You Started TOA.CMD
  ECHO Without A Replaceable Parameter
  ECHO This Information Is Required
  ECHO For TOA.CMD To Run
  ECHO
  ECHO When You Start TOA.CMD
  ECHO List The Names Of The Files
  ECHO To Copy On The Command Line
  ECHO After The TOA Command
GOTO END
```

Now you have a visual clue that this section is an integral section of code.

The FOR command

Once we cover logic testing in chapter 17, you'll have everything you need to know to write complex loops using the GOTO command. However, one limitation of looping via the GOTO command is that you must provide the parameters of the loop when you code the batch file. For example, you can't go through the loop once for each .DOC file or for every file on the B: drive. For that, you need the FOR command.

Looping with FOR

In its simplest form, the FOR command causes OS/2 to loop through a series of files and perform a single action on those files. There are two forms of the command. The first takes a list of files:

```
FOR %%h IN (CHAPTER1.BAK CHAPTER2.BAK) DO ERASE %%h
```

and the second uses wildcards to calculate all applicable files:

```
FOR %%j IN (*.BAK) DO DEL %%j
```

In general, the command is:

```
FOR %%variable IN (set) DO Command
```

The FOR command must be on one line. Unlike DOS, OS/2 FOR loops can be nested. In fact, the commands:

```
FOR %%A IN (0 1 2 3 4 5 6 7 8 9) DO
FOR %%B IN (0 1 2 3 4 5 6 7 8 9) DO
FOR %%C IN (0 1 2 3 4 5 6 7 8 9) DO
ECHO %%A%%B%%C
```

when entered all on one line from a batch file will cause OS/2 to count from 000 to 999. You can see this by running the batch file COUNT.CMD that's included on the disk that comes with this book. By replacing all the dual percent signs with single percent signs, this command will also work from the command line.

The FOR command must be all on one line.

The %%*variable* must be a single character: for example, %%A through %%Z. In addition, if you reference the %%*variable* after the DO command, you must use the same capitalization you used in the beginning. For example:

```
FOR %%J IN (*.*) DO ECHO %%J
```

and:

```
FOR %%j IN (*.*) DO ECHO %%j
```

are valid because both %%Js are the same case, but the command:

```
FOR %%J IN (*.*) DO ECHO %%j
```

is invalid because one J is uppercase and the other is lowercase.

You must be consistent with your capitalization of the variables used in your FOR loops.

OS/2 will let you use %0 through %9 as variables in the FOR command, but it's a bad programming habit because OS/2 uses these as replaceable parameters. You can also use the FOR command from the command-line prompt without a batch file. The only change is that you use only one percent sign rather than two, so %%*variable* must be %*variable*.

OS/2 allows you to use %0–%9 as the variable in a FOR command. Don't do it. This is very poor programming.

Local variables

When you worked with replaceable parameters back in chapter 11, you saw that replaceable parameters were global variables. That is, you can use %1 anywhere in your batch file and the command will have access to the value stored in %1. However, the variables created by the FOR command are local variables. Their value is usable only while the FOR loop is running. Therefore, the following batch file segment:

```
@ECHO OFF
FOR %%J in (1 2 3) DO ECHO %%J
ECHO %%J
```

would not have a value for %%J to echo when it reached the third line, so it would simply echo %J. (Recall that you use two percent signs in an ECHO command to echo a single percent sign.)

FOR variables are local variables whose value is usable only within the FOR loop.

Running commands with a FOR loop

Every so often, computer magazine "hint columns" will have suggestions from people who have just discovered that the things you put in the list of variables for a FOR command can be commands themselves. They're excited because the batch file runs faster this way; if you remember, OS/2 processes batch files one line at a time, and this strategy puts more commands on a single line.

Don't be fooled. While the batch files *are* a little faster, this method has a couple of drawbacks that greatly outweigh this slight dose of speed, the biggest one being human readability. You could probably look at a batch file with the lines:

```
DIR
CHKDSK
CD\
```

and tell exactly what it was supposed to do. However, the function of a batch file with the line:

```
FOR %%j IN (DIR CHKDSK CD\) DO %%j
```

isn't nearly so clear. In the end, you'll waste more time writing and debugging such complex code than you'd save by stacking more commands on a single line.

This method has another drawback; you can't use the trick with any command that requires more than one word. For example, you might want to run CHKDSK and then beep the bell by echoing a ^G. With two lines, you would enter the commands:

```
CHKDSK
ECHO ^G
```

Using the FOR command, you would enter the command:

```
FOR %%j IN (CHKDSK ECHO ^G) DO %%j
```

but because of the space, OS/2 would actually try to run:

```
CHKDSK
ECHO
^G
```

For a quick reference chart for the FOR command, see the following list:

- The syntax of the command is FOR %%J (SET) DO *command.*
- The (SET) can contain a list of files, wildcards, or simply a list of items to process.
- The command to execute might use the %%J variable.
- FOR commands can also be issued from the command line. Just replace the %%J variable with a %J variable.
- If the %%J variable is referenced by the command, that reference must use the same capitalization as was used at the beginning of the FOR command.
- The variables %0–%9 should not be used as FOR command variables.
- The %%J variable is a local variable that no longer contains a value once the command terminates.
- Actual commands can be used in the (SET) and executed by the FOR commands; however, that is poor programming.

Watching for wildcards in replaceable parameters

The FOR command loops through all the elements in its set and performs its command once per element. When an element in the set contains wildcards, the FOR command first expands the wildcards. For example, the command:

```
FOR %%J IN (*.*) DO DEL %%J
```

in a batch file will delete every file in the current subdirectory without triggering the "Are you sure (Y/N)?" message. The batch file TESTWILD.CMD illustrates how to avoid this problem:

```
@ECHO OFF
IF (%1)==() ECHO Requires Parameter To Work
IF (%1)==() GOTO END

IF NOT EXIST %1 ECHO File Does Not Exist
IF NOT EXIST %1 GOTO END

FOR %%J IN (%1) DO SET FROMFOR=%%J
IF %1==%FROMFOR% ECHO %1 Does Not Contain Wildcards
IF NOT %1==%FROMFOR% ECHO %1 Contains Wildcards

:END
```

Logic testing will be covered later, but a brief explanation of the batch file is in order here. First, it uses an IF (%1)==() test to make sure a replaceable parameter was entered. Is so, it goes to the next stage, using an IF NOT EXIST %1 test to exit if no files matching the replaceable parameter exist. If at least one file matches the replaceable parameter, it loops through all of them using a FOR command and sets an environmental variable equal to the expanded value. If no wildcards were used, the name of the file and the name of the expended file from the FOR command are identical and the IF %1==%FROMFOR% test passes. If the FOR command had to expand wildcards, then the name of the file and the replaceable parameter won't match and the test will fail.

This gives you a way to test to see if a replaceable parameter contains wildcards. This is especially useful when creating directories or deleting files when a wildcard could wreak havoc.

DOS FOR command quirks

Under DOS, the FOR command has two quirks. I'll mention them briefly because they can be useful under DOS and they sometimes appear in batch files. However, OS/2 doesn't have either of them so any batch files that depend on them will have to be rewritten.

The first quirk is how a DOS FOR loop processes elements of its set when those elements are preceded with a forward slash (/). The variable is split in two, with the first element being the first character and the second element being the remainder. For example, if you enter the following from the command line:

```
FOR %J IN (/ABC /XYZ /123) DO ECHO %J
```

you might expect to see three messages—/ABC, /XYZ, and /123—but you'd actually see six—A, BC, X, YZ, 1, and 23. Not only is the first character separated, but the forward slash is stripped off as well.

The second quirk involves what the DOS FOR command actually runs after the DO component. Only internal commands and programs are allowed after the DO component—no batch files. You can put a batch file there but the FOR loop will abort after processing the first element in its set.

While DOS exhibits these quirks, OS/2 treats an element with a forward slash as a single element and has no trouble running a batch file as the command following the DO component of the FOR loop.

Summary

- Pseudocode is the process of outlining programs in English without worrying about which language will be used to create the program. Pseudocode is later turned into a program.
- You can name lines in a batch file by preceding an eight-character or shorter name with a colon.
- The GOTO command causes control to jump from the current line to the line named as part of GOTO.
- You can use the GOTO command to loop or permanently transfer control to another section of the batch file.
- Loops created with GOTO need some logic added to tell the batch file when to stop looping.
- Once the zero-length file QUIT.CMD has been created in a subdirectory in your path, you can use the QUIT command to quickly terminate a batch file without a GOTO END command and the corresponding :END label.
- When creating loops with the GOTO command, it's useful to indent everything between the label and the GOTO command to visually represent the loop.
- The FOR command constructs a single-line loop that's automatically executed once for each item in the set of items specified with the command.
- The FOR command must be all on one line.
- You must use consistent capitalization for the loop variable.
- FOR variables are local to the FOR command that creates them.
- By using the code shown in TESTWILD.CMD, you can test replaceable parameters to see if they contain wildcards before using them in a FOR loop.

14
The environment

OS/2 sets aside a portion of memory for storing system-wide variables. This area is called the *environment*, and the variables stored there are called *environmental variables*. For example, the contents of my environment are as follows:

```
WP_OBJHANDLE=188248
USER_INI=F:\OS2\OS2.INI
SYSTEM_INI=F:\OS2\OS2SYS.INI
OS2_SHELL=F:\OS2\CMD.EXE
AUTOSTART=PROGRAMS,TASKLIST,FOLDERS,CONNECTIONS
RUNWORKPLACE=F:\OS2\PMSHELL.EXE
COMSPEC=F:\OS2\CMD.EXE
PATH=F:\OS2;F:\OS2\SYSTEM;F:\OS2\MDOS\WINOS2;
 F:\OS2\MDOS;F:\OS2\APPS;F:\UTILITY;F:\BAT
DPATH=F:\OS2\BITMAP;F:\OS2\MDOS;F:\OS2\APPS;
PROMPT=$i[$p]
HELP=F:\OS2\HELP;F:\OS2\HELP\TUTORIAL;
GLOSSARY=F:\OS2\HELP\GLOSS;
IPF_KEYS=SBCS
KEYS=ON
BOOKSHELF=F:\OS2\BOOK;
EPMPATH=F:\OS2\APPS;
VIO_8514A=DEVICE(BVHVGA,BVH8514A)
VIDEO_DEVICES=VIO_8514A
WORKPLACE__PROCESS=NO
```

I don't plan on going through all these variables since most of them won't affect your batch files. However, I do want to take a look at several of them. After that, I'll discuss how to create environmental variables and how to use them in your batch files.

The prompt

The default prompt is [C:*directory*], which tells you the current drive and directory inside square brackets. It also displays a help bar along the top of the screen. If you want to change this, you can with the PROMPT command. You can include any printable character string in the PROMPT command. In fact, one of the first tricks most computer users learn is to include their name or company name in the prompt. You can also include special characters in the prompt with the commands in TABLE 14-1. Later on in chapter 22, you'll see how to use the PROMPT command to develop even fancier prompts using ANSI escape sequences.

Table 14-1 A listing of the PROMPT metacharacters.

Symbol	Action
$$	Displays a dollar sign.
$_	Includes a carriage return and line feed.
$a	Displays an at symbol (@).
$b	Displays a vertical bar, or pipe (¦).
$c	Displays an open parenthesis.
$d	Displays the date.
$e	Includes an escape. This is useful for sending ANSI escape sequences via the PROMPT command.
$f	Displays a close parenthesis.
$g	Displays a greater-than sign.
$h	Displays a backspace—thus deleting the prior character.
$i	Displays a blue bar at the top of the screen, with help and window-switching information.
$l	Displays a less-than sign.
$n	Displays the current drive.
$p	Displays the current subdirectory.
$q	Displays an equal sign.
$r	Shows the return code (errorlevel) of the last action.
$s	Displays a space.
$t	Displays the time.
$v	Displays the version.

The path

OS/2 will accept three types of commands: internal commands, program names, and batch file names. Every time OS/2 receives a command, it checks to see if the command is an internal command, like ERASE. If so, it executes it. If the command isn't an internal command, OS/2 checks the current subdirectory for a program with that name. It checks first for a .COM program, then an .EXE program, and finally for a .CMD batch or REXX file. If OS/2 finds a program, batch file, or REXX file with the correct name, it executes that program. If OS/2 doesn't find one in the current directory, it searches the path for a .COM, .EXE, or .CMD file. The first subdirectory is searched, then the second, and so on until a program, batch file, or REXX file matching the given name is found or until the end of the path is reached.

The path is stored in the environment. The normal syntax for creating environmental variables will work, so the command:

```
SET PATH=C:\;C:\OS2
```

will work just fine. A shortcut is also available. The command:

```
PATH=C:\;C:\OS2
```

will also create a path.

COMSPEC

COMSPEC is short for *command specification*. In an OS/2 session, this variable tells OS/2 what program to load as the command processor. Usually this is C:\OS2\CMD.EXE, but you can load an alternative command processor like 4OS2 by specifying an alternative value for the COMSPEC variable. In a DOS session, the COMSPEC variable points to COMMAND.COM or an alternative command processor like 4DOS.

Environmental variables

Think of the environment as a scratch pad, where the operating system leaves notes for itself. As you'll see, batch files can also use this scratch pad.

Many programming languages distinguish between different types of variables. For example, you generally don't use the same type of variable for a string of characters as you do for numbers. The environment doesn't make this distinction. Every environmental variable is treated as a string of characters—even if it's all numbers.

Environmental variable names aren't limited to a few characters, so it's a good idea to use descriptive names like SourceDrive and TargetDrive. Of course, these longer names take up more space in the environment and, as you'll see, environmental variable names are converted to uppercase.

If an environmental variable is used temporarily by a batch file, it's also a good idea for that batch file to delete the environmental variable once it no longer needs it so it isn't using environmental memory. However, if a batch file is simply run from the OS/2 desktop to start a program and that session is terminated when the program terminates, there's no need to reset the environmental variables because all environmental variables are lost when a session is terminated.

☑ The environment is a scratch pad for the operating system.

Some notes on names

A lot of the batch files in this book use environmental variables and almost every one uses them without concern for the name. That is, they go ahead and use a name without first checking to see if the name is already in use. That's okay for demonstration batch files and batch files that are run from the desktop because their changes are lost when that session terminates.

You need to be more careful on your system if you're designing multiple batch files to run during the same session. If a batch file depends on an environmental variable when it runs, then you don't want another batch file altering its contents or even wiping it out!

Since environmental variable names can be long, you can avoid this problem by putting the name of the batch file that creates them in important environmental variable names. So if a password batch file created an environmental variable called ALLOWED, you might name the environmental variable PASSWORD_ALLOWED. Since every batch file would use its unique name for a portion of environmental variable names, they would all be unique.

You can also avoid problems by deciding on some names—like JUNK or TEMP—that you'll never use for permanent information. That way, you can always overwrite them without concern for their contents.

While you don't want to accidently overwrite a permanent environmental variable, you also want to avoid filling up your environment with environmental variables you no longer need. It's important that batch files clean up after themselves and delete any environmental variables that aren't needed later. This will go a long way in keeping you from running out of environmental space.

Not all environmental variables are permanent

Environmental variables fall into two categories, those created by OS/2 when it first starts and those created by a batch file or the user once OS/2 is running. I'll call the environmental variables created by OS/2 while booting *permanent environmental variables* and those created by a batch file or the user *transient environmental variables.*

When DOS is booting, environmental variables are usually created by the AUTOEXEC.BAT batch files, but DOS 6 allows the CONFIG.SYS file to also create environmental variables. Additionally, because DOS has only one session, there's no difference between permanent and transient environmental variables. Any change made to the environment by a batch file or the user remains in effect until the computer is turned off or rebooted or another change is made.

Under OS/2, permanent environmental variables are created by the CONFIG.SYS file rather than by a batch file. Permanent environmental variables always exist, unless a batch file or user specifically deletes them. Permanent environmental variables always have the value assigned to them in the CONFIG.SYS file unless a batch file or user specifically alters that value. Changes made to permanent environmental variables are reflected only in that session and aren't lost as soon as that session is terminated. The only way to make a lasting change to a permanent environmental variable is to alter the value assigned to it in the CONFIG.SYS file and reboot OS/2.

OS/2 creates it path and other environmental variables in the CONFIG.SYS file rather than in an AUTOEXEC.BAT batch file—the way DOS does.

When you have more than one session running and you make a change to an environmental variable—either permanent or transient—in one session, that change is not reflected in the other sessions. In order to change the contents of an environmental variable in all your sessions, you must manually make the change in each and every session.

Changes made to permanent environmental variables are temporary. As soon as the session is closed, those changes are lost.

Transient environmental variables are those variables created by the user or a batch file with the SET command. Transient environmental variables are available only in the session where they're created. Additionally, their contents are lost as soon as that session is closed or the computer is turned off or rebooted. Still, transient environmental variables are a very useful way for batch files to communicate with each other.

Transient environmental variables are temporary and exist only in the session where they're created. As soon as that session is closed, their contents are lost.

Putting variables into the environment

Permanent environmental variables can be created only by the CONFIG.SYS file while OS/2 is booting. On the other hand, you can place transient environmental variables into the environment either with a batch file or interactively from the command-line prompt. Either way, the syntax to place an environmental variable into the environment is:

SET *variable=value*

Note that the only space is between SET and the variable name. Don't use spaces around the equal sign. If you do, the name of your variable and its contents will be corrupted. With the command:

```
SET RONNY = Test
```

you'll end up with a variable named RONNY (followed by a space) containing the value Test (preceded with a space).

☠ When using the SET command, be sure not to use a space before or after the equal sign.

Once you store a variable in the environment, you can't edit its value. However, you can replace the contents of an environmental variable using the same command—thus overwriting the contents of the environmental variable with a new value. You can also delete an environmental variable with the command:

```
SET variable=
```

where nothing follows the equal sign. Finally, you can view the contents of the environment by issuing the SET command by itself from the command line or in a batch file.

Using the environment in batch files

When you surround an environmental variable name with percent signs, OS/2 replaces the environmental variable name with its contents. So the command ECHO %PATH% will display your path and not the phrase %PATH%. Under DOS and in a DOS compatibility box, this trick works from within a batch file but not from the command line. With OS/2, it works both from a batch file and from the command line.

You can use a similar approach when transferring data between environmental variables. For example, if the environmental variable BEFORE contains a value you want to store in the environmental variable AFTER, the command to do this in a batch file is:

```
SET AFTER=%BEFORE%
```

Because of the percent signs, OS/2 replaces the %BEFORE% environmental variable with its contents; because of the SET command, it then stores this value to AFTER. Note first that the BEFORE environmental variable is surrounded by percent signs because you want to use its value, but the AFTER environmental variable isn't because you're using that name. Second, this command doesn't change the contents of the BEFORE environmental variable, so now you have the same information stored under two names. Of course, you could go ahead and work with either environmental variable to alter its contents.

➠ Under OS/2, you can access the contents of an environmental variable by surrounding its name with percent signs. This works from within a batch file or on the command line. Under DOS, this works only from a batch file.

What you can do with environmental variables

Environmental variables can be used for the following:

Display You can have a batch file display the contents of any environmental variable by surrounding its name with percent signs. For example, ECHO %PATH% will display the path.

Combining strings Two or more environmental variables can be displayed together. The technique is the same: just surround the respective names with percent signs. For example, if there are environment variables named Drive and File, the command ECHO %DRIVE%%FILE% will display them both, side by side.

In place of text You can use environmental variables anywhere text would be used. For example, the command PATH=%PATH%;C:\123 would append C: \123 onto the current path because the %PATH% is used just like the batch file entering the current path, and the command COPY C:\CONFIG.SYS % DRIVE%%FILE% would copy your CONFIG.SYS to the drive and filename stored under these environmental variables.

In place of commands A batch file can run a command stored to an environmental variable by having that environmental variable, surrounded by percent signs, on a line by itself.

Restoring the environment in a batch file

Sometimes you need to make temporary changes to the environment. OS/2 makes that easy. When a batch file issues a SETLOCAL command, OS/2 stores the current status of the environment, as well as the current drive and subdirectory. After that, the batch file can make any changes to either. Once the batch file is ready to restore the environment, drive, and subdirectory, an ENDLOCAL command returns them all to their exact state just before the SETLOCAL command was issued.

☑ The SETLOCAL and ENDLOCAL commands make it easy to restore the environment, drive, and subdirectory.

If a batch file terminates with a SETLOCAL command in effect, OS/2 behaves as though the last command were an ENDLOCAL and goes ahead and restores the environment in effect when the SETLOCAL command was in effect.

The biggest use of the SETLOCAL and ENDLOCAL commands in a batch file is to return a batch file that must change subdirectories to its original subdirectory when it's done. It's also important to note that the SETLOCAL and ENDLOCAL commands are two of the few batch file commands that won't run from the command line.

➡ The SETLOCAL and ENDLOCAL commands won't run from the command line.

On the disk, you'll find a batch file called LOCAL.CMD to illustrate these commands. LOCAL.CMD first displays the environment. Then it issues a

SETLOCAL command, deletes a number of environmental variables, and displays the rest so you can see that a number of changes were made. After that, it restores the original environment with the ENDLOCAL command and displays the restored environment. It also displays the current subdirectory, changes it to and displays the \OS2\INSTALL subdirectory, and then changes back to and displays the current subdirectory with the ENDLOCAL command.

Using the environment when shelling out of a program

While batch files work with the original—or master—copy of the environment, every time you start a program, OS/2 passes that program a full copy of the environment. The program is free to alter its copy of the environment, but when the program terminates, its copy of the environment is also terminated without passing the changes back to the master copy.

Remember comparing the environment to a scratch pad? Well, when OS/2 runs a program, it provides that program with a photocopy of its scratch pad in case the program needs any of the information it contains. When the program terminates, OS/2 tosses that photocopy into the memory recycling bin without even looking at it!

Using the environment in a batch file

The environment is commonly used as an common exchange ground—allowing one batch file to place information into the environment for another batch file to use. Looking at this in more depth requires that you understand both the errorlevel and logic testing, so I'll postpone this topic until later.

Batch files can use environmental variables just like replaceable parameters, including using them as filenames or even commands. This allows environmental variables to be used as a shortcut.

➡ Batch files can use environmental variables just like replaceable parameters.

Imagine that you're writing a large database program. You usually work on one program for most of the day, trying to get out all the bugs. You use batch files to start Microsoft Word in order to edit your program and to run Quicksilver in order to compile the program. If you store the name of the program in the environment as COMPILE, then batch files can automate much of the work for you.

A batch file segment to compile the program for you, called COMPILE.CMD, would look like this:

```
@ECHO OFF
COMPILE %COMPILE%
```

You could write a similar batch file segment, called WORD2QS.CMD, to similarly automate loading the program into Microsoft Word for editing. It would look like this:

```
@ECHO OFF
WORD %COMPILE%
```

Because Word defaults to ASCII mode when editing an ASCII file, no special switches are required.

Summary

- The environment is a portion of memory set aside for storing system-wide variables—much like a scratch pad for the operating system.
- There are a number of special metacharacters for creating fancy prompts.
- The path is a list of subdirectories for OS/2 to search for a program to run.
- The COMSPEC environmental variable tells OS/2 where to find CMD.EXE.
- The values of environmental variables are lost when the computer is turned off or rebooted.
- Permanent environmental variables have the same value for each session.
- A copy of the environment is provided to each program, but any changes made to it are lost when the program terminates.
- The SET command is used to store data in the environment. It also erases or changes existing data in the environment.
- Batch files and the command line can access the contents of the environment if you surround the environmental variable name with percent signs.
- Batch files can display environmental variables, combine them together, transfer values between them, and even use them as commands.
- Batch files can use the environment to pass information between themselves.
- A batch file can store the current contents of the environment, as well as the current drive and subdirectory, with the SETLOCAL command.
- The environment and current drive and subdirectory can be restored with the ENDLOCAL command once it has been saved with the SETLOCAL command.
- Batch files can use the environment to store data that will be accessed by more than one batch file or that a single batch file needs to access each time it runs.

15
The errorlevel

While a nice place for batch files, the environment is a very inhospitable place for programs to store information so they can communicate with each other. Each program is provided with a copy of the environment when it's first loaded. When a program reads from or writes to the environment, it's dealing with a copy of the environment and not with the original. When the program terminates, its copy of the environment—along with all the changes the program made to it—are destroyed.

The errorlevel value (also called a return code) is provided to overcome this problem. The errorlevel is a single byte of memory that can contain only a single character. Normally, the content of errorlevel is referred to as an ASCII value rather than a character representation. ASCII values 0–255 are therefore possible.

Errorlevel and return code are the same thing.

How the errorlevel works

When a program terminates, it can store a number in the errorlevel to indicate its status at termination. When programs use the errorlevel, the usual rule is to set it to zero for a successful execution and to higher values for different types of errors.

The errorlevel isn't stored in the environment, so changes made to it aren't lost when a program terminates. Unlike the environment, there's only one copy of the errorlevel per session, and every program in a single session changes the same one. However, each different OS/2 session has its own unique errorlevel slot.

The errorlevel doesn't change unless a program changes it, you start another program, or you reboot, so you can perform multiple tests on it.

However, the errorlevel is automatically reset to zero by OS/2 each time you start a new program, so each time a program runs, the prior errorlevel value is lost. Under OS/2, you can reset the errorlevel by running an internal command. This is not the case under DOS and a few batch files might not work properly as a result.

Under OS/2, internal commands reset the errorlevel to zero. This is not the case under DOS. As a result, some batch files translated from DOS might need to be modified.

You don't need the errorlevel when running programs from the command line because you'll see any error messages. However, a batch file won't "see" an error message, so the errorlevel gives it a way to respond to errors.

OS/2 errorlevel support

OS/2 has eleven commands that are documented to support the errorlevel. They are BACKUP, CHKDSK, COMP, EAUTIL, FORMAT, GRAFTABL, RECOVER, REPLACE, RESTORE, UNPACK, and XCOPY. The errorlevels for these eleven commands are shown in TABLES 15-1 through 15-11, along with their associated meanings.

Table 15-1 BACKUP errorlevels.

Errorlevel	Meaning
0	Normal completion.
1	No files were found to back up.
2	Some files or directories weren't processed because of file errors.
3	Ended by the user.
4	Ended because of an error.
5	This return code wasn't used.
6	BACKUP was unable to process the FORMAT command.

Table 15-2 CHKDSK errorlevels.

Errorlevel	Meaning
0	Normal completion.
1	This return code wasn't used.
2	This return code wasn't used.
3	Ended by the user.
4	Ended because of an error.
5	This return code wasn't used.
6	CHKDSK was unable to execute the file system's CHKDSK program.

Table 15-3 COMP errorlevels.

Errorlevel	Meaning
0	Normal completion.
1	No files were found to compare.
2	Some files or directories weren't processed because of file errors.
3	Ended by the user.
4	Ended because of an error.
5	Files didn't compare correctly.

Table 15-4 EAUTIL errorlevels.

Errorlevel	Meaning
0	Normal completion.
1	Files not found.
2	This return code not used.
3	This return code not used.
4	Ended because of an error.

Table 15-5 FORMAT errorlevels.

Errorlevel	Meaning
0	Normal completion.
1	This return code not used.
2	This return code not used.
3	Ended by the user.
4	Ended because of an error.
5	Ended due to no response when user was prompted to format a hard disk.
6	CHKDSK was unable to execute the file system's format program.
7	Volume not supported by another file system's format program.

Table 15-6 GRAFTABL errorlevels.

Errorlevel	Meaning
0	No previously loaded character table exists and a code page is not resident.
1	A previously loaded character table exists. If a new table was requested, it replaces the previous table at its original location.
2	No previously loaded character table exists and no new table is loaded.
3	An incorrect parameter was used.
4	An incorrect version of the program was used.

Table 15-7 RECOVER errorlevels.

Errorlevel	Meaning
0	Normal completion.
1	This return code wasn't used.
2	This return code wasn't used.
3	Ended by the user.
4	Ended because of an error.
5	Unable to read or write to one of the file-allocation tables.
6	Unable to execute another file system's recovery program.

Table 15-8 REPLACE errorlevels.

Errorlevel	Meaning
0	Normal completion.
1	No files found to replace.
2	Some files weren't replaced (or added) due to file errors.
3	This return code not used.
4	Ended because of an error.

Table 15-9 RESTORE errorlevels.

Errorlevel	Meaning
0	Normal completion.
1	No files found to restore.
2	Some files weren't processed due to file errors.
3	Ended by the user.
4	Ended because of an error.

Table 15-10 UNPACK errorlevels.

Errorlevel	Meaning
0	Normal completion.
1	No files found to unpack or copy.
2	Some files or directories weren't unpacked or copied due to file errors.
3	Ended by the user.
4	Ended because of an error.

Table 15-11 XCOPY errorlevels.

Errorlevel	Meaning
0	Normal completion.
1	No files found to XCOPY.
2	Some files or directories weren't copied due to file or directory errors.
3	Ended by the user.
4	Ended because of an error.

OS/2 also has a number of internal commands with undocumented errorlevel support. For example, the DIR command returns an errorlevel of one if you use an invalid switch and an errorlevel of eighteen if it doesn't find the file you specify after the DIR command. Because no documentation on the errorlevels exists and support in future releases is not guaranteed since they're undocumented, I elected not to include errorlevel tables on these internal commands. If you need to know about a specific command, include a $R in your prompt and experiment with the command to see if it produces an errorlevel when you use the command incorrectly or get an error message. I'd like to see IBM document all the errorlevel values it plans on supporting in future releases.

Only a few commercial programs use the errorlevel. If a commercial program uses it, it will be listed in the program documentation. While OS/2 makes little use of errorlevel, it's crucial to become familiar with it. Many batch utilities use the errorlevel to communicate results back to batch files.

To help you experiment with the errorlevel, OS/2 includes a nice feature. Include a $R in your prompt and your prompt will include the errorlevel for the last command you issued. Additionally, I've included a REXX program called GET-ONE.CMD on the disk. This program will take a single keystroke from the user and store its ASCII value in the errorlevel. To run it from within a batch file, use the command CALL GET-ONE and make sure the program is either in the current subdirectory or is in your path. Of course, it can also be run from the command line without the CALL command.

☑ Many batch utilities use the errorlevel to communicate results back to batch files.

Summary

- The errorlevel is a single byte of information that's common to all programs and batch files.
- Including a $R in your prompt will cause OS/2 to display the errorlevel for the last command you entered.
- The REXX program GET-ONE.CMD, included on the disk, allows your batch files to call a program that will set the errorlevel to any value you specify.

16 Command-line punctuation

DOS and OS/2 have some pretty cryptic command-line commands, which is part of why the graphical user interface of OS/2 is so popular. However, its punctuation is far more cryptic than the commands. If you've ever tried to direct input from one file into a filter and then direct the output to another file, then you know what I mean. Because punctuation is often used in batch files, I've devoted this chapter to helping you understand the topic.

Piping and redirection

Normally, you enter input from the keyboard and output goes to the screen, printer, or disk drive. This input and output is often called I/O. OS/2 has the ability, however, to redirect I/O to and from nonstandard locations. This is called *redirection* or *piping*. When you cause input to come from a nonstandard location, it's *input redirection* and when you cause output to go to an nonstandard location, it's *output redirection*. Anything else, which usually involves taking output from one program and using it as input for another program is referred to as *piping*.

☑ Input and output redirection and piping cause OS/2 to handle file inputs and outputs differently.

OS/2 maintains two file handles for I/O, with file handle 0 reserved for input and 1 reserved for output. When you boot, they're both automatically mapped to the console. What redirection and piping really do is replace one of these standard file handles with a different file handle for I/O processing.

The available piping symbols

There are four symbols used for either redirection or piping:

> The greater-than symbol causes output from one location to flow to another location. Many times it's treated as input by the receiving program. When the alternative location is a file, this causes the file to be overwritten if it exists. For this reason, you must be very careful when using a greater-than symbol in a batch file. You should always test first, using an IF test, before piping to a file. If the file exists, you can issue an error message and stop, rename the existing file, or pipe to an alternative file—after checking to make sure the file doesn't exist.

>> The dual greater-than symbol is used to route output to alternative locations. It's the same as the greater-than symbol, except that, when the alternative location is a file, dual greater-than piping causes the messages to be appended to the end of the existing file. This is a safer alternative if you're trying to store error messages or other information in a file. Since the dual greater-than symbol is really just a special case of the greater-than symbol, I'll consider just the greater-than symbol for most of this chapter.

< The less-than symbol causes a program to get its input from the specified device or file.

| Instead of creating a permanent file like the greater-than or dual greater-than symbol, the vertical bar creates a temporary file that's read and erased by the following program. A common use is in the command DIR|MORE. Another use of vertical bar symbol is to pipe data that a program needs to run into that program. For example, ECHO Y|DEL *.* will erase all the files in the current directory without asking. That's because the DEL command requires you to confirm the deletion when deleting all the files, but that confirmation is piped into the DEL command using the ECHO Y command. Basically, the vertical bar means that you're using the output of what's on the left as input to what's on the right.

Devices to pipe to and from

Generally, redirection and piping involves either an OS/2 system device driver or a filename. OS/2 system device drivers are device drivers that are automatically created by the system. They are:

AUX This is an auxiliary device that's normally treated as COM1.

CLOCK$ This is the real-time clock.

COM# This is the serial port. COM1 is the first port, and COM2 is the second. You can also use AUX as the default serial port.

CON Depending on the usage, this is either the screen or the keyboard. When used as the target, it's the screen. When used as the source, CON is the keyboard.

LPT# This is the printer port. LPT1 is the first port, and LPT2 is the second port. You can also use PRN to specify the default printer port.

NUL This is an output device that causes any output sent to it to be discarded.

PRN This is the printer and is normally mapped to LPT1.

If the target of a redirection or pipe is not one of these, then OS/2 knows it is a filename.

How OS/2 handles a pipe

When OS/2 encounters a less-than symbol, it means a program is going to receive its input from the alternative device specified by the pipe. OS/2 then closes the standard input device and opens the alternative one specified on the command line because only one input device can be open at a time. That is why when inputs are redirected into a program from a file, that file must contain all the inputs required by the program. Since the file is the only active source of inputs, no others are available.

The receiving program (the one on the left of the less-than symbol) doesn't know data is being redirected to it. All it knows is that data is coming in from the input device. OS/2 handles altering the input device before turning control over to the program.

Output redirection works in a similar fashion except, of course, it's the output file handle that gets replaced rather than the input file handle. For example, if you issue the command COPY *.* A: to copy some files to the A: drive, you'd expect to see each filename scroll by on the screen as it was copied and then to see the # file(s) copied message when copying was done. Now, change the command to:

```
COPY *.* A: > NUL
```

and you'll see absolutely nothing extra appear on the screen as the command works—and when it's done all you'll see to indicate it is the return of your prompt! Don't worry, the files were still copied. The > NUL told OS/2 to turn off the standard output device—the console—and turn on the alternative output device—NUL in this case. None of this affects the actions of the COPY command itself. This technique is a good way of hiding these sorts of OS/2 messages from new users in batch files.

If you had wanted to log these messages, you could have redirected them to a file with > *filename* if it were a one-time log or >> *filename* if you didn't want to overwrite the log file first. The second approach is particularly useful for accumulating multiple messages in a single file.

When OS/2 encounters a vertical bar (¦), it takes the output of one command and passes (or pipes) it on to another command. For example, you can use piping to display directory information one screenful at a time. (Yes, I know DIR/P will do this, but it's a nice easy example.) First, get a file listing with the command DIR > FILE. This will direct the output of the DIR command into a file named FILE. Then send this file through the MORE filter with the command TYPE FILE > MORE and you'll get exactly what you want.

However, OS/2 makes it easier. The command DIR | MORE does the same thing. OS/2 runs the DIR command, stores its output in memory, and then passes that to MORE for display. This is different from DOS, which uses temporary disk files—rather than memory—to handle pipes.

Piping and redirection, and the command processor

As you experiment with redirection and piping, you're going to find circumstances where it looks like you've done everything right but the command just doesn't work and all you end up with is a zero-length file. For example, start Lotus with the command 123 > LOG and, no matter what you do in Lotus, when you exit, LOG will be a zero-length file! If you start Lotus with the command 123 < LOG, Lotus still expects input from you and won't accept it from the LOG file—which must exist or OS/2 will object and not run the command.

There's nothing wrong here with either OS/2 or Lotus and there's no problem with the way the commands are constructed. Rather, there's confusion about what redirection and piping does.

For output, OS/2 offers several character output services, or programs can use video BIOS routines or write information straight to the video buffer. As you might expect, these latter methods are faster and most programs use them. For input, programs can let OS/2 read the keyboard for them or they can take the faster approach of using interrupt 16h BIOS services. Output can be piped only when it goes through the standard OS/2 output device and input can be piped only when it comes from the OS/2 standard input device. Since most programs bypass these, most programs are immune to piping. However, most OS/2 utilities and command-line utilities do use standard OS/2 I/O so you can pipe these. When a properly constructed pipe fails to work, the flaw is usually that the program being piped bypasses standard OS/2 I/O.

This also explains why you can't use redirection or piping to capture data intended for the printer into a file. Since a printer isn't the standard OS/2 output device but an alternative one, piping doesn't affect it.

Filters to use in pipes

OS/2 includes three filters you can use to manipulate the data coming out of or going into a pipe:

FIND Searches each line of a file for specified text.

MORE Displays one screen of information, pauses until you press any key, and then displays another screen of information. This continues until all the information has been displayed. MORE can't scroll backwards. The more common usages are DIR | MORE and TYPE *filename* | MORE.

SORT Sorts the file (or input) into ASCII order.

Problems with redirection and piping

Redirection and piping can cause problems, the major one being a "hung" computer. If you use piping to tell a program to get its input from a file, then that file must contain all the input the program requires. If it doesn't, you'll have to press Ctrl–Break to abort the program you're running. In addition, redirection and piping can get around the usual warning. For example, the command:

```
ECHO Y | DEL *.*
```

will delete all your files without asking you if you want to because the ECHO command supplies the necessary response. Those warnings are generally in place for a good reason, and it isn't a good idea to avoid them. Also, redirecting error messages doesn't always work.

Under DOS, another problem would crop up when you specify an invalid command, such as:

```
DATE < NUL
PROGRAM < LPT1
```

In the first example, NUL is used as an input device, but NUL can never supply input. In the second case, the printer is used for input and, like NUL, can't supply input. DOS, unfortunately, won't spot either of these problems; the programs or commands will wait forever for a response (or until you press Ctrl–Break or reboot). However, OS/2 is more intelligent and will ignore invalid pipes such as these.

Finally, you can destroy data by using redirection and piping improperly. For example, if you wanted to take the data in FILE.DAT and sort it using SORT.EXE, you might issue the command:

```
SORT < FILE.DAT > FILE.DAT
```

This tells OS/2 to run SORT.EXE and supply it with input from the file FILE.DAT. When SORT.EXE finishes, it's supposed to write the results back to the FILE.DAT file. However, what happens is that FILE.DAT gets erased!

When OS/2 goes to process a command line or batch file command, the first thing it does is replace any environmental variables or replaceable parameters with its value. There are neither in the previous line. The next thing it does is check for redirection and piping and, if it finds any, it initializes the files. Since the above command pipes data into FILE.DAT, it creates FILE.DAT and in the process erases the existing copy. Since all this happens prior to OS/2 actually running the command line, data has not yet been read out of FILE.DAT and piped into SORT.

This is actually a handy way to create zero-length files if you need them. A zero-length file is a file with a directory entry and valid name but no contents, so it doesn't take up any disk space. By typing a nonexistent file with a command like TYPE NOFILE > TARGET, OS/2 goes ahead and creates the TARGET file—but there's nothing to put into it, so it remains a zero-length file.

Command-line operators

OS/2 offers three very useful command-line operators that aren't available in DOS: &, &&, and ¦¦. The & operator allows you to place two commands on the same line and have them both executed. So the command:

```
ECHO First Line & ECHO Second Line
```

is functionally equivalent to these two lines:

```
ECHO First Line
ECHO Second Line
```

The && operator is similar to the & operator only the second command is executed only if the first command is successful. So the second command in:

```
DIR Z*.* && ECHO Z*.* Found
```

would execute only if the current subdirectory contained a file matching the Z*.* file specification.

The ¦¦ operator allows you to place two commands on the same line, where the second command is executed only if the first command fails. So in the command:

```
DIR Z*.* ¦¦ ECHO Z*.* Not Found
```

only the first or second line would execute, but not both. If a file matching the Z*.* file specification exists, the first command would execute; otherwise, the second command would execute.

Like the pipe symbols, in order to display these symbols in an ECHO statement, they must be preceded with a caret. The batch file SHOW-PIPE.CMD illustrates using these commands in a batch file. Its operational commands are shown as follows:

```
@ECHO OFF
ECHO Showing ^¦^¦ Command
ECHO Runs Command Only If Prior Command Failed
DIR A*.* ¦¦ ECHO No A*.* Files Found
DIR Z*.* ¦¦ ECHO No Z*.* Files Found
DIR ZQZ*.* ¦¦ ECHO No ZQZ*.* Files Found

ECHO Showing ^& Command
ECHO Runs One Command After Another On Same Line
ECHO 1 & ECHO 2 & ECHO 3 & ECHO 4 & ECHO 5
```

```
ECHO Showing ^&^& Command
ECHO Runs Another Command On Same Line
ECHO Only If First Successful
ECHO 1 && ECHO 2 && ECHO 3 && ECHO 4
```

I found that these three symbols didn't work consistently when used in conjunction with an IF test so I don't recommend you use them in that context.

> The &, &&, and ¦¦ operators didn't work consistently when used in conjunction with an IF test.

The plus sign is used to perform file concatenation, which is a fancy name for combining two or more files together. For example, the command:

```
COPY File1+File2+File3 File4
```

will copy the first three files into one larger file, File4. This can cause problems if either of these first three files contains an end-of-file (EOF) marker; most editors won't allow you to go beyond the point in a file where the first EOF marker is located.

You can also use file concatenation to append information to the bottom of a batch file without loading an editor. For example, the command:

```
COPY CONFIG.SYS+CON
```

copies the current contents of the CONFIG.SYS file plus whatever you type after issuing this command (press F6 or ^Z to quit entering text) into a new version of the CONFIG.SYS file.

Use this approach to appending text with care. If the file you're appending text to is large, the operation might not work properly. Plus, if the file doesn't end with a Return, you must first press Return, or the text you enter will be appended to the last line of the file. The rest of the command-line operators are as follows:

: The colon is used to name lines in a batch file. This is explained in detail in chapter 13.

. DOS 3 and later will usually display a blank line in response to an ECHO. command, so you might see this in batch files you receive from others. This trick also works under OS/2, so you don't need to modify these batch files to use them.

@ The at character is used to turn off command echoing for a single command in a batch file, regardless of the global status of command echoing. This is covered in chapter 6.

% A single percent sign is used to mark replaceable parameters in a batch file, as covered in chapter 11. It is also used to name the variable in a FOR loop when issued from the command line rather than in a batch file. This usage is covered in chapter 13.

%% Dual percent signs are used to name the variable in a FOR loop when the FOR loop is used as part of a batch file. See chapter 13.

%*variable*% Percent signs surrounding a variable allow the value of that variable to be used in a batch file or on the command line. This usage is covered in chapter 14. This does not work from the command line.

= The single equal sign is used to assign values to environmental variables and to erase those values. See chapter 14.

== Dual equal signs are used in IF tests to test to see if two strings are equal. See chapter 17.

Summary

- By using piping, OS/2 can get input from alternative sources as well as send output to alternative locations.
- The greater-than sign causes OS/2 to pipe output to an alternative location. When that location is a file, the file is overwritten.
- Dual greater-than signs also cause OS/2 to pipe output to an alternative location. When that location is a file, the file is not overwritten.
- The less-than sign causes a program to obtain its input from an alternative location.
- The vertical bar causes the output of one program to be sent to another program without creating a permanent file.
- Devices that can be used as alternative sources for pipes include the console (CON), the printer (LPT or PRN), the serial port (COM), nothing (NUL), and a file.
- OS/2 includes three filters that work with pipes: FIND for locating specific text, MORE for displaying text one screen at a time, and SORT for placing data in order.
- Improper use of piping can cause files to be overwritten.
- The & operator allows you to enter two commands on one line and have them both unconditionally executed.
- The && operator allows you to enter two commands on one line and have the second executed only if the first is successful.
- The || operator allows you to enter two commands on one line and have the second execute only if the first isn't successful.
- The &, &&, and || operators didn't work consistently with IF tests, and their use in that context is not recommended.
- The plus sign is used to perform file concatenation.
- The colon is used to name lines in a batch file.
- A period directly following an ECHO causes either OS/2 or MS-DOS to display a blank line in a batch file.
- The @ sign is used to turn off command echoing for a single command in a batch file regardless of command echoing being turned on.

- The single percent sign is used to mark replaceable parameters in batch files and for the variable name in a FOR loop issued from the command line.
- Dual percent signs are used for the variable name in a FOR loop issued in a batch file.
- Surrounding an environmental variable name with percent signs allows the contents of that variable to be used in a batch file.
- The equal sign is used to assign values to environmental variables and to erase those values.
- Dual equal signs are used in IF tests to see if two strings are equal.

17
Logic testing

Basically, logic testing in a batch file means that you should be able to specify a statement and then have the batch file react differently depending on whether the statement is true or false. An IF test allows a batch file to accomplish this. The basic syntax of an IF test is:

```
IF statement action
```

If the statement being tested is false, then the batch file will skip to the next line and continue processing. If the statement is true, then the batch file will process the rest of this line.

The *action* portion of the IF test can be a GOTO command. GOTO allows the batch file to take different paths through the batch file—and thus do different things—depending on the conditions the batch file finds while it's running. Logic testing can take one of four forms:

- Are two strings of characters the same?
- What is the errorlevel? (Recall that the errorlevel and return code are the same thing.)
- Does a file exist?
- Does a subdirectory exist?

When you compare two strings of characters, you can acquire these strings from several different sources. They can be:

- Hardwired into the batch file
- Replaceable parameters
- From the environment

Are two values the same?

Batch files can test to see only if two character sets are the same; they can't perform numeric calculations to see if two equations are equal. For that you need REXX. A set of characters is called a *string*, and comparing two strings is called a *string comparison*. The format of the IF test when used for string comparisons is:

```
IF string1==string2 action
```

where *string1* is the source of the first string, *string2* is the source of the second string, and *action* is the command to be formed when the two strings are the same. Notice that two equal signs are used—not one. If you forget and use a single equal sign, OS/2 will give you an error message.

One of the strings in this comparison almost always comes from either replaceable parameters or the environment—with replaceable parameters being the most common source. The other string is generally hardwired into the batch file. I generally put the replaceable parameter on the left side of the two equal signs and the hardwired value on the right side.

One of the things I'll use this for throughout the remainder of this book is to add help to batch files. I'll use /? to be consistent with OS/2, but let's look at the problem associated with using the older form of /H found in some programs.

When a user starts a batch file with a /H, you want to briefly display a help message and then exit the batch file. You might think the command to do this is:

```
IF %1==/H GOTO HELP
```

and this indeed might work. However, it suffers from two problems—one minor and one more serious.

The minor problem is that string comparisons in a batch file are case-sensitive. Recall that a batch file simply replaces the replaceable parameters with the values entered on the command line. When a user starts this batch file with /H, this test becomes:

```
IF /H==/H GOTO HELP
```

which is true. However, when a user starts the batch file with /h, this test becomes:

```
IF /h==/H GOTO HELP
```

which is not true. The solution to this problem is to test for both possible values, so the test becomes:

```
IF %1==/H GOTO HELP
IF %1==/h GOTO HELP
```

In this case, if the user enters /H, the first test passes and the batch file jumps to the help section without ever reaching the second test. If the first test fails because the user enters /h, the batch file runs the second test and now finds the two strings equal, jumping to the help section. Of course, if the user enters some other replaceable parameter, both tests would fail and the batch file would continue without executing either GOTO command.

String comparisons in a batch file are case-sensitive.

While it's not difficult to check the different capitalizations for a single letter, it can become burdensome when multiple letters are involved. For example, if the first replaceable parameter is either daily, weekly, or monthly, then it would take nine IF tests to test for just the likely capitalization combinations of all lowercase, all uppercase, and first letter capitalized. The disk that comes with this book includes a utility called CAPITAL.CMD to deal with the problem, which is explored in chapter 26.

When you compare strings where one or both of the values comes from replaceable parameters, you'll have more problems dealing with the way OS/2 treats replaceable parameters. Recall from chapter 11 that everywhere you enter a %1 in the batch file, OS/2 replaces that %1 with the first replaceable parameter entered on the command line. Thus, if you have the test:

```
IF %1==/H GOTO HELP
```

and the user enters a replaceable parameter, then the test works properly—as shown earlier.

Unfortunately, OS/2 isn't very smart in making these comparisons. When the user doesn't enter a replaceable parameter, OS/2 substitutes nothing for %1 and the above comparison becomes:

```
IF ==/H GOTO HELP
```

When this happens, OS/2 thinks you left off part of the IF test and issues an error message.

The solution to this minor dilemma is simple: surround the comparison with a set of symbols so OS/2 will compare something to something. I always use parentheses, but some users prefer quotation marks. The advantage to surrounding both items to compare with a set of parentheses is that you allow a single test to compare the two strings, while avoiding any problems when one—or even both—of the strings in the comparison are empty. It even allows testing for an empty string because ()==() is a valid test. Thus, the command:

```
IF (%1)==() GOTO NONE
```

would successfully test for a blank first replaceable parameter and return the correct result.

OS/2 has problems performing string comparisons when one of the strings is a nul string. The solution is to surround both the strings with parentheses.

In addition to testing the replaceable parameters, you can use the same IF test to test environmental variables. The only difference is that the environmental variable must be surrounded by percent signs. So the IF test to see if the prompt is PG is this:

```
IF (%PROMPT%)==($P$G) ECHO Prompt Is $P$G
```

The percent signs around PROMPT tell OS/2 to replace it with the value of the PROMPT environmental variable. Of course, like all other IF tests, this one is case-sensitive.

What is the errorlevel?

As you saw in chapter 15, the errorlevel has room for only one byte, so only an ASCII value of 0 to 255 can be stored in it. Using the statement:

```
IF ERRORLEVEL #
```

a batch file can test the contents of the errorlevel and make decisions based on that content. Unfortunately, the test isn't straightforward.

The test IF ERRORLEVEL 5 doesn't test to see if the errorlevel is equal to 5, as you might expect from the section on string comparisons. Rather, it tests for an errorlevel of 5 or higher, so any number from 5 to 255 will result in a true response to this test.

☑ The IF ERRORLEVEL test is a greater-than-or-equal-to test and not an equality test.

Because the IF ERRORLEVEL test is a greater-than-or-equal-to test, you must always test from the highest possible errorlevel value to the lowest. In addition, you must branch away from the testing after the first match. CHECKERR.CMD is a batch file that will test for every possible errorlevel value and display that value on the screen. A small segment of CHECKERR.CMD is shown here:

```
@ECHO OFF
IF ERRORLEVEL 255 ECHO 255
IF ERRORLEVEL 255 GOTO END
IF ERRORLEVEL 254 ECHO 254
IF ERRORLEVEL 254 GOTO END
IF ERRORLEVEL 253 ECHO 253
IF ERRORLEVEL 253 GOTO END
--- and so on ---
```

Notice how CHECKERR.CMD operates. It first tests for a value of 255. Because the maximum value of errorlevel is 255, this first test is an equality test rather than the normal greater-than-or-equal-to test. If the value is 255, it displays that information and jumps to the end of the batch file. If the value is not 255, it tests for 254. If the value is 254, it displays that value and jumps to the end of the batch file. If not, it tests for 253, 252, and so on down the line. By testing from the highest possible value to the lowest possible value, you can avoid the problems associated with the greater-than-or-equal-to errorlevel test.

While CHECKERR.CMD is very long, most batch files will be able to test every possible errorlevel value while remaining fairly short. The reason is that most OS/2 programs that use the errorlevel use only a few values. So the batch file has to check for only these few values in declining order, not every possible value.

Does a file exist?

The third possible type of IF test tests to see if a file exists. The format for the command is:

```
IF EXIST filename action
```

so the command:

```
IF EXIST C:\CONFIG.SYS ECHO CONFIG.SYS File Exists
```

would check to see if your CONFIG.SYS file existed in the root directory of the C: drive and display a message if it did.

The IF test won't have any problem testing to see if a file exists, even if the replaceable parameter used in the test doesn't have a value. Thus, the test:

```
IF EXIST %1 action
```

doesn't need anything special to protect it in case the user doesn't enter a replaceable parameter. If fact, putting the filename inside parentheses would cause the test to always fail. The IF test can use wildcards, so the test:

```
IF EXIST C:\BAT\*.CMD ECHO Batch Files Found
```

would be true if at least one .CMD file existed in the C:\BAT subdirectory. If no path is specified in the IF EXIST test, it looks for only the file in the current subdirectory on the current drive. If you like, you can specify the full path to the file, as is the case in the earlier tests.

Does a subdirectory exist?

Unlike DOS, the OS/2 IF EXIST command handles subdirectories without any problem. If you have a subdirectory called C:\BAT, then the command:

```
IF EXIST C:\BAT
```

would properly consider that a true statement. Under DOS, the command:

```
IF EXIST C:\BAT\NUL
```

was to "trick" DOS into performing this test. This should be converted under OS/2.

Earlier batch files revisited

Back in chapter 11, you looked at three batch files: A.CMD, RONNYMD .CMD, and TOA.CMD. A.CMD worked fine, but the other two had problems. You've looked at TOA.CMD a couple of times since then, but it still has some problems. You now have enough tools to revisit these three files and put them into final form.

A.CMD

When last you examined A.CMD, it looked like this:

```
@ECHO OFF
REM NAME:     A.CMD
REM PURPOSE: Directory Of A: Drive
REM VERSION: 1.00
REM DATE:     May 12, 1993

DIR A:%1 /P
```

This batch file runs fine, but you can make it better. You can add command-line help and also assume that if the user enters a %2 he wants to specify the switches, so leave off the /P. The resulting, and final, version of TOA.CMD is shown next:

```
@ECHO OFF
REM NAME:     A.CMD
REM PURPOSE: Directory Of A: Drive
REM VERSION: 2.00
REM DATE:     May 12, 1993

IF (%1)==(/?) GOTO HELP

IF (%2)==() DIR A:%1 /P
IF (%2)==() GOTO END

DIR A:%1 %2 %3 %4 %5
GOTO END

:HELP
  ECHO Performs A Directory Of The A: Drive
  ECHO Allows You To Specify Files And Switches
  ECHO On The Command Line
GOTO END

:END
```

This new version has a line added at the top to jump to a help section if the user requests help, plus lines to display that help. It has an IF test added to the front of the old DIR line and performs that line only when the user enters a single replaceable parameter. The next line exits the batch file if the user enters a single replaceable parameter. Finally, it performs a directory using five replaceable parameters. It reaches this point only if the user enters two or more replaceable parameters; if the user enters less than five, the extra ones in the batch file are ignored.

RONNYMD.CMD

When you last examined RONNYMD.CMD, it looked like this:

```
@ECHO OFF
REM NAME:     RONNYMD.CMD
REM PURPOSE: Make And Change To A Subdirectory
REM VERSION: 1.00
REM DATE:     May 12, 1993

MD %1
CD %1
```

The major problem with this batch file is it doesn't confirm that the user entered the name of a subdirectory to create. A minor problem—which you can now completely solve—is that it also fails to check to see if the user specified a subdirectory that already exists. The resulting, and final, version of RONNYMD.CMD is shown next:

```
@ECHO OFF
REM NAME:     RONNYMD.CMD
REM PURPOSE: Make And Change To A Subdirectory
REM VERSION: 2.00
REM DATE:     May 12, 1993

IF (%1)==(/?)  ECHO Makes And Changes To A Subdirectory
IF (%1)==(/?)  GOTO END
IF (%1)==()   ECHO No Subdirectory Specified
IF (%1)==()   GOTO END
IF EXIST %1   ECHO %1 Subdirectory Exists
IF EXIST %1   GOTO END

MD %1
CD %1

:END
```

The most interesting aspect of this modified version is the way it handles help and errors. Rather than jumping to a special section, it uses two IF tests: the first displays a brief message and the second jumps to the end of the batch file. This approach works when your messages are short. When you need more than one or maybe two lines of messages, you're better off jumping to a special section to handle it.

TOA.CMD

When you last saw TOA.CMD, it looked like this:

```
@ECHO OFF
REM NAME:     TOA.CMD
REM PURPOSE: Copy .CMP And .DOC Files To The A: Drive
REM          While Deleting .BAK Files
REM VERSION: 3.00
REM DATE:    May 12, 1993
:TOP
  DEL %1.BAK
  COPY %1.DOC A:
  COPY %1.CMP A:
  SHIFT
GOTO TOP
```

The batch file performs its assigned tasks of deleting the .BAK file and then copying the .DOC and .CMP files to the A: drive for the first replaceable parameter. The SHIFT command then brings the next replaceable parameter into the %1 slot and the process is repeated. The one problem is that the batch file doesn't know when to stop. Even after using all the replaceable parameters, it continues trying to use nonexistent replaceable parameters to copy nonexistent files until the user presses Ctrl–Break.

Fixing TOA.CMD is as easy as adding two lines. First, it needs a label at the end of the batch file to jump to, and it needs an IF test to jump to the end label when the batch file runs out of replaceable parameters. The corrected, and final, version of TOA.CMD is shown next:

```
@ECHO OFF
REM NAME:     TOA.CMD
REM PURPOSE: Copy .CMP And .DOC Files To The A: Drive
REM          While Deleting .BAK Files
REM VERSION: 4.00
REM DATE:    May 12, 1993

IF (%1)==(/?) GOTO HELP

:TOP
  IF (%1)==() GOTO END
  DEL %1.BAK
  COPY %1.DOC A:
  COPY %1.CMP A:
  SHIFT
GOTO TOP

:HELP
  ECHO Copies All The .DOC And .CMP Files
  ECHO You Specify On The Command Line
GOTO END

:END
```

Notice that the batch file tests for a blank replaceable parameter at the top of the loop before processing. That's important in case the user starts the batch file without any replaceable parameters. If the logic testing were at the end and the user started the program without a replaceable parameter, the first journey through the loop would generate error messages.

Preview of chapter 19

Logic testing is so important to successful batch files that, after the review in chapter 18, chapter 19 is also devoted to logic testing. The techniques in chapter 19 are more advanced than this chapter, but often these techniques make a complex problem easier to solve, so it's important to understand them.

Summary

- An IF test is used to perform logic testing in a batch file.
- An IF test can test to see if two strings are the same, what the errorlevel is, or if a file exists.
- Batch file string comparisons are case-sensitive.
- In a string comparison, the variables on both sides of the dual equal signs should be surrounded by parentheses to avoid problems when one of the strings is empty.
- An IF test can test the errorlevel value; however, the test is a greater-than-or-equal-to test and not an equality test.
- Because the IF test on errorlevel is a greater-than-or-equal-to test, errorlevel tests must cascade from largest to smallest.
- The IF test can test to see if a single file, a group of files specified with a wildcard, or a subdirectory exists.
- Command-line help can be added by either jumping to a special section to display the help or by having an IF test display the help and a second IF test exit the batch file.

18
Review #2

While we've covered only seven chapters since the last review, these seven chapters have contained a tremendous amount of material. You now know how to squirt information into a batch file from the command line, how to use that information in a batch file (no matter how much of it was entered on the command line), how to loop, and how to perform logic testing.

It's important to take a few moments and make sure that you're up to speed before continuing. What follows are three quick problems. Take a few moments and try to work them out. If you get stuck, glance back through the last few chapters. You need to have the skills necessary to solve these problems before you continue through the book; otherwise, you'll run into difficulty.

Problem 4

A friend of yours has a new computer. He's going away for the weekend but wants to run the computer continually while he's gone. He purchased a diagnostic program called Check It Out; the command to run the program is CHKITOUT. This program performs a complete diagnostic on the computer. It creates a file containing a full report and sets the errorlevel to 1 when it encounters a problem, but it doesn't display any information on the screen.

Your friend has asked you to write him a batch file to run CHKITOUT continually. Each time CHKITOUT terminates with an errorlevel of 1, the batch file should display an error message on the screen.

Problem 5

Your boss is having problems with her computer. It has a C: and D: drive, but sometimes she has to reboot the computer several times before the D: drive is operational. She has found a utility program called BOOT.COM that reboots the computer, and has asked you to write a batch file she can call from her startup folder to reboot the computer if the D: drive isn't operational. That way, each time it boots the computer will automatically reboot itself until the D: drive is operational.

Problem 6

You did such a good job on the last problem that your boss has asked you for another favor. It seems that she spends a lot of time on bulletin-board systems and acquires a lot of ASCII files to read. Normally, she reads them with the command:

```
TYPE file | MORE
```

but she's finding that method to be difficult when she has a lot of files. She has asked you for a batch file that loops through and displays all the files that she specifies on the command line.

Answers

There are a number of ways to tackle each of these problems. My solutions are included in appendix A in the back of the book. You don't need to match my answers; if you developed a working solution to the problem, then your solution is just as good as mine and might even be better.

PART 4
Advanced batch file topics

Now that you've seen the intermediate batch file commands, it's time to take a look at the advanced commands. By the time you finish this section, you'll have seen all the native batch subcommands that are available for you to use in batch files.

Chapter 19: Advanced logic testing Chapter 17 covered simple logic testing. This chapter expands logic testing to include all the available logic-testing commands OS/2 offers.

Chapter 20: Advanced ways to get information from users OS/2 makes it fairly difficult to get information from the user, giving you just replaceable parameters and Ctrl–Break to do the job. This chapter shows how to use the utility programs that come with the book to greatly expand the ability of a batch file to interact with the user.

Chapter 21: Advanced screen design Most batch files use a series of ECHO commands to communicate with the user in a very boring fashion. This chapter covers things you can do to improve your boring batch file screens.

Chapter 22: ANSI This chapter continues where chapter 21 leaves off by showing you how to used advanced ANSI commands to construct colorful and highly formatted screens. It also briefly covers other uses for ANSI.

Chapter 23: Batch file subroutines Subroutines are one of the most powerful approaches to writing complex batch files. This chapter shows you how to use them.

Chapter 24: When batch files don't work Even after reading a book like this one, you're going to occasionally have problems with the batch files you write. While nothing can eliminate the need for you to work through the logic of your batch file to resolve a problem, this chapter shows you some ways to expedite the process.

Chapter 25: Review #3 Before moving on, you should understand the commands and concepts covered so far. This chapter is a quick test. Pass it, and you're ready to move on.

19
Advanced logic testing

In chapter 17, you began looking at logic testing in batch files. You saw that batch files could test for four conditions and that when you compare two strings of characters you can acquire them from several different sources.

In this chapter you'll examine logic testing in even more detail, and I'll be introducing you to some of the utilities included on the disk that comes with this book. As you'll see, these utilities can make your batch files extremely powerful.

NOT

The NOT modifier is used to reverse an IF test. If an IF EXIST test is true, then the corresponding IF NOT EXIST test is false. If an IF EXIST test is false, then the IF NOT EXIST test is true. For example, the batch file segment:

```
IF EXIST C:\CONFIG.SYS ECHO CONFIG.SYS Exists
IF NOT EXIST C:\CONFIG.SYS ECHO CONFIG.SYS Missing!
```

will tell the user about her CONFIG.SYS no matter if it exists or not.

Interbatch communications

You can have batch files communicate with each other by placing values into the environment. ACCOUNT1.CMD performs monthly closing. The program CLOSE.EXE sets the errorlevel to show whether or not it ran without errors. ACCOUNT1.CMD needs to communicate that information to ACCOUNT2.CMD. It could depend on the errorlevel, but that could be reset if you ran another program in between the two batch files. To avoid that problem, ACCOUNT1.CMD places a value into the environment. The portion of ACCOUNT1.CMD that runs the closing program and creates the environmental variable is shown here:

```
CLOSE
IF ERRORLEVEL 1 SET ACCOUNT=NO
IF ERRORLEVEL 1 GOTO END
SET ACCOUNT=YES
```

ACCOUNT2.CMD then checks for that value and won't run without a correct setting. The portion of ACCOUNT2.CMD that handles this is :

```
IF (%ACCOUNT%)==() GOTO ERROR
IF (%ACCOUNT%)==(NO) GOTO NO
IF (%ACCOUNT)==(YES) CLOSE2
GOTO END

:ERROR
  ECHO Run ACCOUNT1.CMD First
  PAUSE
GOTO END

:NO
  ECHO Warning: Close Did Not Run Successfully
  ECHO Fix These Errors Before Running Account2
  PAUSE
GOTO END

:END
SET ACCOUNT=
```

Capitalization is not a problem here because ACCOUNT1.CMD always creates the variables in uppercase. Also note that ACCOUNT2.CMD resets the ACCOUNT environmental variable after running, which keeps ACCOUNT2 .CMD from being run twice.

A logical question is "Why didn't CLOSE.EXE set the information into the environment itself?" Well, each program is passed a copy of the environment when it starts. When the program terminates, that copy of the environment is erased. So CLOSE.EXE couldn't set the environment directly because those changes would have been lost when CLOSE.EXE terminated. The errorlevel isn't stored in the environment, so it isn't lost when CLOSE.EXE terminates. Also note that all programs and batch files must be run in the same session for this to work.

Dealing with capitalization

Managing capitalization in batch files is a real pain. As I said in chapter 17, just testing for the likely capitalization of three possible replaceable parameters—Daily, Monthly, and Annual—takes nine IF tests. That means the code just to handle the most likely capitalizations takes up nine lines, where three would work if capitalization were not a problem.

Even this elaborate scheme won't respond properly to replaceable parameters such as DAIly. There are a number of ways of dealing with the capitalization problem quickly without a lot of extra code. Each method has unique advantages.

GOTO %1

The first way to avoid the capitalization problem is to use the replaceable parameter as a label for the GOTO command because labels are case-insensitive. Keep in mind that OS/2 always replaces replaceable parameters with their value. Take a look at this batch file segment:

```
GOTO %1

:DAILY
  DAILY
GOTO END

:MONTHLY
  MONTHLY
GOTO END

:ANNUAL
  ANNUAL
GOTO END

:END
```

If you run this batch file with the command line:

```
BATCH daily
```

OS/2 will replace the GOTO %1 line with GOTO daily and the batch file will run properly—no matter what capitalization you use.

This method is only a partial solution. If the user starts the batch file with an invalid parameter—yearly, for example—it will abort on the line GOTO %1 with an error message. Because the batch file bombs after a GOTO %1 command if the specified label doesn't exist, no commands are needed under the GOTO %1 other than the sections that are being jumped.

While there's no absolute protection against invalid labels when using this approach, there is partial protection. Each section can use multiple labels with all the labels the user is likely to use. For example, the Annual section might look like this:

```
:ANNUAL
:ANNUALLY
:YEAR
:YEARLY
:ENDOFYEAR
  ANNUAL
:GOTO END
```

This helps prevent the "label not found" problem by putting as many possible labels in the batch file as the user is likely to use. Because label lines are not executed, having the batch file jump to the :ANNUAL or the :ENDOFYEAR line has the same effect on the execution of the batch file.

Environmental variables

A second method is to store the selected option in the environment as an environmental variable. The next batch file segment illustrates this:

```
SET DAILY=
SET MONTHLY=
SET ANNUAL=
SET %1=YES

IF (%DAILY%)==(YES)  GOTO DAILY
IF (%MONTHLY%)==(YES) GOTO MONTHLY
IF (%ANNUAL%)==(YES) GOTO ANNUAL
GOTO ERROR

:DAILY
  DAILY
GOTO END

:MONTHLY
  MONTHLY
GOTO END

:ANNUAL
  ANNUAL
GOTO END

:ERROR
  ECHO You Entered An Invalid Parameter
GOTO END

:END
```

First, each possible environmental is deleted and then the line SET %1=YES creates a single environmental variable with the name of the replaceable parameter and a value of YES.

This method works well for most replaceable parameters and avoids the missing label problem associated with the GOTO %1 method, but has a minor problem of its own. If the replaceable parameter the user enters can be a number, the batch file will end up making unexpected tests. Suppose you wanted to run Lotus 1-2-3, so the user would be expected to 123 as a replaceable parameter. The SET %1=YES line would work properly. In order to run Lotus, you would need a test line of IF %123%==YES. However, OS/2 would translate the %1 portion of this test as the first replaceable parameter.

Running a program

I became so frustrated trying to deal with capitalization that I wrote a REXX program called CAPITAL.CMD to cure the problem once and for all. CAPITAL takes a single word as an input, converts it to all uppercase, and stores the results in the environment under the environmental variable RETURN.

CAPITAL.CMD works only one word at a time. Send it more than one word, and it will ignore everything after the first word. This is true even if everything is enclosed inside quotation marks. Since filenames are case-insensitive, CAPITAL.CMD doesn't need to be compatible with them. The next batch file segment illustrates using CAPITAL:

```
CALL CAPITAL %1
IF (%RETURN%)==(DAILY)  GOTO DAILY
IF (%RETURN%)==(MONTHLY) GOTO MONTHLY
IF (%RETURN%)==(ANNUAL) GOTO ANNUAL
GOTO ERROR
```

Of course, somewhere near the end of the batch file you'll want a SET RETURN= command to reset this variable once you no longer needed it.

Each of these approaches has good points and bad points. The one you select really depends on your needs. However, I find that most of my batch files can be written using just the CAPITAL.CMD approach.

Multiple IF tests

Several IF tests can be combined to handle a complex decision or to help overcome the case problem associated with string comparisons. The format of a two-deep multiple IF test is:

```
IF statement1 IF statement2 action
```

When the first IF test fails, control flows to the next line in the batch file as it normally does. When the first IF statement is true, control passes to the remainder of the command as it normally does—only in this case, the remainder of the command is another IF test. Now, if the second IF test fails, control flows to the next line in the batch file, but if the second IF test is true the *action* command is executed. So each IF test acts as a gate, and the *action* executed only when every IF test before it is true. If just one of the IF tests is false, the entire test fails and the *action* isn't executed.

OS/2 doesn't place a direct limit on the number of IF tests you can combine in this fashion. You can use three or four or even five if you like. However, the command must be shorter than the 300-character limit OS/2 places on all batch file commands. In addition, the logic must be clear enough that the batch file author and anyone who later needs to maintain the batch file can understand it.

A shorter way to show the errorlevel

Consider the following example:

```
IF ERRORLEVEL 3 IF NOT ERRORLEVEL 4 ECHO Errorlevel Is 3
```

Three conditions are possible: the errorlevel is less than 3, the errorlevel is greater than 3, or the errorlevel equals 3.

When the errorlevel is less than 3, the first IF test fails and the batch file moves on to the next line. When the errorlevel is greater than 3, the first IF test passes. When an IF test passes, the batch file executes the remainder of the line—which in this case contains another IF test. For this second IF test, the test IF ERRORLEVEL 4 is true, but the NOT modifier changes the results to false. Thus, the second IF test fails and the batch file continues on to the next line.

Now, when the errorlevel is equal to 3, the first IF test passes and again the batch file moves on to the remainder of the IF test. In this case, the test IF ERRORLEVEL 4 is false because the errorlevel is 3, so the test fails. However, the NOT modifier changes the results to true. Having passed both IF tests, the batch file moves on the next portion of the line and displays the errorlevel value. In general, the IF test:

```
IF ERRORLEVEL n IF NOT ERRORLEVEL n+1 action
```

is true only for an errorlevel value of exactly *n*. Take a look at CHECKER1.CMD, a brief segment of which is shown below. This batch file takes advantage of these multiple IF tests to considerably reduce the number of lines needed to display all possible errorlevel values over CHECKERR.CMD in chapter 17.

```
IF ERRORLEVEL 255                        ECHO 255
IF ERRORLEVEL 254 IF NOT ERRORLEVEL 255 ECHO 254
IF ERRORLEVEL 253 IF NOT ERRORLEVEL 254 ECHO 253
IF ERRORLEVEL 252 IF NOT ERRORLEVEL 253 ECHO 252
--- and so on ---
```

While CHECKER1.CMD is shorter, it will take much longer to run—especially when the errorlevel is a high number. When CHECKERR.CMD processes a high errorlevel number—say 250—it has to go through only a few IF tests before it finds a match. For a value of 250, it would go through twelve IF tests before jumping out of the batch file. However, for each errorlevel value, CHECKER1.CMD processes all 255 of the first IF tests. In addition, it processes the second IF test for all errorlevel tests with lower test values than the errorlevel value. That is, for errorlevel test values of 0–250, CHECKER1.CMD must move on to the second IF test because the first is true. So for 250, CHECKER1.CMD ends up processing 305 IF tests rather than the twelve CHECKERR.CMD required and so it runs slower.

Summary

- The NOT modifier reverses the decision of any IF test.
- By creating environmental variables, batch files can communicate with each other even when there's a time lapse between each of them running.
- One way to deal with capitalization of replaceable parameters is with a GOTO %1 command.
- When using GOTO %1 to deal with capitalization of replaceable parameters, the batch file will bomb when the label doesn't exist. The chance of this can be reduced by using multiple labels.
- Another way to deal with capitalization of replaceable parameters is by creating an environmental variable with the name of the replaceable parameter because environmental variable names are always converted to uppercase.
- A final way to deal with capitalization of replaceable parameters is to run the CAPITAL.CMD program included on the disk that comes with this book.
- Multiple IF tests can be combined on a single line.
- When multiple IF tests are combined, the command is not executed unless all of the IF tests are true.
- When multiple IF tests are combined, their length must not exceed 300 characters.

20
Advanced ways to get information from users

The errorlevel is one of the more useful items available to batch file authors, yet it's also one of the least used. Part of the reason that it's avoided is because of its idiotic name, which tells the user nothing about what it actually does and probably scares off a lot of potential users. OS/2 is trying to improve this by beginning to call it a return code. The other reason that the errorlevel is rarely used is that OS/2 gives you no tool to set it. At best, a very few OS/2 programs set the errorlevel when they exit.

So far, you've seen only two ways to get information from the user: replaceable parameters and Ctrl–Break. With replaceable parameters, the user must remember the questions in advance—before running the batch file—in order to enter that information on the command line. Of course, it's easier from the desktop where OS/2 can be configured to prompt you for the information. That's asking for a lot! I have trouble remembering what batch file I need to run, much less what questions it's going to ask me. And often the questions change each time the batch file runs. "Do you really want to delete these files?" can take on a lot of different meanings depending on which files the batch file shows me, so asking the question from the desktop is not always the answer.

Pausing the batch file and asking the user to press any key to continue or Ctrl–Break to stop is one way of getting a yes/no response. It's inelegant but it works. However, because the batch file stops in response to a Ctrl–Break, it cannot perform any other tasks if the user wants to stop the operation.

All in all, the batch file tools OS/2 gives you to query the user are a pretty sorry lot! However, the single byte of errorlevel memory gives you a way to improve the situation, and the programming language REXX that comes with OS/2 gives you a method of accessing the errorlevel.

Working with the errorlevel

OS/2 includes an advanced batch-like language called REXX. REXX is very powerful and is covered separately in my book *Writing OS/2 REXX Programs*, available from McGraw-Hill. Chapter 26 provides you with an introduction to the power of REXX. The only thing of interest to us here is that REXX gives you the power to write utilities to overcome the limitations of the OS/2 batch language.

REXX lets you write utilities to overcome the limitations of the OS/2 batch language.

Don't worry, you don't have to be able to write REXX programs or even understand them. In fact, I'm not even going to show you a listing of the REXX programs in this chapter. I've already written the programs so all you need to know is how to use them. You'll find all the programs on the disk that comes with this book in the A:\UTILITY subdirectory.

In order to use these utility programs, they need to be in a subdirectory that's in your path. Since REXX programs are very much like batch files, I suggest you copy them to your batch subdirectory.

If you had a program called BATUTIL that you wanted to run as part of a batch file, you would just add the command BATUTIL to a line by itself in your batch file. That works with programs, but REXX programs aren't really programs. Rather, they're a cross between programs and batch files. If you have a REXX program called BATUTIL.CMD, you must run it with the command CALL BATUTIL. Other than that, they run just like other programs.

To run a REXX program from within a batch file, you must precede the name of the REXX program with a CALL command.

Any character with GET-ONE.CMD

Occasionally, you'll need to get a character of information from the user, where that character can be most anything. Since the OS/2 desktop can handle your menus for you, you'll need this a lot less than under DOS. Nevertheless, I've included a program to handle this just in case you need it. The program is called GET-ONE.CMD.

GET-ONE.CMD prompts the user to press any keystroke. It takes that keystroke, converts it to its ASCII value, and stores that value in the errorlevel. You'll find a complete ASCII chart in FIG. 8-1 back in chapter 8.

To use GET-ONE.CMD, place the CALL GET-ONE command in your batch file. Of course, GET-ONE.CMD must be in your path. Once the user has pressed a key, you can test for its value using a series of IF ERRORLEVEL tests, as was discussed in chapters 17 and 19.

Just a letter with GETA2Z.CMD

Many times, you want the user to select from a limited number of options. When that is the case, going through the entire 256 possible errorlevel values with GET-ONE.CMD can be just too much work. For those occasions, GETA2Z.CMD can make things easier. To keep you from having to remember ASCII codes, GETA2Z.CMD even reports an A with an errorlevel of 1, B with an errorlevel of 2, and so on. Plus, GETA2Z.CMD is case-insensitive so an a and A are treated the same.

Just a number with GET_0-9.CMD

Sometimes, even the 26 options of GETA2Z.CMD are too many. When you need fewer options, GET_0-9.CMD can make things easier still. To keep you from having to remember ASCII codes, a zero is reported with an errorlevel of 0, a one is reported with an errorlevel of 1, and so on.

Just a yes or no with YESORNO.CMD

Occasionally, you'll just need to ask the user a yes/no question like "Do you really want to do this?" For those occasions, even GET_0-9.CMD is too much work. When asking the user a question, YESORNO.CMD can make things as easy as possible. A no is reported with an errorlevel of 1 and a yes is reported with an errorlevel of 0. YESORNO.CMD is case-insensitive and needs only the first letter of the response.

More information with the environment

Sometimes, you need more information from the user than you can easily get using the single byte of the errorlevel. On those occasions, the environment is the perfect place to get that information. While an OS/2 batch file doesn't have the tools for getting information from the user and placing it into the environment, once again REXX programs come to the rescue and provide just this enhancement.

One word with GET.CMD

Oftentimes, it's useful for a batch file to ask the user a question where the user can enter an entire word or filename. Questions like "Please enter your first name" can make batch file messages more personal, and questions like "Enter the name of the file to load into your word processor" can greatly expand the power of your batch files.

To run GET.CMD, just put the CALL GET command in your batch file. GET.CMD will prompt the user for information, strip off everything except the first word entered, and place that word into the environment under the environmental variable name RETURN. If this contains a filename or word—like a first name—you want to include directly in a command, you can reference it by surrounding the RETURN environmental variable name with percent signs. For example:

```
DEL %RETURN%
```

or:

```
ECHO Welcome To The Batch File %RETURN%
```

If you need to get several pieces of information—like first and last name—from the user, run GET.CMD once per word. After getting the first word, transfer its contents to another variable with the command SET FIRST=%RETURN% and then get the next word. Following this pattern, you can use GET.CMD to get as many words as you need.

Converting to uppercase with CAPITAL.CMD

In the last chapter, I discussed the problems you can have with capitalization and replaceable parameters. If your batch file expects the word *daily* as one of several possible replaceable parameters, as a minimum you must test on daily, Daily, and DAILY, and you still won't spot some unusual capitalizations. If you could convert replaceable parameters to all uppercase, you would greatly reduce the number of IF tests required in your batch files. Well, CAPITAL.CMD does just that.

Run CAPITAL.CMD and pass it text with the command CALL CAPITAL *text* so you can pass it a replaceable parameter with the command CALL CAPITAL %1. CAPITAL.CMD takes the first word and ignores the rest. It converts that word to all uppercase and stores it in the environment under the environmental variable name RETURN. So to test the first replaceable parameter for a value of *daily*, you would just need the following two lines:

```
CALL CAPITAL %1
IF (%RETURN%)==(DAILY) GOTO DAILY
```

no matter how the user capitalized the word. If you need to capitalize more than one word, you can use the technique described with GET.CMD to get more than one word.

You can change these

You can see all six of these utilities in action by running the demonstration batch file SHOWGETS.CMD that's included on the disk with this book. Just be sure the six utility programs are in a subdirectory that's in your path. To give you a better idea how to include these utilities in your batch file, the operation of SHOWGETS.CMD is explained in detail in FIG. 20-1.

Batch File Command	Explanation
@ECHO OFF	Turn command-echoing off.
REM NAME: SHOWGETS.CMD REM PURPOSE: Show Using Different REXX Programs REM PURPOSE: To Get Information From The User REM VERSION: 1.00 REM DATE: May 31, 1993	Documentation remarks.
IF (%1)==(/?) GOTO HELP IF (%1)==(?) GOTO HELP	If the user requested help, jump to a special section to display help information.
CLS	Clear the screen.
ECHO Press Any Key When Ready To Start	Tell the user what to do.
CALL GET-ONE	Run GET-ONE.CMD to get a single keystroke from the user.
ECHO The Batch File Is Going Into A Loop ECHO The Only Way Out Is To Press ECHO A Capital Z ECHO But First Try Several Other Characters	Tell the user what will happen next.
:TOP1	Label marking the top of a loop.
CALL GET-ONE	Run GET-ONE.CMD to get a single keystroke from the user.
IF ERRORLEVEL 90 IF NOT ERRORLEVEL 91 ECHO Z-Pressed! IF ERRORLEVEL 90 IF NOT ERRORLEVEL 91 GOTO OUT1	Test to see if the user pressed a Z. If so, display a message and exit the loop.
GOTO TOP1	Continue looping.

20-1 SHOWGETS.CMD illustrates using six of the REXX utility programs that come on the disk with the book.

20-1 Continued.

Batch File Line	Explanation
`:OUT1`	Label used to edit the loop above when a Z is pressed.
`CLS`	Clear the screen.

`ECHO The Following Program Accepts Only Letters`
`ECHO But Try Some Numbers First`
`ECHO Again Only A Capital Z Will Get You`
`ECHO Out Of The Loop`
	Tell the user what will happen next.

`:TOP2`	Label marking the top of a loop.
`CALL GETA2Z`	Run GETA2Z.CMD to get a letter from the user.
`IF ERRORLEVEL 26 ECHO Z-Pressed` `IF ERRORLEVEL 26 GOTO OUT2`	Test to see if the user pressed a Z. If so, display a message and exit the loop.
`GOTO TOP2`	If the user did not press a Z, continue looping.
`:OUT2`	Label used to exit the loop above when the user presses a Z.
`CLS`	Clear the screen.

`ECHO The Following Program Accepts Only Numbers`
`ECHO 0-9 But Try Some Letters First`
`ECHO This Time A 9 Will Get You Out Of The Loop`
	Tell the user what will happen next.

`:TOP3`	Label used as the top of a loop.
`CALL GET_0-9`	Run GET_0-9.CMD to get a number from the user.

`IF ERRORLEVEL 0 IF NOT ERRORLEVEL 1 ECHO 0 Pressed`
 	
`Continues 1-7`
 	
`IF ERRORLEVEL 8 IF NOT ERRORLEVEL 9 ECHO 9 Pressed`
`IF ERRORLEVEL 9 ECHO 9 Pressed`
	Uses a series of errorlevel tests to tell the user what number was selected.

Batch File Line	Explanation
`IF ERRORLEVEL 9 GOTO OUT3`	If the user selected 9, exit the loop.
`GOTO TOP3`	If the user did not select 9, continue looping.
`:OUT3`	Label used to exit the loop above.
`ECHO Do You Want To Continue`	Ask the user about continuing.
`CALL YESORNO`	Run YESORNO.CMD to get a response from the user.
`IF ERRORLEVEL 1 GOTO END`	If the user selected no, exit the batch file.
`ECHO Thanks For Sticking With It!`	If the user selected yes, display a message.
`PAUSE`	Pause the program until the user presses a key.
`CLS`	Clear the screen.
`ECHO What Is Your First Name?`	Display a question.
`CALL GET`	Run GET.CMD to get the answer.
`SET FIRST=%RETURN%`	Store the answer under a different name in the environment.
`ECHO What Is Your Last Name?`	Display another question.
`CALL GET`	Run GET.CMD again to ask another question.
`SET LAST=%RETURN%`	Store the answer under a different name in the environment.
`ECHO Are You A MR.?`	Ask another question.
`SET TITLE=MR.`	Set a default title.
`CALL YESORNO`	Run YESORNO.CMD to get a response.
`IF ERRORLEVEL 1 SET TITLE=MS.`	If the user answered no, change the title.

`ECHO Hello %TITLE% %LAST%`
`ECHO Your Name Is %FIRST% %LAST%`
`ECHO In All Uppercase Your Name Is`
	Display the user's name.

20-1 Continued.

Batch File Line	Explanation
`CALL CAPITAL %FIRST%`	Run CAPITAL.CMD to convert the first name to all uppercase.
`SET FIRST=%RETURN%`	Store the uppercase first name to another environmental variable.
`CALL CAPITAL %LAST%`	Run CAPITAL.CMD to convert the last name to all uppercase.
`SET LAST=%RETURN%`	Store the uppercase last name to another environmental variable.
`ECHO %FIRST% %LAST%`	Display the uppercase name.
`PAUSE`	Pause the program until the user presses a key.

`SET RETURN=`
`SET FIRST=`
`SET LAST=`
`SET TITLE=`
	Clear the environmental variables used by the batch file.

`GOTO END`	Exit the batch file.

`:HELP`
`ECHO Shows Using Different REXX Programs`
`ECHO To Get Information From The User`
`ECHO Requires The Following REXX Programs`
`ECHO To Be In Your Path:`
`ECHO GET-ONE.CMD GETA2Z.CMD GET_0-9.CMD`
`ECHO YESORNO.CMD GET.CMD CAPITAL.CMD`
`GOTO END`
	Display a help screen and exit the batch file when the user requests help.

`:END`	Label marking the end of the batch file.

Chapter 26 has an introduction to REXX programming and, if you're interested in modifying these programs, you'll want to take a look at that chapter. Plus, keep an unmodified backup of the utility you're going to modify in case you make a mistake.

One simple change you might want to make is changing the prompt to something more meaningful for your application. Prompts work similarly to the prompts in batch files with two exceptions: First, the SAY command is used instead of the ECHO command and, second, messages must be enclosed in double quotation marks or they're converted to uppercase. As long as you change only the words between the quotation marks to the prompt you want to use, you shouldn't have any problems.

Summary

- GET-ONE.CMD lets you get any character from the user and place its ASCII value in the errorlevel.
- GETA2Z.CMD lets you get a letter from the user and store A in errorlevel as 1, B as 2, and so on.
- GET_0-9.CMD lets you get a single-digit number from the user and store that number in the errorlevel.
- YESORNO.CMD lets you ask the user a simple question and store a yes in the errorlevel as 0 and a no as 1.
- GET.CMD lets you ask the user a question and store an entire word or filename in the environment.
- CAPITAL.CMD lets you convert a single word to all uppercase and store the results in the environment.
- If you want to alter the prompts for these programs, it's as easy as editing the .CMD file.

21
Advanced screen design

The main tool for displaying messages in a batch file is a series of ECHO commands, which works well for a few messages but soon gets old if your batch file has to display a lot of information. Fortunately, you have several alternatives. You can:

- Create a text file and use the TYPE command to send that file to the screen.
- Write a custom program.
- Use ANSI.

The alternative you select depends on your specific needs and skills.

Text files

Probably the easiest way to quickly display a screen full of information is to use the OS/2 Enhanced Editor or your word processor to create each screen as a separate ASCII file. That way, you can add blank lines where you want them, center text, and otherwise visually arrange the elements on the screen. Once you have the screens looking the way you want, just type them to the screen from your batch file. Of course, you'll need a PAUSE command between each screen. Using this method, the batch file TXTSCRN.CMD might look like this:

```
@ECHO OFF
CLS
TYPE C:\BAT\INTRO.TXT
PAUSE
CLS
```

```
TYPE C:\BAT\SCREEN1.TXT
PAUSE
CLS
TYPE C:\BAT\SCREEN2.TXT
PAUSE
```

Notice that this batch file segment specifies the full path to each text file. Because batch files are usually designed to run from anywhere on your hard disk, you cannot depend on the batch file and associated text files being in the same subdirectory from which the batch file is executed.

This method is easier than a series of ECHO commands but it has several drawbacks. One is simply remembering to send copies of all the associated text files when you send someone a copy of the batch file. A second drawback is that users wanting to run your batch file on their systems must have a subdirectory of the same name you used to store your text files, and must copy the text files to that subdirectory. That's a lot to expect users to do. Of course, you could write a batch file to install this batch file on their systems. Finally, the method lacks the ability to control the screen color.

☑ Typing an ASCII file to the screen is an easy way for a batch file to display a screen full of information, but creates unique problems when batch files are distributed to other users.

Writing a program

You can also display text by using a high-level programming language. Writing high-level programs is beyond the scope of this book so I won't cover it in any detail. Most high-level programs compile to an executable .EXE file, so all you have to do to display the text is include the name of the .EXE file in a batch file. In addition, most high-level languages can control the screen color and execute very quickly.

This approach means you don't need a specific directory name in which to store the file. As long as the resulting screen is anywhere in the path, it will execute whenever the batch file issues the command to run the program. However, while this solves one problem, it introduces another—namely the programing tools and abilities this approach requires, which are one thing that many batch file users lack.

☑ Writing a program is a nice way to create custom screens, but it also requires skills and tools that many users don't have.

ANSI

The best way to design complex screens with full control over colors and cursor location is to use ANSI. ANSI is covered in detail in the next chapter.

Summary

- You can display a screen full of information with a series of ECHO commands.
- Another way to display a screen full of information is by creating an ASCII file and typing it to the screen.
- Using an ASCII file to display text when the batch file is shared with other users requires sharing the text files as well as having users install the text files in the same subdirectory as was used on the original system.
- Another way to display a screen full of information is by writing your own program. This requires programming tools and experience with a programming language.
- Using a program to display a screen full of information requires that the program be shared with other users of the batch file, but it can be placed in any subdirectory along the path.

22
ANSI

In the last chapter, you saw that you could use text files, the TYPE command, and custom programs to design screens. Another method of screen design is ANSI. Because ANSI is such a complex program, I decided to cover it here in a separate chapter instead of including it with the other methods.

ANSI basics

Under DOS, the device driver ANSI.SYS (ANSI for short) gives you an incredible amount of power over the appearance of the screen. By using that power, you can produce very attractive and eye-catching screens and messages in your batch files. However, writing batch files for others using ANSI is asking for problems because so few users load ANSI. Nothing looks worse than seeing ANSI escape sequences stream across a screen when ANSI isn't running. The reason for ANSI's lack of popularity is that it's saddled with the worst user interface of any program on the market—ANSI makes even Edlin look user-friendly!

Things are a little better under OS/2. ANSI still has its terrible interface but ANSI support is automatically included in OS/2 so you don't have to worry about the user loading ANSI.SYS. It can, however, be turned off with the ANSI OFF command. If you're writing batch files for others, it's a good idea to add an ANSI ON command to any batch file using ANSI commands.

ANSI is a great way to create colorful screens if you can get past its terrible interface.

Getting started with ANSI

Before reading about ANSI, you might want to try a little experiment. Go to an OS/2 full screen and run the ANSIDEMO.CMD batch file, shown in FIG. 22-1.

If you have a color display, ANSIDEMO.CMD will give you a blue background with bright white letters for the text. There should be a red title at the top of the menu and a bright yellow message at the bottom telling you to make your selection. Now to see the real power of ANSI, issue a CLS command.

With other utilities that set the color of the display, CLS returns the display to white characters on a black background. However, ANSI color assignments are permanent, at least until you reboot or issue a new ANSI

Batch File Command	Explanation
`@ECHO OFF`	Turn command-echoing off.

`REM NAME:     ANSIDEMO.CMD`
`REM PURPOSE:  Show ANSI.SYS`
`REM           Power To Control`
`REM           The Screen`
`REM VERSION:  2.00`
`REM DATE:     July 22, 1993`
	Documentation remarks.

`IF (%1)==(/?) GOTO HELP` `IF (%1)==(?)  GOTO HELP`	If the user requested help, jump to a special section to display help information.
`REM Change The Screen Colors` `REM Bright White On Blue`	Documentation remarks.

`ECHO ESC[37m`
`ECHO ESC[44m`
`ECHO ESC[1m`
	Issue the ANSI escape sequences.

`REM Clear the Screen`
`REM Set Colors First So CLS`
`REM Would Use New Colors`
	Documentation remarks.

`ECHO ESC[2J`	Issue the ANSI escape sequence.
`REM Change To Flashing Red` `REM Display Message And Reset`	Documentation remarks.

`ECHO ESC[1;30HESC[31mESC[5mA`
`Very Special`
`MenuESC[0mESC[37mESC[44m`
`ESC[1m`
	Issue the ANSI escape sequences.

22-1 ANSIDEMO.CMD runs an ANSI demonstration that prints text on the screen in different colors at different positions on the screen.

Batch File Line	Explanation
REM Position Cursor And Display Options	Documentation remarks.
ECHO ESC[6;20H1. Run Word Processing ECHO ESC[7;20H2. Run Spreadsheet ECHO ESC[8;20H3. Run Database ECHO ESC[9;20H4. Play Games ECHO ESC[10;20H5. Format A Disk ECHO ESC[11;20H6. Backup Hard Disk To Floppies	Issue the ANSI escape sequences to draw the menu.
ECHO ESC[15;20HESC[33mPress The Number of The Program You WantESC[37m	Issue the ANSI escape sequences to draw the message at the bottom.
ECHO	Display a blank line by echoing an Alt-255.
PAUSE	Pause the program until the user presses a key.
GOTO END	Exit the batch file.
:HELP ECHO This Batch File Is A ECHO Demonstration Of ANSI ECHO It Requires That You Load ECHO ANSI.SYS In Your CONFIG.SYS File GOTO END	Display a help screen and exit the batch file when the user requests help.
:END	Label marking the end of the batch file.

command, so the CLS command retains the blue background with bright white lettering. Because ANSIDEMO.CMD uses nothing but OS/2 and ANSI commands, this batch file will run on any computer running OS/2. As a result, you don't have to worry about the user owning a utility program that will change colors or position the cursor. You also don't have to worry about any supporting files.

✍ ANSI is a great way to set screen colors.

If you like what you saw, read on: what follows is a tutorial on ANSI. ANSI functions fall into four broad categories (explained in detail later in this chapter):

Screen control You've already seen this in the example. ANSI controls screen colors nicely and allows you to display different text on the screen in different colors. It also allows you to change your prompt to those far fancier than the pitiful (by comparison) prompts that OS/2 allows without ANSI.

Cursor control ANSI allows you to position the cursor anywhere on the screen. ANSIDEMO.CMD used this to center text and otherwise control its position on the screen without the need to pad with spaces or issue a specific number of ECHO commands to move the cursor down the screen.

Video control ANSI allows you to change the display mode and attributes.

Keyboard control ANSI allows you to remap your keyboard.

First a warning: ANSI is very difficult to learn to use, due to the poor explanation in the documentation plus its unusual user interface. Plan on spending a lot of time studying this tutorial and your on-line documentation—along with doing a lot of experimenting—before you can consider yourself an ANSI master.

While very powerful, ANSI has a very poor interface that is difficult to learn and hard to use.

Entering ANSI commands

Every ANSI command starts with an Escape followed by a left square bracket. The ANSI command to clear the screen, for example, is ESC[2J. (For all the commands and batch file listings that follow, I've used ESC to stand for the Escape character so you can read it, both in the text and the batch file listings. However, the batch file or command must have the Escape character, which has an ASCII value of 27 and a hexadecimal value of 1B.) Because the first character in an ANSI command is always an Escape, the commands are often called *escape sequences*.

ANSI commands are called *escape sequences*.

You should immediately see the first problem with ANSI: You can't enter any ANSI commands from the keyboard because when you press the Esc key OS/2 thinks you want to abort the current command. Typing Alt–27 on the number pad doesn't bypass this problem; it's just another way of entering an Escape. So you can experiment, I've included a batch file called SENDANSI.CMD on the disk that comes with this book. It has command-line help and remarks, so it's fairly long, but the only command it contains is ECHO ESC[%1. To use it, enter the ANSI command you want to run without the Escape and left bracket that begins the command. SEND ANSI.CMD adds those two characters and issues the command. SEND ANSI.CMD won't work with ANSI keyboard reassignment commands or any other ANSI commands that include a semicolon or require more than one word in the command.

Word processors, editors, and the "escape" problem

Many word processors and editors make it difficult to create batch files with ANSI commands because they refuse to let you place an Escape character in the file. There's a trick to get around that. When you enter the CLS command, OS/2 responds with an ESC[2J command. You can redirect that to a file with the command CLS > *filename*. Then you can edit the file with your word processor. While many word processors don't allow you to enter an Escape, most will edit a file containing an Escape without any problem. Just copy the escape character anywhere you need it.

Redirect a CLS command to a file to easily get an Escape in a file.

The OS/2 Enhanced Editor lets you enter the Escape directly. Make sure the NumLock key is on. Hold down the Alt key and enter 27 from the keypad—not the numbers along the top of the keyboard. You'll see a reverse arrow in the center of the line. That is the Escape character. Then enter the rest of the ANSI escape sequence.

With the OS/2 Enhanced Editor, press Alt–27 to enter an Escape character into a file.

Sending ANSI commands by typing a file

While ANSI is loaded, all the text written to the screen through OS/2 is processed through ANSI. ANSI watches for the ESC[sequence. Anything beginning with ESC[is treated as an ANSI command and anything else is sent to the screen. That gives you a number of ways to send ANSI sequences to the screen. Issue the following two commands:

```
CLS > TEMP.CMD
TYPE TEMP.CMD
```

If you look at the file TEMP.CMD with an editor, you'll see that it contains the text sequence ESC[2J. However, when you try to display it with the TYPE command, ANSI sees the sequence beginning with ESC[as a command, and executes it. So in addition to echoing ANSI commands to the screen with the ECHO command, you can put them in an ASCII file and type them to the screen. You can also copy these ASCII files to the screen with the command:

```
COPY TEMP.CMD CON
```

☑ You can issue ANSI commands by placing the escape sequences in an ASCII file and typing or copying that file to the screen.

Sending ANSI commands using the environment

To continue with the experiment, load TEMP.CMD into an editor. Add the command SET TEMP= in front of the ANSI sequence so the line looks like this: SET TEMP=ESC[2J. Then exit and run the batch file. Because you didn't turn command-echoing off, OS/2 will try to echo the command to the screen, and ANSI will again intercept and execute it. However, the environmental variable will be successfully created.

Now enter the SET command. OS/2 will display the other environmental variables properly. However, when it reaches the TEMP variable and tries to display its contents, ANSI will again intercept and execute the escape sequence. In addition to ECHO, TYPE, and COPY, this gives you a fourth way to issue ANSI commands. It also turns out to be the easiest way.

☑ You can give ANSI commands by placing the escape sequences in an environmental variable and using the SET command to display the environmental variables.

Sending ANSI commands via the prompt

Most environmental variables are rarely displayed. There is, however, one exception. The prompt is an environmental variable that is displayed after every OS/2 command. It's also displayed for each batch file command if command-echoing is on. The prompt is particularly useful for ANSI commands. The metacharacter $e issues an escape, so you can avoid the problem of having to get an Escape into the sequence. In addition, the prompt command has other metacharacters to spice up a prompt. Refer back to TABLE 14-1 for a list.

☑ You can give ANSI commands by placing the escape sequences in the prompt. This is especially easy because the prompt offers the $e metacharacter that represents the Escape character.

You can see an example of the fancy prompts ANSI is capable of generating by issuing the following command from the command-line prompt with ANSI loaded (replace the periods with an equal number of spaces):

```
PROMPT=$e[s$e[1;1H$e[K$d..$t..$p$e[u$p$g$e[44m$e[37m$e[1m
```

This prompt shows the day of the week, the date, the time, and the current drive and subdirectory on the top line of the screen. It also sets the screen colors to bright white on blue and uses the standard PG prompt on the current line of the screen!

The prompt also uses a couple of ANSI sequences I haven't yet mentioned, but you can see how elements of the prompt metacharacters and ANSI can be combined to produce an exceptional prompt. In case you don't want to take the time to enter and debug this complex prompt, the batch file NICEPROM.CMD on the disk that comes with this book will issue it for you.

You should be aware of a problem, however, with using the prompt to send ANSI escape sequences in a batch file. Normally, the first command of a batch file is @ECHO OFF to turn command-echoing off. However, this also causes OS/2 to stop displaying the prompt, which prevents ANSI escape sequences stored in the prompt from being sent to the screen so they can be processed. The solution is to issue an ECHO ON command when you want to send ANSI escape sequences with the prompt. After sending the ANSI escape sequence, you can turn echoing back off so that your batch file will execute cleanly.

When using the PROMPT command in a batch file to send ANSI escape sequences, command-echoing must be turned on. Otherwise, the prompt will never be displayed.

As you can see, entering ANSI commands takes a little planning. You can use the above mentioned SENDANSI.CMD to enter very simple ANSI commands. For more complex ANSI commands, I created a batch file called SENDANS2.CMD so you can experiment with all the combinations of ANSI commands you like. To run it, enter the command:

SENDANS2 *command1 command2* . . .

at the command line. SENDANS2.CMD will add the ESC[to the beginning of each command, so you should leave it off all commands. It builds a large environmental variable containing the entire command string and then issues it all at once, so there are no line feeds between commands. Since SENDANS2 strips off one character from each parameter (the leading space) and adds two (ESC[), the environmental variable will be longer than the command you issue. If that causes it to exceed the 300-character limit OS/2 places on commands, the computer could behave in some unpredictable manner.

Like SENDANSI.CMD, you cannot use SENDANS2.CMD to send ANSI commands containing a semicolon because OS/2 treats the semicolon as a divider and strips it off before passing the replaceable parameter to the batch file. As a result, there's no way to get a semicolon for the command line into the batch file.

Screen control

The most common ANSI command is the one to change colors. The command is ESC[#m, where # is the number of the foreground or background color to use. The color numbers are all two digits; all foreground colors start with a 3 and all background colors start with a 4. The colors are shown in TABLE 22-1. So the command ESC[44mESC[37m will set the screen to white letters on a blue background—my personal favorite. Two notes are in order here:

- The clear screen command ends with an uppercase J, and the color command ends with a lowercase m. Most ANSI commands are case-sensitive, so pay attention to case when writing them.
- An m ends every ANSI attribute setting command, but you need only one per line. Thus, the previous command could be shortened to ESC[44;37m. The m terminates the command. You don't have to reissue the ESC[after the 44—the ANSI command isn't terminated because there's no m.

Table 22-1 ANSI color codes.

Number	Color
0	Black
1	Red
2	Green
3	Yellow
4	Blue
5	Magenta
6	Cyan
7	White

Being able to control screen colors leads to two somewhat useful utilities. BLANK.CMD uses ANSI sequences to blank the screen at the command-line prompt by converting the screen to black text on a black background:

```
@ECHO OFF
ECHO ESC[0m
ECHO ESC[30m
ECHO ESC[40m
CLS
```

This will keep amateur snoops from looking at your files. I should note that the blank screen is really only blank at the command line and the few programs that use ANSI color settings. Most programs, however, display fine while ANSI is set for a blank screen. Of course, the user must be able to load the program without seeing the prompt of the commands being entered. Plus, anyone marginally familiar with OS/2 will be able to switch out of that window with a Ctrl–Esc keystroke. Finally, BLANK.CMD won't work if you already issued ANSI commands to set the screen color in your prompt since those settings will overwrite the BLANK.CMD settings. Typing UNBLANK runs UNBLANK.CMD:

```
@ECHO OFF
ECHO ESC[37m
ECHO ESC[44m
ECHO ESC[1m
CLS
```

UNBLANK.CMD uses ANSI commands to restore the screen to bright white letters on a blue background. (You must, of course, be able to run UNBLANK.CMD without being able to see the screen.)

Cursor control

ANSI lets you position the cursor anywhere on the screen and move it around the screen as you see fit. In their simplest form, these commands are:

ESC[A	Moves the cursor up one row
ESC[B	Moves the cursor down one row
ESC[C	Moves the cursor to the right one column
ESC[D	Moves the cursor to the left one column

If you precede the A through D with a number, the cursor will be moved that many times, so ESC[5A would move the cursor up five rows. The command ESC[r;cH would move the cursor to row r and column c, ESC[1;1H would move it to the top left corner of the screen, and ESC[24,80H would move it to the bottom right corner. One note: the lowercase f works identically to the uppercase H, so ESC[10;10H and ESC[10;10f do the same thing.

ANSI can also save the current cursor position with the command ESC[s. This command can save only one cursor position, so each time you use it, you overwrite the prior position it has saved. The ESC[u command returns to the position saved with the ESC[s command. You can also have ANSI report the cursor position with an ESC[6n command. This is generally used by programs and is of little value in a batch file.

Video control

ANSI has several commands to control other aspects of how the screen appears:

ESC[=7h	Causes lines longer than 80 characters to wrap around to the next line. This is the default mode.
ESC[=7l	Causes lines longer than 80 characters to be truncated so they don't wrap. Note that the last character is a lowercase L and not a one.

ESC[0m	Turns off all screen attributes, returning the screen to white on black.
ESC[1m	Turns on high-intensity foreground colors.
ESC[2m	Returns the foreground colors to normal intensity.
ESC[4m	Turns on underlining on a monochrome display.
ESC[5m	Causes the foreground text to blink.
ESC[7m	Converts the display to inverse video.
ESC[8m	Blanks the screen by setting the foreground color to the background color.

☑ ANSI offers a lot of control over video attributes.

Keyboard control

With ANSI, you can also reconfigure your keyboard. This topic is unrelated to batch files, so I'll cover it only briefly. By default, OS/2 doesn't support ANSI keyboard remapping. Instead, it supports advanced command-line editing. You must turn off this advanced command-line editing in order to enable ANSI keyboard remapping. A single command does both things at once. The command KEYS OFF turns off ANSI keyboard remapping and restores advanced command-line editing. Any ANSI remapped keys are returned to their normal operation. Most users prefer the default advanced command-line editing to ANSI keyboard support. The general format of the command is:

```
ESC[m;np
```

where *m* is the ASCII value of the key to reassign and *n* is the ASCII value the key is to take on. For example, most of the time in OS/2, you use the parentheses more than the brackets (although the left bracket gets a workout under ANSI). You can switch them in OS/2 by using the commands:

```
ECHO ESC[91;40p
ECHO ESC[93;41p
ECHO ESC[40;91p
ECHO ESC[41;93p
```

The reassignment works at the OS/2 command line and with a few programs that get their input from OS/2—but not in programs like Microsoft Word or the Enhanced Editor that bypass OS/2 for keystrokes. To reset the keyboard reassignments, issue the commands:

```
ECHO ESC[91;91p
ECHO ESC[93;93p
ECHO ESC[40;40p
ECHO ESC[41;41p
```

For experimenting purposes, you'll find these two batch files on the disk under the names KEY-1.CMD and KEY-2.CMD. Under DOS, you can also remap these using the actual keystrokes. So the commands would have been:

```
ECHO ←["[";"("p
ECHO ←["]";")"p
ECHO ←["(";"["p
ECHO ←[")";"]"p
```

However, OS/2 doesn't support this form of the command. In fact, if you were to put these commands into a batch file and run it, OS/2 would become confused and wouldn't display any of the four characters.

The disk that comes with this book has a batch file that will help you experiment with ANSI keyboard reassignments, ANSIKEY1.CMD. It takes pairs of numbers associated with the various keystrokes: The first number is the keystroke to modify, and the second keystroke is its new value. It issues the ANSI command necessary to make the first assignment, issues two SHIFT commands, and checks to see if another pair of numbers is waiting:

```
:TOP
  IF (%2)==() GOTO END
  ECHO ←[%1;%2p
  SHIFT
  SHIFT
GOTO TOP
```

To remap the square brackets and parentheses mentioned earlier, enter the command:

```
ANSIKEY1 91 40 93 41 40 91 41 93
```

To restore the keys to their original value, enter:

```
ANSIKEY1 40 40 41 41 91 91 93 93
```

ANSIKEY1.CMD will accept over fifty reassignments on a single line, making it easy to reassign a lot of keys at once. If you find yourself using the same reassignment command more than once or twice, you might want to write a custom batch file either to issue the ANSI commands or just to store the commands you use to call one of these batch files.

Under DOS, in addition to remapping standard keys, you can also remap extended keystrokes like Ctrl–F1. OS/2 doesn't support this either.

An example

You can use ANSI keyboard remapping to construct a very useful batch file. Computer magazines often publish debugging scripts for you to enter to create small utilities. Since these are in hexadecimal, the numbers you must enter range from 0–9 and A–F, but not all of these are on your numeric keypad. ENTERHEX.CMD remaps the /, *, –, +, =, and Del keys that surround the number pad as keys A–F so you can quickly enter the letters as well as the numbers. While this remapping works from the command line, it won't work inside the Enhanced Editor. The code for the operational portion of ENTERHEX.CMD follows:

```
KEYS OFF
ECHO ←[47;65p
ECHO ←[42;66p
ECHO ←[45;67p
ECHO ←[43;68p
ECHO ←[61;69p
ECHO ←[46;70p
ECHO Number Pad Ready For Hex Entry
```

UNENTER.CMD will restore the keys to normal. The code for the operational portion is:

```
KEYS OFF
ECHO ←[47;47p
ECHO ←[42;42p
ECHO ←[45;45p
ECHO ←[43;43p
ECHO ←[61;61p
ECHO ←[46;46p
ECHO Number Pad Restored
```

As you've seen, ANSI offers some very powerful abilities to control the screen, but its ability to control the keyboard is much, much weaker.

Summary

- You can use ANSI to control the screen, cursor, video, and keyboard.
- You can use ANSI escape sequences to change the foreground and background colors of the screen.
- When you use ANSI to change the color of the screen, a CLS command doesn't reset the colors to white on black.
- ANSI commands are called *escape sequences*.
- You cannot enter ANSI commands from the keyboard because they start with the Escape character.
- If your word processor can't enter an Escape character in a file, pipe the CLS command to a file and incorporate the Escape from that file in your document.
- ANSI processes any line sent to the screen that begins with an Escape character followed by an open bracket, no matter how the characters are displayed.
- You can display ANSI escape sequences using the ECHO command.
- You can display ANSI escape sequences by storing them in an ASCII file and typing that file to the screen.
- You can display ANSI escape sequences by storing them in environmental variables and then using the SET command or ECHO %*variable*% command to display one or more environmental variables.
- You can display ANSI escape sequences using the PROMPT command, which has a built-in Escape character.

- When ANSI escape sequences are displayed in a batch file via the PROMPT command, command-echoing must be turned on while the prompt is being used to send the ANSI commands.
- ANSI lets you move the cursor in any direction as well as save and recall the cursor position.
- ANSI also allows you to remap the keyboard, although it won't work with many programs that avoid OS/2 to get their keystrokes.
- OS/2 support for ANSI keyboard remapping is more limited than DOS and less useful than ANSI's ability to control the screen.

23
Batch file subroutines

In programming, a subroutine is a special type of program. When a program calls a subroutine, control is passed to the subroutine. When the subroutine is finished, control is passed back to the program that called the subroutine. The calling program continues from the point where it passed control to the subroutine. Figure 23-1 illustrates this graphically.

Subroutines are a way of writing a section of code once, storing it in a special way, and reusing it as many times as needed. In a batch file, this often makes the logic much easier to follow and the batch file easier to write and debug.

For example, if you want to perform multiple commands based on the errorlevel value, you could have a series of IF tests for each possible error-

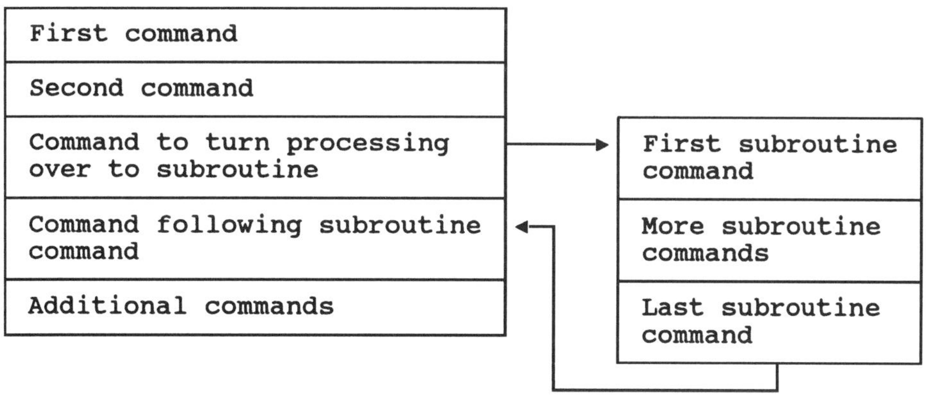

23-1 A subroutine is a "mini" program that's run by another program. When a subroutine is done, it returns control to the original program that ran it.

level value. Each IF test would jump to a different section of the batch file to perform the multiple commands, and then the sections would re-converge. Unlike DOS, OS/2 gives you the ability to overcome this by placing multiple commands on a single line—see chapter 16 for details. With subroutines, the batch file would have a single command for each IF test where that command ran a subroutine. Consider the following example:

```
IF ERRORLEVEL 3 SUB-3
IF ERRORLEVEL 2 SUB-2
IF ERRORLEVEL 1 SUB-1
IF ERRORLEVEL 0 SUB-0
```

Of course, as you learn to write subroutines, you'll replace the commands after the errorlevel tests with the actual commands to run subroutines.

Subroutines allow you to reuse your batch file code.

What is a subroutine, and how do I write one?

A subroutine is nothing more than one or more lines of batch file commands—exactly like any other batch file commands. The question is not "What is it?" but rather "How do you use it?" You can either store the subroutine as a separate batch file, or store it inside the original batch file and use IF tests to jump to the section of code.

Later on, you'll see that you can also run a REXX program from within a batch file as a subroutine. It's run the same way but must be stored as a separate file.

Storing a subroutine as a separate batch file

The easiest way to write a subroutine is to write that subroutine as a stand-alone batch file. The method's biggest advantage is that it allows multiple batch files to call on a common subroutine; its worst disadvantage is that it uses more hard disk space because each batch file is allocated a full cluster of space no matter how small it is. However, this size penalty is minimal under the high-performance file system (HPFS). Additionally, when you give a copy of your batch file to someone else, you have to remember to get them copies of all the subroutines.

The easiest way to write a subroutine is to write that subroutine as a stand-alone batch file.

The batch command to run a subroutine batch file in a separate file is the CALL command. Thus, a batch file can call another batch file with:

```
CALL batch
```

where *batch* is the name of the subroutine. Once the subroutine batch file terminates, control automatically returns to the batch file that called it.

The CALL command makes it easy for one batch file to run another batch file and regain control when it terminates.

An example

Look back at TOA.CMD. This was a batch file you began looking at in chapter 11 as a way to copy .DOC and .CMP files to the A: drive and delete the associated .BAK file when the user entered just the filename. This batch file evolved over the next several chapters, reaching its ultimate form in chapter 17. That version of TOA.CMD is shown here:

```
@ECHO OFF
:TOP
  IF (%1)==() GOTO END
  DEL %1.BAK
  COPY %1.DOC A:
  COPY %1.CMP A:
  SHIFT
GOTO TOP

:END
```

The same batch file but with internal documentation and command-line help is included on the disk that comes with this book.

The purpose of this batch file is to copy the modified versions of files to a floppy disk to be transported to another location. As it exists, it does not enforce this. If a .DOC file has been modified, then—on my system using Microsoft Word—a .BAK file always exists. Suppose you want to add the logic necessary to skip copying the file if a .BAK file doesn't exist. The new version of TOA.CMD might look like this:

```
@ECHO OFF
:TOP
  IF (%1)==() GOTO END
  IF NOT EXIST %1.BAK ECHO %1 Not Modified So Not Copied
  IF NOT EXIST %1.BAK GOTO SKIP
  DEL %1.BAK
  COPY %1.DOC A:
  COPY %1.CMP A:
:SKIP
  SHIFT
GOTO TOP

:END
```

Now suppose you want to add logic to the copying portion of the batch file to detect minor errors—like a full diskette—and warn the user. And what if you want to make sure the user enters the name right by warning him if the .DOC file doesn't exist. As you can imagine, the original three lines of the batch file that handled the repetitive tasks of copying and deleting files, shown here, are going to become very complex:

```
DEL %1.BAK
COPY %1.DOC A:
COPY %1.CMP A:
```

Predictably, because this chapter covers subroutines, the solution is to place these three commands in a separate batch file and treat them as a subroutine. The original version of TOA.CMD has these three lines stripped out and a single command added to call the subroutine TOA-SUB.CMD. (Recall that different versions of TOA.CMD are stored in the appropriate chapter subdirectories in the \BAT\TOA subdirectory on the disk that comes with this book.)

Within TOA.CMD, the files to be copied are known as %1. However, this replaceable parameter is only global while inside TOA.CMD and is not available to the subroutine. In order to make the name of the file available to TOA-SUB.CMD, you must pass it to that batch file as a replaceable parameter. The resulting TOA.CMD looks like this:

```
@ECHO OFF
:TOP
  IF (%1)==() GOTO END
  CALL TOA-SUB %1
  SHIFT
GOTO TOP
:END
```

A version of TOA.CMD with internal documentation and command-line help is included on the disk that comes with this book. A preliminary version of TOA-SUB.CMD looks like this:

```
@ECHO OFF
DEL %1.BAK
COPY %1.DOC A:
COPY %1.CMP A:
```

Two notes about this subroutine are important. First, it doesn't need to test to see if %1 exists because TOA.CMD takes care of that prior to calling the subroutine. Second, the @ECHO OFF command isn't really necessary because command-echoing is always off when a batch file with command-echoing turned off calls another batch file as a subroutine. You'll see why I've added it later.

Because this subroutine is shorter and not already convoluted by the looping performed in TOA.CMD, you can add additional checks without the batch file becoming as complicated as TOA.CMD would have become. First, let's add the logic to test and make sure the file has been modified by testing to see if the .BAK file exists. The pseudocode for this is:

```
If .BAK does not exist, tell user and exit subroutine
If .BAK exists, continue normally
```

and the resulting subroutine looks like this:

```
@ECHO OFF

IF NOT EXIST %1.BAK ECHO File Not Modified--Not Copied
IF NOT EXIST %1.BAK GOTO END

DEL %1.BAK
COPY %1.DOC A:
COPY %1.CMP A:

:END
```

Next, you want to make sure the file actually exists before you try to copy it. If the file was created by Lotus or dBASE, a .BAK file might still exist but a .DOC file might not. If the .DOC file doesn't exist, you want to exit without copying anything; if the .CMP file doesn't exist, you want to simply skip that COPY command because not all documents have .CMP files. The pseudocode for this is:

```
If .DOC file does not exist, warn user and exit subroutine
If the .CMP file exists, copy it to the diskette
```

and the resulting subroutine looks like this:

```
@ECHO OFF

IF NOT EXIST %1.BAK ECHO File Not Modified--Not Copied
IF NOT EXIST %1.BAK GOTO END

IF NOT EXIST %1.DOC ECHO %1.DOC File Not Found
IF NOT EXIST %1.DOC GOTO END

DEL %1.BAK
COPY %1.DOC A:
IF EXIST %1.CMP COPY %1.CMP A:

:END
```

Because the second set of IF tests makes sure the .DOC file exists, no IF test is used in front of that COPY command. However, when it's time to copy the .CMP file, the batch file hasn't verified that it exists, so this COPY command is preceded by an IF test.

As the last modification, you want to make sure that the file was successfully copied to the A: drive. The COPY command sets the errorlevel to one if a copy fails (this is undocumented) so, rather than depend on an undocumented feature, I elected to perform this test manually. The pseudocode for this is:

```
If file is on current drive but not A: drive warn user
```

and the resulting subroutine looks like this:

```
@ECHO OFF
IF NOT EXIST %1.BAK ECHO File Not Modified--Not Copied
IF NOT EXIST %1.BAK GOTO END

IF NOT EXIST %1.DOC ECHO %1.DOC File Not Found
IF NOT EXIST %1.DOC GOTO END

DEL %1.BAK
COPY %1.DOC A:
IF EXIST %1.CMP COPY %1.CMP A:

IF NOT EXIST A:%1.DOC ECHO %1.DOC Not Copied Successfully
:END
```

This test will spot occasions when the file was too big to fit on the A: drive, but won't handle situations where there's a version of the file already on the A: drive and some other problem prevented the successful copying—all because the batch file will find that A:%1.DOC exists.

While errorlevel support for the COPY is undocumented, the XCOPY command has documented errorlevel support. A zero represents a successful copy, while a higher value represents some sort of problem. You can use that information to modify this subroutine to spot any copying problem by using XCOPY and errorlevel tests. The resulting subroutine looks like this:

```
@ECHO OFF

IF NOT EXIST %1.BAK ECHO File Not Modified--Not Copied
IF NOT EXIST %1.BAK GOTO END

IF NOT EXIST %1.DOC ECHO %1.DOC File Not Found
IF NOT EXIST %1.DOC GOTO END

DEL %1.BAK
IF EXIST %1.CMP XCOPY %1.CMP A:
XCOPY %1.DOC A:

IF ERRORLEVEL 1 ECHO %1.DOC Not Copied Successfully
:END
```

In addition to converting the COPY commands to XCOPY and converting the final IF EXIST test to IF ERRORLEVEL, I also reversed the copying order of the .CMP and .DOC files. The errorlevel used in the IF ERRORLEVEL test is the final errorlevel value, and the .DOC document file is far more important than the .CMP dictionary file. So by copying the .DOC file last, its errorlevel is the one tested. Interested readers might want to add tests on both values if the first XCOPY has a problem.

These are all the modifications the subroutine needs if it's to function solely as a stand-alone subroutine. However, because it exists as a stand-alone batch file, users are likely to try and run it to see what it does. You can avoid this by adding command-line help with the now familiar /? switch, but this time also display the help if the batch file is started without a replaceable parameter. This final test works because TOA.CMD always calls it with a replaceable parameter; the batch file knows it's being run improperly if it doesn't receive a replaceable parameter. The final version of the batch file is shown next:

```
@ECHO OFF

IF (%1)==()   GOTO HELP
IF (%1)==(/?) GOTO HELP
IF (%1)==(?)  GOTO HELP

IF NOT EXIST %1.BAK ECHO File Has Not Been Modified--Not Copied
IF NOT EXIST %1.BAK GOTO END

IF NOT EXIST %1.DOC ECHO %1.DOC File Not Found
IF NOT EXIST %1.DOC GOTO END

DEL %1.BAK
IF EXIST %1.CMP XCOPY %1.CMP A:
XCOPY %1.DOC A:
IF ERRORLEVEL 1 ECHO %1.DOC Not Copied Successfully
GOTO END

:HELP
 ECHO This Batch File Is A Subroutine Used By TOA.CMD
 ECHO It Is Not Designed To Be Run By The User
GOTO END

:END
```

This version of TOA-SUB.CMD is included on the disk that comes with the book. The only difference is that the disk version includes some additional internal documentation.

By now, you should also see why I included the @ECHO OFF command in the subroutine, although it's not needed when the batch file is running as a subroutine. If a user runs the batch file from the command line to find out what it does, the help section will take care of that, but everything would look very unattractive without the @ECHO OFF command.

Inside the calling batch file

Placing a subroutine inside the batch file that calls it makes writing batch files much more difficult. This is recommended only for users extremely short on disk space.

Before we get started with this technique, let me begin by recommending that many of you skip this section! Placing batch file subroutines inside the batch files themselves is much more difficult that using stand-alone files for subroutines. Its major advantage is that it saves a little disk space. If you aren't running very short on disk space, I recommend you skip ahead to the next section. Also, if your disk has an HPFS rather than a FAT (file allocation table), then the size penalty for stand-alone subroutines is very small. If your version of OS/2 supports long filenames, then you have HPFS.

With a FAT system, each batch file you write takes up a minimum of one cluster of disk space. Depending on several factors, that can be up to 8K and will most likely be at least 2K. If you're running very short of hard disk space, that can seem like a large price to pay for a relatively small subroutine. You can avoid this by bundling all the subroutines within the main batch file. HPFS allocates space differently—without clusters—so small files don't waste much space.

When you include the subroutine(s) inside the batch file, the batch file ends up running itself. A program or batch file that runs itself is said to be *recursive*. Recursive batch files have two advantages over batch files that call separate batch files as subroutines. First, the resulting batch file is generally smaller than the separate batch file and subroutines under the FAT. This is generally true in spite of the requirement in the recursive batch file for additional IF tests to direct it to the appropriate spot in the batch file to continue processing.

A program or batch file that runs itself is said to be *recursive*.

The second advantage of a recursive batch file is how easy it is to transfer it to different systems. If you need to copy a recursive batch file to another system, then that batch file is all you need to take to the new machine. If you want to transfer a batch file with external subroutines, then you have to remember to copy all the files—something I have trouble with.

There is, however, one very significant drawback to recursive batch files. The resulting batch file is longer, more complex, and can be much more difficult to write. This additional complexity is an important consideration—one you shouldn't overlook.

Building the subroutine inside the main batch file saves space but makes the resulting batch file more complex.

Storing subroutine commands within a batch file

When subroutine commands are stored inside the main batch file, the batch file needs to know if it's being called as a batch file or as a subroutine, and it needs to take different courses of action accordingly. A replaceable parameter functions as a signal to tell the batch file if it's being called by itself as a subroutine. When that signal is missing, the batch file knows it is being called from the command line. A series of IF tests at the beginning of the batch file direct it to the appropriate section of the batch file depending on the flag it receives as a replaceable parameter. That way the batch file can contain more than one internal subroutine.

Let's start with TOA.CMD and include TOA-SUB.CMD as an internal subroutine. We'll call the resulting batch file BIGTOA.CMD. BIGTOA.CMD needs to run exactly like TOA.CMD when it first starts. However, where TOA.CMD calls TOA-SUB.CMD as a subroutine, BIGTOA.CMD needs to call itself. We'll use %2 as a flag to BIGTOA.CMD that it's running as a subroutine—specifically, when BIGTOA.CMD calls itself as a subroutine, it will pass XYZ123ABC as %2.

This means that you have to have several IF tests at the top of BIG TOA.CMD. One will direct the batch file to help if /? is entered, and another will direct the batch file to the subroutine section if %2 is XYZ123ABC. Because BIGTOA.CMD provides this replaceable parameter, capitalization won't be a problem. The end of the subroutine section is a GOTO END command, so the subroutine copy of the batch file will exit and return control to the calling copy of BIGTOA.CMD. Of course, the subroutine no longer needs its own help section. Otherwise, the subroutine section is identical. The resulting batch file is as follows:

```
@ECHO OFF
IF (%1)==(/?) GOTO HELP
:TOP
 IF (%1)==() GOTO END
 IF (%2)==(XYZ123ABC) GOTO SUB
 CALL BIGTOA %1 XYZ123ABC
 SHIFT
GOTO TOP

:HELP
 ECHO This Batch File Requires You To Enter Filenames
 ECHO Without The Extension. For Each Name, It Erases
 ECHO The Associated .CMD File Then It Copies The
 ECHO Associated .DOC And .CMP Files To The A: Drive
GOTO END

:SUB
 IF NOT EXIST %1.BAK ECHO File Not Modified--Not Copied
 IF NOT EXIST %1.BAK GOTO END

 IF NOT EXIST %1.DOC ECHO %1.DOC File Not Found
 IF NOT EXIST %1.DOC GOTO END

 DEL %1.BAK
 IF EXIST %1.CMP XCOPY %1.CMP A:
 XCOPY %1.DOC A:

 IF ERRORLEVEL 1 ECHO %1.DOC Not Copied Successfully
GOTO END

:END
```

BIGTOA.CMD calls itself as a subroutine. It also illustrates the best approach to writing recursive batch files. Because the individual-file approach is easier to write, that's what I used here. Only after TOA.CMD and

TOA-SUB.CMD were finished did I begin working on the single recursive batch file that incorporated both files.

This example also illustrates a habit you might be wondering about, one that I've developed when writing batch files. I've always closed out the last section of the batch file—generally the help section—with a GOTO END command, even when the next line is the :END label. By doing so, I avoid introducing problems when I rearrange the logic of the batch file—as I did when I created BIGTOA.CMD by modifying TOA.CMD to include the subroutine. Without the GOTO END command, the main routine continues on into the subroutine when it's done. By automatically adding a GOTO END to the end of each section, I don't have to remember to do so if I decide to combine them later.

It's also possible to reorder the IF tests in BIGTOA.CMD to make it run more quickly. Because BIGTOA.CMD calls itself as a subroutine for each file, it's likely to run as a subroutine more often than as a stand-alone batch file. As written, when running as a subroutine, it has to first pass through the IF test relating to command-line help. By putting the subroutine IF test first, the IF test is avoided when BIGTOA.CMD runs as a subroutine. In general, when using branching IF tests in a batch file, they should be ordered from the most likely to be true to the least likely.

☑ When using multiple IF tests to branch in a batch file, arrange them so the ones most likely to be true are the first in the series.

A final word on batch file subroutines

No matter how you end up storing your subroutines, it's always easier to write them as stand-alone files and then combine them if necessary. Storing everything as one batch file makes the most sense if you're running a FAT system that's extremely short of disk space or if you're transferring the resulting batch file to other users. Storing the subroutine as a stand-alone batch file makes the most sense when simplicity is important or when the subroutine will be called by more than one batch file.

Running REXX programs

REXX programs are advanced batch files written using the REXX interpreter included with OS/2. A REXX program must have the same .CMD extension as a batch file. REXX program files must have a /* as the first two characters in the file as that is how OS/2 tells the difference between REXX programs and regular batch files. REXX programs cannot use batch commands and batch files cannot use advanced REXX commands; however, a batch file can run a REXX program as a subroutine and the two can even pass parameters back and forth. When batch files run REXX programs as subroutines, they do so with the CALL command.

A batch file can run a REXX program but must run it using the CALL command.

Many of the utilities included with this book are, in fact, REXX programs. For example, CAPITAL.CMD is a REXX program that takes a single word passed to it as a replaceable parameter, converts it to all uppercase, and stores it in the environment under the environmental variable name RETURN. The program SHOW-CAP.CMD illustrates running a REXX program from within a batch file. When you run SHOW-CAP.CMD, be sure to enter a single replaceable parameter with some lowercase letters in it. The program is shown here:

```
@ECHO OFF
CALL CAPITAL %1
ECHO %%1 Was %1
ECHO Uppercase %1 Is %RETURN%
```

As you'll see in chapter 26, REXX is a very powerful language that all batch file programmers would do well to learn a little about.

Summary

- A subroutine is reuseable code that one or more batch files can access when needed to perform some specific function.
- Subroutines can be stored as separate batch files and run with the CALL command.
- Subroutines make the logic of a batch file easier to follow than entering multiple commands on a single line.
- Storing subroutines as stand-alone batch files is the easiest way to write and debug subroutines, but it takes up more disk space and you must remember to provide all the subroutines when you give a batch file to another user.
- When using the CALL command to access another batch file, the called batch file doesn't have access to the replaceable parameters of the original batch file, so it must be passed any information it needs.
- It's important that stand-alone batch file subroutines protect themselves from being run by users from the command line. The safest form of protection is to test for a specific replaceable parameter provided by the batch file that is supposed to call the subroutine batch file.
- Storing the subroutine inside the original batch file saves space and makes it easier to transport the batch file, but it also makes the resulting batch file more complex.
- You can store subroutines inside the original batch file by using a series of IF tests to direct the batch file to the appropriate location each time it starts and using a replaceable parameter as a flag when calling the batch file as a subroutine.

- If you're writing a subroutine that can possibly be called by more than one batch file, it makes sense to create that subroutine as a stand-alone batch file. That way, all the batch files can access that single subroutine. If the subroutine will be used by only one batch file, then it makes more sense to create that subroutine as part of the original batch file.
- OS/2 batch files can run REXX programs and even pass them replaceable parameters, but they must be run like a subroutine using the CALL command.

24
When batch files don't work

By now, you should have a good understanding of the basics of writing and using batch files. You should be able to create a batch file that uses standard OS/2 commands as well as batch-specific commands and even be able to use some of the REXX utility programs that come with this book. You should also know how to use replaceable parameters and IF tests to control the flow of the batch file. As you begin to use this knowledge in your computing, however, you're going to occasionally have a batch file that doesn't work properly—so you need to know what to do.

If your batch file is in a loop or doesn't appear to be doing anything, hit Ctrl–C or Ctrl–Break. This should stop the batch file. OS/2 simply stops the batch file without asking you if it's what you really want, the way DOS does. You can also stop a batch file by double-clicking on the close button to close that OS/2 session. Once you get it stopped, however, you need to locate the problem. You can list the file on screen with the command:

```
TYPE FILE.CMD
```

but you'll need to use an editor to make changes, so you might as well load it into the Enhanced Editor to begin with.

While it isn't possible to give you a list of everything you should do when your batch file fails, following is a list of what I've found to be the most common troubleshooting approaches.

Possible error messages

If you're lucky, the operating system will tell you why your batch file isn't working properly. However, the message is likely to be cryptic and difficult to understand. For example, if your batch file has the invalid command:

```
IF A=B ECHO Invalid
```

Then OS/2 will respond with the error message "SYS1079: ECHO was unexpected at this time." (This line is invalid because it needs two equal signs.) If this error message doesn't tell you enough, you can get more detailed information by requesting help with the command:

```
HELP SYS1079
```

When you request error-message help information, OS/2 repeats the error message and then gives you an explanation and suggests a possible solution. For example, for the SYS1079 error message OS/2 shows the following:

```
SYS1079: *** was unexpected at this time.

EXPLANATION: The command is missing required keywords.
ACTION: Retry the command correctly.
```

I picked this example specifically because accidently dropping one of the two required equal signs is one of the most common batch file mistakes users make. The other is testing a replaceable parameter with a test like:

```
IF %1==A
```

without first making sure the replaceable parameter has a value. You can avoid this error by always surrounding the replaceable parameter you're testing and the test value with parentheses, so there's never a nul value on either side of the test. Thus, this test should be rewritten as:

```
IF (%1)==(A)
```

I won't go through all the possible error messages in detail since OS/2 offers the help itself. If you find an error message you don't understand, just let OS/2 explain it to you, as described.

Check the spelling

The next thing to check is the spelling. It's very easy to make a spelling error, especially when you're copying the file from the console. Sometimes it's visually difficult to spot a misspelled word, like ECHE for ECHO. I use Microsoft Word, a word processor that lets you specify your own dictionaries, so I've developed a dictionary of batch commands and common OS/2 commands and messages. When I think there might be a spelling error, I run the batch file through the spelling checker in Word using this dictionary. If your dictionary allows custom dictionaries, you might try the same thing.

If your word processor doesn't allow custom dictionaries or you don't want to go through the trouble of creating one, you might try an old proofreading trick. When reading anything, you tend to get interested in the content and anticipate the words or spelling that should be there. That makes it harder to catch errors. The solution is to read backwards, or in the case of batch files, where lines usually can't be split up, from the last line to the first. While you won't be able to follow the logic (that's the idea), you'll be much more likely to spot spelling errors.

Look more closely

Sometimes, it's hard to follow the execution of a batch file. With command-echoing turned off and a fast computer, it can be very hard to follow your batch files as they run. When I have this problem, I comment out the @ECHO OFF line by adding a REM, followed by a space, at the beginning of the line and slow my computer down to its slowest speed before running the batch file. If it still goes too fast, try running several endless-loop batch files in other windows to load up the system with work and slow down your session. You can use ENDLESS.CMD on the disk that comes with this book for just this purpose.

Isolate the problem

As you begin taking a closer look at your batch file, you'll most likely find that most of it runs fine but breaks down at some particular point. Once I've isolated the problem to a particular section of the batch file, I turn off command-echoing for the rest of the batch file and just turn it on for that section by using an ECHO ON command at the beginning of the section and an @ECHO OFF at the end. I also insert several PAUSE commands in the problem section so I can take my time examining the information on the screen while the problem section runs.

Split out the problem section

Occasionally, a particular section just seems so wrong that nothing I do will make it work. When that happens, I remove the problem section and make it a separate batch file. That way I can run it by itself—supplying the inputs it needs—without the rest of the batch file getting in the way. I can add ECHO commands to see the values of variables and any number of PAUSE commands to review the screen. When I finally get this batch file working, I merge it back into the original batch file.

Diagram the logic

When you have a problem involving logic testing, the best solution to solving the problem is to draw a "map" of the logic. That way you can make sure all the paths reach their proper conclusion. It's been my experience that "dangling" paths are one of the major sources of logic errors. Figures 24-1 and 24-2 show a map of the logic of COPYTHE2.CMD, the solution to problem 9 in chapter 25.

Put it aside for a while

Sometimes, when nothing seems to work, the best thing you can do is put the batch file aside for a while and come back to it. A number of times, I've

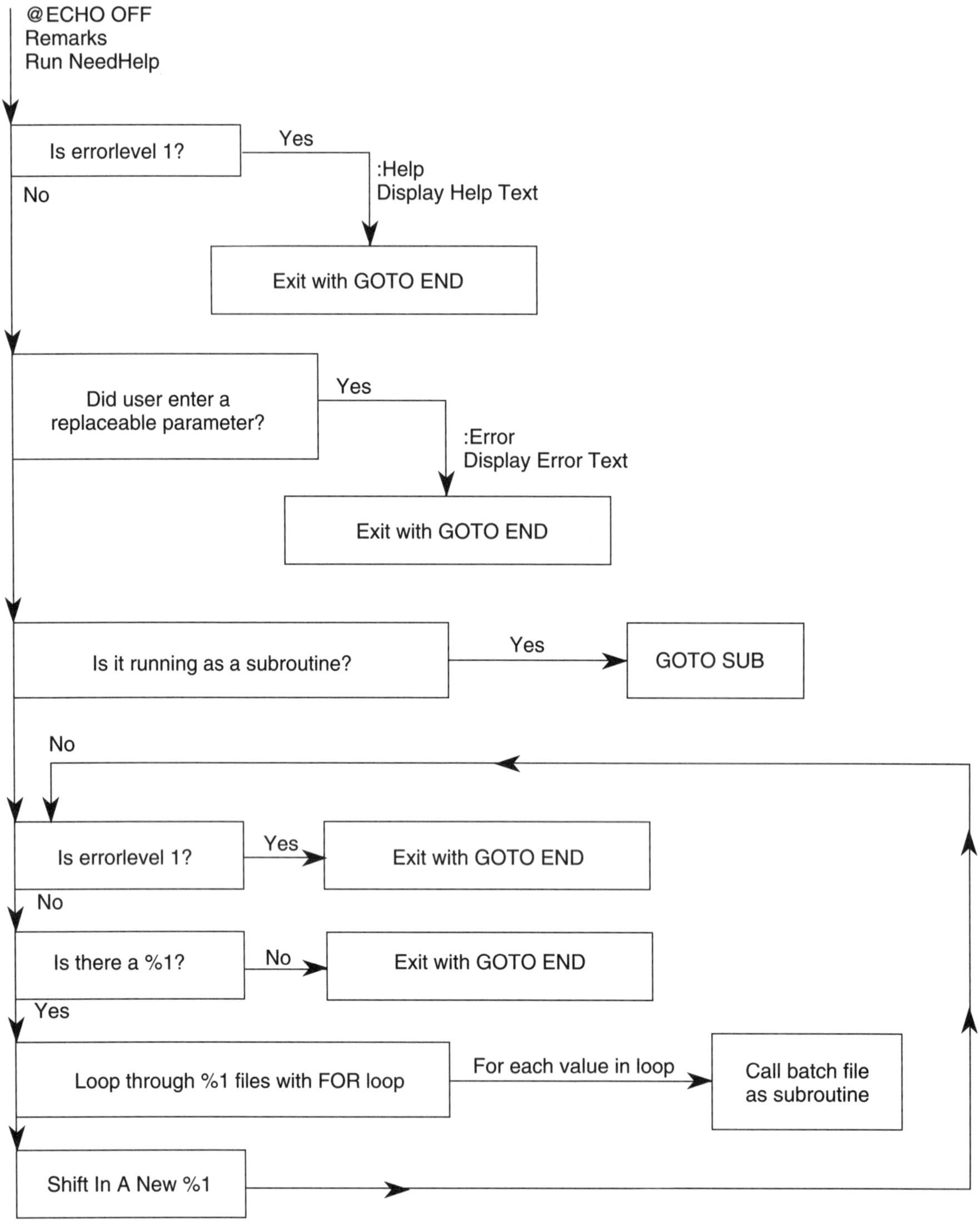

24-1 The logic of the main portion of COPYTHE2.CMD, from chapter 25.

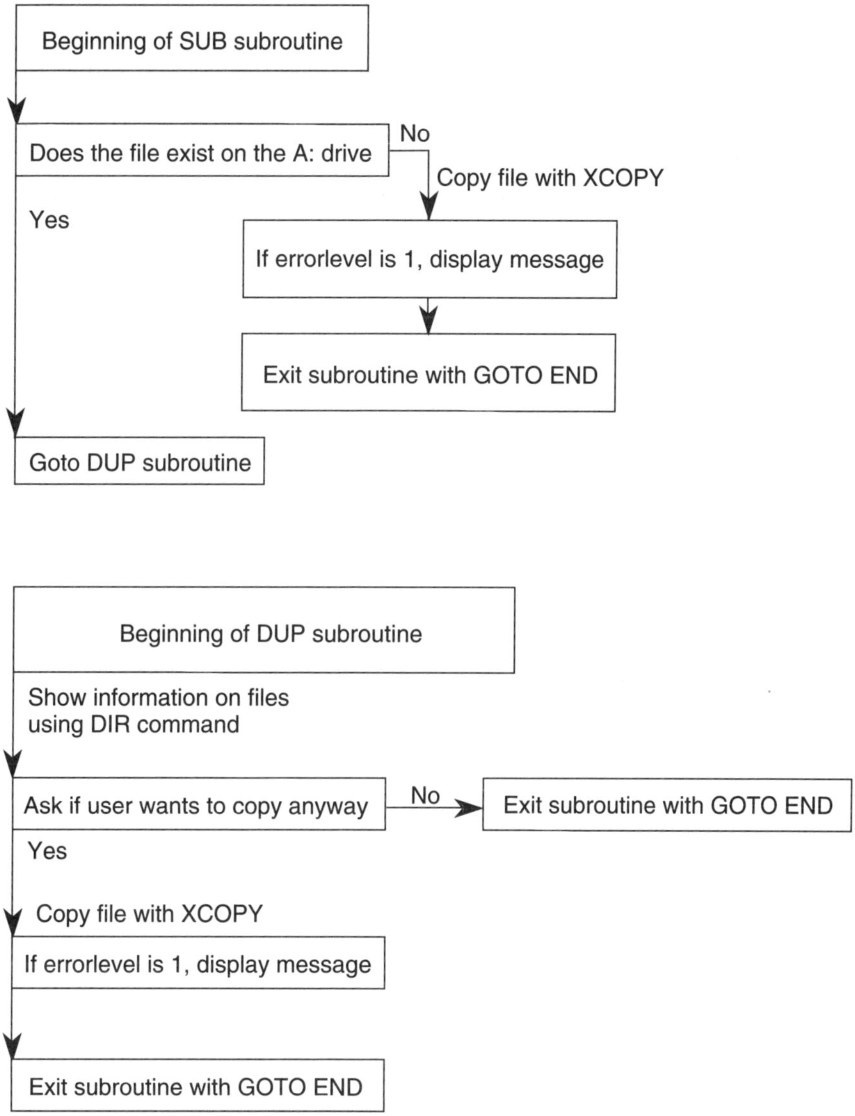

24-2 The logic of the subroutines of COPYTHE2.CMD, from chapter 25.

put aside a batch file with what seemed to be an impossible task only to come back to it later and see an obvious problem. This approach works for many problems, not just batch files.

Start over

If all else fails, the final solution is to erase the problem batch file or batch file segment and start over. Often, this second attempt will turn out better than the first because you have experience with the problem already.

Summary

- If your batch file generates an error message, that message can help you find the problem with your batch file.
- If your batch file appears to lock up, you can often regain control by pressing Ctrl–Break.
- If Ctrl–Break doesn't let you regain control over your batch file, you can always shut down the entire session by double-clicking on the close button.
- When trying to figure out OS/2 error messages, be sure to use the on-line help OS/2 offers.
- After looking for error messages, the next thing to check when a batch file doesn't work is the spelling of the commands.
- When checking the spelling doesn't resolve the problem, try turning command-echoing on and adding PAUSE commands to watch command execution closer.
- When a closer review doesn't solve the problem, try isolating the problem portion of the batch file into a separate batch file.
- When the problem with a batch file involves logic testing, try drawing a map of the logic.
- As a last resort, try putting the problem batch file aside for a while or even starting over.

25
Review #3

What follows are three quick problems. Take a few moments and try to figure them out. It's important that you have the skills necessary to solve these problems before you go on; otherwise, you will find the new material difficult.

Problem 7

A friend of yours is always copying files between two different machines. Several times, she has made the mistake of copying a file to a floppy disk when another version of that very file was already on the floppy disk. She has asked you to write a batch file to copy all the files she specifies on the command line to the A: drive—but only if the file doesn't already exist on the A: drive.

The complete filename with extension will be provided on the command line, so no assumptions about the name should be made. When wildcards are used, the batch file should copy all the files to the A: drive that don't exist, while skipping the ones already on the A: drive. Also, keep the user informed of the process.

Problem 8

You're working with a program you don't normally use, and you find yourself entering the same long command over and over. You decide to write a batch file to handle it.

When you run this new batch file with a command after its name, the batch file will store that command in the environment and then run it. When you run the batch file alone, it will issue the command stored in the environment. Some of your commands are very long, so you want to avoid limiting the commands to nine pieces, corresponding to %1–%9.

Problem 9

Your friend from problem 7 likes your batch file but asks you for a modification. Sometimes, she wants to overwrite the file on the disk with the one on the hard disk. Rather than just skipping all the files that exist on the floppy disk, she wants the batch file to show her information on both versions and ask her what to do.

Hint: Use the REXX program YESORNO.CMD on the disk if you need to ask the user a question. It returns an errorlevel of zero for a yes and one for no.

Answers

My solutions are shown in appendix A in the back of the book. It isn't important that you match my answers; if you develop a working solution to the problem, great!

PART 5
Batch file applications and utilities

You've learned so much about batch files, now it's time to put that into practice. So far, you've seen a number of demonstration batch files that solved very specific problems or just illustrated a point. For the next few chapters, you'll see how batch files can be a part of the solution for larger problems. Before that, however, I'll show you some batch file utilities that can make writing these batch files much easier.

Chapter 26: REXX programming The REXX language that comes with OS/2 is a very powerful language. This chapter provides a brief introduction.

Chapter 27: Batch file utilities The REXX language that comes with OS/2 has allowed me to provide you with some very powerful and useful batch file utilities. This chapter will document their functions, show you the actual source code, and give you modification hints so you can easily customize the utilities for your own use.

Chapter 28: An automated batch file help system One problem with having a lot of batch files is remembering which batch file does what. As it turns out, batch files can solve this problem and, in the process, give you a set of very powerful tools for locating the right batch file for your needs. This chapter documents this most powerful utility.

Chapter 29: A document archival system Never lose an important file again! That is a strong claim, but this chapter will show you how.

Chapter 30: Keeping two computers in synchronization Image that you're working on a project at work and decide to take work home with you. Now you've got to remember to grab copies of all the files that have changed since you last worked on this project at home. Tomorrow morning, you'll face this same problem again as you get ready to bring the finished work back to the office. This chapter will show you how to fully automate this process—even if one machine is running OS/2 and the other is running DOS!

Chapter 31: Simulating DOSKEY with batch files DOS's DOSKEY gives you command-line recall, keyboard macros, and the ability to enter multiple commands on a single command line. OS/2 supports entering multiple commands on one command line and has command-line recall if you have KEYS ON. It doesn't have macro capabilities. In this chapter, you'll see how to add macros and improve command-line recall—even with KEYS OFF—all using nothing but batch files.

Chapter 32: Smaller batch file applications This chapter presents a number of batch file applications that were too small to put in their own chapter.

26
REXX programming

REXX programs can do *anything* a batch file can do—and generally do it with far fewer lines of code. However, writing OS/2 batch files requires no knowledge of REXX—and running the REXX utilities in the next chapter and even changing their prompts requires no knowledge of REXX. So unless you're interested in learning more about REXX, you might want to skip this chapter completely.

➠ It isn't necessary to learn REXX in order to use or even modify the utilities that come with this book.

Covering REXX in detail requires an entire book, so this chapter is only an introduction to REXX. If you're interested in learning more about REXX than is presented in this chapter, check out the on-line documentation that comes with OS/2 or my *Writing OS/2 REXX Programs* book, available from McGraw-Hill.

Background

REXX is short for *restructured extended executor*. REXX was developed as a mainframe language by Mike Cowlishaw of IBM, and became so popular that it was selected as the standard command language for the IBM Systems Application Architecture, or SAA.

With many computer languages, the program's author must take care of a great many details. As an example, variables must be "typed" as either strings or numbers and often declared in advance. These details help ensure that the resulting program is structured properly. REXX was designed to let you get your programming job done quickly with a minimum of up-front fussing with program structure. This makes it easier and quicker to use REXX, but can make working on larger programs more difficult.

Introduction

Both batch files and REXX programs are stored in files with a .CMD extension. The only way OS/2 has to tell them apart is to look at the file itself. OS/2 requires that the first two characters in a REXX program be /*. If the file begins with /*, then OS/2 knows it's a REXX program; otherwise, it assumes it's a batch file.

The selection of the /* characters is not as arbitrary as it seems. REXX comments must begin with a /* and end with a */, so OS/2 is simply requiring that REXX programs begin with a comment. So anything placed between a /* and a */ is a comment and has no impact on program operations.

Like batch files, REXX programs are ASCII files. Additionally, REXX programs are ready-to-run as written and don't need to be compiled. So as soon as you make a modification to one of the utilities in the next chapter, it will be ready to test. Of course, you should keep a backup copy in case your modifications don't work as you expect.

REXX uses the SAY command instead of the ECHO command to display information on the screen. If the information isn't inside quotation marks, it's converted to all uppercase, so you'll want to surround your messages with quotation marks as shown in all the utilities in the next chapter. For the most part, it's the messages you'll want to customize—changing them to request the specific information you want. A simple REXX program using comments and the SAY command would be:

```
/* NAME:    REXX-1.CMD */
/* PURPOSE: Demonstration REXX Program */
/* VERSION: 1.00 */
/* DATE:    June 11, 1993 */

SAY Hello Reader
Say I Am A New REXX Program
```

Since neither line is surrounded by quotation marks, both lines would be displayed in all uppercase.

Unless you surround your prompts and variable information with quotation marks, they are converted to all uppercase.

Variables and branching

In a batch file, the only variables you have access to are environmental variables. REXX can create its own variables by assigning a value to a variable name. From then on, that variable name is replaced with the contents of the variable. The following example will make that clearer:

```
/* NAME:     REXX-2.CMD */
/* PURPOSE: Demonstration REXX Program */
/* VERSION: 1.00 */
/* DATE:     June 11, 1993 */

READER="Ronny"
SAY Hello Reader
Say I Am A New REXX Program
```

In this program, Reader is now a variable name, so the first line it displays will be "HELLO Ronny." (Since "Ronny" is in quotation marks when created, it is not converted to uppercase.)

REXX variables are not limited to strings; they can also contain numbers. Unlike many languages, there's no difference in REXX between a string and numeric variable. In working with numeric variables, REXX can perform the normal mathematical operations of addition, subtraction, multiplication, and division. The results can either be stored to a variable or printed with the SAY command. Consider the following:

```
/* NAME:     REXX-3.CMD */
/* PURPOSE: Demonstration REXX Program */
/* VERSION: 1.00 */
/* DATE:     June 11, 1993 */

First=12
Second=14
SAY "Sum Is" First + Second
Times=First*Second
Say "Product Is" Times
```

In REXX, there's no difference between string and numeric variables.

Like a batch file, REXX programs generally flow from top to bottom in a straight line. REXX programs have two commands to alter program flow: EXIT and SIGNAL. The EXIT command causes a REXX program to immediately terminate and return control to the operating system.

With a batch file, you specify a label with a colon and a name (:TOP), and you can jump to that label with a GOTO TOP command. In REXX, you mark a label with a name and a colon (TOP:), and you can jump to that label with a SIGNAL command, like SIGNAL TOP. In REXX, SIGNAL has many other uses that I won't discuss here.

One way to get input from the user is with the PULL command. The PULL command takes everything the user enters until pressing Return and stores it in a variable, as shown here:

```
/* NAME:  REXX-4.CMD */
/* PURPOSE: Demonstration REXX Program */
/* VERSION: 1.00 */
```

```
/* DATE:     June 11, 1993 */

SAY "Enter Your First Name"
PULL First
SAY "Enter Your Last Name"
PULL Last
Say "Hello" First Last
```

The PULL command can easily handle more than one variable, so this program could be shortened to the following:

```
/* NAME:     REXX-5.CMD */
/* PURPOSE: Demonstration REXX Program */
/* VERSION: 1.00 */
/* DATE:     June 11, 1993 */

SAY "Enter Your Name"
PULL First Last
Say "Hello" First Last
```

Each variable after the PULL command is assigned one word of the response. If the number of words exceeds the number of variables, all the extra words are assigned to the last variable. If there aren't enough words for all the variables, those extra variables aren't created.

The PULL command is used to get information from the user.

Logic testing and looping

REXX supports logic testing with both IF/THEN and IF/THEN/ELSE statements. The following program illustrates logic testing:

```
/* NAME:     REXX-6.CMD */
/* PURPOSE: Demonstration REXX Program */
/* VERSION: 1.00 */
/* DATE:     June 11, 1993 */

SAY "Enter Two Numbers"
PULL One Two
Total=One+Two
IF Total > 20 THEN SAY "Total Over 20"
 ELSE SAY "Total Less Than Or Equal To 20"
```

This program will prompt the user for two numbers. Once it has the two numbers, it totals them and prints a different message if the total is over 20 or less than or equal to 20.

REXX uses DO WHILE and DO UNTIL to loop until specific conditions are met. They work very similarly, only the DO WHILE loop requires the condition to exist first and the DO UNTIL doesn't. For example, the following program is an arithmetic test that prompts the user for two numbers and then keeps prompting for the sum until the right number is entered:

```
/* NAME:     REXX-7.CMD */
/* PURPOSE: Demonstration REXX Program */
/* VERSION: 1.00 */
/* DATE:     June 11, 1993 */

SAY "Enter Two Numbers"
PULL First Second
Answer=First+Second
Respond=0
DO UNTIL Respond = Answer
 SAY "What Is" First "+" Second
 PULL Respond
END
```

The DO UNTIL Respond = Answer line could be replaced with DO WHILE Re spond <> Answer line since Respond has a value before the loop begins. There is also a LEAVE command that causes REXX to immediately exit a loop. This arithmetic test could be rewritten as follows to give the user an option to give up:

```
/* NAME:     REXX-8.CMD */
/* PURPOSE: Demonstration REXX Program */
/* VERSION: 1.00 */
/* DATE:     June 11, 1993 */

SAY "Enter Two Numbers"
PULL First Second
Answer=First+Second
Respond=0
DO UNTIL Respond = Answer
 SAY "What Is" First "+" Second
 PULL Respond
 IF Respond=STOP THEN LEAVE
END
```

Since the PULL command converts the response to uppercase, no conversion is needed before performing the IF test on the response variable.

If you need to loop through a command or series of commands a specific number of times, DO followed by a number does just that, as the following program illustrates:

```
/* NAME:     REXX-9.CMD */
/* PURPOSE: Demonstration REXX Program */
/* VERSION: 1.00 */
/* DATE:     June 11, 1993 */

DO 100
 SAY "Counting To 100"
END
```

If you need to know the line number, then you can modify the DO loop to include a variable to contain the loop number, as shown here:

```
/* NAME:     REXX-10.CMD */
/* PURPOSE: Demonstration REXX Program */
/* VERSION: 1.00 */
/* DATE:     June 11, 1993 */

DO I = 1 TO 100
 SAY "Counting To 100. On Line" I
END
```

Subroutines

Just as it was with batch files, a REXX subroutine is a small section of code designed to be reused. With REXX, the subroutine must be stored as part of the main file. It starts with the subroutine name followed by a colon (just like a line name) and ends with a RETURN command. So a subroutine acts as a special type of GOTO command. The following program illustrates this:

```
/* NAME:     REXX-7.CMD */
/* PURPOSE: Demonstration REXX Program */
/* VERSION: 1.00 */
/* DATE:     June 11, 1993 */

CALL Setup
CALL Problem
EXIT

SETUP:
 SAY "Enter Two Numbers"
 PULL First Second
 Answer=First+Second
 Respond=0
RETURN

PROBLEM:
 DO UNTIL Respond = Answer
 SAY "What Is" First "+" Second
 PULL Respond
 END
RETURN
```

Notice the EXIT command before the beginning of the subroutines. Since REXX processes files from beginning to end unless told to do otherwise, it will run the subroutines again after running the program because they're at the bottom—unless you tell it to quit before reaching them.

You can pass parameters to a subroutine by placing them after the subroutine name. Multiple parameters must be separated with commas, as shown in the following program:

```
/* NAME:     REXX-12.CMD */
/* PURPOSE: Demonstration REXX Program */
/* VERSION: 1.00 */
/* DATE:     June 11, 1993 */
```

```
CALL Count 50, "Ronny"
EXIT

COUNT:
 Count = Arg(1)
 Name = Arg(2)
 SAY "Hello" Name "Counting To" Count
 DO I = 1 To Count
 SAY "Line Number" I "Of" Count
 END
RETURN
```

The Arg function (short for *argument*) is used to transfer the information passed to the subroutine to variables.

This has been just a sample of the power of the REXX language. If you are at all interested in programming, you will find REXX to be a worthwhile language to study.

Summary

- One of the advantages of the REXX programming language is its ability to yield powerful programs while remaining user-modifiable.
- The SAY command is to REXX what the ECHO command is to a batch file.
- REXX can create a variable just by assigning a value to a variable name with an equal sign.
- The EXIT command will immediately terminate a REXX program. Its most common use is to separate the body of a REXX program from subroutines.
- Lines and subroutines are marked in REXX by following a name with a colon on a line by itself.
- The SIGNAL command is used to jump to a named line.
- The PULL command gets information from the user.
- REXX supports logic testing with IF/THEN and IF/THEN/ELSE statements.
- DO WHILE and DO UNTIL loops will repeat a series of statements until some condition is met.
- REXX subroutines must be stored as part of the main program.
- Subroutines are executed with the CALL command.

27
Batch file utilities

In addition to all the sample batch files, ready-to-use batch files, and thousands of icons, the disk that comes with this book provides you with a handful of tools to help you write even more powerful batch files. All of these have been mentioned elsewhere in the book, but this chapter provides more complete documentation for many of the utilities, and will even tell you how you can modify them yourself.

No knowledge of REXX is required to run these batch file utilities—other than knowing you must run the programs with the CALL command. Additionally, the modifications I'll be suggesting don't really require that you know much about REXX.

A brief word on licensing

Unless otherwise indicated, all of these programs are copyrighted by Windcrest. Windcrest grants you, the reader, the right to modify these programs and copy them to any machine you use—even if they'll be running on more than one machine at a time. You may also distribute any of the REXX programs with batch files you write that use these programs, as long as you don't remove the copyright notice from the REXX programs and as long as your work doesn't compete with this or my new REXX book.

Getting information from the user

OS/2 retains many of the limitations of the DOS batch language, which is to say that it's very limited in its ability to get information from the user. The only way users have of entering information into OS/2 batch files is by entering replaceable parameters on the command line or pressing Ctrl–Break to stop a batch file. That's a fairly limited set of tools.

Fortunately, the REXX language that comes with OS/2 fills in the missing gaps of the OS/2 batch language. And because every version of OS/2 comes with REXX, you can easily modify these programs, something you usually can't do with a batch file utility.

Getting words from the user

One of the things you'll want your batch files to do is ask the user for information such as their name or the name of a file to erase, copy, or run. For this task, you need a utility that can accept full words rather than a single character. GET.CMD does just this:

```
/* Name:     GET.CMD */
/* PURPOSE: A REXX Program To Get Information From The User */
/* VERSION: 1.00 */
/* DATE:     May 27, 1993 */
/* Copyright (c) 1994 Windcrest */

SAY "Enter A Single Word"
PARSE PULL Word .
ENV = 'OS2ENVIRONMENT'
LastRC = VALUE('Return',Word,Env)
```

The most likely change for you to make is the "Enter A Single Word" prompt on the first operational line of the program—after all the comments. You can use any message you want inside quotation marks. Unlike batch files, REXX programs don't have a problem with piping symbols inside messages—as long as those messages are inside quotation marks. You can even drop the quotation marks; however, if you do that the prompt will be converted to all uppercase and you must avoid piping symbols.

If you're going to convert the user's response to uppercase anyway, as you might do if you needed to test on it, then it's easy to have the program do that automatically. Just drop the PARSE command on the second operational line, leave the command as PULL Word, and the user's response will be converted to uppercase. If you want to store the response in the environment under a different name, change the Return on the last line to the environmental variable name you want to use.

Additionally, it's not necessary to have just one version of each utility. You might want to take a copy of GET.CMD, which gets a word from the user, and create GET-BIG.CMD to get uppercase responses, GET-FILE .CMD with a different prompt to get filenames, and GET-NAME.CMD with yet a different prompt to get the user's name to include it in messages.

Converting to uppercase

When the information you receive via replaceable parameters must be tested, capitalization can become a problem. If the user is supposed to enter one of several flags, like daily, then you have to test for daily, Daily, and

DAILY—just to catch the common capitalizations. This requires a lot of logic testing and can still miss unusual capitalization. An easier approach is just to force it to be all uppercase.

You call CAPITAL.CMD, pass it a word as a replaceable parameter, and it converts that word to all uppercase and stores it in the environment. CAPITAL.CMD is as follows:

```
/* Name:     CAPITAL.CMD */
/* PURPOSE: Convert A Word To All Uppercase */
/* VERSION: 1.00 */
/* DATE:     May 30, 1993 */
/* Copyright (c) 1994 Windcrest */

Word = ARG(1)
PARSE UPPER VAR Word OutWord Word
/* Delete This Line And The Next Two Lines */
/* If You Do Not Want The Word Echoed */
SAY OutWord
ENV = 'OS2ENVIRONMENT'
LastRC = VALUE('Return',OutWord,Env)
```

CAPITAL.CMD does not have a prompt since it runs without user intervention. As the comments in the program indicate, you can delete the two preceding comments and the SAY OutWord line if you don't want the uppercase word echoed to the screen.

The second operational line strips off all but the first word if more than one is passed to the utility. Since it stores the results in the environment, storing multiple words under a single environmental variable would normally not be very useful. However, it you need this capability, just remove the last Word from this line so it becomes PARSE UPPER VAR Word OutWord, and it will convert everything it's passed to uppercase and store the entire string in the environment under an environmental variable name. Like GET.CMD, you can change the Return on the last line to another name if you want to alter the environmental variable name it uses.

Getting any character from the user

Many times, all you need is a single character from the user—when, for instance, the user needs to pick from a list or answer yes or no to a prompt. GET-ONE.CMD handles this problem when you want to accept any character from the user. The next three utilities do the same thing but take more restricted lists of characters from the user. GET-ONE.CMD is as follows:

```
/* Name:     GET-ONE.CMD */
/* PURPOSE: REXX Program To Get A Single
            Character From User */
/* VERSION: 1.00 */
/* DATE:     May 30, 1993 */
/* Copyright (c) 1994 Windcrest */
```

```
CALL RxFuncAdd 'SysGetKey', 'RexxUtil', 'SysGetKey'
SAY "Enter A Single Character"
Character = SysGetKey(echo)
ASCII = C2D(Character)
Exit ASCII
```

As the PURPOSE comment in this program shows, REXX comments can span more than one line. Once REXX sees a /*, it treats everything it sees as comments until it encounters a */. As written, GET-ONE.CMD echoes the pressed key to the screen. To prevent that, replace the echo on the third operational line with noecho. Of course, you'll want to change the prompt on the second operational line.

GET-ONE.CMD stores its results in the errorlevel. Some of the utilities that follow will show you how to test and modify that value. You might want to review them for ideas.

Getting a letter

Testing on all 256 possible values is a lot of testing for most of the questions you want to ask the user. GETA2Z.CMD reduces the testing by restricting the user to entering just a letter:

```
/* Name:     GETA2Z.CMD */
/* PURPOSE: This Is A REXX Program To Get A Single
            Character From The User */
/* Copyright (c) 1994 Windcrest */
/* PURPOSE: Returning A As 1, B As 2, And So On */
/* VERSION: 1.00 */
/* DATE:     May 30, 1993 */

CALL RxFuncAdd 'SysGetKey', 'RexxUtil', 'SysGetKey'
TOP:
ASCII = 0
SAY "Enter A Single Character A-Z"
AnyCharacter = SysGetKey(echo)
PARSE UPPER VAR AnyCharacter Character
IF Character = "A" then ASCII = 1
IF Character = "B" then ASCII = 2

/* C-X Handled In A Similar Fashion */

IF Character = "Y" then ASCII = 25
IF Character = "Z" then ASCII = 26
SAY
IF ASCII = 0 then SAY "ERROR 1: Enter A - Z ^G"
IF ASCII = 0 THEN SIGNAL TOP
Exit ASCII
```

The AnyCharacter = SysGetKey(echo) is used to obtain the single character from the user just as it was before. Only this time, the AnyCharacter variable name is used instead of Character. Since logic testing will be performed on this variable, the PARSE UPPER VAR AnyCharacter Character is used to convert the character to uppercase and store it under the variable name Character.

After that, a series of 26 tests are performed on the Character variable so see if it's a letter. For example, the IF Character = "A" then ASCII = 1 tests to see both if the character is an A and if it stores a number representing its position in the alphabet to the ASCII variable. After these tests are finished, the program checks the value of the ASCII variable. If it's still zero then the user entered something other than a letter. The utility displays an error message and goes through the loop again with the SIGNAL command. You can alter this error message if you like. In addition to displaying the error message, the prompt has a ^G in it so it beeps the speaker as part of the error message.

When the user enters a letter, the program exits and sets the errorlevel to the value of the ASCII variable. Remember that the ASCII variable stores the letter's position in the alphabet.

Like the other utilities, you're likely to want to change the prompt at the top of the utility. Additionally, you might want to change the error message at the bottom of the utility. You can change them just like any other messages.

If you like, you can reduce the number of letter choices available to the user. To do that, just delete the entire IF Character line for those letters you don't want the user to be able to use. Or even better, just comment out those lines by starting them with a /* and ending them with a */. That way, it's easy to add them back in later if you need them. If you do delete letters, you need to be sure to tell the user so he doesn't get frustrated trying to enter the letter Q, which you have caused the utility not to accept, at the prompt "Enter A Single Character A-Z."

Getting a number

If you want the user to pick from only a few alternatives, a number works better than a letter because there are only ten (0–9) of them. GET_0-9.CMD is the program:

```
/* Name:     GET_0-9.CMD */
/* PURPOSE: This Is A REXX Program To Get
 A Single Number From The User */
/* PURPOSE: Returning 0 As 0, 1 As 1, And So On */
/* VERSION: 1.00 */
/* DATE:     May 30, 1993 */
/* Copyright (c) 1994 Windcrest */

CALL RxFuncAdd 'SysGetKey', 'RexxUtil', 'SysGetKey'
TOP:
ASCII = 999
SAY "Enter A Single Character 0-9"
Character = SysGetKey(echo)
```

```
IF Character = "0" then ASCII = 0
IF Character = "1" then ASCII = 1
IF Character = "2" then ASCII = 2
IF Character = "3" then ASCII = 3
IF Character = "4" then ASCII = 4
IF Character = "5" then ASCII = 5
IF Character = "6" then ASCII = 6
IF Character = "7" then ASCII = 7
IF Character = "8" then ASCII = 8
IF Character = "9" then ASCII = 9
SAY
IF ASCII = 999 then SAY "ERROR 1: Enter 0 - 9 ^G"
IF ASCII = 999 THEN SIGNAL TOP
Exit ASCII
```

GET_0-9.CMD works much like GETA2Z.CMD. Its differences involve the input section. Since numbers cannot be upper- or lowercase, it accepts the user's input directly into the Character variable and doesn't perform a conversion to it. Also, because a 0 entry would result in ASCII having a value of zero, ASCII is first set to 999 instead of 0, and the program knows it gets a value response when ASCII is no longer 999. Otherwise, it works the same as GETA2Z.CMD.

Like GETA2Z.CMD, you can change the prompt and error message and reduce the number of choices available to the user. The process is identical to altering GETA2Z.CMD.

Yes or no

Sometimes, you just want to ask the user "Do you really want to do this?" When all you need is a yes or no response, YESORNO.CMD is the best choice. It sets the errorlevel to zero for a yes and one for a no. YESORNO.CMD is shown below:

```
/* Name:     YESORNO.CMD */
/* PURPOSE: This Is A REXX Program To Get Yes
            Or No From The User */
/* PURPOSE: Returning Yes As 0, No As 1 */
/* VERSION: 1.00 */
/* DATE:    May 30, 1993 */
/* Copyright (c) 1994 Windcrest */

CALL RxFuncAdd 'SysGetKey', 'RexxUtil', 'SysGetKey'
TOP:
ASCII = 999
SAY "Enter A Single Character Y)es or N)o"
Character = SysGetKey(echo)
IF Character = "Y" then ASCII = 0
IF Character = "y" then ASCII = 0
IF Character = "N" then ASCII = 1
IF Character = "n" then ASCII = 1
```

```
SAY
IF ASCII = 999 then SAY "ERROR 1: Enter Y)es or N)o ^G"
IF ASCII = 999 THEN SIGNAL TOP
Exit ASCII
```

YESORNO.CMD is a modified version of GET_0-9.CMD. Rather than converting the letter to uppercase as GETA2Z.CMD does, it just tests for the upper- and lowercase versions of both letters. Other than testing for two letters rather than ten digits, it's identical to GET_0-9.CMD. You might want to modify the prompt, error message, or errorlevel values it returns for a yes or no.

Finding ASCII characters

When you're using high-ordered ASCII characters to add formatting to your batch files, it's nice to have a handy reference. ASCII.EXE is just such a reference. It's a DOS program that pops up and shows all the ASCII characters except a few of the nonprintable codes below 30. Be sure to run it in DOS full-screen mode. Unlike the REXX programs above, ASCII.EXE cannot be altered by the user.

Summary

- GET.CMD is a REXX program that lets the batch file get names and filenames from the user.
- CAPITAL.CMD takes a single word and converts it to all uppercase for easy IF testing.
- GET-ONE.CMD gets a single character from the user and returns its ASCII value via the errorlevel.
- GETA2Z.CMD gets a single letter from the user and returns an errorlevel of one for A, two for B, and so on. It is not case-sensitive.
- GET_0-9.CMD gets a single number from the user and returns an errorlevel of zero for zero, one for one, and so on.
- YESORNO.CMD gets a yes or no from the user and returns an errorlevel of zero for yes and one for no.

28 An automated batch file help system

One problem with having a lot of batch files is that it's difficult to remember which batch file does what. This is much less of a problem under OS/2 than it was under DOS because you can install your batch files onto the desktop with long descriptions and illustrative icons to help you remember what they do. Unless a specific batch file needs to run from the command line, this is the best approach for dealing with those batch files you use enough to make it worth doing all this.

☑ A good approach to providing batch file help is to install all your batch files to the OS/2 desktop.

Some batch files are run so infrequently that you might not want to bother cluttering up your desktop with them.

Help files

Another approach is to write your own help file, like HELP.CMD, without documentation and command-line help (the disk version has both):

```
@ECHO OFF
CLS
ECHO DISCARD.CMD
ECHO -----------
ECHO Will Move All Unwanted Files
ECHO To A Directory For Holding
ECHO SYNTAX: DISCARD FILE1 FILE2
ECHO
```

```
ECHO MAINTAIN.CMD
ECHO -----------
ECHO Will Erase Temporary Files,
ECHO Sort Files, And Run Your
ECHO File Defragmentation Program
ECHO SYNTAX: MAINTAIN
ECHO WARNING: Takes Two Hours To Run
ECHO

ECHO PRINT.CMD
ECHO -----------
ECHO Will Print ASCII Files Automatically
ECHO SYNTAX: PRINT FILE1 FILE2 FILE3
ECHO WARNING: Make Sure Printer Is On
ECHO Or Computer Will Lock Up
```

This batch file displays a friendly reminder of the purpose of each batch file. Note that the lines that appear to have just an ECHO command by itself actually display a blank line by echoing an Alt–255.

A second approach to providing batch file help is a batch file that displays topical information.

As written, HELP.CMD simply displays a brief explanation of each batch file. If you've accumulated a lot of batch files, it can be time-consuming to read through all those messages looking for a specific batch file. As HELP1.CMD in FIG. 28-1 shows, you can use IF tests to make this help batch file somewhat context-sensitive. However, the help is limited to the few categories preprogrammed into the batch file.

Batch File Line	Explanation
`@ECHO OFF`	Turn command-echoing off.

`REM NAME:     HELP1.CMD`
`REM PURPOSE: Display Batch Help`
`REM VERSION: 1.00`
`REM DATE:     January 3, 1992`
	Documentation remarks.

`IF (%1)==(?)  GOTO HELP`
`IF (%1)==(/?) GOTO HELP`
`IF (%1)==(/h) GOTO HELP`
`IF (%1)==(/H) GOTO HELP`
	If the user requested help, jump to a special section to display help information.

`IF (%1)==()   GOTO NOTHING`	If the user did not request help on a specific topic, jump to a special section.

28-1 HELP1.CMD displays help on only the topic you select when you run the batch file.

Batch File Line	Explanation
CALL CAPITAL %1	Use CAPITAL.CMD to convert the first replaceable parameter to all uppercase and store in environment.
IF %RETURN%==UTILITY GOTO UTILITY IF %RETURN%==UTILITIES GOTO UTILITY IF %RETURN%==PRINTING GOTO PRINTING IF %RETURN%==PRINT GOTO PRINTING IF %RETURN%==BACKUP GOTO BACKUP IF %RETURN%==BACK GOTO BACKUP IF %RETURN%==MISC GOTO MISC	Jump to the section of information the user requested.
GOTO WRONG	If the batch file reaches this point, the user did not request a valid section of information so jump to an error-handling routine.
:UTILITY ECHO DISCARD.CMD ECHO -------- ECHO Will Move All Unwanted ECHO Files To A Directory ECHO For Holding SYNTAX: ECHO DISCARD FILE1 FILE2... ECHO ECHO MAINTAIN.CMD ECHO -------- ECHO Will Erase Temporary ECHO Files, Sort Files,And ECHO Run Your File ECHO Defragmentation Program ECHO SYNTAX: MAINTAIN ECHO WARNING: Takes Two ECHO Hours To Run GOTO END	Section to explain the utility batch files and then exit.
:PRINTING ECHO PRINT.CMD ECHO ------- ECHO Will Print ASCII ECHO Files Automatically	Section to explain the printing batch file and then exit.

28-1 Continued.

Batch File Line	Explanation
ECHO SYNTAX: PRINT FILE1 FILE2 ECHO WARNING: Make Sure ECHO Printer Is On ECHO Or Computer Will Lock Up GOTO END	
:BACKUP ECHO BACKUP.CMD ECHO ------ ECHO Will Backup All (Or ECHO Some) Subdirectories ECHO On Your Hard Disk ECHO SYNTAX: BACKUP ECHO To Backup Hard Disk ECHO SYNTAX: BACKUP Directory ECHO To Backup A Subdirectory GOTO END	Section to explain the back-up batch file and then exit.
:MISC ECHO GAME.CMD ECHO ---- ECHO Bring Up The Game Menu ECHO SYNTAX: GAME GOTO END	Section to explain the miscellaneous batch file and then exit.
:WRONG ECHO INVALID SYNTAX GOTO NOTHING	Display an error message when the user starts the batch file but enters an invalid category.
:NOTHING ECHO SYNTAX: HELP1 CATEGORY ECHO Valid categories are: ECHO Utility, Backup, ECHO Printing, Misc GOTO END	Display an error message when the user starts the batch file without a category.
:HELP ECHO Displays Help On ECHO Specific Batch Files GOTO NOTHING	Display a help screen and exit the batch file when the user requests help.
:END	Label marking the end of the batch file.

Customized help

While writing custom help batch files works, it's a difficult system to maintain. Each time you write a batch file or discard an existing batch file, you must update everything to reflect that change. Otherwise, your help system gets out of sync with your batch files and gives outdated information.

You have the same problem with the desktop. Forget to install one of your batch files or neglect to change the description when you alter a batch file and your desktop and batch files will also be out of sync.

While installing batch files to the desktop or creating topical batch files does work, it's difficult to keep these systems in sync.

One approach allows you to add and delete batch files at will and never gets out of sync, but it requires some special considerations when you create your batch file. First, it helps if you store all your batch files in a common subdirectory. I use the F:\BAT subdirectory for this, although the name does not matter; if you use a different subdirectory name, you'll need to modify the batch files to work with your subdirectory name.

While you don't need to keep all your batch files in one subdirectory, it makes the help system work much better. If you have your batch file arsenal scattered across multiple subdirectories, the help system can give you information on only one subdirectory at a time. Also, for these batch files to work across different subdirectories, you'll need to modify them to either take the subdirectory as an input or always use the current subdirectory.

Second, your batch files must be created with the proper internal documentation. This requirement affects only the first five lines of the batch file, and every batch file should begin with these same first five lines:

```
@ECHO OFF
REM NAME:
REM PURPOSE:
REM VERSION:
REM DATE:
```

Chapter 5 examines this in more detail. If you haven't read chapter 5 yet, do so before continuing with this chapter.

The easiest way to display batch file help is using a system keyed to the information built into the batch file itself.

HELPBAT.CMD in FIG. 28-2 uses this documentation to display custom help about each batch file. It begins with a FOR loop that loops through each batch file in the F:\BAT subdirectory. For each batch file, it calls itself with a special flag that causes HELPBAT.CMD to jump to a special routine the second time through.

Batch File Command	Explanation
`@ECHO OFF`	Turn command-echoing off.

`REM NAME:     HELPBAT.CMD`
`REM PURPOSE: Display Batch`
`     Purpose`
`REM VERSION: 1.00`
`REM DATE:     November 6, 1992`
	Documentation remarks.

`IF (%2)==(DISPLAY) GOTO` `     DISPLAY`	If the batch file is running as a subroutine, jump to a special section.

`IF (%1)==(?)  GOTO HELP`
`IF (%1)==(/?) GOTO HELP`
`IF (%1)==(/h) GOTO HELP`
`IF (%1)==(/H) GOTO HELP`
	If the user requested help, jump to a special section to handle that.

`FOR %%J IN (F:\BAT\.CMD) DO` `     CALL HELPBAT %%J DISPLAY`	Loop through each batch file in the F:\BAT subdirectory and call HELPBAT.CMD as a subroutine for each batch file.
`GOTO END`	After looping through all the batch files, exit HELPBAT.CMD.
`:DISPLAY`	Label marking the beginning of the subroutine.
`   ECHO %1` `   ECHO ——————————`	Display the name of the batch file. (It is passed to the subroutine as a replaceable parameter.)
`TYPE %1 | FIND "PURPOSE:"`	Type the batch file and display the Purpose line.
`   ECHO`	Display a blank line by echoing a high ordered Alt-255.
`GOTO END`	Exit the batch file.

`:HELP`
`  ECHO Reads Batch Files & Displays`
`  ECHO The Name And Purpose Line`
`GOTO END`
	Display help and exit the batch file when the user requests help.

`:END`	Label marking the end of the batch file.

28-2 HELPBAT.CMD uses internal batch file documentation to display custom help about each batch file.

That special subroutine first displays the name of the batch file and underlines it. It has access to the name because the name is passed to it as a replaceable parameter. After displaying the name, it types the batch file using the TYPE command. It pipes this information to the FIND filter, which then displays only the line containing PURPOSE:. This is the reason for the recommendation in chapter 5 to put your entire purpose statement all on one line; that way, this display completely explains the purpose of the batch file.

If you must use multiple lines for your purpose statement, you could start each one with a PURPOSE: to make sure the help batch files display the entire purpose. That does, however, tend to make the help screens look fairly cluttered. After that, control returns to the original version of HELPBAT.CMD that loops through to the next batch file, if any remain.

On a 16-MHz IBM model 80, this system runs slow enough that I can read all the lines as they scroll up the screen. However, on my Gateway 486/66, the lines scroll too fast to read. If that happens to you, you can replace the ECHO %1 line with a TYPE %1 | FIND "NAME:" line. That will cut the speed of the display in half because the batch file now has to type the batch file twice and use the FIND filter twice to locate specific text. If it still runs too fast, you can add lines to display the version and last modified date. If you display all four pieces of information, that version of HELPBAT.CMD will run at one-fourth the speed of the original version.

When you delete a batch file, it ceases to exist, so the FOR loop bypasses any reference to it and it's automatically removed from the system. When you add a new batch file, it contains all the information required by HELPBAT.CMD and the FOR loop automatically includes it. As a result, this system is automatically current with your batch files without any modification when you modify your batch files.

Context-sensitive help

While HELPBAT.CMD is a very effective method of displaying general batch file help, it can be overpowering when you have a lot of batch files. For example, I have well over a thousand batch files for all the books I've written. Finding a specific batch file using HELPBAT.CMD would take a long time and a lot of reading.

Fortunately, narrowing the search is fairly easy. Simply add a filter to the line that types the batch files, as shown by HELPBAT2.CMD in FIG. 28-3. When you don't enter any text, you get all the purpose lines as you do with HELPBAT.CMD. However, when you enter a phrase, HELPBAT2.CMD displays the purpose line for only those batch files that contain that phrase.

HELPBAT2.CMD is very similar to HELPBAT.CMD, but it differs in two areas. First, the batch file must turn the phrase you enter to search on into an environmental variable. This phrase must appear on the purpose line, and it must appear in exactly the same order specified without anything else in the middle. If the purpose line was:

```
REM PURPOSE: Runs The Menu Program
```

Batch File Line	Explanation
`@ECHO OFF`	Turn command-echoing off.

`REM NAME:     HELPBAT2.CMD`
`REM PURPOSE: Display Batch Purpose`
`REM          For Matching Text`
`REM VERSION: 1.00`
`REM DATE:    November 9, 1992`
	Documentation remarks.

`IF (%2)==(DISPLAY) GOTO DISPLAY`	If the batch file is being called as a subroutine, jump to a special section.

`IF (%1)==(?)  GOTO HELP`
`IF (%1)==(/?) GOTO HELP`
`IF (%1)==(/h) GOTO HELP`
`IF (%1)==(/H) GOTO HELP`
	If the user requested help, jump to a special section to display help information.

`SET FIND=`	Clear out the environmental variable that will be used to store the text to search for.
`SET BLANK=YES`	This environmental variable is used to indicate the first word being added to the FIND environmental variable since that word does not need a space in front of it.
`IF (%1)==() GOTO RUN`	If the user did not enter any text to search for, jump to the execution section.
`:TOP`	Label marking the top of the loop to construct the environmental variable to search on.
`   IF %BLANK%==NO  SET FIND=%FIND% %1`	If the flag equals no, then add this word onto the end of the environmental variable with a space before it.
`   IF %BLANK%==YES SET FIND=%1`	If the flag equals yes, then add this word onto the environmental variable without a space before it.

28-3 HELPBAT2.CMD uses internal batch file documentation and the FIND filter to display custom help information on only those topics you request. Due to a limitation of the batch file, it will display the name of all the batch files, even those that don't match the search criteria.

Batch File Line	Explanation
SET BLANK=NO	Now that the batch file has gone through the loop, set the flag to no.
SHIFT	Move all the replaceable parameters down one level.
IF (%1)==() GOTO RUN	If there are no more replaceable parameters, go to the execution section.
GOTO TOP	Continue looping.
:RUN	Label marking the beginning of the section that actually loops through all the batch files.
FOR %%J IN (F:\BAT*.CMD) DO CALL HELPBAT2 %%J DISPLAY	Use a FOR loop to loop through all the batch files and call this batch file as a subroutine.
SET FIND= SET BLANK=	After the batch file runs, reset the environmental variables.
GOTO END	Exit the batch file.
:DISPLAY	Label marking the beginning of the section to display the batch files matching the search criteria.
IF %BLANK%==YES GOTO BLANK	If the user did not enter a search criteria, jump to a special line.
ECHO %1 ECHO ————————	Display the batch file name.
TYPE %1 | FIND /I "%FIND%" | FIND /I "PURPOSE:"	Type the batch file and search for the search criteria.
ECHO	Display a blank line by echoing an Alt-255.
GOTO END	Exit the subroutine.

28-3 Continued.

Batch File Line	Explanation

:BLANK
  ECHO %1
  ECHO ——————
  TYPE %1 | FIND /I "PURPOSE:"
  ECHO
GOTO END
	Display the purpose line when the user does not enter a search criteria—so it replicates HELPBAT. CMD. This is required because the FIND filter does not work properly when the %FIND% environmental variable is blank.

:HELP
  ECHO Reads Batch Files &
  ECHO Displays The Name And
  ECHO Purpose Line And Will
  ECHO Search The Purpose For
  ECHO Text Entered On The
  ECHO Command Line
GOTO END
	Display a help screen and exit the batch file when the user requests help.

:END	Label marking the end of the batch file.

then the phrases Menu, Menu Program, and The Menu would all display this line. However, the phrases Run The Menu (with Run instead of Runs), Runs Menu (without the The), and Menu Program Now (extra word) would all fail to display the line.

The section of batch file code that constructs the environmental variable is shown here:

```
:TOP
 IF %BLANK%==NO SET FIND=%FIND% %1
 IF %BLANK%==YES SET FIND=%1
 SET BLANK=NO
 SHIFT
 IF (%1)==() GOTO RUN
GOTO TOP
```

This code loops around, constructing the FIND environmental variable by adding one word at a time until it runs out of replaceable parameters. After that, this is used as an additional search parameter:

```
:DISPLAY
 IF %BLANK%==YES GOTO BLANK
 ECHO %1
 ECHO --------------------
 TYPE %1 | FIND "%FIND%" /I | FIND "PURPOSE:" /I
```

```
 ECHO
GOTO END
```

Notice how it skips the additional searching by jumping to a different section if there are no replaceable parameters, but includes a second FIND filter search if replaceable parameters are entered. It's required because using a FIND filter to search on an empty replaceable parameter causes an error.

While HELPBAT2.CMD displays the purpose line for only those batch files that contain the text the user specifies on the command line, it displays the underlined file names of every batch file in the subdirectory. This can be avoided, but it requires several steps:

1. The results of the FIND search are piped into a file. If the FIND search is successful, this file will contain the PURPOSE: line; otherwise, it will be a zero-length empty file.
2. The file (called JUNK.000) is checked to see if it's a zero-length file. If so, the batch file currently being processed doesn't match the search criteria, so it's skipped. This checking is possible because OS/2 won't copy a zero-length file. So the file is copied to another name and, if that other name exists, then JUNK.000 wasn't a zero-length file.
3. If the file is not a zero-length file, then the name of the batch file and the PURPOSE: line are displayed by typing JUNK.000 to the screen.

HELPBAT3.CMD, shown in FIG. 28-4, accomplishes this. Since it doesn't display the names of the batch files unless they match the search criteria, HELP BAT3.CMD is an excellent way to get context-sensitive help for your batch files.

Batch File Line	Explanation
`@ECHO OFF`	Turn command-echoing off.

`REM NAME:     HELPBAT3.CMD`
`REM PURPOSE:  Display Batch`
`     Purpose`
`REM          For Matching Text`
`REM          Show Only Matches`
`REM VERSION:  1.00`
`REM DATE:     December 11, 1992`
	Documentation remarks.

`IF (%2)==(DISPLAY) GOTO DIS-` `     PLAY`	If the batch file is being called as a subroutine, jump to a special section.

28-4 By piping the FIND results to a temporary file and trying to copy that file, HELPBAT3.CMD avoids the limitation of HELPBAT2.CMD. It displays context-sensitive help and displays only the names of those batch files containing the information you request.

28-4 Continued.

Batch File Line	Explanation

`IF (%1)==(?)  GOTO HELP`
`IF (%1)==(/?) GOTO HELP`
`IF (%1)==(/h) GOTO HELP`
`IF (%1)==(/H) GOTO HELP`
	If the user requested help, jump to a special section to display help information.

`SET FIND=`	Clear out the environmental variable that will be used to store the text to search for.
`SET BLANK=YES`	This environmental variable is used to indicate the first word being added to the FIND environmental variable since that word does not need a space in front of it.
`IF (%1)==() GOTO RUN`	If the user did not enter any text to search for, jump to the execution section.
`:TOP`	Label marking the top of the loop to construct the environmental variable to search on.
`IF %BLANK%==NO  SET FIND=%FIND% %1`	If the flag equals no, then add this word onto the end of the environmental variable with a space before it.
`IF %BLANK%==YES SET FIND=%1`	If the flag equals yes, then add this word onto the environmental variable without a space before it.
`IF %BLANK%==YES SET BLANK=NO`	Now that the batch file has gone through the loop, set the flag to no.
`SHIFT`	Move all the replaceable parameters down one level.
`IF (%1)==() GOTO RUN`	If there are no more replaceable parameters, go to the execution section.
`GOTO TOP`	Continue looping.
`:RUN`	Label marking the beginning of the section that actually loops through all the batch files.

Batch File Line	Explanation
`FOR %%J IN (F:\BAT\*.CMD) DO CALL HELPBAT3 %%J DISPLAY`	Use a FOR loop to loop through all the batch files and call this batch file as a subroutine.
`SET FIND=` `SET BLANK=`	After the batch file runs, reset the environmental variables.
`IF EXIST JUNK.000 DEL JUNK.000`	If the temporary file exists, erase it.
`GOTO END`	Exit the batch file.
`:DISPLAY`	Label marking the beginning of the section to display the batch files matching the search criteria.
`IF %BLANK%==YES GOTO BLANK`	If the user did not enter a search criteria, jump to a special line.
`TYPE %1 | FIND /I "%FIND%" | FIND /I "PURPOSE:" > JUNK.000`	Type the batch file and search for the search criteria. Pipe the results to a temporary file. This file will be blank unless the search text was found.
`COPY JUNK.000 JUNK.010 > NUL 2>&1`	Try to copy this file to another file. The NUL 2>&1 is required to suppress all error messages.
`IF NOT EXIST JUNK.010 GOTO END`	If the second file exists, then the copy was successful and that means the first file was not a 0-length file. That means the search was successful. If the file does not exist, the batch file exits the loop because the search was not successful.
`ECHO %1` `ECHO ————————`	If the batch file reaches this point, the search was successful so display the batch file name.
`TYPE JUNK.000` `ECHO`	Display the results of the search by typing the piped file to the screen.

28-4 Continued.

Batch File Line	Explanation
`DEL JUNK.010`	Delete the temporary file. This is required so the next time through the loop, the batch file will not see this copy when copying a 0-length file failed.
`GOTO END`	Exit the batch file.

`:BLANK`
`ECHO %1`
`ECHO ——————`
`TYPE %1 | FIND /I "PURPOSE:"`
`ECHO`
`GOTO END`
	Display the purpose line when the user does not enter a search criteria—so it replicates HELPBAT. CMD. This is required because the FIND filter does not work properly when the %FIND% environmental variable is blank.

`:HELP`
`ECHO Reads Batch Files &`
`ECHO Displays The Name And`
`ECHO Purpose Line And Will`
`ECHO Search The Purpose For`
`ECHO Text Entered On The`
`ECHO Command Line`
`GOTO END`
	Display a help screen and exit the batch file when the user requests help.

`:END`	Label marking the end of the batch file.

HELPBAT3.CMD uses the information built into the batch file itself to display help on only those batch files relating to the topic you specify.

Depending on how many batch files you have, you'll find either HELP BAT.CMD or HELPBAT3.CMD a big help in figuring out which batch file does what. I use HELPBAT3.CMD constantly on my system.

Summary

- One way to keep track of all your batch files is to install them to the desktop.
- Another way to track your batch files is to write yet another batch file to provide help on existing batch files. This batch file doesn't need to be context-sensitive, like HELP.CMD, or it can be context-sensitive, like HELP1.CMD.

- Before you can write a more advanced help system, you must store your batch files in a common subdirectory and construct them with the proper internal documentation.
- HELPBAT.CMD automatically displays the purpose line for each batch file automatically. It doesn't require any modifications when you add or delete batch files.
- HELPBAT2.CMD uses the FIND filter to display the purpose line for only batch files that contain a specified piece of text. However, HELPBAT2.CMD still displays the name of all the batch files.
- HELPBAT3.CMD uses the FIND filter to display the purpose line for only batch files that contain a specified piece of text. By using OS/2-specific syntax, HELPBAT3.CMD avoids displaying the names of batch files that don't match the search criteria.

29
A document archival system

What I'm going to describe in this chapter is a complete system for making sure that you never again lose an important file. Because it consists of several major sections, you can adopt only those sections that are critical to your own applications. The major sections to my overall document archival system are listed next.

➡ This is a complete system to make sure you never again lose an important data file!

Periodic backups Absolutely nothing is more important than periodically backing up your hard disk or important floppy disks. This is the only part of this plan that I recommend to everyone. In fact, without periodic backups, the rest of this system is fairly useless. If you don't care enough about your data to protect it with a backup, then why waste time protecting it in any other fashion?

Systematically copy crucial data files Many important data files undergo routine revisions. Prior to making a major revision, I copy the file to be revised to a special holding subdirectory.

Never delete old files I never erase an old file. Instead, I copy it to a special holding subdirectory. When that subdirectory is full of files, I copy the files to a disk and erase them from the subdirectory. I then store the disk in a safe place. I currently have 150 such disks.

Index document files I use a commercial indexing package to index my word processing documents so I can find them faster.

Each part of my overall document archival system is explained in much more detail, as follows next.

Periodic backups

Back when everyone used floppies, the most damage you could do with one mistake was 320K. Like mistakes, bad disks or defective hardware rarely damaged more than 320K. Large hard disks, however, now give us the ability to damage 200M or more of data with one mistake, or as the result of an errant command or defective hardware. 200M is over 135 high capacity floppy disks!

If you don't care enough about your data to back it up, then why waste time protecting it in any other fashion?

I insure my computer with a company called Safeware. Recently, they sent out a newsletter listing some of the more unusual claims they had paid. This list included the following:

- A California man carried some work home with him. He kept the disks in a box that looked like his cat's litter box. As you might expect, the cat used the disk box to relieve himself and destroyed all the data on the disks.
- A California boy was hiding behind the family computer during a friendly game of hide-and-seek. When a friend found him, the boy made a heroic dash to avoid being tagged. While dashing, he tripped over the power cord. That sent a shock through the computer that caused the hard disk to crash.
- A Los Angeles motorist collided with a fire hydrant, sending a column of water into the air. That water entered a nearby office building, damaging several computers.
- A California man knocked his fish tank over, spilling all the water into his computer.
- A Florida man had his laptop out near the pool. The family dog bumped the table and sent the computer to the bottom of the pool.

As you can see, computers can be damaged by a number of unexpected events. While an insurance policy like the one from Safeware can protect your hardware and even your programs, it's up to you to protect your data.

In the last presidential campaign I just saw a graphic reminder of the importance of backups on CNN. CNN reported a break-in at the campaign headquarters of Ross Perot. The only damage reported was the erasure of a file containing the names of 17,000 supporters. As you can imagine, this has the potential of doing millions of dollars of damage to a campaign if these 17,000 supporters are the more generous supporters. In a close race, it could even determine the outcome! However, at the close of the report, the CNN reporter noted that the Perot campaign had a backup disk.

Many small businesses maintain all their records—all the payroll records, tax information, bid information, and more—on a single microcomputer. Imagine the impact to that business if those records were lost. I know of one company that had their three computers stolen. To make matters worse, they didn't have backups. They were so desperate for the data that they ran ads saying that the thieves could keep the computers and they wouldn't press charges if they could just get their data back. They never did, and they ended up going out of business.

I know of a large utility company that maintains a lot of their rate case information on microcomputers. One of the analysts tried to format a floppy with (you guessed it) the FORMAT command at the C prompt and ended up reformatting the hard disk. He was lucky: a recent backup had been made and he lost only a few hours of work. The manager told me that losing the files on his hard disk would have delayed a multi-million-dollar rate case. He now requires daily backups.

➡ Losing the files on a hard disk could cost a great deal of money and permanently damage a business.

I have about twenty articles in progress, the final version of my dissertation, a copy of this book, the related batch files, eleven other finished books and several books in progress on my hard disk. Until recently, I make a daily incremental backup and two full weekly backups. One backup is stored at home and the other is stored at my office.

Is this carrying things too far? I don't think so. An incremental backup takes about two minutes, and the two full backups take less than half an hour. So I spend about an hour a week on backups, this hour being insurance. It would take an experienced typist over twenty hours to rekey just my dissertation, and it would take me thousands of hours to redo the research if I lost the hard disk copy and couldn't locate a printed copy. Even my notes are on the hard disk. Now add in the time to redo all the other files, and you begin to see why I make backups.

As I said, that was my approach until recently. I now have a very fast tape drive that can perform a full backup on my hard disk in about twenty minutes, which is so fast that I've forgone incremental backups. I now make two full backups daily (one during supper and one after I quit for the night), and I keep the three latest versions of these two backup sets. One set is stored at home and the other is stored at the office.

Which files to back up?

You should have copies of most of your software on the original distribution disks, so you don't need to back up these files very often. Just keep the originals in a safe place so they can't be damaged. Even in the worst case of fire or theft, you can always replace your software by buying a new copy, so you will not lose your software. Many software companies will even replace manuals and disks for registered users for a nominal fee with a police or fire report verifying the loss.

> Software comes with its own backup in the form of the distribution disks, making backing up your software less important.

Except during installation, programs don't often change. The software is "tied together" with system files that include batch files, .INI files, the CONFIG.SYS file, and subdirectories. You can safely go a long time between backups of these files. They generally change only when you install new software or remove existing software.

If damaged, these system files can be replaced from an old backup or the original distribution disks. However, things aren't that simple with your data files. You create them and then usually modify them quite often. It's important, therefore, to back up these files frequently.

> You create your data, so it's important to back up these files frequently.

Types of backups

Your first hard-drive backup should be a full backup. This gives you a good copy of installed software and system files, as well as a copy of your data files. When you change a data file, OS/2 automatically changes a flag it maintains to indicate that a current backup no longer exists. At the end of the day (or week, if you want to live dangerously), you can make an incremental backup. The backup software looks through your hard disk for files with the archive flag. The software backs up that file and resets the flag, and then looks for the next file.

This process is fairly painless because incremental backups are very quick. As you continue making incremental backups, the disks will begin to pile up. If you're constantly updating a 300K database, then you'll create a new copy of this file on disk every day. Most backup software won't remove earlier versions of this file from the backup disks during an incremental backup. Another problem is that files you've erased from the hard disk still exist on the backup disks. Files that have been renamed will exist on the backup disks under both names. If you have to restore from backup disks, you can end up with a lot of extra files.

You can reduce these minor problems by using LISTFILE.CMD. LIST FILE.CMD is shown here without command line help or internal documentation but the version on the disk has both.

```
@ECHO OFF
C:
CD\
ATTRIB *.* /S > C:\CHANGED.TXT
```

All LISTFILE.CMD does is create a file containing a list of all the files on the hard disk. On my 386/20 with a bulging 105M hard disk, it takes less than two minutes to run. To avoid tieing up your computer, you can easily LISTFILE.CMD to run in a background session. You might want to install it as a startup file to make sure the list is always up-to-date.

By running it before backing up, this file will also be backed up—even by an incremental backup because you just changed it. If you must restore, you can compare the files that exist after the restore to LISTING.TXT. Any files that exist on the hard disk but not in LISTING.TXT were either erased or renamed, so they can be deleted.

While incremental backups are quick, restoring from them can be cumbersome if they have been going on too long. At some point you'll have so many disks from incremental backups that it will be time to erase them and make another full backup.

These types of backups will protect you from hardware problems and mistakes but not from theft, fire, or other types of damage. For that, you need a second backup set, stored off-site. In order to create a second incremental backup, your backup program must give you the option of not resetting the archive flag, and not all of them do.

Frequent backups alone will not protect your data against fire or theft. For that, you need an off-site backup.

Many organizations with very critical files maintain their three or so newest incremental backups. These are often called the grandfather, father, and son. The purpose of these multiple backups is that you can recreate changes to important files.

Multiple backups also give you a way to recover if your primary backup fails. I once needed to restore from a backup made by a major backup program. That program had not displayed any error messages when making the backup but when I went to restore, not a single file on the backup was recoverable. I sent the diskettes to the software company and they could not recover any data either. Luckily, I had a full backup from the day before, and it restored properly, so all I lost was one day's work. However, without that second backup, all of my data would have been lost.

Systematically copying crucial data files

If you need multiple backups for only a few files, there's a better way than running your backup program several times a day. I have a subdirectory called C:\OLD just for old copies of files. Every time I make a major change to a file, I copy it to this subdirectory with a number extension. So the first version of this chapter is CHAP-29.001, the second is CHAP-29.002, and so on. This way, I can always go back to an earlier version if I decide I don't like the changes I've made.

COPYBACK.CMD is a batch file to automate the copying of important files to the backup subdirectory. The operational portion of COPYBACK .CMD is shown below. Note that it checks to make sure that the target file-name doesn't exist before copying.

```
IF EXIST C:\OLD\%2 GOTO EXISTS
XCOPY %1 C:\OLD\%2/V
IF ERRORLEVEL 1 ECHO Trouble Copying
GOTO END
```

As the files accumulate in the C:\OLD subdirectory, you have a choice. You can erase older versions of the now modified (several times over) files, or you can copy them to floppy disks.

Never delete old files!

One of the things I learned a long time ago is that, just as soon as you erase a file, you end up needing it. As a result, I never completely erase a file unless I can easily recreate it. There are a lot of files on your hard disk that you can easily recreate, such as these:

.BAK files With most word processors, every time you save a file, the prior version is saved under the same name with a .BAK extension. Because I save all critical versions to a special subdirectory (as I explained previously), I routinely erase these files.

.OBJ files When you run most compilers, they first turn your source code into .OBJ files, and then they turn the .OBJ files into .EXE files. If you have the source code, you can easily recreate the .OBJ files by running the compiler again.

.PRN files These are ASCII files created by printing a spreadsheet file to a document. These can easily be recreated by reprinting the spreadsheet.

.$$$ and .TMP files These are working files created by some commercial packages. They're usually erased by the package when you exit, but a re-boot or disk problem can leave them on your hard disk.

Commercial program files These are the files that come on your software disks. If you need to recreate these, you can copy them from the original disks.

These are about all the files I erase. For the rest of my files, when I'm finished using them, I copy them to a holding subdirectory called C:\DIS CARD, and then I erase the original. DISCARD.CMD is the batch file I use for this. It copies all the files I list on the command line. Prior to copying, it checks to make sure that a file doesn't already exist in the \DISCARD subdirectory with the same name. After successfully copying the file, it erases the original. The operational portion of DISCARD.CMD is shown below.

```
:TOP
 IF (%1)==() GOTO END
 IF EXIST C:\DISCARD\%1 GOTO ERROR
 COPY %1 C:\DISCARD\%1 /V
 IF EXIST C:\DISCARD\%1 DEL %1
 SHIFT
GOTO TOP
```

Once I get a lot of files in the C:\DISCARD subdirectory, I copy them to a floppy disk and then delete them from the hard disk. Each of my floppy disks is numbered, from one to my latest one. After copying the files to a floppy disk, I perform three steps. First I erase the copied files from the hard disk. Next, I create a list of the files on the floppy disk. This list stays on the hard disk for easy retrieval when I want to search for a file. Finally, I index the document files on the hard disk.

Deleting all the files on the hard disk that were copied to the discard floppy disk would be easy if all the files were copied—all it would take is a DEL *.* command. However, I sometimes have more files than will fit on a single floppy, but not enough to justify using two. The problem is then to delete only those files that were actually copied to the discard floppy disk. DE LOLD.CMD does just that. While it contains a number of lines to handle command line help and internal documentation, the operational command are

```
A:
FOR %%j IN (*.*) DO DEL C:\DISCARD\%%j
C:
```

The batch file changes to the A drive first because it would be more difficult to write this batch file to run from the C: drive.

To create a file on the hard disk containing a listing of all the files on the floppy disk, I change over to the C:\DIRECTORY subdirectory and issue the command:

```
DIR A: > 99.DIR
```

replacing the 99 with the number of the current floppy disk. By maintaining a directory of all my discard floppy disks on my hard disk, I can rapidly search them for a file.

This might sound like overkill, especially if you rarely go back to a file after you're finished with it. The advantage to this system is that it's dirt cheap. In my area, 1.44M floppy disks currently cost about $10 per box of ten. So I have less than $150 invested in storing every one of my old files. The way I figure it, using just one of those files again saves me much more than $150. I've been using this system for several years now, and I'm very pleased with the results. In fact, I find these disks so useful, I recently started using DISKCOPY to make a duplicate to keep off-site for safety.

➡ I've been using this system for several years now and I'm very pleased with the results.

Indexing document files

Currently, a number of good word processing indexing programs are available. These programs take a word processing file or an ASCII file and create an index of it. These aren't indexes like you find in the back of a book; rather, they're indexes that allow you to search for every document that contains a specific phrase.

ZyIndex is such a package. It will index most word processing documents, using the format they're stored in. All you have to do is tell ZyIndex the format. I use ZyIndex to index all the text files on my discard floppy disks so I can rapidly locate information on them. A big drawback to ZyIndex, and all other indexing programs, is that it will index only text information; it won't index dBASE database files or Lotus spreadsheet files. To get around that problem, I create a small text file with the same name but a different extension that explains what the attached file does. For example, I create .WKT files to explain worksheet (spreadsheet) files. So HP.WKT explains in ASCII text what the file HP.WK1 does. I use .DBT files to explain the function of .DBF dBASE database files.

ZyIndex lets you assign names up to 30 characters to the floppy disks. These names can't include spaces, so I use an underscore to simulate a space. Because all the floppy disks are numbered, I give them the same name combined with their unique number. Disk number 43 would be named DISCARD_DISK_43.

INDEX.CMD runs the indexing program. It is shown below without the command line help or internal documentation of the version on the disk:

```
@ECHO OFF

IF (%1)==() GOTO NONE

CD\ZYINDEX
IF EXIST A:*.DOC ZYINDEX D:\ZYINDEX\ A:*.DOC/03 DISCARD_DISK_%1
IF EXIST A:*.WKT ZYINDEX D:\ZYINDEX\ A:*.WKT/01 DISCARD_DISK_%1
IF EXIST A:*.DBT ZYINDEX D:\ZYINDEX\ A:*.DBT/01 DISCARD_DISK_%1
GOTO END

:NONE
 ECHO You Did Not Enter A Number
 ECHO For The Floppy Disk
GOTO END

:END
```

It knows that the name should include the DISCARD_DISK_ specification, so I don't have to enter that. It also knows a number should be entered, so it checks to make sure that one was.

By following all four steps outlined in this chapter, you can be sure that you will never lose an important data file. Additionally, you will have the tools and techniques to quickly locate any single data file in your set of floppy disks that you use to store the old data files. I would be interested in hearing from any users who have success with this system or who find ways to improve this system.

Summary

- The major steps to this plan are periodic backups, duplicating critical data files before modification, copying old files to floppy disks rather than erasing them, and indexing data files with a commercial indexing program.
- Periodic backups are critical to the health of your data.
- Regular full backups and daily incremental backups will ensure the safety of your data.
- For further protection, you must keep rolling backups where you keep the last two or backups.
- For full protection, you need to keep both on-site and off-site copies of all your backups.
- Program files and the batch files that support the operation of your system need backing up far less frequently than your data files.
- LISTFILE.CMD makes sure every incremental backup includes a list of all the files currently on the hard disk.
- If you make a backup copy of critical data files before modifying them by copying the file to a new name in a backup subdirectory, you can always revert to the prior version if you decide you do not like the changes you made.
- COPYBACK.CMD automates the copying of important files to the backup subdirectory so you can keep multiple copies of those important files as you make modifications to them. This allows you to revert to earlier versions as needed.
- For additional protection, as this subdirectory of prior versions of critical files grows, it can be copied to floppies rather than simply deleting files.
- Program files can be safely deleted because you can restore them from the distribution diskettes as required.
- Data files that are easily recreated, such as .PRN and .OBJ, can safely be deleted as required.
- All other data files should be moved to a holding subdirectory rather than being deleted.
- As this holding subdirectory fills up or when you need additional space on the hard disk, the files can be copied to floppy disks and then deleted from the hard disk.
- A list of files for each floppy disk can be maintained on the hard disk to make locating a specific file quicker.
- A commercial program can index the data files on the floppy disk to speed file location even more.

30 Keeping two computers in synchronization

In addition to writing computer books, I'm also a college professor. I have a computer at the college that I use to write lecture notes, syllabi and tests. Sometimes, I like to work on my books at school and often I like to work on my class work at home. My problem is how to keep these two computers in synchronization.

This problem is not limited to just taking work home. Salespeople or others with jobs requiring travel might have a big desktop computer for the office and a small notebook computer for the road that need to be kept synchronized.

One solution is to connect a modem to each computer and either synchronize the two computers over the phone or at least use the phone to call the other computer and retrieve the needed files. That can be an expensive solution if you commute a long distance to work and the call is a long distance call. Salespeople are likely to have long distance calls when they forget a file.

If the computers can be located side-by-side, as with a notebook and desktop, then you can connect them with a nul modem cable and use one of the many file-transfer packages—like Laplink—to synchronize the computers. This wouldn't work in my case since both machines are desktop. Most workers carrying work home have a desktop machine at home, so it wouldn't work for them either.

Another solution is to buy a commercial synchronization package like FileRunner. Synchronization packages like FileRunner are very useful and if your needs are straightforward, they can be a good solution.

If you're looking for the cheapest and most powerful solution, then the batch file approach I'm going to show you is the best. It's able to fully synchronize two computers or just certain subdirectories on two computers.

The example I'll show you handles all the files on the D: drive and several subdirectories on the C: drive. This approach isn't as automatic as programs like FileRunner, but it does give you more control. And once you modify the batch files to match your hard disk structure, you have everything you need.

When you're doing the same work on more than one computer, it's important to keep those computers synchronized.

Preparing the computers

The synchronization system runs fairly painlessly using three batch files: PREPARE.CMD, GETFILES.CMD, and DOTHIS.CMD. However, running the batch files, the two computers must be prepared and two of the batch files (PREPARE.CMD and GETFILES.CMD) must be customized for your file structure. Let's look at preparing the two computers for synchronization first.

Get a subdirectory list

The first step you need to take is to develop a list of all the subdirectories you need to keep in synchronization on the two computers. List these subdirectories at the lowest possible level, so if you have three subdirectories C:\PROJECT1\WORD, C:\PROJECT1\LOTUS, and C:\PROJECT1\D BASE, then it would be enough to list C:\PROJECT1 as needing to be kept in synchronization.

Since each subdirectory will generate a separate set of entries in the batch files, you want to keep the list as short as possible. At the same time, you want to avoid having any program subdirectories in the synchronization list. There are three reasons for this. First, your license probably doesn't allow you to transfer program files in this fashion. Second, when the computers have different configurations—as a desktop and notebook computer are likely to have—then transferring programs this way will transfer the wrong configuration data to the target computer. Third, program files take up a lot of room and require a lot of floppy disks to transfer. If you limit yourself to data files, it rarely takes more than one or two disks to fully synchronize two computers.

Careful selection of the subdirectories to keep synchronized is the most important step in this process.

My computer has a large number of subdirectories that need to be kept synchronized—far too many, in fact, to list in a batch file. Also, I wanted an easy way to make backups of all my data files without making backups of program files. That way I could make frequent, quick backups of my data files and only infrequent, lengthier backups of my program files.

My solution was to repartition my hard disk into two logical drives, C: and D:. The C: drive is a massive 800Mb partition where I have all my software installed. Backing it up takes two hours with my tape drive. Fortunately, its contents don't change very much so I only rarely need to make a backup. The D: drive is a smaller 200Mb partition. It's smaller because there's no software installed there, just data.

That data changes frequently, so I make daily backups. Because data compresses much more than programs, my tape backup is able to back up the entire D: drive in about twenty minutes.

I have the same structure on my office computer, only I have fewer programs there and a smaller C: drive. However, it's mostly the D: drive I'm interested in keeping synchronized. Anytime anything changes on either D: drive, I want that change to be reflected on the other machine. In addition to the entire D: drive, I keep the following subdirectories on the C: drive in synchronization:

C:\BAT Most of my batch files are designed for a generic purpose (like keeping my computers synchronized), so they can run on both machines.

C:\CSERVE\FCABINET\CABINET These are all my data files from CompuServe. Only my home machine has the CompuServe software, but by maintaining a duplicate set of data files on my office machine I have an excellent backup. This data is not stored on the D: data drive because the CompuServe software prefers to have everything stored off a common subdirectory—so I had to choose between installing software on my data drive or data on my software drive.

C:\FTIES This is a genealogy program my wife sometimes uses. We have only one licensed copy and it's installed at home. This program wants its data files in the program subdirectory, so the synchronization program synchronizes only the *.IFT data files.

C:\TAKENOTE TakeNotes works much better if its database files are stored in the same subdirectory as the program. Only the data files need to be synchronized, so the batch files deal only with the *.TN files.

C:\WINWORD I have a licensed copy of Microsoft Word for Windows for both sites, but I don't need to transfer program files. So the synchronization batch file transfers only *.DOT (template) and *.BMP (toolbar) files since these are the only files I need synchronized.

C:\WORD I have a licensed copy of Microsoft Word for both sites. I certainly don't need to transfer program files from this subdirectory. However, I do want to keep my dictionary and macro files in synchronization. Again, Word prefers to keep those in its own program subdirectory.

C:\WORD\NORMAL A long time before I started using a data drive, I stored all my Word style sheets in this subdirectory. Rather than trying to change old habits, I've left them there so this subdirectory needs to stay synchronized.

Since these different subdirectories could offer insights for problems you might have, I've left them all in the batch files for this system.

Get everything synchronized

Batch files aren't smart enough to look at two files and figure out which is older or anything like that. Before a batch file can be used to keep two computers synchronized, those two computers are going to have to be manually synchronized.

Before a batch file can be used to keep two computers synchronized, you have to manually synchronize those two computers.

If the task of getting the two computers synchronized sounds too daunting, you might want to look into a commercial synchronization program like FileRunner that can handle everything for you. It has limits the batch files don't have, but does more of the work for you.

My approach was to make a full backup of the data subdirectories on both computers and do a full restore to the other computer with the software configured to overwrite only older files. That way, newer files got transferred, as well as files that existed on the source computer but not the target—but newer files didn't get overwritten by older files. Because this method transfers everything that's newer or doesn't exist from one computer to the other, afterwards both computers have an identical file structure and are fully synchronized.

Back up both computers

Even if you made backups to synchronize the computers, you now need to make another one on both computers. While it's always good to make as many backups as you can, the primary reason for this backup is to turn off all the archive bits. OS/2 maintains an archive bit marking every file that has been modified since the last backup. All those files you restored to each computer after the backup will have this archive bit turned on. Since both computers are currently fully synchronized, the files don't need to be transferred so the backup will reset the archive bit. If you really don't want to do backups at this time, you can also reset the archive bit by issuing the command:

```
ATTRIB *.* -A
```

in each synchronized subdirectory and adding a /S switch if all the subdirectories below that subdirectory are to be synchronized.

Using the system

Using the system is extremely simple. At the end of each work session, run the PREPARE.CMD batch file. This copies all the modified files in the synchronized subdirectories to a floppy disk. As long as you continue using that computer, just continue running PREPARE.CMD at the end of each session. If the floppy disk fills up, just start another one.

☑ PREPARE.CMD copies all modified files to the floppy disk.

When you finally sit down to use the second system, insert the floppy disk and run GETFILES.CMD. If there are more than one disk, you must run GETFILES.CMD on each one in order, starting with the earliest one. Again, if there are more than one disk, once their contents have been transferred to the second system you no longer need any of the disks except the last one, so you can reformat the remainder to use again.

☑ GETFILES.CMD transfers all modified files from the floppy disk to the hard disk of the computer not used to modify those files.

After transferring the files using GETFILES.CMD, transfer any modified files back to the last floppy using PREPARE.CMD at the end of each session. Once you get back to the first system, use GETFILES.CMD to transfer those modified files on the disk back to the first computer.

In case that explanation was hard to follow, let's work through a simple example using my system:

Day 1 On my home system, I modify CHAPTE30.DOC, CHAPTE31.DOC, and CHECKBOK.WK3. OS/2 turns on the archive bits for these three files. At the end of the day, PREPARE.CMD copies all the files with the archive bit turned on to the floppy disk while turning off the archive bit on the hard disk. After running PREPARE.CMD, no archive bits are turned on anywhere on my hard disk. On the floppy disk, CHAPTE30.DOC, CHAPTE31.DOC, and CHECKBOK.WK3 have their archive bit turned on because copying files to the floppy turns on the archive bit.

Day 2 I stay home and work on CHAPTE30.DOC again, as well as TEST12.DOC and SYLLABUS.DOC. At the end of the day, PREPARE.CMD copies these three files to the floppy disk and resets their archive bits on the hard disk. CHAPTE30.DOC overwrites an older version on the floppy disk so there are five files on the floppy disk (CHAPTE30.DOC, CHAPTE31.DOC, CHECKBOK.WK3, SYLLABUS.DOC, and TEST12.DOC) with the archive bit turned on.

Day 3, a.m. I go to the college and run GETFILES.CMD. It looks over the entire floppy disk and finds the five files with the archive bit turned on and copies them to the hard disk there. That process turns off the archive bit on the floppy disk so these files won't be transferred again. Copying these files to the hard disk turns their archive bit on, and GETFILES.CMD turns it back off. The files have not been modified so they don't need to be transferred.

Day 3, p.m. After running GETFILES.CMD, I modify TEST12.DOC again and create a new document called CHAPTE32.DOC. At the end of the day, I run PREPARE.CMD. It finds the two files on my hard disk with the archive bit turned on, copies them to the floppy disk, and resets the archive bit on the hard disk.

Day 4 I run GETFILES.CMD at home to synchronize that computer. It finds the files on the floppy disk that need copying, copies them to the hard disk, and resets the archive bit on both the floppy disk and the hard disk.

PREPARE.CMD is shown in detail in FIG. 30-1, and GETFILES.CMD is shown in detail in FIG. 30-2. Since these two files are so crucial to this process, let's briefly discuss these files in more general terms. You'll understand FIGS. 30-1 and 30-2 better if you read this discussion first.

Batch File Line	Explanation
`@ECHO OFF`	Turn command-echoing off.

`REM NAME:     PREPARE.CMD`
`REM PURPOSE: Get Hard Disk`
`     Ready For Backup`
`REM VERSION: 1.00`
`REM DATE:     May 27, 1993`
	Documentation remarks.

`IF (%1)==(?)  GOTO HELP`
`IF (%1)==(/?) GOTO HELP`
`IF (%1)==(/h) GOTO HELP`
`IF (%1)==(/H) GOTO HELP`
	If the user requested help, jump to a special section to display help information.

`D:`	Change to the D: drive.
`CD\`	Change to the root directory.
`IF (%1)==() GOTO NOCHECK`	If the user did not enter a replaceable parameter, skip checking to see if it was a SKIP.
`CAPITAL %1`	Run CAPITAL.CMD to convert the first replaceable parameter to all uppercase.
`IF %RETURN%==SKIP GOTO SKIP`	If the first replaceable parameter was SKIP, jump over the hard disk preparation section.

30-1 PREPARE.CMD copies modified files from the hard disk to the floppy disk and resets the archive bit on the hard disk.

Batch File Line	Explanation
`:NOCHECK`	Label used to jump over checking when no replaceable parameter was entered.
`ECHO Changing Attributes Of Files *.TMP`	Tell the user what is happening now.
`ATTRIB *.TMP -A /S`	Use the ATTRIB command to remove the archive bit on all *.TMP files in all subdirectories on the D: drive.
`ECHO Changing Attributes Of Selected Files`	Tell the user what is happening now.
`ATTRIB C:\CSERVE\FCABINET\CABINET\*.* -A`	Use the ATTRIB command to remove the archive bit on CompuServe files on the C: drive.
`ATTRIB C:\WORD\*.INI -A` `ATTRIB C:\WORD\*.TMP -A`	Use the ATTRIB command to remove the archive bit on Microsoft Word*.INI and *.TMP files.
`ECHO Changing Attributes Of *.BAK Files`	Tell the user what is happening now.
`ATTRIB *.BAK -A /S`	Use the ATTRIB command to remove the archive bit on all *.BAK files in all subdirectories on the D: drive.

`ATTRIB C:\BAT\*.BAK -A`
`ATTRIB C:\BAT\*.OBJ -A`
`ATTRIB C:\FTIES\*.BAK -A`
`ATTRIB C:\WORD\NORMAL\*.BAK-A`
`ATTRIB C:\WORD\*.BAK -A`
`ATTRIB C:\WINWORD\*.BAK -A`
	Use the ATTRIB command to remove the archive bit on selected files on the C: drive.

`ECHO Changing Attributes Of JUNK*.* Files`	Tell the user what is happening now.

30-1 Continued.

Batch File Line	Explanation
ATTRIB JUNK*.* -A /S	Use the ATTRIB command to remove the archive bit on all JUNK*.* files in all subdirectories on the D: drive.
ECHO Changing Attributes Of Files IMAGE.*	Tell the user what is happening now.
ATTRIB IMAGE.* -A	Use the ATTRIB command to remove the archive bit on the IMAGE.* files created by the Norton Utilities in the root directory.
ECHO Changing Attributes Of Files TREEINFO.*	Tell the user what is happening now.
ATTRIB TREEINFO.NCD -A	Use the ATTRIB command to remove the archive bit on the NCD file.
:SKIP	Label marking the point to skip to when the SKIP option is used.
ECHO Copying Modified Files From D: Drive	Tell the user what is happening now.
XCOPY *.* A:\ /M /S	Copy all the modified files from the D drive to the A: drive.
IF NOT ERRORLEVEL 1 GOTO NOERROR	If there was not a copying error, jump over the error section that follows.
ECHO ^G^G^G^G	When there is an error, ring the bell several times.
ECHO Not All Files Copied! ECHO Copying Stopped PAUSE	Display warning messages.
GOTO END	Exit the batch file.
:NOERROR	Label used to jump over the error section when no error occurred.
ECHO Copying Selected Modified Files From C: Drive	Tell the user what is happening.

Batch File Line	Explanation

XCOPY C:\FTIES*.IFT
    A:\FTIES*.* /M
XCOPY C:\BAT*.* A:\BAT*.* /M
XCOPY C:\WORD\NORMAL*.STY
    A:\WORD\NORMAL*.* /M
XCOPY C:\WORD*.* A:\WORD*.*
    /M
XCOPY C:\WINWORD*.DOT
    A:\WINWORD*.* /M
XCOPY C:\WINWORD*.BMP
    A:\WINWORD*.* /M
XCOPY C:\TAKENOTE*.TN
    A:\TAKENOTE*.* /M
XCOPY C:\CSERVE\FCABINET\
    CABINET*.* A:\CSERVE\
    FCABINET\CABINET*.* /M/S
	Copy selected files from the C: drive to the A: drive.

ECHO Done!	Tell the user the copying is done.
GOTO END	Exit the batch file.

:HELP
  ECHO Copies Modified Files
  ECHO To Floppy Disk To Take
  ECHO To Other Computer
GOTO END
	Display a help screen and exit the batch file when the user requests help.

:END	Label marking the end of the batch file.

Batch File Line	Explanation
@ECHO OFF	Turn command-echoing off.
REM NAME: GETFILES.CMD REM PURPOSE: Copy Files From A:Drive To D:Drive REM VERSION: 1.00 REM DATE: June 13, 1993	Documentation remarks.

IF (%1)==(?) GOTO HELP
IF (%1)==(/?) GOTO HELP
IF (%1)==(/h) GOTO HELP
IF (%1)==(/H) GOTO HELP
	If the user requested help, jump to a special section to display help information.

30-2 GETFILES.CMD copies modified files from the floppy disk to the hard disk and resets the archive bit on both disks.

30-2 Continued.

Batch File Line	Explanation
`IF (%1)==() SET SKIP=NO` `IF (%1)==() GOTO NOSKIP`	If the user did not enter a replaceable parameter, then the skip option not selected so skip testing replaceable parameter.
`CAPITAL %1` `IF (%RETURN%)==(SKIP) SET SKIP=YES`	Convert the replaceable parameter to uppercase and test to see if the user selected the skip option.
`:NOSKIP`	Label used to jump over testing the first replaceable parameter when one is not entered.
`A:` `CD\`	Make sure the A: drive is at the root directory.
`D:` `CD\`	Make sure the D: drive is the root directory.
`REM This Needs To Remain First`	Documentation remarks.
`IF EXIST A:\DOTHIS.CMD ECHO ON`	If the file A:DOTHIS.CMD exists, turn command-echoing on so the user can see what commands are executed.
`IF EXIST A:\DOTHIS.CMD CALL A:\DOTHIS.CMD`	If the file A:DOTHIS.CMD exists, run it with the CALL command so control returns to this batch file.
`IF EXIST A:\DOTHIS.CMD DEL A:\DOTHIS.CMD`	If the file A:DOTHIS.CMD exists, delete it now that it has been processed.
`@ECHO OFF`	Turn command-echoing off in case the file A:DOTHIS.CMD existed and it was turned on.
`REM This Needs To Remain Second`	Documentation remarks.

`C:`
`CD\BAT`
`CD`
`XCOPY A:\BAT\*.* /M`
	Copy any batch files from the A: drive to the C:\BAT subdirectory.

Batch File Line	Explanation
`IF ERRORLEVEL 2 GOTO ERROR`	If files were not copied properly, jump to an error-handling section.
`IF %SKIP%==NO ATTRIB -A *.*`	Now that the copying is finished, if the user did not select the skip option, reset all the archive bits in this subdirectory.

`C:`
`CD\CSERVE`
`CD`
	Change to the C:\CSERVE CompuServe subdirectory. The CD command is used to tell the user what subdirectory is being processed.

`XCOPY A:\CSERVE\*.* /M /S`	Copy the modified files and reset the archive bit on the hard disk.
`IF ERRORLEVEL 2 GOTO ERROR`	If files were not copied properly, jump to an error-handling section.
`IF %SKIP%==NO ATTRIB -A *.* /S`	Now that the copying is finished, if the user did not select the skip option, reset all the archive bits in this subdirectory.
`CD\TAKENOTE` `CD`	Change to the C:\TAKENOTE TakeNotes subdirectory.
`XCOPY A:\TAKENOTE\*.* /M`	Copy the modified files and reset the archive bit on the hard disk.
`IF ERRORLEVEL 2 GOTO ERROR`	If files were not copied properly, jump to an error-handling section.
`IF %SKIP%==NO ATTRIB -A *.*`	Now that the copying is finished, if the user did not select the skip option, reset all the archive bits in this subdirectory.
`CD\FTIES` `CD`	Change to the C:\FTIES Family Ties subdirectory.
`XCOPY A:\FTIES\*.* /M`	Copy the modified files and reset the archive bit on the hard disk.

30-2 Continued.

Batch File Line	Explanation
IF ERRORLEVEL 2 GOTO ERROR	If files were not copied properly, jump to an error-handling section.
IF %SKIP%==NO ATTRIB -A *.*	Now that the copying is finished, if the user did not select the skip option, reset all the archive bits in this subdirectory.
CD\WORD CD	Change to the C:\Word Microsoft Word subdirectory.
XCOPY A:\WORD*.* /M /S	Copy the modified files and reset the archive bit on the hard disk.
IF ERRORLEVEL 2 GOTO ERROR	If files were not copied properly, jump to an error-handling section.
IF %SKIP%==NO ATTRIB -A *.* /S	Now that the copying is finished, if the user did not select the skip option, reset all the archive bits in this subdirectory.
CD\WINWORD CD	Change to the C:\WINWORD Microsoft Word for Windows subdirectory.
IF ERRORLEVEL 2 GOTO ERROR	If files were not copied properly, jump to an error-handling section.
XCOPY A:\WINWORD*.* /M /S	Now that the copying is finished, if the user did not select the skip option, reset all the archive bits in this subdirectory.
IF %SKIP%==NO ATTRIB -A *.DOT /S IF %SKIP%==NO ATTRIB -A *.BMP /S	Now that the copying is finished, if the user did not select the skip option, reset all the archive bits on selected files in this subdirectory. These are the only files copied so they are the only ones that must be reset.

Batch File Line	Explanation
`CD\`	Change back to the root directory since the batch file is finished with the C: drive.

`D:`
`CD\`
`CD`
	Change to the root directory of the D: drive.

`XCOPY A:*.* /S /M`	Copy the modified files and reset the archive bit on the hard disk.
`IF ERRORLEVEL 2 GOTO ERROR`	If files were not copied properly, jump to an error-handling section.
`IF %SKIP%==NO ECHO Resetting Archive Bits` `IF %SKIP%==NO ECHO This May Take A Few Moments`	It takes a long time to do the entire D: drive so tell the user what will be happening next.
`IF %SKIP%==NO ATTRIB -A *.* /S`	Now that the copying is finished, if the user did not select the skip option, reset all the archive bits on this drive.
`GOTO END`	Exit the batch file.

`:ERROR`
`ECHO Copying Error ^G^G^G`
`GOTO END`
	Display an error message and exit.

`:HELP`
`ECHO This Batch File Copies`
`ECHO Files From The`
`ECHO B:Drive To The D:Drive`
`ECHO With Selected Files`
`ECHO Copied To C:Drive`
`GOTO END`
	Display a help screen and exit the batch file when the user requests help.

`:END`	Label marking the end of the batch file.
`SET SKIP=`	Before exiting, reset the environmental variable used by the batch file.

PREPARE.CMD

The basic task PREPARE.CMD has to perform is copying modified files from the hard disk to the floppy disk. However, not every modified file gets copied. First, the copying is limited to synchronized subdirectories. Second, while not necessary, it's a good idea to avoid copying temporary files like .BAK, .OBJ, and .TMP.

When I first wrote PREPARE.CMD, it was PREPARE.BAT and I was running it under Windows. I started out erasing the temporary files but Windows would often crash when a .TMP file was erased, and Microsoft Word would crash if any of its .BAK files were erased. To avoid these problems, I just reset the archive bit on these files and I've continued doing that since I've moved to OS/2.

You'll notice a lot of ATTRIB commands at the top of PREPARE.CMD turning off the archive bit for a lot of different files. I've been using this process for about two years now and I'm always on the lookout for files that don't really need to be synchronized. When I find such a file, I add its name to my list of ATTRIB commands to turn off its archive bit too.

If you enter Skip as the first replaceable parameter to PREPARE.CMD, it will skip all the ATTRIB commands. If you run PREPARE.CMD and it fills up a floppy disk without finishing, you're going to want to insert another disk and immediately run it again. When you do this, running through all the ATTRIB commands will just slow down this second execution. This is the only time the Skip switch should be used. Use it any other time and you'll get all the files you don't really want.

After running or skipping all the ATTRIB commands, PREPARE.CMD starts doing the actual copying. It uses the XCOPY command since it handles subdirectories and file attributes. By using the /M switch, XCOPY automatically copies only those files with the archive bit turned on and automatically turns off the archive bit after copying the file.

XCOPY is used once for each of the synchronized subdirectories. Since the entire D: drive is synchronized, it can be handled with a single XCOPY command.

GETFILES.CMD

The basic operation of GETFILES.CMD is to copy modified files from the floppy disk to the hard disk of the computer to be synchronized—the target computer. Its operation is simpler than that of PREPARE.CMD because PREPARE.CMD doesn't allow any unchanged files to reach the floppy disk so GETFILES.CMD doesn't have to exclude any files on the floppy disk.

The first thing GETFILES.CMD does is to check for a file called A:DOTHIS.CMD. If it finds this batch file, it runs it and then erases it. The operation of DOTHIS.CMD is discussed in the next section.

Understanding the logic of GETFILES.CMD requires a brief look at the operation of PREPARE.CMD. For the sake of simplicity, let's assume that PREPARE.CMD works only with the D: drive and the C:\BAT subdirectory.

When PREPARE.CMD copies everything modified from the D: drive to the floppy disk, it does so with an XCOPY D:*.* /S /M A:\ command. When it next copies the modified files in the C:\BAT subdirectory, it does so with an XCOPY C:\BAT*.* A:\BAT*.*/M command.

Now, if GETFILES.CMD were to try and copy the D: drive files first with an XCOPY A:*.* D:\ /S /M command, it would also get the modified files in A:\BAT—which should be going to the D:\BAT subdirectory. To avoid this problem, GETFILES.CMD must copy the A:\BAT files to C:\BAT first. That way, by the time GETFILES.CMD is ready to copy everything to the D: drive, the files in A:\BAT (and all the other individual subdirectories) have had their archive bit reset and GETFILES.CMD gets only the files intended for the D: drive. So GETFILES.CMD must always copy the individual subdirectories first and then the D: drive.

GETFILES.CMD must always copy the individual synchronized subdirectories first, while holding the entire D: drive to the very end.

XCOPY automatically resets the archive bit on the floppy disk when it copies those modified files to the hard disk. However, the process of copying them to the hard disk turns on the archive bit on the hard disk. In order to prevent PREPARE.CMD from copying those files right back to the floppy disk the next time it's executed, GETFILES.CMD must reset the archive bit in each subdirectory. It uses the ATTRIB command for this.

GETFILES.CMD takes a "brute force" approach to resetting the archive bit and simply resets all the archive bits in each synchronized subdirectory. It can do this because you run GETFILES.CMD before you modify any files, so none of the files other than the ones transferred by GET FILES.CMD should have their archive bit turned on.

DOTHIS.CMD

This system will do an excellent job of keeping two computers synchronized, but it suffers from the same flaw as most other synchronization systems: files erased on one computer remain on the other. After all, if I erase CHAPTE30.DOC on my home computer and forget to erase it at school, there's nothing in either batch file to do the erasing for me.

Without A:DOTHIS.CMD, erased files would remain on one of the two computers.

This is where A:DOTHIS.CMD comes in. I tend to do all my file maintenance from the command line—old habits die hard I guess—so after issuing a DEL D:\BOOK11\CHAPTE30.DOC command, it's quite easy to issue an ECHO DEL D:\BOOK11\CHAPTE30.DOC>>A:DOTHIS.CMD command.

Using OS/2 command-line editing, it's easy to pull the old line up and add an ECHO to the front of the command, and an >>A:DOTHIS.CMD to the end. This stores a copy of all the file-maintenance commands I issue on the synchronization disk, and GETFILES.CMD automatically repeats them on the other computer. That way, erased files disappear from both computers. By using the >> append pipe rather than the > overwrite pipe, I can insert as many commands into this file as I like.

Dealing with disks

Surprisingly, the disks don't fill up very quickly. I work on the computer a lot and a single disk keeps me going for a week or more. Think about it. A lot of the day-to-day work you do involves modifying the same files. Each day when PREPARE.CMD copies these to the floppy disk, they take up about the same space, using a little more or less depending on how you modified them. So you'll be surprised at how long a single disk lasts—unless you work with very large files.

PREPARE.CMD automatically detects when the disk is full using XCOPY. XCOPY aborts and sets the errorlevel when the next file to be copied won't fit on the disk, and PREPARE.CMD uses that to signal an error. XCOPY automatically resets the hard disk archive bit on those files that were successfully copied and not on those it failed to copy so you can just insert another disk and run PREPARE.CMD again.

I have four disks devoted to file transfer. When the first is full, I go to the second, and so on. Once the fourth is full, I loop back to the first. I reformat the disks right before I use them. That way I have an extra incremental backup of a lot of my recent data files if I need it. The more disks you devote to synchronization, the longer incremental backup you'll have. Since XCOPY doesn't alter a file it copies to disk, that backup file is immediately available with either the COPY or XCOPY commands.

Backup warning!

PREPARE.CMD keys off of the archive bit—which a backup program resets. If you run your backup program with files waiting to be synchronized, PREPARE.CMD won't be able to spot any of those files after the backup. The solution is to run PREPARE.CMD before any backup. In fact, you should add the CALL PREPARE command to the top of each of your backup batch files.

Always run PREPARE.CMD before any backup.

Adding compression

This method of synchronization breaks down if you work with very large files. The screen shots I took for this book were bit-mapped graphics and

780K each! Only one of them would fit on a 1.44Mb floppy disk. When I was creating the icon appendix, I created 41 files requiring 32Mb. Since only one would fit on a floppy, transferring them with PREPARE.CMD would have required 41 floppies—and since PREPARE.CMD aborts each time a floppy fills up, I would have had to restart it 41 times! Happily, bit-mapped graphics files compress nicely and PkZip got all 41 files down to 1.12Mb, which fit easily on one floppy disk.

I only occasionally deal with large graphics files and never with any other types of large files, so I handle them manually—outside of PREPARE.CMD—when the occasion arises. If you deal with larger files more often, you might want to modify PREPARE.CMD and GETFILES.CMD to use compression. As it turns out, the modifications are minor and quite easily made. For that reason, I'll describe them here.

None of the logic or preparations of either batch file needs to be changed. In PREPARE.CMD, replace the XCOPY lines with a command to compress the modified files. For example, if you were using PkZip 1.01-OS/2, the following command would compress all the modified files on the D: drive onto a single file on the A: drive, and reset the archive bits on the D: drive just like XCOPY:

```
PKZIP A:\D-DRIVE G:\*.* -p -i -r
```

In GETFILES.CMD, the command to uncompress these files and retain their directory structure is:

```
PKUNZIP A:\D-DRIVE D:\ -d
```

Since each synchronized subdirectory is compressed to a separate .ZIP file, there's none of the previously discussed problem.

There *is* one problem you may run into, however. PkZip isn't as smart as XCOPY when it fills a disk. If the disk fills up in the middle of a compression, PkZip simply aborts and erases its working files so nothing is compressed. If the compressed file is too large to fit on a single floppy, then you have to manually compress the files into smaller sets outside of PREPARE.CMD. A future version of PkZip should allow compressed volumes to span across multiple disks the way the DOS version currently does.

➡ PREPARE.CMD and GETFILES.CMD can easily use data compression.

Resynchronization

It's easy for one computer to get out of sync. You bring home some modified files from the office and, without thinking, alter some files on the home computer. Now you have some altered files on both the hard disk and the floppy. What to do?

If you run GETFILES.CMD, the modified files on the hard disk will have their archive bit reset and never be transferred to the office computer.

Run PREPARE.CMD first to put all the modified files on the floppy disk. But if you now run GETFILES.CMD to put them onto the home computer, the archive bits on the floppy disk will be reset and you won't be able to get them to the office computer. Is all lost? Must you start over and resynchronize both computers?

Happily, the answer is no. As long as the same file isn't modified on both the floppy and hard disk, you can painlessly resynchronize both computers.

> As long as the same file is not modified in two places, you can painlessly correct the problem.

GETFILES.CMD has a "skip" option just for this occasion. As soon as you realize there's a problem, run GETFILES.CMD using this option. This will transfer all the modified files to the computer you're working on without resetting any archive bits on that computer. That way when you run PRE PARE.CMD, the files you've modified on that computer will be properly copied to the floppy disk. The files you brought to that computer will also be transferred back to the floppy disk since their archive bit wasn't reset, but that's the small price you must pay. You won't hurt anything by transferring these extra files back to the original computer.

The GETFILES.CMD skip option is also useful when you have more than one synchronization disk to transfer. Resetting the archive bits takes time and it really needs to be done only after the last disk is processed, so run all but the last with the skip option. Just be sure to run the last disk normally or PREPARE.CMD will want to transfer all those files back again.

Now, if you've modified the same files on both computers so the floppy disk has one version and the current computer has another, you have a bigger problem. Rename the version that's on the current computer and then proceed as above. One you run GETFILES.CMD, you're going to have to manually reconcile the duplicated file and then delete the extra copy. After that, you can run PREPARE.CMD and everything will be on track again.

Dealing with more than two computers

Using this system with two computers works beautifully since each computer can reset the other's archive bit. When you want to synchronize three (or more) computers, the task becomes much more complicated. Here is an abbreviated version of the problem:

1. Files A, B, and C modified on computer 1 are copied to a synchronization disk.
2. Modified files A, B, and C are copied to computer 2. Files B, C, and D are then modified and copied to disk.
3. Modified files A–D are copied back to computer 1, where D is modified and E and F are created. Files D–F are copied to the floppy disk.

4. Modified files D–F are copied to computer 3, where F is modified and copied back to the disk.
5. The disk is taken back to computer 1. Which files need to be copied back?

Without being able to reset the archive bit after synchronization, the pool of files to be transferred will just keep growing. I can't in good faith recommend a batch file solution when more than two computers are involved. At this point, you need a commercial program like FileRunner.

A few words on ethics and privacy

As I mentioned at the beginning of the chapter, I have a computer both at home and at the office that I keep synchronized. The college where I teach doesn't object to my keeping personal files on my office computer because I own it. However, if you use these programs to store your personal data on your office computer, your company might not be as understanding. In fact, I know of some companies where storing personal files on the computer is grounds for dismissal! So be very careful about the files you're transferring. Even if you're transporting only work files back and forth to your house to work on at night, you might want to get clearance from your company to do so.

Besides risking your company's ire if they catch you storing personal data on a company computer, there's the risk of someone seeing something you really want to keep private—like your family budget, love letters, or even a diary. So be very careful about any personal files you're transferring—even if you have the company's permission to store them on your computer.

And don't think that a password will protect you. I know several major programs with built-in passwords that I can bypass in seconds, and it's likely that the folks who maintain your computer know more tricks than I do. They don't even have to be snooping. You might ask them to take a look at a hard disk problem and they'll just happen on that very steamy love letter or novel you recently started with your boss as the villain. At best it's embarrassing, and at worst can get you in serious trouble. So be careful!

Summary

- One way to synchronize two computers is to connect them via a modem and grab the files you need.
- Another way to synchronize two computers when one of them is portable is to connect them with a nul modem cable and use a file-transfer package.
- Another way to synchronize two or more computers is with a commercial synchronization package.

- You can synchronize two computers using three batch files: PRE PARE.CMD, GETFILES.CMD, and DOTHIS.CMD.
- The first step is to obtain a list of subdirectories to be synchronized. PREPARE.CMD and GETFILES.CMD must be modified to work with these subdirectories.
- This synchronization system should not be used with program subdirectories.
- The second step is to prepare both computers. This system works only when it's started with both computers properly configured.
- The third step is to make a full backup of both computers. This not only gives you two backups, but it resets all the archive bits on both computers.
- After modifying files on a computer, run PREPARE.CMD to transfer the modified files to the floppy disk.
- GETFILES.CMD transfers the modified files on the floppy disk to the hard disk of the computer not used to modify the files.
- DOTHIS.CMD stores all those file-maintenance commands you need to execute on the second computer.
- By rotating synchronization disks, you can use the disks as an incremental backup of your data.
- Backups reset the archive bit that PREPARE.CMD depends on. You should always run PREPARE.CMD before any backups.
- PREPARE.CMD and GETFILES.CMD need only minor modifications to use file compression in order to fit larger files onto the floppy disk.
- If a computer gets out of synchronization, running GETFILES.CMD with the skip option and then running PREPARE.CMD should correct the problem.

31
Simulating DOSKEY with batch files

DOS 5 comes with a wonderful keyboard enhancement program called DOSKEY, as does DOS 6. This memory-resident program gives you three major command-line enhancements:

Command-line macros OS/2 offers no such feature.

Recall of prior command lines With KEYS ON, OS/2 supports command-line recall but, like DOS, this feature is cumbersome to use.

Entering multiple commands on a single line Of course, OS/2 supports this without DOSKEY. Just separate each command with a &. Since OS/2 supports longer command lines than DOS, you can even stack more commands on a single line if you're so inclined. As an additional benefit, OS/2 lets you stack commands like this inside your batch files, something you can't do with DOS.

When I've talked to MS-DOS users who've switched to OS/2, the most common complaint I hear is about having to give up DOSKEY. OS/2 has some nice command-line editing features, but DOSKEY is nicer!

Well, I have a solution for you. In this chapter, you'll see how to write batch files that give you most of the functionality of DOSKEY in OS/2 without any memory-resident component. In some cases, the batch files will even out-perform DOSKEY! Of course, since OS/2 already supports entering multiple commands on a single line, I won't address that aspect of DOSKEY.

Command-line macros

With a command-line macro, you enter a macro name and a command or series of commands on the command line. Unlike a command-line recorder, a macro isn't run immediately after it's created—it's merely stored in memory for later use. After that, every time you enter the macro name at the start of a command line, DOSKEY replaces it with the command assigned to it.

With DOSKEY, these assignments are stored in memory. That means they're lost when you turn the computer off or reboot. While you can save them to a file, you must edit that file before you can recall the definitions.

In order to recreate command-line macros with a batch file, the batch file will have to be able to do the following things:

Store a new macro It can do this by piping the commands entered on the command line to a batch file.

Run a macro stored in a file It can do this by running the batch file containing the macro.

Display the available macros It can do this by simply typing the contents of each macro to the screen.

MACRO.CMD in FIG. 31-1 does all this. It restricts you to the macro names of 0–9, but this can be easily modified. Each macro can be as long as the command line allows.

Batch File Line	Explanation
`@ECHO OFF`	Turn command-echoing off.

`REM NAME:     MACRO.CMD`
`REM PURPOSE: Run Macro In File`
`REM VERSION: 1.00`
`REM DATE:     November 6, 1992`
	Documentation remarks.

`IF (%1)==(?)  GOTO HELP`
`IF (%1)==(/?) GOTO HELP`
`IF (%1)==(/h) GOTO HELP`
`IF (%1)==(/H) GOTO HELP`
	If the user requested help, jump to a special section to display help information.

`IF NOT EXIST C:\MACRO MD C:\MACRO`	If the storage subdirectory does not exist, create it.
`IF (%1)==()  GOTO MISSING`	The batch file requires at least one parameter so if none is entered, jump to an error handling routine.

31-1 MACRO.CMD allows you to define, view, and run keyboard macros.

Batch File Line	Explanation
`IF (%1)==(D) GOTO DISPLAY` `IF (%1)==(d) GOTO DISPLAY`	If the user requests a display of available macros, jump to a section to handle that.
`IF (%1)==(ABC123XYZ) GOTO` `    SHOWTHEM`	If the batch file is running as a subroutine, jump to a section to handle that.
`IF (%2)==()  GOTO RUN`	If the second replaceable parameter is blank, then user is requesting the batch file to run a macro so jump to a section to handle that.

`FOR %%J IN (0 1 2 3 4 5 6 7 8`
`    9) DO IF (%1)==(%%J) GOTO`
`    DEFINE`
	If the batch file reaches here, the user is defining a macro so check first replaceable parameter against 0–9 to ensure a valid name was used. If so, jump to definition section.

`GOTO ERROR1`	If the batch file reaches this point, the user entered an invalid macro name to create so jump to an error handling section.

`:ERROR1`
` ECHO You Entered An Invalid`
` ECHO Code On The Command Line`
` ECHO`
`GOTO MISSING`
	Display an error message.

`:ERROR2`
`  ECHO The Command You Entered`
`  ECHO Was Too Long And Every-`
`  ECHO thing After The %9 Is`
`  ECHO Missing From The Macro`
`  ECHO`
`  ECHO Shorten Your Command`
`GOTO END`
	Display an error message and exit the batch file.

`:ERROR3`
`   ECHO The Macro You Selected`
`   ECHO (%1) Does Not Exist`
`   ECHO`
`GOTO MISSING`
	Display an error message.

`:RUN`	Beginning of the section to run a macro.

`   IF NOT EXIST`
`    C:\MACRO\%1.CMD GOTO`
`    ERROR3`
	If the requested macro does not exist, jump to an error handling section.

31-1 Continued.

Batch File Line	Explanation
`C:\MACRO\%1.CMD`	Run the macro batch file. Note that the batch file is run without the CALL command so control never returns to this batch file.
`GOTO END`	Since control never returns this line is not needed—it is added just for safety.

`:MISSING`
`ECHO To Define A Macro, Enter`
`ECHO The Number Followed By`
`ECHO The Macro Definition`
`ECHO Numbers 0-9 Are Allowed`
`ECHO To Run Existing Macro,`
`ECHO Enter Number Of Macro`
`ECHO Available Macros Are:`
`GOTO DISPLAY`
	Display an error message.

`:DISPLAY`	Beginning of the section to display the available macros.
`FOR %%J IN (0 1 2 3 4 5 6 7 8 9) DO CALL MACRO ABC123XYZ %%J`	Loop through all available macros and call this batch file as a subroutine.
`GOTO END`	Exit the batch file.
`:SHOWTHEM`	Label marking the beginning of a subroutine section to display the macros.
`IF NOT EXIST C:\MACRO\%2.CMD GOTO END`	If the macro does not exist, exit the subroutine.
`ECHO —%2—`	Display the macro name.
`TYPE C:\MACRO\%2.CMD│FIND /V "@ECHO OFF"`	Display the contents of the macro, but skip the @ECHO OFF line.
`ECHO`	Display a blank line by echoing an Alt-255.
`GOTO END`	Exit the subroutine.
`:DEFINE`	Label marking the beginning of the section to create a macro file.
`SET MACRO=`	Reset the environmental variable used to store the commands.

Batch File Line	Explanation
`SET NAME=%1`	Store the name to an environmental variable so the SHIFT command can be used.
`SHIFT`	Move all the replaceable parameters down one level.
`:TOPLOOP`	Label marking the top of a loop to create an environmental variable containing the macro commands.
`SET MACRO=%MACRO% %1`	Add the first replaceable parameter to the command.
`SHIFT`	Move all the replaceable parameters down one level.
`IF NOT (%1)==() GOTO TOPLOOP`	If there are more commands, continue looping.
`ECHO @ECHO OFF > C:\MACRO\%NAME%.CMD`	Pipe the first line to the macro file to turn off command-echoing.
`ECHO %MACRO% >> C:\MACRO\%NAME%.CMD`	Pipe the actual macro command to the macro file.
`SET MACRO=` `SET NAME=`	Reset the environmental variables.
`GOTO END`	Exit the batch file.

`:HELP`
`ECHO MACRO.CMD Allows You To Define`
`ECHO Up To Ten Macros (0-9) That Are`
`ECHO Stored On Disk So They Do Not`
`ECHO Use Any Memory`
`GOTO END`
	Display a help screen and exit the batch file when the user requests help.

`:END`	Label marking the end of the batch file.

If you enter MACRO D, it displays all the available macros. If you enter MACRO #, it runs the macro stored under the number you enter on the command line. And if you enter MACRO # commands, it stores those commands in a macro without executing them. Macros are stored in the C:\MACRO subdirectory. The subdirectory should not be in your path. They remain until you overwrite them or manually erase them, so macros are retained if you reboot. Plus, macros created by one session can immediately be used in another session.

Users interested in implementing this system but concerned about being allowed to enter just one line of commands should note that once MACRO.CMD has created a macro, nothing prevents you from going back and enhancing it because it's nothing but a regular batch file. Additionally, there's nothing preventing you from creating one or more of the macro batch files yourself without using MACRO.CMD. You'll still be able to use MACRO.CMD to display and run the resulting batch file.

Command-line recorder

I really dislike the way DOSKEY and every other keyboard program I've seen store old command lines. Every single command line gets stored. I tend to enter a lot of short commands, like DIR or D:, and I prefer not to have to search through all these looking for one or two long commands to reuse. You end up punching in so many keystrokes to find the line you want that you might as well have typed it in again!

One of the nice things about a batch file approach is that only those command lines you enter via the batch file are stored, so you control which ones are stored. Enter the command normally and it bypasses the macro program, which is just perfect for short commands. Enter the command after the batch file name and the command is executed, plus it's stored for later use, which is just perfect for longer commands.

Like the macro batch file, old command lines are kept in batch files so they aren't affected by rebooting or turning the computer off, and command lines entered in one session are immediately available to run in any other session. In addition, for especially complex command lines, you can edit the batch file directly.

In fact, the command-line recorder is very similar to the macro recorder. It does have three differences:

- After storing a command line, that command line is immediately executed.
- You assign macro names but command lines are stored in the next available name.
- After all the names have been used, the oldest command line is discarded and the remaining ones are moved down one name to make room for the new command line to be stored rather than you deciding where to store each macro.

As it turns out, all three of the differences are easy to accomplish with a batch file. To run a command line after storing it requires only one additional line in the batch file—a line to run the just-created batch file. Assigning the name to the command line requires searching for the first available name and, if none is found, deleting 0.CMD, renaming the remaining batch files to a number one lower, and then using the name of 9.CMD to store the current command line. Beyond this, the batch file, called CL.CMD, is very similar to MACRO.CMD, explained earlier. CL.CMD is reviewed in detail in FIG. 31-2.

Batch File Line	Explanation
`@ECHO OFF`	Turn command-echoing off.

`REM NAME:     CL.CMD`
`REM PURPOSE:  Store Command`
`REM           Lines Using`
`REM           Files Not Memory`
`REM VERSION:  1.00`
`REM DATE:     November 6, 1992`
	Documentation remarks.

`IF (%1)==(ABC123XYZ) GOTO SHOWTHEM`	If the batch file is running as a subroutine, jump to a section to handle that.

`IF (%1)==(?)  GOTO HELP`
`IF (%1)==(/?) GOTO HELP`
`IF (%1)==(/h) GOTO HELP`
`IF (%1)==(/H) GOTO HELP`
	If the user requested help, jump to a special section to display help information.

`IF (%1)==(D)  GOTO DISPLAY` `IF (%1)==(d)  GOTO DISPLAY`	If the user requests a display of available macros, jump to a section to handle that.
`SET USE=`	Reset the environmental variable that will store the name to use. Unlike MACRO.CMD, CL.CMD automatically selects the name to use.
`IF NOT EXIST C:\CL MD C:\CL`	If the storage subdirectory does not exist, create it.
`FOR %%J IN (0 1 2 3 4 5 6 7 8 9) DO IF (%1)==(%%J) GOTO RUN`	Since the user does not enter the name of the command-line file to define, if he enters a 0-9 as the first replaceable parameter, he is asking the batch file to run that command line so jump to a section to do that.

31-2 CL.CMD stores, displays, and reruns command lines.

31-2 Continued.

Batch File Line	Explanation
`FOR %%J IN (9 8 7 6 5 4 3 2 1 0) DO IF NOT EXIST C:\CL\%%J.CMD SET USE=%%J`	If it reaches this point, the user is storing a command line so search for a name. Searching backwards and resetting the environmental variable for each match will find the lowest free number.
`IF NOT (%USE%)==() GOTO USE`	If the line above found a number, then jump to a definition section.
`GOTO ALLUSED`	If it reaches this point, then no numbers were free to store the command line. Jump to a special section to handle this.
`:RUN`	Label marking the beginning of the section to run the command line.
`C:\CL\%1.CMD`	Run the command-line batch file. Note that the batch file is run without the CALL command so control never returns to this batch file. The batch file does not make sure it exists first. Interested users might want to add this error-checking.
`GOTO END`	Since control never returns here, this line is not needed—it is added just for safety.
`:USE`	Label marking the beginning of the section to create a command-line file.
`SHIFT`	Move the replaceable parameters down one level so %0 contains the first command.

Batch File Line	Explanation
`ECHO @ECHO OFF > C:\CL\%USE%.CMD`	Pipe the first line to the command-line file to turn off command-echoing.
`ECHO %0 %1 %2 %3 %4 %5 %6 %7 %8 %9 >> C:\CL\%USE%.CMD`	Pipe the commands to the command-line file. Users expecting to store more than ten commands would want to modify this section to operate the way MACRO.CMD does.
`C:\CL\%USE%.CMD`	Since the user expects the command line to be executed after it's created, run it. It's run without a CALL command so control does not return to this batch file.
`GOTO END`	Since control never returns here, this line is not needed—it is added for safety.
`:ALLUSED`	Label marking the beginning of the section to handle there not being any free numbers to store the command line file in.
`DEL C:\CL\0.CMD`	Since command lines are stored first in, first out, delete the oldest file.

`REN C:\CL\1.CMD 0.CMD`
`REN C:\CL\2.CMD 1.CMD`
`REN C:\CL\3.CMD 2.CMD`
`REN C:\CL\4.CMD 3.CMD`
`REN C:\CL\5.CMD 4.CMD`
`REN C:\CL\6.CMD 5.CMD`
`REN C:\CL\7.CMD 6.CMD`
`REN C:\CL\8.CMD 7.CMD`
`REN C:\CL\9.CMD 8.CMD`
	Rename the remaining files to keep the sequence correct.

`SET USE=9`	Use the 9-slot that was freed when 9.CMD was renamed to 8.CMD.
`GOTO USE`	Jump to a section to define the command-line file.
`:DISPLAY`	Beginning of the section to display the available command lines.

31-2 Continued.

Batch File Line	Explanation
`FOR %%J IN (0 1 2 3 4 5 6 7 8 9) DO CALL CL ABC123XYZ %%J`	Loop through all available command lines and call this batch file as a subroutine.
`GOTO END`	Exit the batch file.
`:SHOWTHEM`	Label marking the beginning of a subroutine section to display the command lines.
`IF NOT EXIST C:\CL\%2.CMD GOTO END`	If the command line does not exist, exit the subroutine.
`ECHO -%2-`	Display the command-line name.
`TYPE C:\CL\%2.CMD | FIND /V "@ECHO OFF"`	Display the contents of the command line, but skip the @ECHO OFF line.
`ECHO`	Display a blank line by echoing an Alt-255.
`GOTO END`	Exit the subroutine.

`:MISSING`
`ECHO You Did Not Enter`
`ECHO Anything After`
`ECHO The Name So CL Does`
`ECHO Not Know What To Do!`
`ECHO`
`GOTO EXPLAIN`
	Display an error message.

`:EXPLAIN`
`ECHO Enter CL D To Display`
`ECHO Existing Command Lines`
`ECHO`
`ECHO Enter CL # To Reuse`
`ECHO One Of The Existing`
`ECHO Command Lines Where #`
`ECHO Is The Number Of The`
`ECHO Command Line To Reuse`
`ECHO`
`GOTO DISPLAY`
	Display an error message.

Batch File Line	Explanation

`:HELP`
`    ECHO Enter CL D To Display`
`    ECHO Existing Command Lines`
`    ECHO`
`    ECHO Enter CL # To Reuse`
`    ECHO One Of The Existing`
`    ECHO Command Lines Where #`
`    ECHO Is The Number Of The`
`    ECHO Command Line To Reuse`
`GOTO END`
	Display a help screen and exit the batch file when the user requests help.

`:END`	Label marking the end of the batch file.

Summary

- Between MACRO.CMD, CL.CMD, and the built-in OS/2 support for multiple commands on a single command line, you have most of the functions of MS-DOS DOSKEY program.
- With MACRO.CMD and CL.CMD, you also have the advantage of storing information between sessions automatically without having to do anything special.

32 Smaller batch file applications

This chapter presents a number of shorter batch file applications, some of them mundane and others unique. This diversity has two purposes. First, I want you to see how you can use fairly simple batch files to solve everyday problems. Second, by presenting you with batch files that solve unusual problems, I hope to make you think about how you can solve your own unique problems with a batch file.

Screen savers

A screen saver is a program that blanks the screen until you press a key. Screen savers are currently very popular, and you can buy them with all kinds of pictures displayed on the screen instead of a completely blank screen. You can also construct your own screen saver with a very short batch file. NOBURN.CMD does just this. While it has lines for command-line help, its two operational lines are:

```
CLS
PAUSE > NUL
```

The CLS blanks the screen and PAUSE > NUL keeps the prompt from reappearing until you press a key.

NOBURN.CMD can be run from the command line or installed as an icon on your desktop. If installed on the desktop, be sure to configure it to run in full-screen mode. While NOBURN.CMD isn't as fancy as commercial programs, it's free and requires no memory when you aren't using it. It's also an excellent way to keep casual snoops from reading your screen if you must step away from your computer for a few moments.

Changing subdirectories

Many users have a very complex directory structure that's nested several levels deep. They often need to leave one subdirectory to check something in another subdirectory and then switch back, and are looking for a way to automate this.

If you need or want to tackle the problem with batch files, you have a couple of alternatives. If you're always switching between just a couple of subdirectories, you can write a custom batch file to change to each subdirectory. For example, you could write a batch file called 0-9.CMD with the single command:

```
CD\D\LOTUSFIG\0-9
```

to change to that subdirectory. I use this method to change back to my home directory on the network at the office, because entering CD\D\USERS\MKTEVAL\RICHARDS is a bit much.

Of course, this can become a complex solution if you have a lot of subdirectories to change between. You can also write a batch file to partially solve this problem. This batch file marks the current directory as home and builds a second batch file to always return you to the home directory. The next time you run this batch file, it will create a new home directory and a new batch file to change you to there. The batch file RETURN.CMD:

```
COPY C:\BAT\RETURN C:\BAT\RETURNTO.CMD
CD >> C:\BAT\RETURNTO.CMD
```

copies a file called RETURN to the batch file named RETURNTO.CMD. RETURN contains the single line:

```
CD ^z
```

where ^z is an end-of-file marker. Because there's no return in the file, when the next line of RETURN.CMD pipes in the subdirectory, it gets added to the same line as the CD. The result is a line similar to this:

```
CD C:\D\LOTUSFIG\0-9
```

Even though this path includes the drive, this approach won't change drives. That is, if you're trying to change to the \D\LOTUSFIG\0-9 subdirectory on the C: drive but issue this command from the D: drive, OS/2 will remain on the D: drive and won't change to the appropriate subdirectory.

Because the batch file must be in a subdirectory in the path in order for it to work, RETURN.CMD is configured to always use the C:\BAT subdirectory. For that reason, every time you run RETURN.CMD, it overwrites RETURNTO.CMD with a new version. You can expand RETURN.CMD to handle multiple subdirectories by using a replaceable parameter on the command line and creating RETURN1.CMD, RETURN2.CMD, and so on. I'll leave this up to you.

If you don't want to create a custom batch file, you can use the batch file RETURN2.CMD as follows:

```
@ECHO OFF
%DRIVE%
CD %HOME%
```

This batch file requires you to issue the commands:

```
SET HOME=\D\LOTUSFIG\0-9
SET DRIVE=C:
```

to tell RETURN2.CMD which subdirectory is home. The only real drawback to RETURN2.CMD is that you have to manually type the home subdirectory into the environment. Of course, if you'll be using the same home subdirectory for a long period of time, you can place these SET commands in your CONFIG.SYS file.

You can avoid having to enter the home subdirectory into the environment by using RETURN3.CMD to change to a subdirectory originally—which you must do anyway. When RETURN3.CMD changes to a subdirectory, it must be passed the drive (with the colon) and the subdirectory separately. It first records these in the environment with the commands:

```
SET DRIVE=%1
SET HOME=%2
```

and then changes to that drive and subdirectory with the commands:

```
%1
CD\
CD %2
```

When you use RETURN3.CMD without a subdirectory, it changes back to the last subdirectory stored in the environment, using the same commands. Since RETURN3.CMD changes back to the root directory first, it doesn't matter if you precede the subdirectory with a backslash or if you leave it off. If you like, you can modify RETURN3.CMD to record multiple home subdirectories in the environment.

If you routinely change between only a few subdirectories, it is possible to duplicate the power of the Norton Utilities NCD program with a batch file. The batch file RCD.CMD does just this. Run RCD.CMD by including a shortcut name of a subdirectory to change to after the batch file name. So RCD.CMD consists of a number of different sections, all looking similar to the following:

```
:BAT
 C:
 CD\BAT
GOTO END
```

RCD.CMD uses a GOTO %1 to jump to that label, where it issues a command to change to that subdirectory. Because you can have multiple labels together in a batch file, it's possible to assign multiple shortcut names to a single subdirectory. The problem with RCD.CMD is that you must manually append each new subdirectory. Additionally, if you specify a shortcut name that doesn't exist, the batch file will abort with a "The system cannot find the batch label specified" error message. RCD.CMD has no trouble changing drives because you can easily program that into the batch file.

Finding files

While the batch file isn't as flexible as some comparable commercial programs, you can use it as a fast file-searching program. The ATTRIB (short for *attribute*) program was designed to change the attributes of files. It works across subdirectories using an /S switch. Because running ATTRIB without any switches to change the status of files causes it to list all the files it finds matching your file specification, ATTRIB can work as a file-finding utility. FASTFIND.CMD uses the ATTRIB command for just this purpose. Its single operational line is:

```
ATTRIB \%1 /S | MORE
```

Batch file floppy-disk catalog

You can use a batch file to catalog disks, and it works fairly well if you have only a few disks. If you have more than a few, however, you're probably better off buying one of the many shareware disk-cataloging programs that are available because the batch file method is fairly slow and lacks important error-checking. Be careful when you use it and make frequent backups.

CATALOG.CMD is the batch file that creates the catalog. After some error-checking, it changes to the C:\CATALOG subdirectory and issues the following command to create the catalog:

```
FOR %%j in (A:\*.*) DO ECHO %%j
 %1 %2 %3 %4 %5 %6 %7 %8 %9 >> C:CATALOG.TXT
```

CATALOG.CMD lacks any error-checking at all—I've left this for you to add. The batch file should determine that it's logged into the proper drive and subdirectory before running. As written, the batch file makes sure the user enters a name and then uses the FOR loop to cycle through all the files on the A: drive.

REMOVE.CMD is a batch file for removing entries. It also lacks much error-checking, but it's impossible to add some with batch commands. The basic problem is using the FIND command to select lines to delete. If you start the batch file with the replaceable parameter OFFICE, it not only deletes the lines with the added label OFFICE, it also deletes the file OF FICE.TAX and any other line containing the line OFFICE. For this reason, use this cataloging method with a great deal of care and frequent backups.

REMOVE.CMD first copies CATALOG.TXT to CATALOG.BAK as a backup in case there's a problem. Then it types CATALOG.TXT, using a FIND filter to locate all the lines not containing the TXT specified, and pipes that to a temporary file with the command:

```
TYPE CATALOG.TXT | FIND /V "%FIND%" > JUNK.TMP
```

It then deletes CATALOG.TXT and renames JUNK.TMP to CATALOG.TXT.

Adding to and deleting from your path

Most people simply include every subdirectory they need to search through in the path and forget it. There are occasions, however, when you might want to have two separate paths (for example, if you're testing a new program and don't want OS/2 to search anywhere other than the current subdirectory, if you've added a subdirectory for a special program and want it in the path for only a short period of time, or if you have so many subdirectories to search that you want to have a separate path for each task). The plan of attack is the same for each of these problems. The steps are as follows:

1. Store the current path to a variable in the environment.
2. Replace the path with a new path or modify the existing path.
3. Restore the old path from the environment.

A batch file can store the current path to another environmental variable with the command:

```
SET OLDPATH=%PATH%
```

Of course, at this point, two versions of your path exist—one stored under OLDPATH and one stored under PATH.

If you want to create a new path, it will be easier to either write a custom batch file for each alternative path or simply enter it from the command line. However, if you have two or three alternative paths that you use a lot, you might want to have a batch file that uses a replaceable parameter to let you select between them. For example:

```
@ECHO OFF
IF (%1)==(1) SET PATH=C:\;C:\DBASE
IF (%1)==(2) SET PATH=C:\;C:\WORD
IF (%1)==(3) SET PATH=C:\;C:\NORTON
```

would let you switch rapidly between three different paths. You could even use this same batch file to restore the original path with two modifications:

```
@ECHO OFF
IF (%1)==() SET PATH=%OLDPATH%
IF (%1)==() SET OLDPATH=
```

```
IF (%1)==(1) SET PATH=C:\;C:\DBASE
IF (%1)==(2) SET PATH=C:\;C:\WORD
IF (%1)==(3) SET PATH=C:\;C:\NORTON
```

A batch file can also remove subdirectories from your path, although the process is a little tricky. A batch file has access to the %PATH% environmental variable but has no way to strip it into its component parts. However, the different subdirectories in a path are separated by semicolons, which OS/2 treats as legal dividers for replaceable parameters. So if you issue the command:

```
BATCH %PATH%
```

and have OS/2 treat %PATH% as the environmental variable, then the first subdirectory in the path would be %1, the second would be %2, and so on. The batch file EDITPATH.CMD uses this to loop through the subdirectories in your path, one at a time. It uses YESORNO.CMD to ask if you want to keep each subdirectory in your path, and removes those you don't want. EDITPATH.CMD is shown in FIG. 32-1. You must run EDITPATH .CMD with the command:

```
EDITPATH %PATH%
```

As you elect to keep each subdirectory, EDITPATH.CMD stores that subdirectory in a temporary environmental variable called P. Only when you finished making all your selections is the contents of the PATH environmental variable replaced with the contents of the P environmental variable.

Batch File Line	Explanation
`@ECHO OFF`	Turn command-echoing off.

`REM NAME:     EDITPATH.CMD`
`REM PURPOSE: Selectively`
`REM          Delete Path`
`REM          Subdirectories`
`REM VERSION: 1.00`
`REM DATE:    December 14, 1992`
	Documentation remarks.

`IF (%1)==(?)  GOTO HELP`
`IF (%1)==(/?) GOTO HELP`
`IF (%1)==(/h) GOTO HELP`
`IF (%1)==(/H) GOTO HELP`
	If the user requested help, jump to a special section to display help information.

`IF (%1)==()   GOTO HELP`	This batch file must be passed %PATH% as the first replaceable parameter so if no replaceable parameter is passed, it's being run wrong so jump to the help section.

32-1 EDITPATH.CMD lets you select subdirectories to keep in your path one at a time.

Batch File Line	Explanation

`REM The Environmental Variable`
`REM P Will Contain The New`
`REM Path - You Must Maintain The Path`
`REM So Utilities Will Work - P`
`REM Is Used So "SET P=" Is As`
`REM Close In Length To "PATH="`
`REM As Is Possible`
	Documentation remarks.

`SET P=`	Reset the environmental variable used to construct the new path.

`REM FLAG Environmental`
`REM Variable Used To Track`
`REM Additions Since First`
`REM Addition To Path Must`
`REM Skip Leading Semicolon`
	Documentation remarks.

`SET FLAG=0`	Set the environmental variable that is used as a flag to zero.
`:TOP`	Label marking the top of the loop used to process the path.
`IF (%1)==() GOTO ENDLOOP`	If no more subdirectories remain in the path, exit the loop.
`ECHO`	Display a blank line by echoing an Alt-255.
`ECHO Keep %1 In Path (Y/N)?`	Ask the user about keeping the next subdirectory in the path.
`CALL YESORNO`	Run YESORNO.CMD to get an answer.
`IF ERRORLEVEL 1 GOTO SKIP`	If the user answers no, skip over the section used to append this subdirectory to the path.
`IF %FLAG%==1 SET FLAG=2`	If the flag environmental variable equals one, exactly one subdirectory has been appended to path so increase to two.
`IF %FLAG%==0 SET FLAG=1`	If the flag environmental variable equals zero, increase to one to indicate the first subdirectory has been added.

32-1 Continued.

Batch File Line	Explanation
`IF %FLAG%==1 SET P=%1`	If the flag environmental variable equals one, batch file is appending first subdirectory so do not add semicolon to front.
`IF %FLAG%==1 GOTO SKIP`	If the flag environmental variable equals one, skip the next command.
`SET P=%P%;%1`	If the batch file reaches this point, then a subdirectory other than the first subdirectory is being appended to the path so insert a semicolon in front of subdirectory.
`:SKIP`	Label used to mark the spot to skip to when the user does not want to keep a subdirectory in the path.
`SHIFT`	Move all the replaceable parameters down one level.
`GOTO TOP`	Continue looping.
`:ENDLOOP`	Label used to mark the section to jump to when all the subdirectories have been processed.
`PATH %P%`	Change the path to the value stored in the P environmental variable.
`ECHO PATH Now Set To:` `PATH`	Tell the user the new path.
`SET FLAG=` `SET P=`	Reset the environmental variables used by the batch file.
`GOTO END`	Exit the batch file.

`:HELP`
`ECHO This Batch File Is`
`ECHO Used To Remove`
`ECHO Subdirectories From`
`ECHO PATH Run With Command`
`ECHO EDITPATH %%PATH%%`
`GOTO END`
	Display a help screen and exit the batch file when the user requests help.

`:END`	Label marking the end of the batch file.

There are two problems that EDITPATH.CMD has to avoid. First, the first subdirectory added to the path is not preceded by a semicolon while all the remaining subdirectories are. Second, the length of any command line cannot exceed 300 characters, yet the path itself can be 295 characters. (Five characters are needed for the PATH and space that precedes the path when you create it.)

When I first started writing this batch file, I tried to avoid adding the semicolon before the first subdirectory with these two IF tests:

```
IF NOT (%PATH%)==() SET PATH=%PATH%;%1
IF (%PATH%)==() SET PATH=%1
```

This approach works well as long as the path is fairly short. However, the path environmental variable is used twice in the first IF test, so a moderately long path could cause this statement to exceed the 300-character limit on the command line. EDITPATH.CMD avoids this problem by setting the FLAG environmental variable to zero and then incrementing it to one the first time through and to two after that. The leading semicolon is avoided only when FLAG has a value of one.

EDITPATH.CMD constructs a second environmental variable called P to contain the modified path until the end of the batch file when the path is replaced with the contents of the P environmental variable. The reason for this is quite pragmatic. If the path was reset at the beginning of the batch file and reconstructed in the batch file—rather than using P—then YESORNO wouldn't run because it's no longer in your path!

Summary

- NOBURN.CMD is a simple screen saver that runs from the command line and requires so little memory that you can run it while shelled out of another program.
- One way to quickly change to a single subdirectory is with a custom batch file.
- A batch file like RETURN.CMD can store the current subdirectory in a batch file for instant return.
- A batch file like RETURN2.CMD can store a single subdirectory in the environment for quick changes.
- A batch file like RCD.CMD can quickly switch between a number of subdirectories.
- Combining the ATTRIB command with a batch file gives you a quick and powerful file-location program.
- CATALOG.CMD and REMOVE.CMD function as simple batch file floppy-disk cataloging programs.
- Passing the path to a batch file as a replaceable parameter gives the batch file access to the subdirectories in the path as individual replaceable parameters.
- A batch file like EDITPATH.CMD lets you pick subdirectories individually to keep in or discard from the path.

Appendices

Well, you've almost reached the end of the book. I hope you enjoyed reading it as much as I enjoyed writing it. Hopefully, you'll find the reference material in this section useful.

Appendix A: Solutions to review problems This appendix explains my solutions to the various problems I asked you to attempt. You could have a different solution that is just as good or even better, so don't worry if your solution doesn't match mine.

Appendix B: Batch file documentation This appendix briefly documents all the batch files and other utilities you'll find on the disk.

Appendix C: Icons Many batch files run other programs. In order to assign the appropriate icon to many of your batch files, you're going to need many general-purpose icons. These are included on the disk. To help you quickly find the right one, this appendix shows all the icons and their associated filenames.

Appendix D: Batch file icons The batch files that come with this book have their own icons. Each icon has the same name as the batch file, only with an .ICO extension. This appendix shows all the batch file icons and their associated filenames.

Appendix E: Utility icons The utilities that come with this book have their own icons, each with the same name as the utility only with an .ICO extension. This appendix shows all the batch file icons and their associated filenames.

A
Solutions to review problems

Problem	Figure	Batch file	Notes
1	A-1	FORMAT.CMD	Safely formats a floppy disk in A:
2	A-2	PROBLEM2.CMD	Performs environmental management tasks.It takes several lines to set the path, but could be done in one.
3	A-3	ACCTHELP.CMD	Provides information about several accounting problems.
4	A-4	RUNCHECK.CMD	Continually runs a diagnostic program.
5	A-5	BOOT-4-D.CMD	Checks to see if D: is operational and reboots if not.
6	A-6	READFILE.CMD	Automates displaying ASCII files.
7	A-7	COPYTHEM.CMD	Copies all files entered on the command line to A: only if they don't already exist there.
8	A-8	USEOVER.CMD	Allows you to reuse commands.
9	A-9	COPYTHE2.CMD	Modification of #7; prompts user whether or not to overwrite files that already exist on A:.

I hope you've enjoyed working on these nine problems. I expect some of your answers are very different from mine. I also expect that many of you came up with even better solutions! If you can successfully tackle these problems, then you're ready for any batch file challenges your computing is likely to toss your way.

Batch File Line	Explanation
`@ECHO OFF`	Turn command-echoing off.

`REM NAME:     FORMAT.CMD`
`REM PURPOSE: Format Disk In A:`
`     Drive`
`REM VERSION: 1.00`
`REM DATE:     May 17, 1993`
	Documentation remarks.

`IF (%1)==(?)  GOTO HELP`
`IF (%1)==(/?) GOTO HELP`
`IF (%1)==(/h) GOTO HELP`
`IF (%1)==(/H) GOTO HELP`
	If the user requested help, jump to a special section to display help information.

`ECHO Insert A New Disk In A:`
`ECHO Drive. Remember That`
`ECHO Formatting Will Erase`
`ECHO Anything Already Stored`
`ECHO On This Disk`
`ECHO`
`ECHO To Abort Formatting Just`
`ECHO Press Ctrl-Break`
`ECHO`
`ECHO Press Any Other Key Once`
`ECHO Disk Is In The A: Drive`
	Tell the user what is happening.

`PAUSE`	Pause the program until the user presses a key.
`XYZ A: /ONCE`	Format a disk in the A: drive.
`GOTO END`	Exit the batch file.

`:HELP`
`   ECHO Formats Disk In A:`
`   ECHO Drive Using HPFS Fat`
`GOTO END`
	Display a help screen and exit the batch file when the user requests help.

`:END`	Label marking the end of the batch file.

A-1 Answer to problem 1. FORMAT.CMD gives some general information on formatting a disk and then pauses before the actual formatting in case the user wants to press Ctrl–Break.

Batch File Line	Explanation
`@ECHO OFF`	Turn command-echoing off.

`REM NAME:     PROBLEM2.CMD`
`REM PURPOSE: Solution To`
`     Problem 2`
`REM VERSION: 1.00`
`REM DATE:    May 27, 1993`
	Documentation remarks.

`IF (%1)==(?)  GOTO HELP`
`IF (%1)==(/?) GOTO HELP`
`IF (%1)==(/h) GOTO HELP`
`IF (%1)==(/H) GOTO HELP`
	If the user requested help, jump to a special section to display help information.

`PATH;`	Reset the path.

`SET PATH=C:\`
`SET PATH=%PATH%;C:\NORTON`
`SET PATH=%PATH%;C:\123`
`SET PATH=%PATH%;C:\WP`
`SET PATH=%PATH%;C:\UTILITY`
`SET PATH=%PATH%;C:\BAT`
	Create a new path.

`SET TEMP=C:\TEMP`
`SET DOSONLY=NO`
`SET LIB=D:\BLDLITE`
`SET OBJ=D:\BLDLITE`
	Create environmental variables.

`CONFIGPT`	Run a program to configure the printer.
`GOTO END`	Exit the batch file.

`:HELP`
` ECHO Performs Several Tasks:`
` ECHO 1. Resets Path`
` ECHO 2. Creates Set Variables`
` ECHO 3. Configures Printer`
`GOTO END`
	Display a help screen and exit the batch file when the user requests help.

`:END`	Label marking the end of the batch file.

A-2 Answer to problem 2. PROBLEM2.CMD changes the path, creates several environmental variables, and runs the CONFIGPT.EXE program.

Batch File Line	Explanation
@ECHO OFF	Turn command-echoing off.
REM NAME: ACCTHELP.CMD REM PURPOSE: Provide Accounting Help REM VERSION: 1.00 REM DATE: May 12, 1993	Documentation remarks.
CLS	Clear the screen.
ECHO Introduction ECHO ——— ECHO ECHO This Accounting System Uses	Display information for the user.
ECHO Daily ECHO ECHO This Program Performs The ECHO Closing That Is Required ECHO Each Day. It Can Be Run ECHO By Any Clerk Using The ECHO Clerical Password. Note ECHO That It Must Be Run ECHO After 4PM And Not Before. ECHO	Display information for the user.
PAUSE	Pause the program.
CLS	Clear the screen.
ECHO Weekly ECHO ECHO This Program Performs The ECHO Closing That Is Required ECHO Each Week. It Can Be ECHO Run By Only A Senior Clerk Or ECHO Above And Requires A ECHO Management-1 Password. It ECHO Must Be Run On The Last ECHO Working Day Of The Month ECHO And Must Be Run After ECHO Running The Daily ECHO Closing Program. ECHO	Display information for the user.

A-3 Answer to problem 3. ACCTHELP.CMD explains how to use three accounting programs stored on the computer.

Batch File Line	Explanation
ECHO Annual ECHO ECHO This Programs Performs ECHO The Annual Closing ECHO Required At The End ECHO Of Each Year. It Can ECHO Be Run By Only A Branch ECHO Manager And Requires ECHO A Management-4 Password. ECHO It Must Be Run On The ECHO Last Day Of The Year ECHO After Running The ECHO Daily Closing Program. ECHO	Display information for the user.
PAUSE	Pause the program until the user presses a key.
CLS	Clear the screen.
ECHO Backups ECHO ------- ECHO ECHO Corporate Policy Requires ECHO Two Backups To Be ECHO Performed After A Weekly ECHO Closing. One Backup Must ECHO Be Sent To The IS ECHO Department At ECHO Headquarters (24/185) ECHO And The Other Retained ECHO Locally. Three Backups ECHO Are Required After An ECHO Annual Closing. In ECHO Addition To The IS And ECHO Local Copies, A Copy Is ECHO To Be Sent To The Legal ECHO Department (28/185). ECHO	Display information for the user.
ECHO More Help ECHO --------- ECHO If You Need More Help, ECHO Contact: ECHO ECHO Mark Williams ECHO 24/185 ECHO Extension 256	Display information for the user.
PAUSE	Pause the program until the user presses a key.

Batch File Line	Explanation
`@ECHO OFF`	Turn command-echoing off.

`REM NAME:     RUNCHECK.CMD`
`REM PURPOSE: Run Check-It-Out`
`    Program`
`REM          And Report Errors`
`REM          Solution To Problem #4`
`REM VERSION: 1.00`
`REM DATE:    May 17, 1993`
	Documentation remarks.

`IF (%1)==(?)  GOTO HELP` `IF (%1)==(/?) GOTO HELP`	If the user requested help, jump to a special section to display help information.
`CLS`	Clear the screen.
`:TOP`	Label marking top of loop.
`   CHKITOUT`	Run Check-It-Out program.
`   IF ERRORLEVEL 1 ECHO Check-It-Out Had Problems`	If an error is reported, display error message.
`   IF ERRORLEVEL 1 GOTO TOP`	If an error is reported, continue looping.
`   ECHO Check-It-Out Ran Fine` `GOTO TOP`	The batch file reaches this point only if no error occurred so it displays a message and continues looping.

`:HELP`
`   ECHO Continually Runs CHKITOUT`
`GOTO END`
	Display a help screen and exit the batch file when the user requests help.

`:END`	Label marking the end of the batch file.

A-4 Answer to problem 4. RUNCHECK.CMD continually runs a program called Check-It-Out and displays the results on the screen.

Batch File Line	Explanation
`@ECHO OFF`	Turn command-echoing off.

`REM NAME:     BOOT-4-D.CMD`
`REM PURPOSE: Reboot Until D:`
`    Drive Works`
`REM          Solution To`
`    Problem #5`
`REM VERSION: 1.00`
`REM DATE:    May 17, 1993`
	Documentation remarks.

`IF (%1)==(?)  GOTO HELP` `IF (%1)==(/?) GOTO HELP`	If the user requested help, jump to a special section to display help information.
`IF EXIST D:\*.* GOTO END`	If any files on the D: drive exist, the D: drive must exist so exit the batch file.
`BOOT`	Run the BOOT program to reboot.

`REM Since The Computer Reboots`
`    Here`
`REM The Rest Of This Batch`
`    File`
`REM Is Not Processed`
	Documentation remarks.

`:HELP`
`   ECHO Reboots If D:Drive`
`   ECHO Not Working`
`GOTO END`
	Display a help screen and exit the batch file when the user requests help.

`:END`	Label marking the end of the batch file.

A-5 Answer to problem 5. BOOT-4-D.CMD is called from the Startup folder and reboots the computer if the D: drive is not working.

Batch File Line	Explanation
`@ECHO OFF`	Turn command-echoing off.

`REM NAME:     READFILE.CMD`
`REM PURPOSE: Display ASCII Files`
`REM VERSION: 1.00`
`REM DATE:     May 17, 1993`
	Documentation remarks.

`IF (%1)==(?)  GOTO HELP` `IF (%1)==(/?) GOTO HELP`	If the user requested help, jump to a special section to display help information.
`:TOP`	Label marking the top of the loop to display the files.
`CLS`	Clear the screen.
`IF (%1)==() GOTO END`	If there are no more files to display, exit the batch file.
`ECHO Displaying %1`	Tell the user the name of the file to be displayed.
`TYPE %1 | MORE`	Use the MORE filter to display the next file.
`SHIFT`	Move all the replaceable parameters down one level.
`GOTO TOP`	Continue looping.

`:HELP`
`ECHO Display ASCII Files`
`GOTO END`
	Display a help screen and exit the batch file when the user requests help.

`:END`	Label marking the end of the batch file.

A-6 Answer to problem 6. READFILE.CMD displays the files entered on the command line one at a time by typing them to the screen and using the MORE filter to display them one screen at a time.

Batch File Line	Explanation
`@ECHO OFF`	Turn command-echoing off.

`REM NAME:     COPYTHEM.CMD`
`REM PURPOSE: Copy Files To A: Drive`
`REM VERSION: 1.00`
`REM DATE:     May 26, 1993`
	Documentation remarks.

`IF (%1)==(/?) GOTO HELP`
`IF (%1)==(?)  GOTO HELP`
`IF (%1)==(/h) GOTO HELP`
`IF (%1)==(/H) GOTO HELP`
`IF (%1)==()   GOTO ERROR`
	If the user requested help, jump to a special section to display help information.

`IF (%1)==(XYZ123ABC) GOTO SUB`	If the batch file is being called as a subroutine, jump to a special section to handle that.
`:TOP`	Label marking the top of the main processing loop.
`   IF ERRORLEVEL 1 GOTO END`	If XCOPY reports an error, then exit the batch file.
`   IF (%1)==() GOTO END`	Once there are no more files to copy, exit the batch file.
`   FOR %%J in (%1) DO CALL COPYTHEM XYZ123ABC %%J`	Loop through all the files in the first replaceable parameter and call this batch file as a subroutine.
`   SHIFT`	Move all the replaceable parameters down one level.
`GOTO TOP`	Continue looping.
`:SUB`	Label marking the top of the subroutine.
`   IF EXIST A:%2 ECHO %2 Is Already On A:Drive` `   IF EXIST A:%2 GOTO END`	If the file already exists on the A: drive, display an error message and exit. (Remember that when running as a subroutine, %1 is the flag and %2 is the filename.)
`   XCOPY %2 A:`	Perform the actual copying.

A-7 Answer to problem 7. COPYTHEM.CMD copies all the files specified on the command line to the A: drive only if they don't already exist on the A: drive.

A-7 Continued.

Batch File Line	Explanation
`IF ERRORLEVEL 1 ECHO Problem Copying %2`	If XCOPY reports an error, display an error message. The actual exiting will be performed in the main routine.
`GOTO END`	Exit the subroutine.

`:ERROR`
`ECHO Must Specify Files To`
`ECHO Copy On Command Line`
`GOTO END`
	Display an error message when the user does not enter the names of any files to process.

`:HELP`
`ECHO Copies The Files You`
`ECHO Specify On The Command`
`ECHO Line To The A:Drive`
`ECHO Without Writing`
`ECHO Over Any Files`
`GOTO END`
	Display a help screen and exit the batch file when the user requests help.

`:END`	Label marking the end of the batch file.

Batch File Line	Explanation
`@ECHO OFF`	Turn command-echoing off.

`REM NAME:    USEOVER.CMD`
`REM PURPOSE: Use A Command Over And Over`
`REM VERSION: 1.02`
`REM DATE:    August 3, 1992`
	Documentation remarks.

`IF (%1)==(/?) GOTO HELP`
`IF (%1)==(?)  GOTO HELP`
`IF (%1)==(/h) GOTO HELP`
`IF (%1)==(/H) GOTO HELP`
	If the user requested help, jump to a special section to display help information.

`IF (%1)==() IF (%COMMAND%)==() GOTO NOTHING`	If the user did not enter any commands, and no command is stored in the environment, jump to an error-handling section.

A-8 Answer to problem 8. When run with a command following its name, USEOVER.CMD stores that command to an environmental variable and then runs the command. When run alone, USEOVER.CMD runs the command stored in the environment.

Batch File Line	Explanation
`IF (%1)==() GOTO JUSTCMD`	If the user did not enter any command and it reaches this point, a command is stored in the environment so jump to a section to run that command.
`REM Construct Command in` `REM Environmental Variable`	Documentation remarks.
`SET COMMAND=`	Reset the environmental variable.
`:TOP`	Label marking the top of a loop to construct the command.
`   SET COMMAND=%COMMAND% %1`	Store the first replaceable parameter to the environmental variable.
`   SHIFT`	Move all the replaceable parameters down one level.
`   IF (%1)==() GOTO JUSTCMD`	If there are no more parts to the command, jump to the section to run the command.
`GOTO TOP`	Continue looping.
`:JUSTCMD`	Label marking the beginning of the section to run the command.
`%COMMAND%`	Run the command stored in the environment.
`GOTO END`	Exit the batch file.

`:HELP`
`   ECHO JUSTCMD`
`   ECHO Runs Stored Command`
`   ECHO JUSTCMD Part1...PartN`
`   ECHO Stores And Runs The`
`   ECHO New Command`
`GOTO END`
	Display a help screen and exit the batch file when the user requests help.

`:NOTHING`
`   ECHO No Command Stored In`
`   ECHO Environment`
`   ECHO Before Using You Must`
`   ECHO Store A Command`
`GOTO END`
	Tell the user a command must be stored in environment before it can be run.

`:END`	Label marking the end of the batch file.

Batch File Line	Explanation
`@ECHO OFF`	Turn command-echoing off.

`REM NAME:     COPYTHE2.CMD`
`REM          Modified For`
`REM          Problem 9 With`
`REM          Name COPYTHE2.BAT`
`REM PURPOSE: Copy Files To A: Drive`
`REM VERSION: 2.00`
`REM DATE:    May 26, 1993`
	Documentation remarks.

`IF (%1)==(/?) GOTO HELP`
`IF (%1)==(?)  GOTO HELP`
`IF (%1)==(/h) GOTO HELP`
`IF (%1)==(/H) GOTO HELP`
`IF (%1)==()   GOTO ERROR`
	If the user requested help, jump to a special section to display help information.

`IF (%1)==(XYZ123ABC) GOTO SUB`	If the batch file is being called as a subroutine, jump to a special section to handle that.
`:TOP`	Label marking the top of the main processing loop.
`IF ERRORLEVEL 1 GOTO END`	If XCOPY reports an error, then exit the batch file.
`IF (%1)==() GOTO END`	Once there are no more files to copy, exit the batch file.
`FOR %%J in (%1) DO CALL COPYTHE2 XYZ123ABC %%J`	Loop through all the files in the first replaceable parameter and call this batch file as a subroutine.
`SHIFT`	Move all the replaceable parameters down one level.
`GOTO TOP`	Continue looping.
`:SUB`	Label marking the top of the subroutine.
`IF EXIST A:%2 GOTO DUP`	If the file already exists on the A: drive, jump to another section.

A-9 Answer to problem 9. COPYTHE2.CMD copies all the files specified on the command line to the A: drive. Unlike COPYTHEM.CMD, COPYTHE2.CMD will ask the user what to do if there's already a version of the files on the A: drive.

Batch File Line	Explanation
`XCOPY %2 A:`	Perform the actual copying.
`IF ERRORLEVEL 1 ECHO Problem Copying %2`	If XCOPY reports an error, display an error message. The actual exiting will be performed in the main routine.
`GOTO END`	Exit the subroutine.
`:DUP`	Label marking the beginning of the section that handles the file already existing on the A: drive.

`ECHO %2 Already Exists On A:Drive`
`ECHO A:Drive`
`ECHO ----`
`DIR A:%2`
`ECHO Current Drive`
`ECHO -------`
`DIR %2`
`ECHO Overwrite %2 On A: Drive (Y/N)?`
	Explain the problem, show the user both files with the DIR command, and ask what to do.

`CALL YESORNO`	Run YESORNO.CMD to get a response from the user.
`IF ERRORLEVEL 1 GOTO END`	If the user answers no (do not copy) then exit subroutine.
`XCOPY %2 A:`	It reaches this point only if the user answers yes to copy the file.
`IF ERRORLEVEL 1 ECHO Problem Copying %2`	If XCOPY reports an error, display an error message. The actual exiting will be performed in the main routine.
`GOTO END`	Exit the subroutine.

`:ERROR`
`ECHO Must Specify Files To`
`ECHO Copy On Command Line`
`GOTO END`
	Display an error message when the user does not enter the names of any files to process.

A-9 Continued.

Batch File Line	Explanation

`:HELP`
`   ECHO Copies The Files You`
`   ECHO Specify On The Command`
`   ECHO Line To The A:Drive`
`   ECHO Without Writing`
`   ECHO Over Any Files`
`GOTO END`
	Display a help screen and exit the batch file when the user requests help.

`:END`	Label marking the end of the batch file.

B

Batch file documentation

Batch file	Explanation
0-9.CMD	A demonstration batch file to quickly change to the C:\D\LOTUSFIG\0-9 subdirectory. Its main purpose is to show how to use batch files to quickly move around a hard disk.
2-THINGS.CMD	A demonstration batch file that shows batch files can run more than one command. This batch file simply runs CHKDSK followed by DIR.
A.CMD	A demonstration batch file for performing a directory of the A: drive. This batch file is used to illustrate improvements that can be made to batch files with more advanced commands.
ACCOUNT1.CMD	A demonstration batch file from chapter 19 that illustrates transferring the errorlevel to the environment by setting an environmental variable.
ACCOUNT2.CMD	A demonstration batch file from chapter 19 that uses the information put into the environment by AC COUNT1.CMD to make a decision.
ACCTHELP.CMD	A demonstration batch file that shows using a batch file to provide information to the user. This batch file provides information on a fictitious accounting system.
ANSIDEMO.CMD	A demonstration batch file that shows how much power ANSI has over screen colors, position, and formatting.

ANSIHIDE.CMD	A demonstration batch file that uses ANSI to hide command-line messages.
ANSIKEY1.CMD	A batch file to send pairs of ANSI keyboard reassignment codes. The numbers must be entered on the command line as replaceable parameters.
B.CMD	A demonstration batch file to perform an incremental backup.
BATCH.CMD	A demonstration batch file that uses the GOTO command to jump over some documentation remarks.
BLANK.CMD	A batch file that uses ANSI commands to blank the screen.
BOOT-4-D.CMD	A demonstration batch file designed to be used on a system with a problem D: drive that sometimes doesn't work when the computer is booted. This batch file checks for the D: drive on startup and reboots if it doesn't exist.
CAPITAL.CMD	A REXX program that will convert one word to uppercase and store it in the environment under the environmental variable RETURN.
CATALOG.CMD	A batch file for cataloging files on floppy disks.
CHECK.CMD	A batch file to run CHKDSK.
CHECKERR.CMD	A batch file to display the errorlevel.
CHECKER1.CMD	Another batch file to display the errorlevel.
CL.CMD	Stores up to ten command lines using files rather than memory. That allows them to be used across sessions. They are retained even if the computer is rebooted or turned off.
COMMANDS.CMD	A demonstration batch file that shows using replaceable parameters as commands. While possible, this technique is not recommended since the batch file author loses all control over the batch file.
COMPILE.CMD	A demonstration batch file designed to compile a program.
COPYBACK.CMD	Copies files to a backup subdirectory using a name specified on the command line.
COPYTHEM.CMD	Copies the files specified on the command line to the A: drive only if those files don't already exist on the A: drive.
COPYTHE2.CMD	Copies the files specified on the command line to the A: drive. If the files already exist on the A: drive, it asks the user what to do.
COUNT.CMD	A demonstration batch file that uses three nested FOR loops to count from 000 to 999.

DELOLD.CMD	A batch file to delete all the files in the C:\DISCARD subdirectory that were successfully copied to the A: drive.
DISCARD.CMD	A batch file to move unwanted files to the C:\DIS CARD subdirectory rather than erasing them.
EDITPATH.CMD	A batch file that loops through all the subdirectories in your path, asking you if you want to keep each one. Only those you elect to keep are left in your path. It must be started with the EDITPATH %PATH% command.
ENDLESS.CMD	A demonstration batch file that runs an endless loop. You must press Ctrl–Break to get out of the loop. It's useful to run in a window to slow down the computer if the need arises.
ENTERHEX.CMD	A demonstration batch file that alters certain keys on the number pad to make entering hexadecimal code easier. It has limited usefulness since it uses ANSI and most programs ignore ANSI keyboard reassignments.
FASTFIND.CMD	A batch file that uses ATTRIB to find files on your hard disk. The file to look for must be specified on the command line.
FORMAT.CMD	A demonstration batch file to handle floppy disk formatting. It handles only files on the A: drive, and FORMAT.COM must be renamed to XYZ.COM before it will work.
GET.CMD	A REXX program that gets one word from the user and stores it in the environment under the environmental variable name RETURN.
GET-ONE.CMD	A REXX program that gets one character from the user and sets the errorlevel equal to its ASCII value.
GET_0-9.CMD	A REXX program that gets a one-digit number from the user and stores that number in the errorlevel.
GETA2Z.CMD	A REXX program that gets one letter from the user and sets the errorlevel equal to one for A, two for B, and so on.
GETFILES.CMD	A demonstration batch file that is part of a collection of batch files to keep two hard disks in synchronization. It copies the files from the A: drive to the C: and D: drives.
HELLO.CMD	A demonstration batch file that says hello.
HELP.CMD	A demonstration batch file that provides limited information on other batch files.
HELP1.CMD	A demonstration batch file that provides limited context-sensitive information on other batch files.

HELPBAT.CMD	A batch file that displays the PURPOSE: line for every batch file in the F:\BAT subdirectory. This is a very good way to display batch file help. You might want to alter the F:\BAT subdirectory to the one you use for your batch files.
HELPBAT2.CMD	A demonstration batch file. It makes HELPBAT.CMD context-sensitive. While it displays only information about batch files that match the search criteria, it has the flaw of displaying all the batch file names.
HELPBAT3.CMD	A batch file that uses an OS/2 trick to overcome the limitation of HELPBAT2.CMD. This batch file is fully context-sensitive and displays the name and information on just the batch files that match the search criteria.
HI-ASCII.CMD	A demonstration batch file that shows using high-ordered ASCII characters to draw boxes in batch files.
I.CMD	A demonstration batch file that performs an incremental backup using the XCOPY command.
ISITZERO.CMD	A REXX program that sets the errorlevel to one if a file is a zero-length file, and zero if not.
KEY-1.CMD	A demonstration batch file that remaps the [] and () keys using ANSI. KEY-2.CMD returns them to their normal functions.
KEY-2.CMD	A demonstration batch file that returns the [] and () keys to normal after they were remapped using KEY-1.CMD. Requires ANSI to run.
LISTFILE.CMD	Pipes a list of all files to C:\CHANGED.TXT. This is useful prior to an incremental backup. Since CHANGED.TXT was just created, it's always backed up by an incremental backup.
LOCAL.CMD	A demonstration batch file showing how to use the SETLOCAL and ENDLOCAL commands in a batch file to save and restore the current environmental settings.
LOTUS.CMD	A demonstration batch file that runs Lotus with an altered prompt. That way, anyone shelling out of Lotus with the /S command will have a reminder that they've shelled out of another program.
MACRO.CMD	Stores up to ten macros using files rather than memory, which allows them to be used across sessions. They are retained even if the computer is rebooted or turned off.
NICEPROM.CMD	A demonstration batch file that displays a very colorful and fancy prompt using ANSI.

NOBURN.CMD	A simple screen-saver batch file. It should be run in a full-screen session for best results.
PREPARE.CMD	A demonstration batch file that's part of a collection of batch files to keep two hard disks in synchronization. It copies the files to the A: drive from the C: and D: drives.
PROBLEM2.CMD	A demonstration batch file that performs some environmental maintenance.
RCD.CMD	A demonstration quick subdirectory-changing batch file. Once reconfigured with your own list of subdirectories and nicknames, it can be quite handy.
READFILE.CMD	A demonstration batch file for displaying a series of ASCII files for easy reading.
REMOVE.CMD	A batch file for removing entries as part of a batch file floppy-disk cataloging system.
RETURN.CMD	A demonstration batch file to return to a subdirectory.
RETURN2.CMD	A demonstration batch file to change to the subdirectory stored in the environment.
RETURN3.CMD	A batch file that will change to the subdirectory specified on the command line and store it in the environment. Later, if it's run without a replaceable parameter, RETURN3.CMD changes back to the subdirectory it stored in the environment.
REXX-1.CMD	A demonstration REXX program that displays a message on the screen.
REXX-2.CMD	A demonstration REXX program that uses a variable to display a message on the screen.
REXX-3.CMD	A demonstration REXX program that performs some simple mathematics.
REXX-4.CMD	A demonstration REXX program that gets information from the user.
REXX-5.CMD	Another demonstration REXX program for getting information from the user.
REXX-6.CMD	A demonstration REXX program showing logic testing.
REXX-7.CMD	A demonstration REXX program showing looping.
REXX-8.CMD	A demonstration REXX program showing the LEAVE command for looping.
REXX-9.CMD	A demonstration REXX program showing looping a specific number of times.
REXX-10.CMD	Another demonstration REXX program showing looping a specific number of times, where the program has access to the loop counter.
REXX-11.CMD	A demonstration math text REXX program.

REXX-12.CMD	A demonstration counting REXX program.
RONNYMD.CMD	A batch file that creates a subdirectory branching off the current subdirectory and then changes to it. This batch file is used to illustrate improvements that can be made to batch files with more advanced commands.
RUNCHECK.CMD	A demonstration batch file that runs a fictitious diagnostic program and reports the results to the screen using the errorlevel.
SAMPLE.CMD	A sample batch file used to illustrate using the Enhanced Editor.
SENDANSI.CMD	A batch file for issuing simple ANSI commands without having to enter the Escape or the [.
SENDANS2.CMD	A batch file for issuing multiple ANSI commands. SENDANSI.CMD issues only one command at a time.
SHOW-A.CMD	A demonstration batch file that performs a directory of the A: drive.
SHOW-CAP.CMD	A demonstration batch file that illustrates using the CAPITAL.CMD REXX program in a batch file.
SHOWGETS.CMD	A demonstration batch file that shows how to use all the REXX utilities included with this book in a batch file.
SHOWPIPE.CMD	A demonstration batch file that shows using the three more unusual and useful command symbols available in OS/2: ||, &, and &&.
SHOWREPL.CMD	A demonstration batch file for showing replaceable parameters.
SHOWSHIFT.CMD	A demonstration batch file for showing the SHIFT command.
TEMP.CMD	A demonstration batch file used as part of the tutorial on ANSI.
TEMPLATE.CMD	A batch file template you can use as the basis for starting your own batch files.
TESTWILD.CMD	A demonstration batch file that will test to see if the first replaceable parameter is a wildcard.
TOA.CMD	This batch file copies files to the A: drive. It illustrates improvements that can be made to batch files with more advanced commands.
TXTSCRN.CMD	A demonstration batch file that displays three screens using the TYPE command and three ASCII files.
UNBLANK.CMD	A demonstration batch file that reverses the blanking effects of BLANK.CMD.
UNENTER.CMD	A demonstration batch file that uses ANSI to reverse the effects of the ENTERHEX.CMD batch file.

USEOVER.CMD	A batch file for reusing a command over and over.
WORD2QS.CMD	A demonstration batch file for loading a program into Microsoft Word for editing and then running it through a compiler.
WP.CMD	A demonstration batch file for starting Microsoft Word.
YESDOC.CMD	A demonstration batch file for copying files to the A: drive.
YESORNO.CMD	A REXX program that gets a Y or N response from the user and sets the errorlevel to one for no and zero for yes.

C
Icons

In order for your batch files to look their best under OS/2, you need icons to represent them. The disk that comes with this book contains 2,818 icons for popular programs and topics. These are public-domain icons downloaded from several popular OS/2 bulletin-board systems. To help you find the icons that best fit your needs, I've taken 41 screen shots showing all the icons on the disk. Those screen shots are at the end of this appendix.

The icons take up too much space (2.6Mb) to store on one floppy disk so I've compressed them into one file (ICONS.LZH) in the \ICONS subdirectory of the disk. The compression was performed with LHA version 2.13, copyright 1991 by Haruyasu Yoshizaki. So you can decompress the icons, a full copy of LHA is included in the \LHA subdirectory.

LHA is a DOS program that must be run in a DOS session. Since the icons take up so much space, I suggest you decompress just the ones you want. To decompress a single icon, use the command:

```
LHA e ICONS name
```

where *name* is the name of the icon you want to decompress. Of course, LHA.EXE must be in the current subdirectory or your path, and ICONS.LZH must be in the current subdirectory or you must specify a full path to it. Wildcards are allowed as part of the icon name, and using *.* will decompress all 2,818 icons.

The file ICONS.LZH does not contain the icons for the batch files or utilities. These are stored uncompressed in the same directory as their associated batch file or utility.

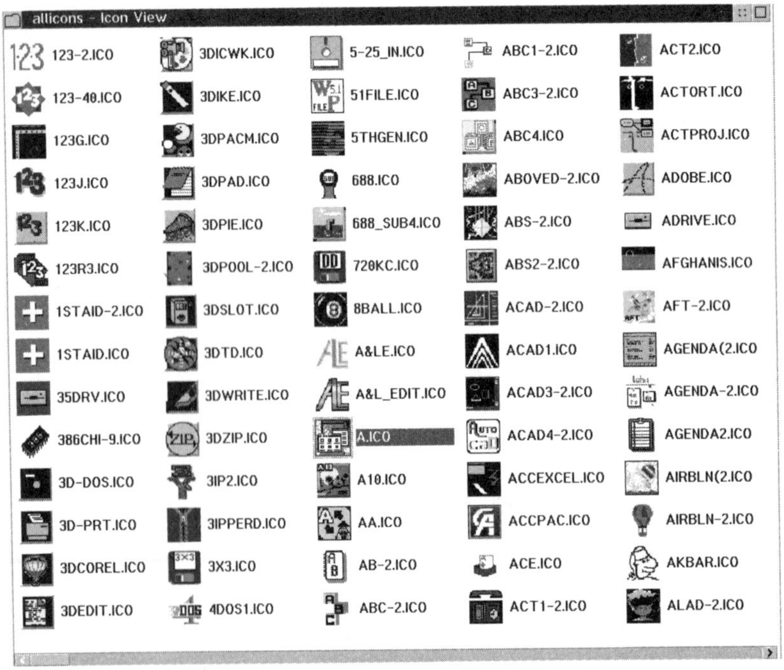
allicons - Icon View
123-2.ICO
123-40.ICO
123G.ICO
123J.ICO
123K.ICO
123R3.ICO
1STAID-2.ICO
1STAID.ICO
35DRV.ICO
386CHI-9.ICO
3D-DOS.ICO
3D-PRT.ICO
3DCOREL.ICO
3DEDIT.ICO
3DICWK.ICO
3DIKE.ICO
3DPACM.ICO
3DPAD.ICO
3DPIE.ICO
3DPOOL-2.ICO
3DSLOT.ICO
3DTD.ICO
3DWRITE.ICO
3DZIP.ICO
3IP2.ICO
3IPPERD.ICO
3X3.ICO
4DOS1.ICO
5-25_IN.ICO
51FILE.ICO
5THGEN.ICO
688.ICO
688_SUB4.ICO
720KC.ICO
8BALL.ICO
A&LE.ICO
A&L_EDIT.ICO
A.ICO
A10.ICO
AA.ICO
AB-2.ICO
ABC-2.ICO
ABC1-2.ICO
ABC3-2.ICO
ABC4.ICO
ABOVED-2.ICO
ABS-2.ICO
ABS2-2.ICO
ACAD-2.ICO
ACAD1.ICO
ACAD3-2.ICO
ACAD4-2.ICO
ACCEXCEL.ICO
ACCPAC.ICO
ACE.ICO
ACT1-2.ICO
ACT2.ICO
ACTORT.ICO
ACTPROJ.ICO
ADOBE.ICO
ADRIVE.ICO
AFGHANIS.ICO
AFT-2.ICO
AGENDA(2.ICO
AGENDA-2.ICO
AGENDA2.ICO
AIRBLN(2.ICO
AIRBLN-2.ICO
AKBAR.ICO
ALAD-2.ICO

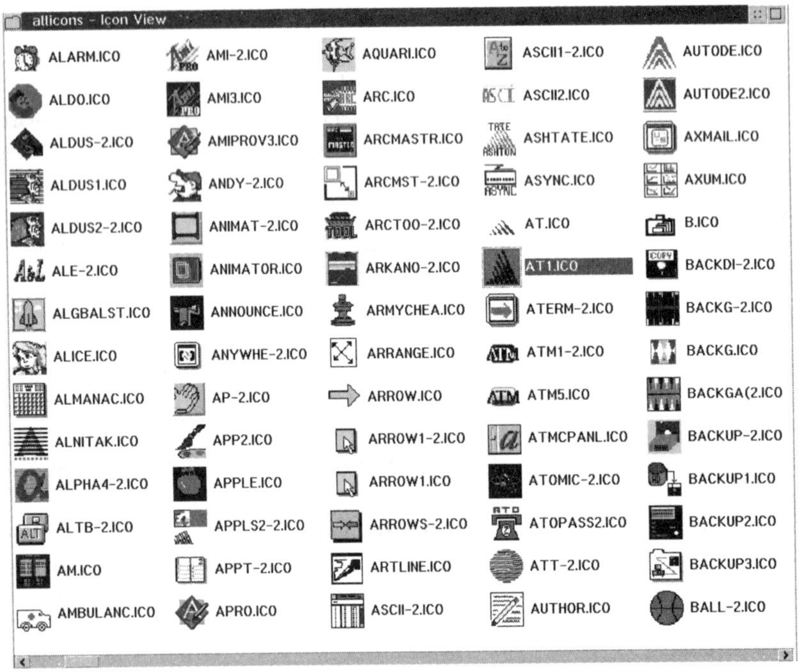
allicons - Icon View
ALARM.ICO
ALDO.ICO
ALDUS-2.ICO
ALDUS1.ICO
ALDUS2-2.ICO
ALE-2.ICO
ALGBALST.ICO
ALICE.ICO
ALMANAC.ICO
ALNITAK.ICO
ALPHA4-2.ICO
ALTB-2.ICO
AM.ICO
AMBULANC.ICO
AMI-2.ICO
AMI3.ICO
AMIPROV3.ICO
ANDY-2.ICO
ANIMAT-2.ICO
ANIMATOR.ICO
ANNOUNCE.ICO
ANYWHE-2.ICO
AP-2.ICO
APP2.ICO
APPLE.ICO
APPLS2-2.ICO
APPT-2.ICO
APRO.ICO
AQUARI.ICO
ARC.ICO
ARCMASTR.ICO
ARCMST-2.ICO
ARCTOO-2.ICO
ARKANO-2.ICO
ARMYCHEA.ICO
ARRANGE.ICO
ARROW.ICO
ARROW1-2.ICO
ARROW1.ICO
ARROWS-2.ICO
ARTLINE.ICO
ASCII-2.ICO
ASCII1-2.ICO
ASCII2.ICO
ASHTATE.ICO
ASYNC.ICO
AT.ICO
AT1.ICO
ATERM-2.ICO
ATM1-2.ICO
ATM5.ICO
ATMCPANL.ICO
ATOMIC-2.ICO
ATOPASS2.ICO
ATT-2.ICO
AUTHOR.ICO
AUTODE.ICO
AUTODE2.ICO
AXMAIL.ICO
AXUM.ICO
B.ICO
BACKDI-2.ICO
BACKG-2.ICO
BACKG.ICO
BACKGA(2.ICO
BACKUP-2.ICO
BACKUP1.ICO
BACKUP2.ICO
BACKUP3.ICO
BALL-2.ICO

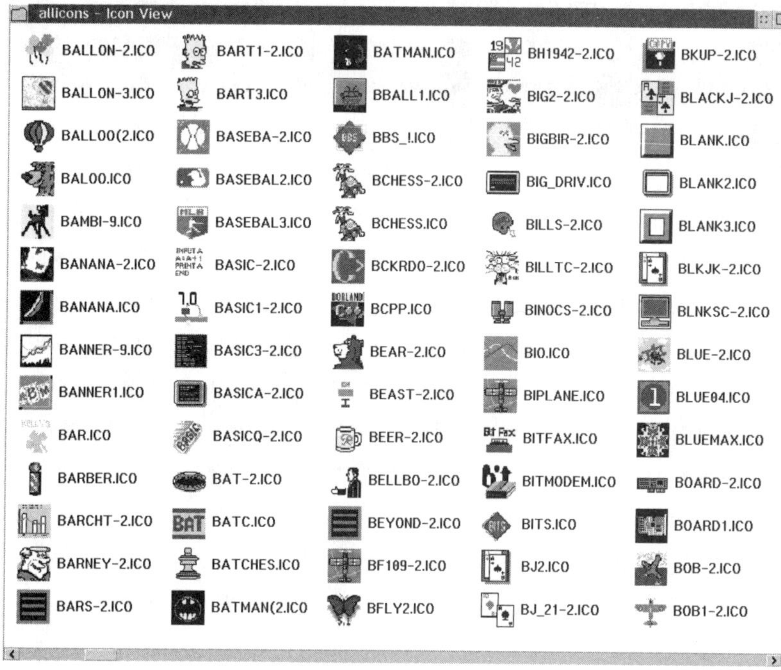
allicons - Icon View
BALLON-2.ICO
BALLON-3.ICO
BALLOO(2.ICO
BALOO.ICO
BAMBI-9.ICO
BANANA-2.ICO
BANANA.ICO
BANNER-9.ICO
BANNER1.ICO
BAR.ICO
BARBER.ICO
BARCHT-2.ICO
BARNEY-2.ICO
BARS-2.ICO
BART1-2.ICO
BART3.ICO
BASEBA-2.ICO
BASEBAL2.ICO
BASEBAL3.ICO
BASIC-2.ICO
BASIC1-2.ICO
BASIC3-2.ICO
BASICA-2.ICO
BASICQ-2.ICO
BAT-2.ICO
BATC.ICO
BATCHES.ICO
BATMAN(2.ICO
BATMAN.ICO
BBALL1.ICO
BBS_I.ICO
BCHESS-2.ICO
BCHESS.ICO
BCKRDO-2.ICO
BCPP.ICO
BEAR-2.ICO
BEAST-2.ICO
BEER-2.ICO
BELLBO-2.ICO
BEYOND-2.ICO
BF109-2.ICO
BFLY2.ICO
BH1942-2.ICO
BIG2-2.ICO
BIGBIR-2.ICO
BIG_DRIV.ICO
BILLS-2.ICO
BILLTC-2.ICO
BINOCS-2.ICO
BIO.ICO
BIPLANE.ICO
BITFAX.ICO
BITMODEM.ICO
BITS.ICO
BJ2.ICO
BJ_21-2.ICO
BKUP-2.ICO
BLACKJ-2.ICO
BLANK.ICO
BLANK2.ICO
BLANK3.ICO
BLKJK-2.ICO
BLNKSC-2.ICO
BLUE-2.ICO
BLUE04.ICO
BLUEMAX.ICO
BOARD-2.ICO
BOARD1.ICO
BOB-2.ICO
BOB1-2.ICO

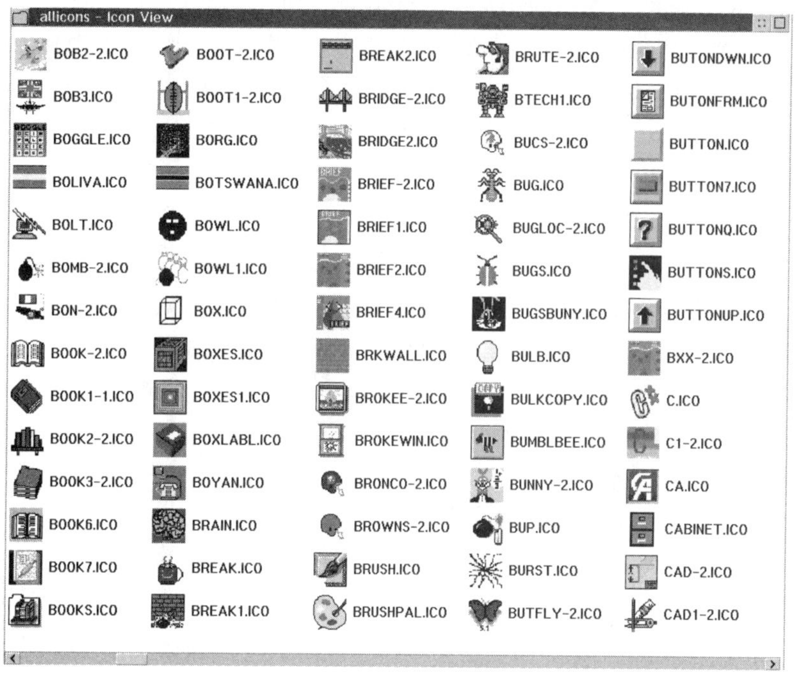
allicons - Icon View
BOB2-2.ICO
BOB3.ICO
BOGGLE.ICO
BOLIVA.ICO
BOLT.ICO
BOMB-2.ICO
BON-2.ICO
BOOK-2.ICO
BOOK1-1.ICO
BOOK2-2.ICO
BOOK3-2.ICO
BOOK6.ICO
BOOK7.ICO
BOOKS.ICO
BOOT-2.ICO
BOOT1-2.ICO
BORG.ICO
BOTSWANA.ICO
BOWL.ICO
BOWL1.ICO
BOX.ICO
BOXES.ICO
BOXES1.ICO
BOXLABL.ICO
BOYAN.ICO
BRAIN.ICO
BREAK.ICO
BREAK1.ICO
BREAK2.ICO
BRIDGE-2.ICO
BRIDGE2.ICO
BRIEF-2.ICO
BRIEF1.ICO
BRIEF2.ICO
BRIEF4.ICO
BRKWALL.ICO
BROKEE-2.ICO
BROKEWIN.ICO
BRONCO-2.ICO
BROWNS-2.ICO
BRUSH.ICO
BRUSHPAL.ICO
BRUTE-2.ICO
BTECH1.ICO
BUCS-2.ICO
BUG.ICO
BUGLOC-2.ICO
BUGS.ICO
BUGSBUNY.ICO
BULB.ICO
BULKCOPY.ICO
BUMBLBEE.ICO
BUNNY-2.ICO
BUP.ICO
BURST.ICO
BUTFLY-2.ICO
BUTONDWN.ICO
BUTONFRM.ICO
BUTTON.ICO
BUTTON7.ICO
BUTTONQ.ICO
BUTTONS.ICO
BUTTONUP.ICO
BXX-2.ICO
C.ICO
C1-2.ICO
CA.ICO
CABINET.ICO
CAD-2.ICO
CAD1-2.ICO

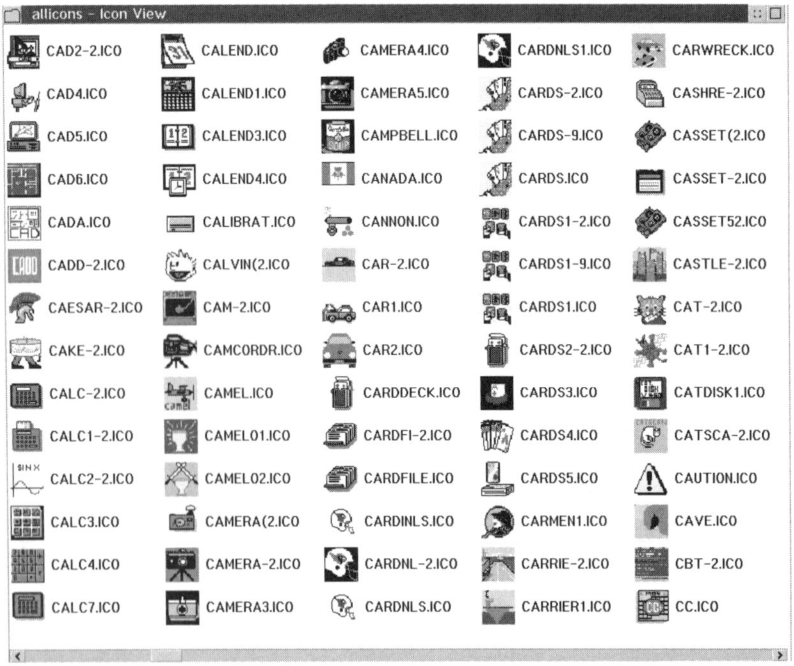
allicons - Icon View
CAD2-2.ICO
CAD4.ICO
CAD5.ICO
CAD6.ICO
CADA.ICO
CADD-2.ICO
CAESAR-2.ICO
CAKE-2.ICO
CALC-2.ICO
CALC1-2.ICO
CALC2-2.ICO
CALC3.ICO
CALC4.ICO
CALC7.ICO
CALEND.ICO
CALEND1.ICO
CALEND3.ICO
CALEND4.ICO
CALIBRAT.ICO
CALVIN(2.ICO
CAM-2.ICO
CAMCORDR.ICO
CAMEL.ICO
CAMEL01.ICO
CAMEL02.ICO
CAMERA(2.ICO
CAMERA-2.ICO
CAMERA3.ICO
CAMERA4.ICO
CAMERA5.ICO
CAMPBELL.ICO
CANADA.ICO
CANNON.ICO
CAR-2.ICO
CAR1.ICO
CAR2.ICO
CARDDECK.ICO
CARDFI-2.ICO
CARDFILE.ICO
CARDINLS.ICO
CARDNL-2.ICO
CARDNLS.ICO
CARDNLS1.ICO
CARDS-2.ICO
CARDS-9.ICO
CARDS.ICO
CARDS1-2.ICO
CARDS1-9.ICO
CARDS1.ICO
CARDS2-2.ICO
CARDS3.ICO
CARDS4.ICO
CARDS5.ICO
CARMEN1.ICO
CARRIE-2.ICO
CARRIER1.ICO
CARWRECK.ICO
CASHRE-2.ICO
CASSET(2.ICO
CASSET-2.ICO
CASSET52.ICO
CASTLE-2.ICO
CAT-2.ICO
CAT1-2.ICO
CATDISK1.ICO
CATSCA-2.ICO
CAUTION.ICO
CAVE.ICO
CBT-2.ICO
CC.ICO

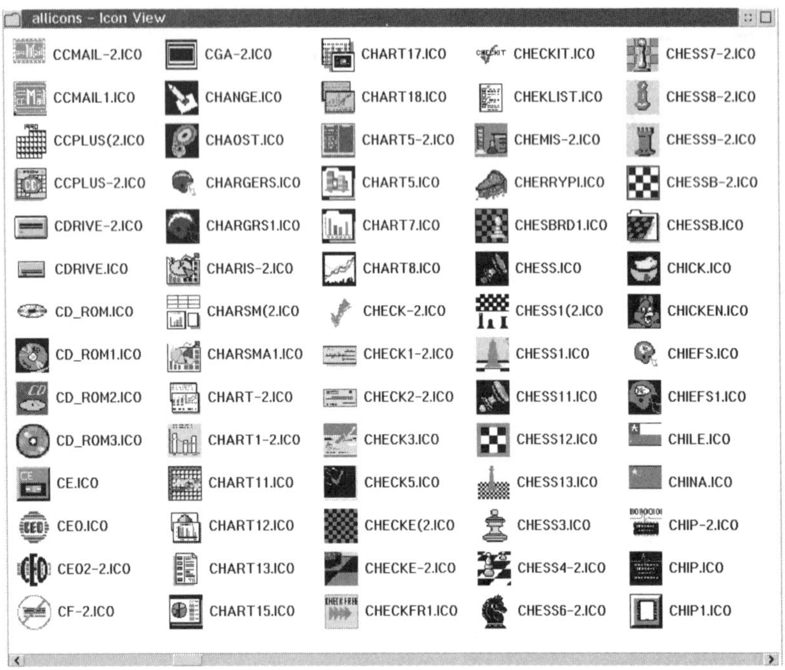
allicons - Icon View
CCMAIL-2.ICO
CCMAIL1.ICO
CCPLUS(2.ICO
CCPLUS-2.ICO
CDRIVE-2.ICO
CDRIVE.ICO
CD_ROM.ICO
CD_ROM1.ICO
CD_ROM2.ICO
CD_ROM3.ICO
CE.ICO
CEO.ICO
CEO2-2.ICO
CF-2.ICO
CGA-2.ICO
CHANGE.ICO
CHAOST.ICO
CHARGERS.ICO
CHARGRS1.ICO
CHARIS-2.ICO
CHARSM(2.ICO
CHARSMA1.ICO
CHART-2.ICO
CHART1-2.ICO
CHART11.ICO
CHART12.ICO
CHART13.ICO
CHART15.ICO
CHART17.ICO
CHART18.ICO
CHART5-2.ICO
CHART5.ICO
CHART7.ICO
CHART8.ICO
CHECK-2.ICO
CHECK1-2.ICO
CHECK2-2.ICO
CHECK3.ICO
CHECK5.ICO
CHECKE(2.ICO
CHECKE-2.ICO
CHECKFR1.ICO
CHECKIT.ICO
CHEKLIST.ICO
CHEMIS-2.ICO
CHERRYPI.ICO
CHESBRD1.ICO
CHESS.ICO
CHESS1(2.ICO
CHESS1.ICO
CHESS11.ICO
CHESS12.ICO
CHESS13.ICO
CHESS3.ICO
CHESS4-2.ICO
CHESS6-2.ICO
CHESS7-2.ICO
CHESS8-2.ICO
CHESS9-2.ICO
CHESSB-2.ICO
CHESSB.ICO
CHICK.ICO
CHICKEN.ICO
CHIEFS.ICO
CHIEFS1.ICO
CHILE.ICO
CHINA.ICO
CHIP-2.ICO
CHIP.ICO
CHIP1.ICO

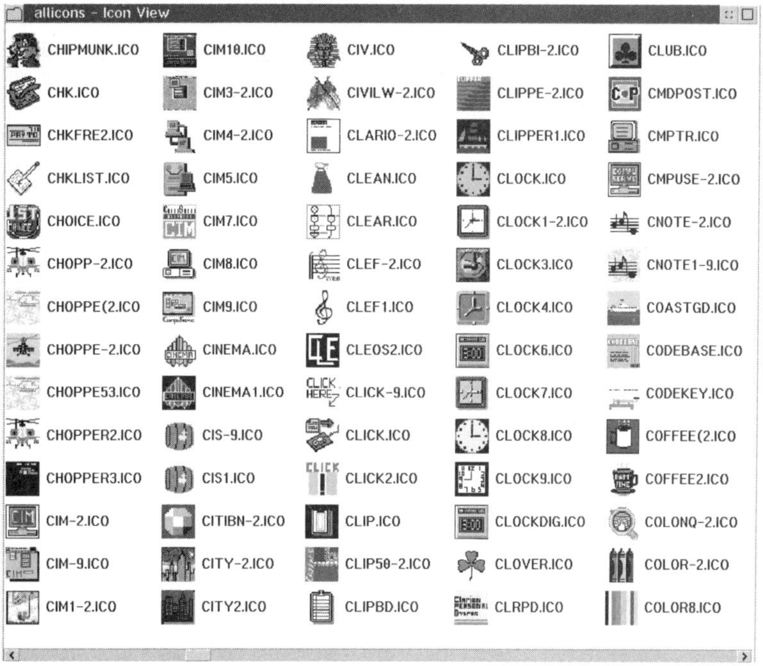
allicons - Icon View
CHIPMUNK.ICO
CHK.ICO
CHKFRE2.ICO
CHKLIST.ICO
CHOICE.ICO
CHOPP-2.ICO
CHOPPE(2.ICO
CHOPPE-2.ICO
CHOPPE53.ICO
CHOPPER2.ICO
CHOPPER3.ICO
CIM-2.ICO
CIM-9.ICO
CIM1-2.ICO
CIM10.ICO
CIM3-2.ICO
CIM4-2.ICO
CIM5.ICO
CIM7.ICO
CIM8.ICO
CIM9.ICO
CINEMA.ICO
CINEMA1.ICO
CIS-9.ICO
CIS1.ICO
CITIBN-2.ICO
CITY-2.ICO
CITY2.ICO
CIV.ICO
CIVILW-2.ICO
CLARIO-2.ICO
CLEAN.ICO
CLEAR.ICO
CLEF-2.ICO
CLEF1.ICO
CLEOS2.ICO
CLICK-9.ICO
CLICK.ICO
CLICK2.ICO
CLIP.ICO
CLIP50-2.ICO
CLIPBD.ICO
CLIPBI-2.ICO
CLIPPE-2.ICO
CLIPPER1.ICO
CLOCK.ICO
CLOCK1-2.ICO
CLOCK3.ICO
CLOCK4.ICO
CLOCK6.ICO
CLOCK7.ICO
CLOCK8.ICO
CLOCK9.ICO
CLOCKDIG.ICO
CLOVER.ICO
CLRPD.ICO
CLUB.ICO
CMDPOST.ICO
CMPTR.ICO
CMPUSE-2.ICO
CNOTE-2.ICO
CNOTE1-9.ICO
COASTGD.ICO
CODEBASE.ICO
CODEKEY.ICO
COFFEE(2.ICO
COFFEE2.ICO
COLONQ-2.ICO
COLOR-2.ICO
COLOR8.ICO

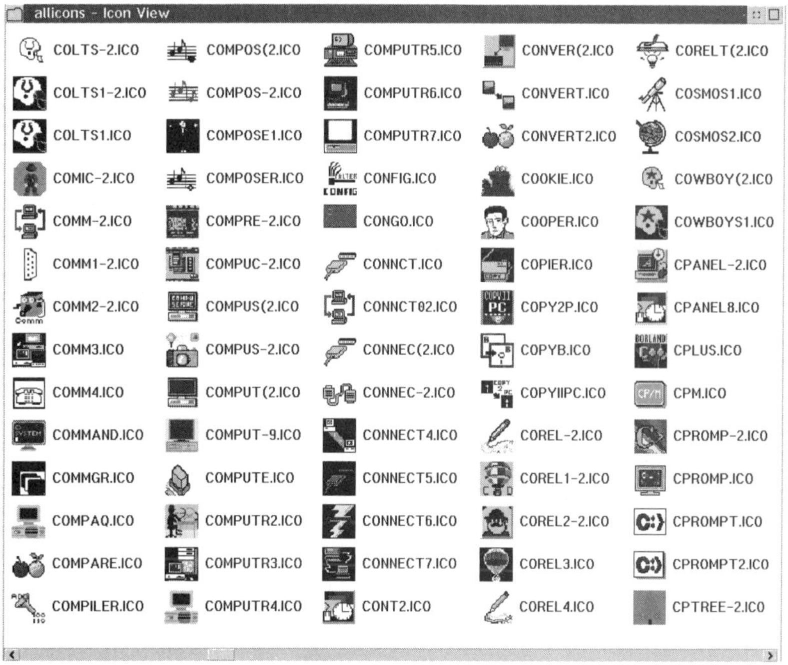
allicons - Icon View
COLTS-2.ICO
COLTS1-2.ICO
COLTS1.ICO
COMIC-2.ICO
COMM-2.ICO
COMM1-2.ICO
COMM2-2.ICO
COMM3.ICO
COMM4.ICO
COMMAND.ICO
COMMGR.ICO
COMPAQ.ICO
COMPARE.ICO
COMPILER.ICO
COMPOS(2.ICO
COMPOS-2.ICO
COMPOSE1.ICO
COMPOSER.ICO
COMPRE-2.ICO
COMPUC-2.ICO
COMPUS(2.ICO
COMPUS-2.ICO
COMPUT(2.ICO
COMPUT-9.ICO
COMPUTE.ICO
COMPUTR2.ICO
COMPUTR3.ICO
COMPUTR4.ICO
COMPUTR5.ICO
COMPUTR6.ICO
COMPUTR7.ICO
CONFIG.ICO
CONGO.ICO
CONNCT.ICO
CONNCT02.ICO
CONNEC(2.ICO
CONNEC-2.ICO
CONNECT4.ICO
CONNECT5.ICO
CONNECT6.ICO
CONNECT7.ICO
CONT2.ICO
CONVER(2.ICO
CONVERT.ICO
CONVERT2.ICO
COOKIE.ICO
COOPER.ICO
COPIER.ICO
COPY2P.ICO
COPYB.ICO
COPYIIPC.ICO
COREL-2.ICO
COREL1-2.ICO
COREL2-2.ICO
COREL3.ICO
COREL4.ICO
CORELT(2.ICO
COSMOS1.ICO
COSMOS2.ICO
COWBOY(2.ICO
COWBOYS1.ICO
CPANEL-2.ICO
CPANEL8.ICO
CPLUS.ICO
CPM.ICO
CPROMP-2.ICO
CPROMP.ICO
CPROMPT.ICO
CPROMPT2.ICO
CPTREE-2.ICO

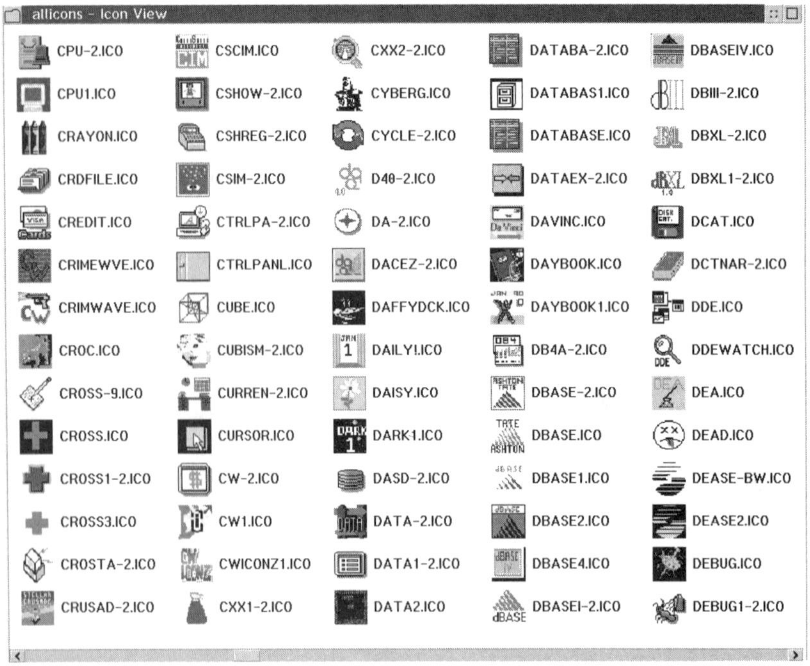
allicons - Icon View
CPU-2.ICO
CSCIM.ICO
CXX2-2.ICO
DATABA-2.ICO
DBASEIV.ICO
CPU1.ICO
CSHOW-2.ICO
CYBERG.ICO
DATABAS1.ICO
DBIII-2.ICO
CRAYON.ICO
CSHREG-2.ICO
CYCLE-2.ICO
DATABASE.ICO
DBXL-2.ICO
CRDFILE.ICO
CSIM-2.ICO
D40-2.ICO
DATAEX-2.ICO
DBXL1-2.ICO
CREDIT.ICO
CTRLPA-2.ICO
DA-2.ICO
DAVINC.ICO
DCAT.ICO
CRIMEWVE.ICO
CTRLPANL.ICO
DACEZ-2.ICO
DAYBOOK.ICO
DCTNAR-2.ICO
CRIMWAVE.ICO
CUBE.ICO
DAFFYDCK.ICO
DAYBOOK1.ICO
DDE.ICO
CROC.ICO
CUBISM-2.ICO
DAILY!.ICO
DB4A-2.ICO
DDEWATCH.ICO
CROSS-9.ICO
CURREN-2.ICO
DAISY.ICO
DBASE-2.ICO
DEA.ICO
CROSS.ICO
CURSOR.ICO
DARK1.ICO
DBASE.ICO
DEAD.ICO
CROSS1-2.ICO
CW-2.ICO
DASD-2.ICO
DBASE1.ICO
DEASE-BW.ICO
CROSS3.ICO
CW1.ICO
DATA-2.ICO
DBASE2.ICO
DEASE2.ICO
CROSTA-2.ICO
CWICONZ1.ICO
DATA1-2.ICO
DBASE4.ICO
DEBUG.ICO
CRUSAD-2.ICO
CXX1-2.ICO
DATA2.ICO
DBASEI-2.ICO
DEBUG1-2.ICO

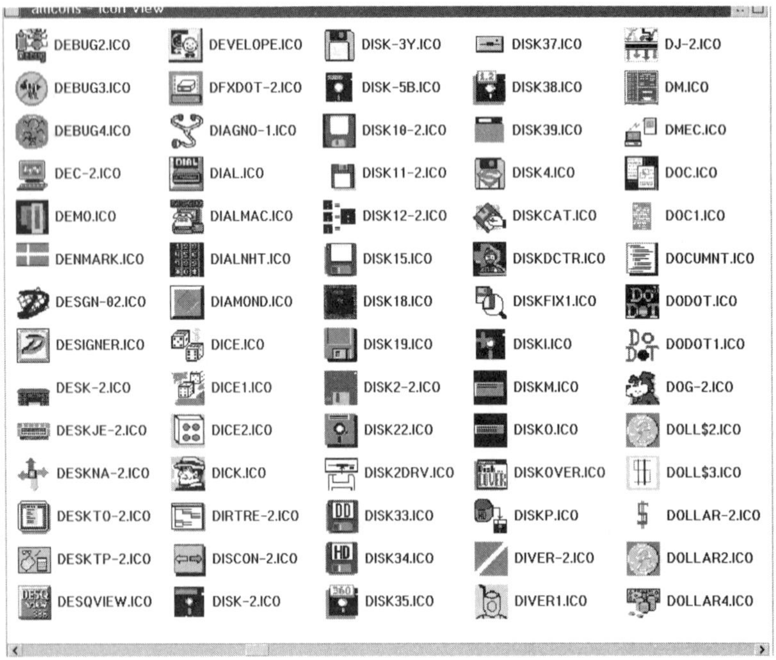
DEBUG2.ICO
DEVELOPE.ICO
DISK-3Y.ICO
DISK37.ICO
DJ-2.ICO
DEBUG3.ICO
DFXDOT-2.ICO
DISK-5B.ICO
DISK38.ICO
DM.ICO
DEBUG4.ICO
DIAGNO-1.ICO
DISK10-2.ICO
DISK39.ICO
DMEC.ICO
DEC-2.ICO
DIAL.ICO
DISK11-2.ICO
DISK4.ICO
DOC.ICO
DEMO.ICO
DIALMAC.ICO
DISK12-2.ICO
DISKCAT.ICO
DOC1.ICO
DENMARK.ICO
DIALNHT.ICO
DISK15.ICO
DISKDCTR.ICO
DOCUMNT.ICO
DESGN-02.ICO
DIAMOND.ICO
DISK18.ICO
DISKFIX1.ICO
DODOT.ICO
DESIGNER.ICO
DICE.ICO
DISK19.ICO
DISKI.ICO
DODOT1.ICO
DESK-2.ICO
DICE1.ICO
DISK2-2.ICO
DISKM.ICO
DOG-2.ICO
DESKJE-2.ICO
DICE2.ICO
DISK22.ICO
DISKO.ICO
DOLL$2.ICO
DESKNA-2.ICO
DICK.ICO
DISK2DRV.ICO
DISKOVER.ICO
DOLL$3.ICO
DESKTO-2.ICO
DIRTRE-2.ICO
DISK33.ICO
DISKP.ICO
DOLLAR-2.ICO
DESKTP-2.ICO
DISCON-2.ICO
DISK34.ICO
DIVER-2.ICO
DOLLAR2.ICO
DESQVIEW.ICO
DISK-2.ICO
DISK35.ICO
DIVER1.ICO
DOLLAR4.ICO

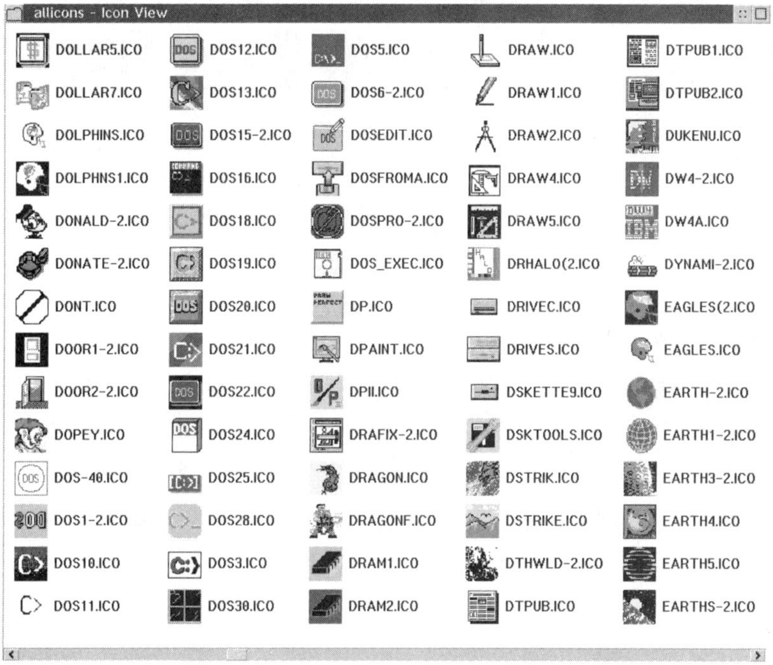
allicons - Icon View
DOLLAR5.ICO
DOLLAR7.ICO
DOLPHINS.ICO
DOLPHNS1.ICO
DONALD-2.ICO
DONATE-2.ICO
DONT.ICO
DOOR1-2.ICO
DOOR2-2.ICO
DOPEY.ICO
DOS-40.ICO
DOS1-2.ICO
DOS10.ICO
DOS11.ICO
DOS12.ICO
DOS13.ICO
DOS15-2.ICO
DOS16.ICO
DOS18.ICO
DOS19.ICO
DOS20.ICO
DOS21.ICO
DOS22.ICO
DOS24.ICO
DOS25.ICO
DOS28.ICO
DOS3.ICO
DOS30.ICO
DOS5.ICO
DOS6-2.ICO
DOSEDIT.ICO
DOSFROMA.ICO
DOSPRO-2.ICO
DOS_EXEC.ICO
DP.ICO
DPAINT.ICO
DPII.ICO
DRAFIX-2.ICO
DRAGON.ICO
DRAGONF.ICO
DRAM1.ICO
DRAM2.ICO
DRAW.ICO
DRAW1.ICO
DRAW2.ICO
DRAW4.ICO
DRAW5.ICO
DRHALO(2.ICO
DRIVEC.ICO
DRIVES.ICO
DSKETTE9.ICO
DSKTOOLS.ICO
DSTRIK.ICO
DSTRIKE.ICO
DTHWLD-2.ICO
DTPUB.ICO
DTPUB1.ICO
DTPUB2.ICO
DUKENU.ICO
DW4-2.ICO
DW4A.ICO
DYNAMI-2.ICO
EAGLES(2.ICO
EAGLES.ICO
EARTH-2.ICO
EARTH1-2.ICO
EARTH3-2.ICO
EARTH4.ICO
EARTH5.ICO
EARTHS-2.ICO

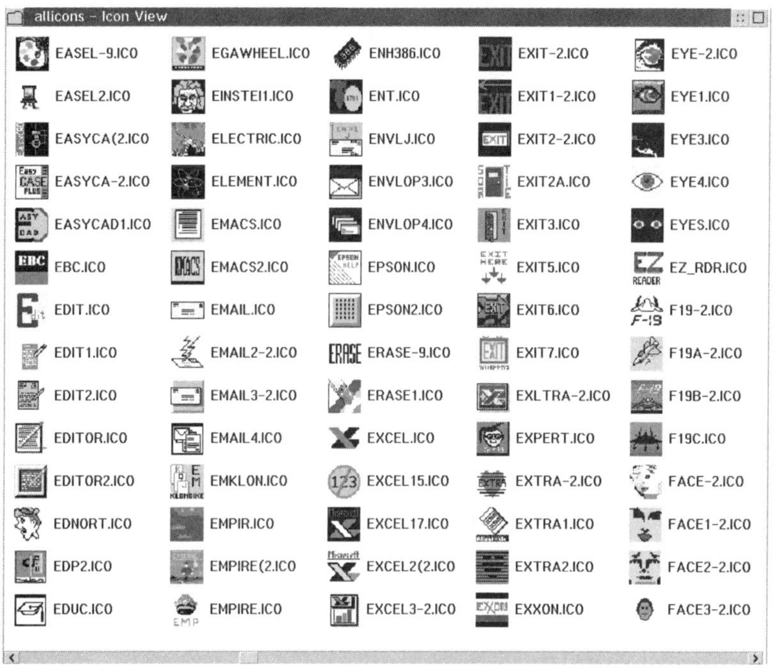
allicons - Icon View
EASEL-9.ICO
EASEL2.ICO
EASYCA(2.ICO
EASYCA-2.ICO
EASYCAD1.ICO
EBC.ICO
EDIT.ICO
EDIT1.ICO
EDIT2.ICO
EDITOR.ICO
EDITOR2.ICO
EDNORT.ICO
EDP2.ICO
EDUC.ICO
EGAWHEEL.ICO
EINSTEI1.ICO
ELECTRIC.ICO
ELEMENT.ICO
EMACS.ICO
EMACS2.ICO
EMAIL.ICO
EMAIL2-2.ICO
EMAIL3-2.ICO
EMAIL4.ICO
EMKLON.ICO
EMPIR.ICO
EMPIRE(2.ICO
EMPIRE.ICO
ENH386.ICO
ENT.ICO
ENVLJ.ICO
ENVLOP3.ICO
ENVLOP4.ICO
EPSON.ICO
EPSON2.ICO
ERASE-9.ICO
ERASE1.ICO
EXCEL.ICO
EXCEL15.ICO
EXCEL17.ICO
EXCEL2(2.ICO
EXCEL3-2.ICO
EXIT-2.ICO
EXIT1-2.ICO
EXIT2-2.ICO
EXIT2A.ICO
EXIT3.ICO
EXIT5.ICO
EXIT6.ICO
EXIT7.ICO
EXLTRA-2.ICO
EXPERT.ICO
EXTRA-2.ICO
EXTRA1.ICO
EXTRA2.ICO
EXXON.ICO
EYE-2.ICO
EYE1.ICO
EYE3.ICO
EYE4.ICO
EYES.ICO
EZ_RDR.ICO
F19-2.ICO
F19A-2.ICO
F19B-2.ICO
F19C.ICO
FACE-2.ICO
FACE1-2.ICO
FACE2-2.ICO
FACE3-2.ICO

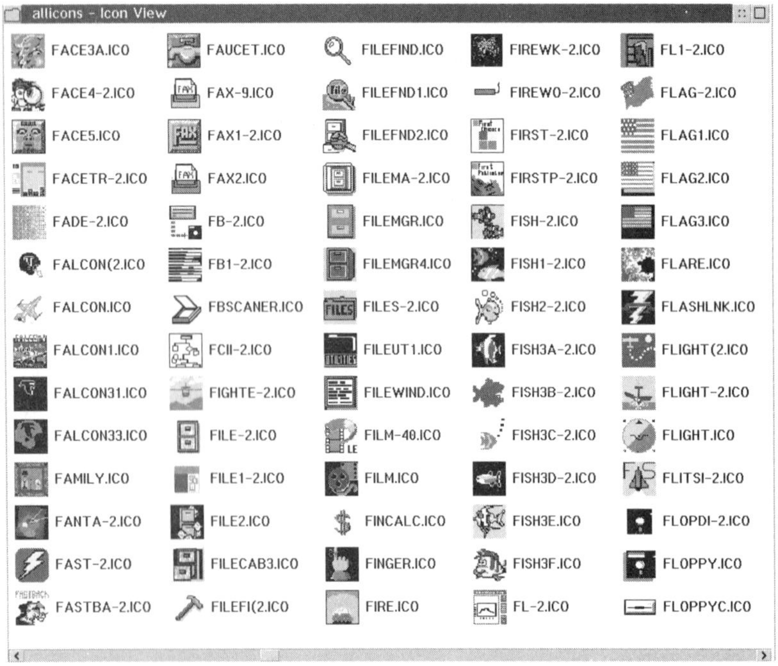
allicons - Icon View
FACE3A.ICO
FACE4-2.ICO
FACE5.ICO
FACETR-2.ICO
FADE-2.ICO
FALCON(2.ICO
FALCON.ICO
FALCON1.ICO
FALCON31.ICO
FALCON33.ICO
FAMILY.ICO
FANTA-2.ICO
FAST-2.ICO
FASTBA-2.ICO
FAUCET.ICO
FAX-9.ICO
FAX1-2.ICO
FAX2.ICO
FB-2.ICO
FB1-2.ICO
FBSCANER.ICO
FCII-2.ICO
FIGHTE-2.ICO
FILE-2.ICO
FILE1-2.ICO
FILE2.ICO
FILECAB3.ICO
FILEFI(2.ICO
FILEFIND.ICO
FILEFND1.ICO
FILEFND2.ICO
FILEMA-2.ICO
FILEMGR.ICO
FILEMGR4.ICO
FILES-2.ICO
FILEUT1.ICO
FILEWIND.ICO
FILM-40.ICO
FILM.ICO
FINCALC.ICO
FINGER.ICO
FIRE.ICO
FIREWK-2.ICO
FIREWO-2.ICO
FIRST-2.ICO
FIRSTP-2.ICO
FISH-2.ICO
FISH1-2.ICO
FISH2-2.ICO
FISH3A-2.ICO
FISH3B-2.ICO
FISH3C-2.ICO
FISH3D-2.ICO
FISH3E.ICO
FISH3F.ICO
FL-2.ICO
FL1-2.ICO
FLAG-2.ICO
FLAG1.ICO
FLAG2.ICO
FLAG3.ICO
FLARE.ICO
FLASHLNK.ICO
FLIGHT(2.ICO
FLIGHT-2.ICO
FLIGHT.ICO
FLITSI-2.ICO
FLOPDI-2.ICO
FLOPPY.ICO
FLOPPYC.ICO

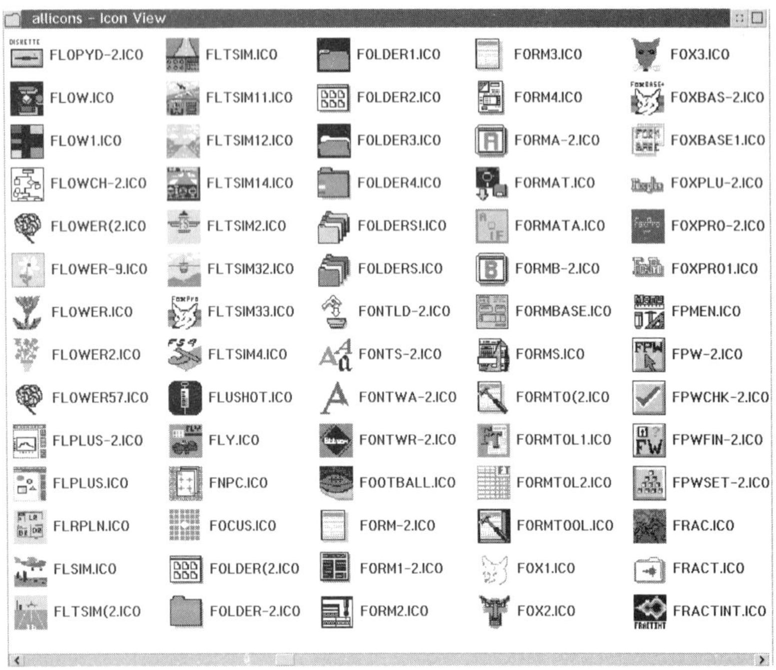
allicons - Icon View
FLOPYD-2.ICO
FLOW.ICO
FLOW1.ICO
FLOWCH-2.ICO
FLOWER(2.ICO
FLOWER-9.ICO
FLOWER.ICO
FLOWER2.ICO
FLOWER57.ICO
FLPLUS-2.ICO
FLPLUS.ICO
FLRPLN.ICO
FLSIM.ICO
FLTSIM(2.ICO
FLTSIM.ICO
FLTSIM11.ICO
FLTSIM12.ICO
FLTSIM14.ICO
FLTSIM2.ICO
FLTSIM32.ICO
FLTSIM33.ICO
FLTSIM4.ICO
FLUSHOT.ICO
FLY.ICO
FNPC.ICO
FOCUS.ICO
FOLDER(2.ICO
FOLDER-2.ICO
FOLDER1.ICO
FOLDER2.ICO
FOLDER3.ICO
FOLDER4.ICO
FOLDERS!.ICO
FOLDERS.ICO
FONTLD-2.ICO
FONTS-2.ICO
FONTWA-2.ICO
FONTWR-2.ICO
FOOTBALL.ICO
FORM-2.ICO
FORM1-2.ICO
FORM2.ICO
FORM3.ICO
FORM4.ICO
FORMA-2.ICO
FORMAT.ICO
FORMATA.ICO
FORMB-2.ICO
FORMBASE.ICO
FORMS.ICO
FORMTO(2.ICO
FORMTOL1.ICO
FORMTOL2.ICO
FORMTOOL.ICO
FOX1.ICO
FOX2.ICO
FOX3.ICO
FOXBAS-2.ICO
FOXBASE1.ICO
FOXPLU-2.ICO
FOXPRO-2.ICO
FOXPRO1.ICO
FPMEN.ICO
FPW-2.ICO
FPWCHK-2.ICO
FPWFIN-2.ICO
FPWSET-2.ICO
FRAC.ICO
FRACT.ICO
FRACTINT.ICO

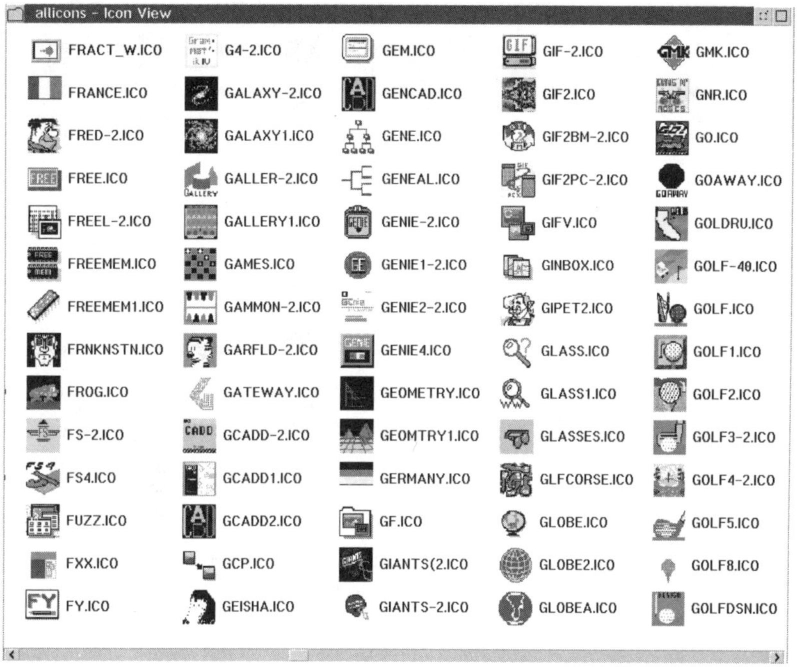
allicons - Icon View
FRACT_W.ICO
FRANCE.ICO
FRED-2.ICO
FREE.ICO
FREEL-2.ICO
FREEMEM.ICO
FREEMEM1.ICO
FRNKNSTN.ICO
FROG.ICO
FS-2.ICO
FS4.ICO
FUZZ.ICO
FXX.ICO
FY.ICO
G4-2.ICO
GALAXY-2.ICO
GALAXY1.ICO
GALLER-2.ICO
GALLERY1.ICO
GAMES.ICO
GAMMON-2.ICO
GARFLD-2.ICO
GATEWAY.ICO
GCADD-2.ICO
GCADD1.ICO
GCADD2.ICO
GCP.ICO
GEISHA.ICO
GEM.ICO
GENCAD.ICO
GENE.ICO
GENEAL.ICO
GENIE-2.ICO
GENIE1-2.ICO
GENIE2-2.ICO
GENIE4.ICO
GEOMETRY.ICO
GEOMTRY1.ICO
GERMANY.ICO
GF.ICO
GIANTS(2.ICO
GIANTS-2.ICO
GIF-2.ICO
GIF2.ICO
GIF2BM-2.ICO
GIF2PC-2.ICO
GIFV.ICO
GINBOX.ICO
GIPET2.ICO
GLASS.ICO
GLASS1.ICO
GLASSES.ICO
GLFCORSE.ICO
GLOBE.ICO
GLOBE2.ICO
GLOBEA.ICO
GMK.ICO
GNR.ICO
GO.ICO
GOAWAY.ICO
GOLDRU.ICO
GOLF-40.ICO
GOLF.ICO
GOLF1.ICO
GOLF2.ICO
GOLF3-2.ICO
GOLF4-2.ICO
GOLF5.ICO
GOLF8.ICO
GOLFDSN.ICO

allicons - Icon View
GOOB-2.ICO
GOOFY.ICO
GOSCRP-2.ICO
GPLAIN-2.ICO
GRADIE-2.ICO
GRAFNBOX.ICO
GRAM-2.ICO
GRAPH.ICO
GRAPH1.ICO
GRAPH2.ICO
GRAPH3.ICO
GRAPH4.ICO
GRAPHP-2.ICO
GRAYFX.ICO
GRAYLINE.ICO
GREEN.ICO
GREMLI-2.ICO
GRID.ICO
GROVER-2.ICO
GT2-2.ICO
GUESSWOT.ICO
GUMBY-2.ICO
GV-2.ICO
GV1-2.ICO
GW.ICO
GWS_1.ICO
HA50S2-1.ICO
HAGAR-2.ICO
HALO.ICO
HAMB-2.ICO
HAMMER-2.ICO
HAND.ICO
HANDHELD.ICO
HANDSC30.ICO
HANDSC31.ICO
HANDSCAN.ICO
HANGMAN.ICO
HANGMAN1.ICO
HARDBALL.ICO
HARDDISK.ICO
HARDDR-2.ICO
HARDNOVA.ICO
HARDRIVE.ICO
HARDUT2.ICO
HARE-2.ICO
HARPON30.ICO
HARPOO(2.ICO
HARPOON.ICO
HARPOON2.ICO
HARVAR(2.ICO
HARVAR-2.ICO
HARVARD2.ICO
HARVARD3.ICO
HARVARD4.ICO
HARVARD6.ICO
HARVARD7.ICO
HDCFOLD.ICO
HDISKB.ICO
HDRIVE(2.ICO
HDRIVE-2.ICO
HEART.ICO
HEARTH.ICO
HELI.ICO
HELLO.ICO
HELP-2.ICO
HERE.ICO
HERO-2.ICO
HEXTRIS.ICO
HF_RIG.ICO
HG.ICO

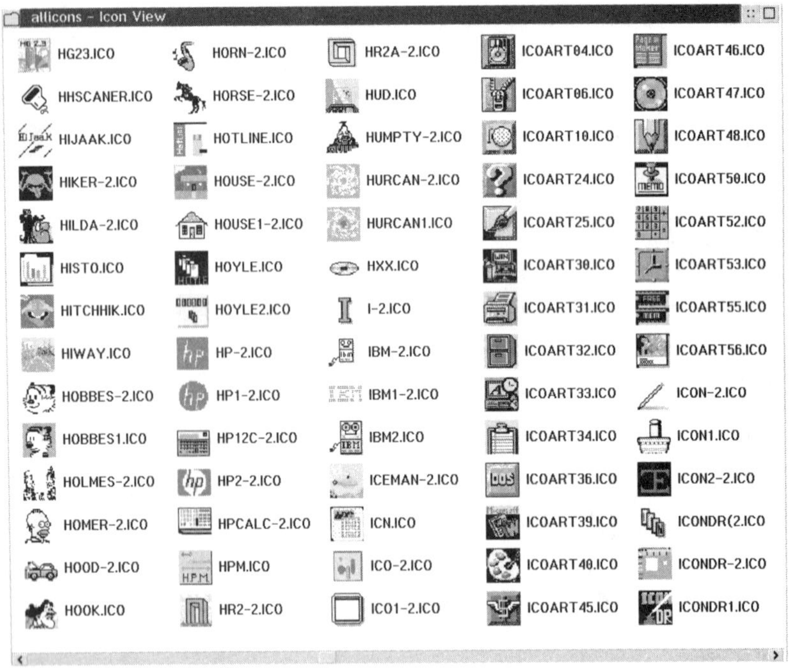
allicons - Icon View
HG23.ICO
HHSCANER.ICO
HIJAAK.ICO
HIKER-2.ICO
HILDA-2.ICO
HISTO.ICO
HITCHHIK.ICO
HIWAY.ICO
HOBBES-2.ICO
HOBBES1.ICO
HOLMES-2.ICO
HOMER-2.ICO
HOOD-2.ICO
HOOK.ICO
HORN-2.ICO
HORSE-2.ICO
HOTLINE.ICO
HOUSE-2.ICO
HOUSE1-2.ICO
HOYLE.ICO
HOYLE2.ICO
HP-2.ICO
HP1-2.ICO
HP12C-2.ICO
HP2-2.ICO
HPCALC-2.ICO
HPM.ICO
HR2-2.ICO
HR2A-2.ICO
HUD.ICO
HUMPTY-2.ICO
HURCAN-2.ICO
HURCAN1.ICO
HXX.ICO
I-2.ICO
IBM-2.ICO
IBM1-2.ICO
IBM2.ICO
ICEMAN-2.ICO
ICN.ICO
ICO-2.ICO
ICO1-2.ICO
ICOART04.ICO
ICOART06.ICO
ICOART10.ICO
ICOART24.ICO
ICOART25.ICO
ICOART30.ICO
ICOART31.ICO
ICOART32.ICO
ICOART33.ICO
ICOART34.ICO
ICOART36.ICO
ICOART39.ICO
ICOART40.ICO
ICOART45.ICO
ICOART46.ICO
ICOART47.ICO
ICOART48.ICO
ICOART50.ICO
ICOART52.ICO
ICOART53.ICO
ICOART55.ICO
ICOART56.ICO
ICON-2.ICO
ICON1.ICO
ICON2-2.ICO
ICONDR(2.ICO
ICONDR-2.ICO
ICONDR1.ICO

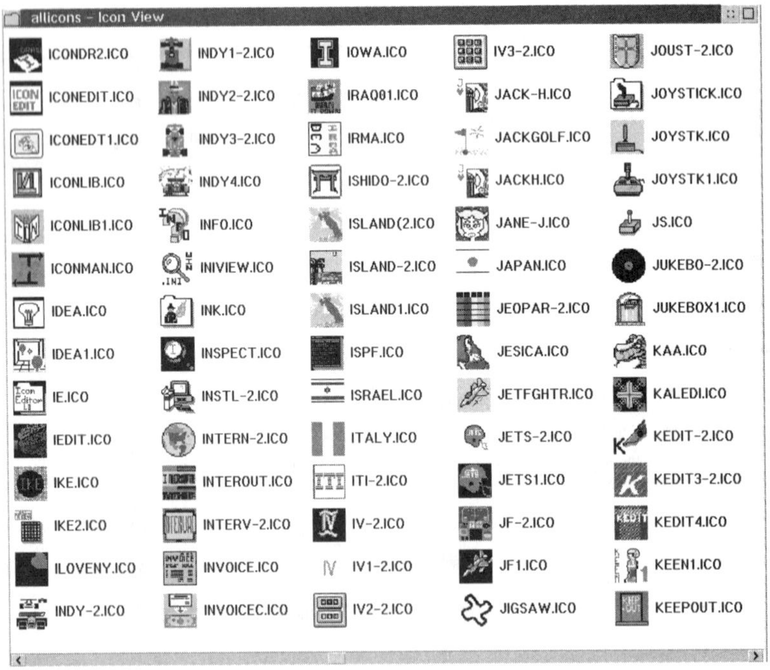
allicons - Icon View
ICONDR2.ICO
ICONEDIT.ICO
ICONEDT1.ICO
ICONLIB.ICO
ICONLIB1.ICO
ICONMAN.ICO
IDEA.ICO
IDEA1.ICO
IE.ICO
IEDIT.ICO
IKE.ICO
IKE2.ICO
ILOVENY.ICO
INDY-2.ICO
INDY1-2.ICO
INDY2-2.ICO
INDY3-2.ICO
INDY4.ICO
INFO.ICO
INIVIEW.ICO
INK.ICO
INSPECT.ICO
INSTL-2.ICO
INTERN-2.ICO
INTEROUT.ICO
INTERV-2.ICO
INVOICE.ICO
INVOICEC.ICO
IOWA.ICO
IRAQ01.ICO
IRMA.ICO
ISHIDO-2.ICO
ISLAND(2.ICO
ISLAND-2.ICO
ISLAND1.ICO
ISPF.ICO
ISRAEL.ICO
ITALY.ICO
ITI-2.ICO
IV-2.ICO
IV1-2.ICO
IV2-2.ICO
IV3-2.ICO
JACK-H.ICO
JACKGOLF.ICO
JACKH.ICO
JANE-J.ICO
JAPAN.ICO
JEOPAR-2.ICO
JESICA.ICO
JETFGHTR.ICO
JETS-2.ICO
JETS1.ICO
JF-2.ICO
JF1.ICO
JIGSAW.ICO
JOUST-2.ICO
JOYSTICK.ICO
JOYSTK.ICO
JOYSTK1.ICO
JS.ICO
JUKEBO-2.ICO
JUKEBOX1.ICO
KAA.ICO
KALEDI.ICO
KEDIT-2.ICO
KEDIT3-2.ICO
KEDIT4.ICO
KEEN1.ICO
KEEPOUT.ICO

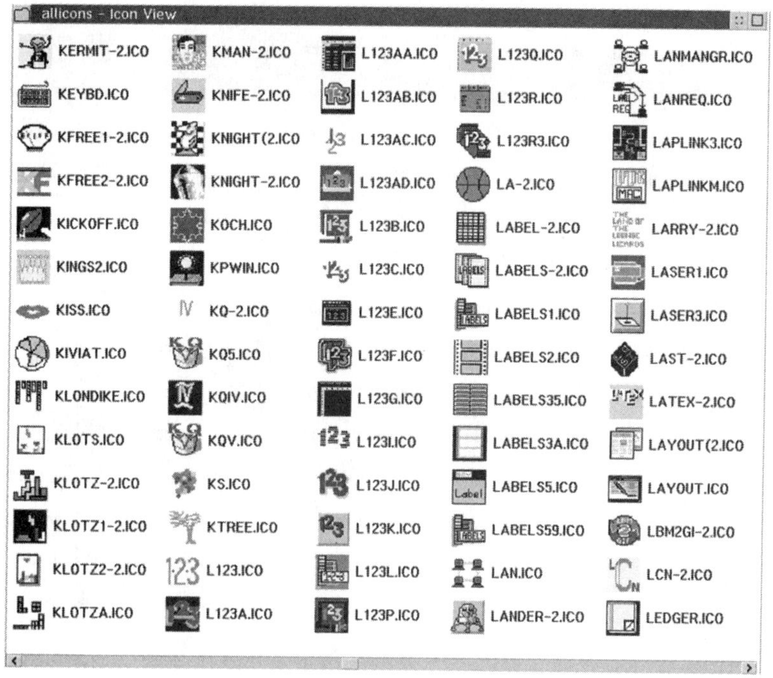
allicons - Icon View
KERMIT-2.ICO
KEYBD.ICO
KFREE1-2.ICO
KFREE2-2.ICO
KICKOFF.ICO
KINGS2.ICO
KISS.ICO
KIVIAT.ICO
KLONDIKE.ICO
KLOTS.ICO
KLOTZ-2.ICO
KLOTZ1-2.ICO
KLOTZ2-2.ICO
KLOTZA.ICO
KMAN-2.ICO
KNIFE-2.ICO
KNIGHT(2.ICO
KNIGHT-2.ICO
KOCH.ICO
KPWIN.ICO
KQ-2.ICO
KQ5.ICO
KQIV.ICO
KQV.ICO
KS.ICO
KTREE.ICO
L123.ICO
L123A.ICO
L123AA.ICO
L123AB.ICO
L123AC.ICO
L123AD.ICO
L123B.ICO
L123C.ICO
L123E.ICO
L123F.ICO
L123G.ICO
L123I.ICO
L123J.ICO
L123K.ICO
L123L.ICO
L123P.ICO
L123Q.ICO
L123R.ICO
L123R3.ICO
LA-2.ICO
LABEL-2.ICO
LABELS-2.ICO
LABELS1.ICO
LABELS2.ICO
LABELS35.ICO
LABELS3A.ICO
LABELS5.ICO
LABELS59.ICO
LAN.ICO
LANDER-2.ICO
LANMANGR.ICO
LANREQ.ICO
LAPLINK3.ICO
LAPLINKM.ICO
LARRY-2.ICO
LASER1.ICO
LASER3.ICO
LAST-2.ICO
LATEX-2.ICO
LAYOUT(2.ICO
LAYOUT.ICO
LBM2GI-2.ICO
LCN-2.ICO
LEDGER.ICO

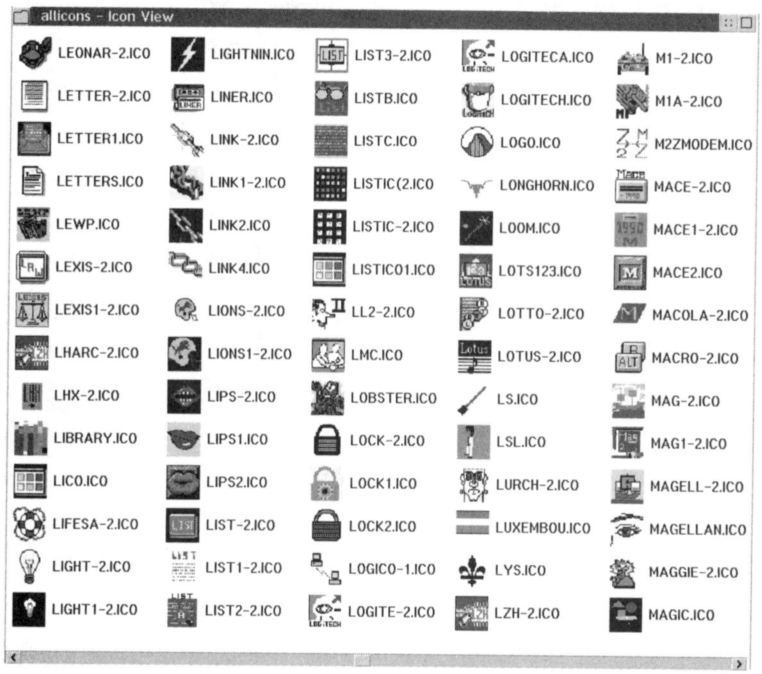
allicons - Icon View
LEONAR-2.ICO
LETTER-2.ICO
LETTER1.ICO
LETTERS.ICO
LEWP.ICO
LEXIS-2.ICO
LEXIS1-2.ICO
LHARC-2.ICO
LHX-2.ICO
LIBRARY.ICO
LICO.ICO
LIFESA-2.ICO
LIGHT-2.ICO
LIGHT1-2.ICO
LIGHTNIN.ICO
LINER.ICO
LINK-2.ICO
LINK1-2.ICO
LINK2.ICO
LINK4.ICO
LIONS-2.ICO
LIONS1-2.ICO
LIPS-2.ICO
LIPS1.ICO
LIPS2.ICO
LIST-2.ICO
LIST1-2.ICO
LIST2-2.ICO
LIST3-2.ICO
LISTB.ICO
LISTC.ICO
LISTIC(2.ICO
LISTIC-2.ICO
LISTIC01.ICO
LL2-2.ICO
LMC.ICO
LOBSTER.ICO
LOCK-2.ICO
LOCK1.ICO
LOCK2.ICO
LOGICO-1.ICO
LOGITE-2.ICO
LOGITECA.ICO
LOGITECH.ICO
LOGO.ICO
LONGHORN.ICO
LOOM.ICO
LOTS123.ICO
LOTTO-2.ICO
LOTUS-2.ICO
LS.ICO
LSL.ICO
LURCH-2.ICO
LUXEMBOU.ICO
LYS.ICO
LZH-2.ICO
M1-2.ICO
M1A-2.ICO
M2ZMODEM.ICO
MACE-2.ICO
MACE1-2.ICO
MACE2.ICO
MACOLA-2.ICO
MACRO-2.ICO
MAG-2.ICO
MAG1-2.ICO
MAGELL-2.ICO
MAGELLAN.ICO
MAGGIE-2.ICO
MAGIC.ICO

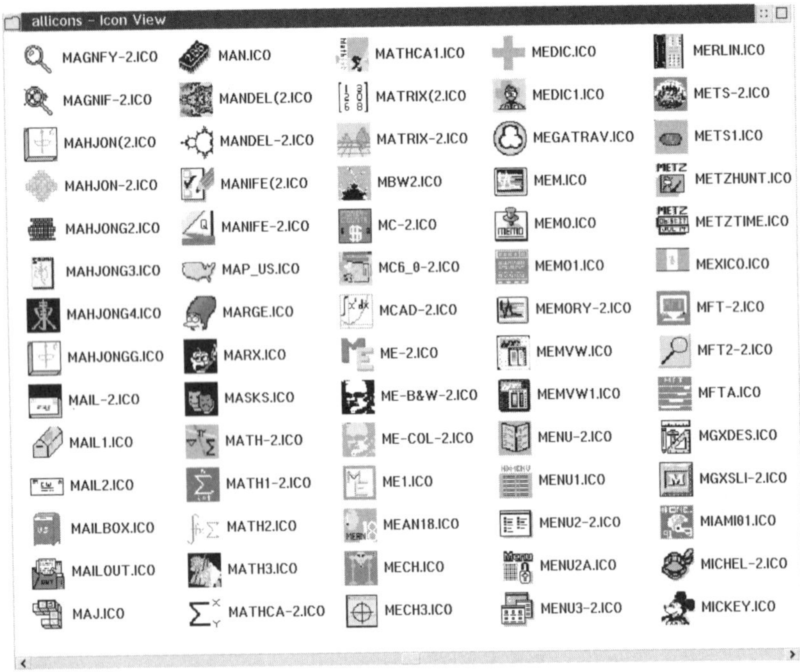
allicons - Icon View
MAGNFY-2.ICO
MAGNIF-2.ICO
MAHJON(2.ICO
MAHJON-2.ICO
MAHJONG2.ICO
MAHJONG3.ICO
MAHJONG4.ICO
MAHJONGG.ICO
MAIL-2.ICO
MAIL1.ICO
MAIL2.ICO
MAILBOX.ICO
MAILOUT.ICO
MAJ.ICO
MAN.ICO
MANDEL(2.ICO
MANDEL-2.ICO
MANIFE(2.ICO
MANIFE-2.ICO
MAP_US.ICO
MARGE.ICO
MARX.ICO
MASKS.ICO
MATH-2.ICO
MATH1-2.ICO
MATH2.ICO
MATH3.ICO
MATHCA-2.ICO
MATHCA1.ICO
MATRIX(2.ICO
MATRIX-2.ICO
MBW2.ICO
MC-2.ICO
MC6_0-2.ICO
MCAD-2.ICO
ME-2.ICO
ME-B&W-2.ICO
ME-COL-2.ICO
ME1.ICO
MEAN18.ICO
MECH.ICO
MECH3.ICO
MEDIC.ICO
MEDIC1.ICO
MEGATRAV.ICO
MEM.ICO
MEMO.ICO
MEMO1.ICO
MEMORY-2.ICO
MEMVW.ICO
MEMVW1.ICO
MENU-2.ICO
MENU1.ICO
MENU2-2.ICO
MENU2A.ICO
MENU3-2.ICO
MERLIN.ICO
METS-2.ICO
METS1.ICO
METZHUNT.ICO
METZTIME.ICO
MEXICO.ICO
MFT-2.ICO
MFT2-2.ICO
MFTA.ICO
MGXDES.ICO
MGXSLI-2.ICO
MIAMI01.ICO
MICHEL-2.ICO
MICKEY.ICO

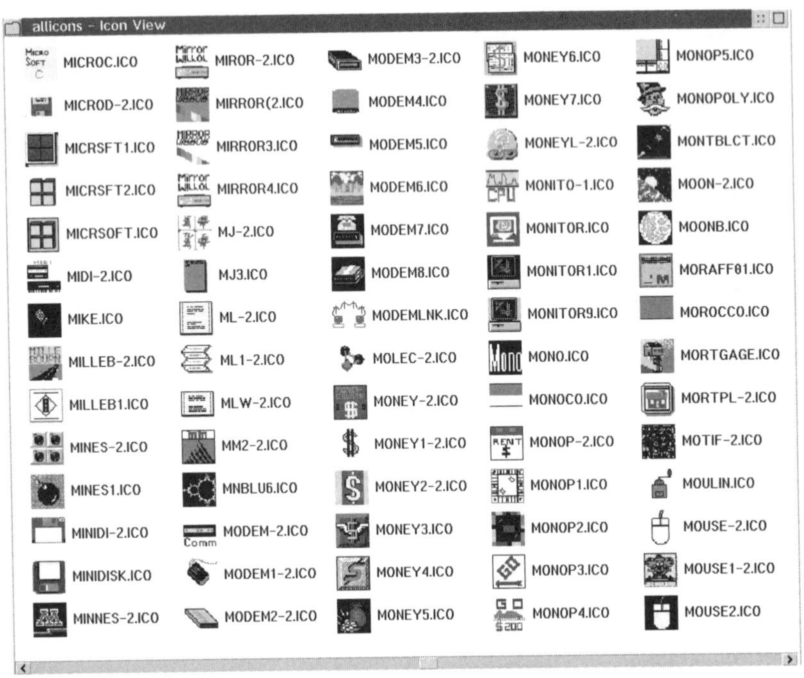
allicons - Icon View
MICROC.ICO
MICROD-2.ICO
MICRSFT1.ICO
MICRSFT2.ICO
MICRSOFT.ICO
MIDI-2.ICO
MIKE.ICO
MILLEB-2.ICO
MILLEB1.ICO
MINES-2.ICO
MINES1.ICO
MINIDI-2.ICO
MINIDISK.ICO
MINNES-2.ICO
MIROR-2.ICO
MIRROR(2.ICO
MIRROR3.ICO
MIRROR4.ICO
MJ-2.ICO
MJ3.ICO
ML-2.ICO
ML1-2.ICO
MLW-2.ICO
MM2-2.ICO
MNBLU6.ICO
MODEM-2.ICO
MODEM1-2.ICO
MODEM2-2.ICO
MODEM3-2.ICO
MODEM4.ICO
MODEM5.ICO
MODEM6.ICO
MODEM7.ICO
MODEM8.ICO
MODEMLNK.ICO
MOLEC-2.ICO
MONEY-2.ICO
MONEY1-2.ICO
MONEY2-2.ICO
MONEY3.ICO
MONEY4.ICO
MONEY5.ICO
MONEY6.ICO
MONEY7.ICO
MONEYL-2.ICO
MONITO-1.ICO
MONITOR.ICO
MONITOR1.ICO
MONITOR9.ICO
MONO.ICO
MONOCO.ICO
MONOP-2.ICO
MONOP1.ICO
MONOP2.ICO
MONOP3.ICO
MONOP4.ICO
MONOP5.ICO
MONOPOLY.ICO
MONTBLCT.ICO
MOON-2.ICO
MOONB.ICO
MORAFF01.ICO
MOROCCO.ICO
MORTGAGE.ICO
MORTPL-2.ICO
MOTIF-2.ICO
MOULIN.ICO
MOUSE-2.ICO
MOUSE1-2.ICO
MOUSE2.ICO

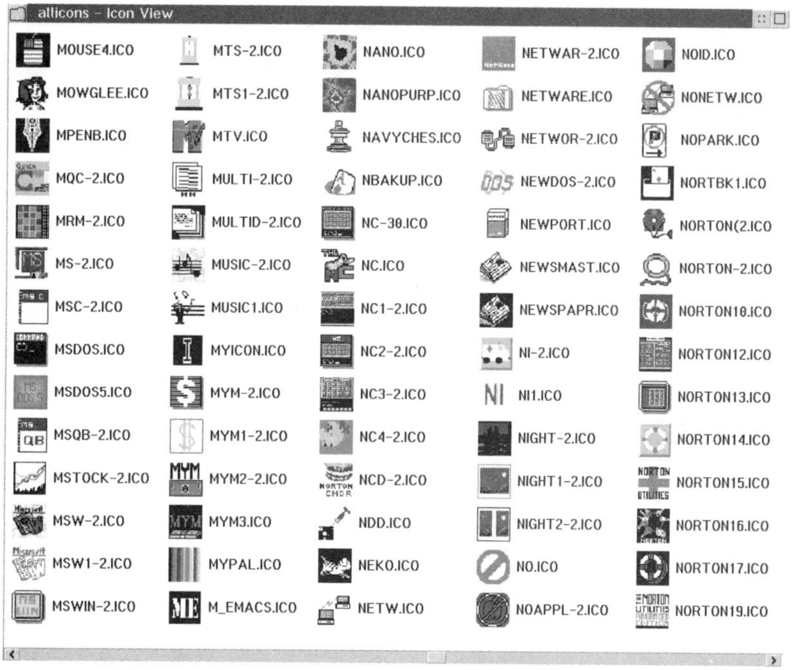
allicons - Icon View
MOUSE4.ICO
MOWGLEE.ICO
MPENB.ICO
MQC-2.ICO
MRM-2.ICO
MS-2.ICO
MSC-2.ICO
MSDOS.ICO
MSDOS5.ICO
MSQB-2.ICO
MSTOCK-2.ICO
MSW-2.ICO
MSW1-2.ICO
MSWIN-2.ICO
MTS-2.ICO
MTS1-2.ICO
MTV.ICO
MULTI-2.ICO
MULTID-2.ICO
MUSIC-2.ICO
MUSIC1.ICO
MYICON.ICO
MYM-2.ICO
MYM1-2.ICO
MYM2-2.ICO
MYM3.ICO
MYPAL.ICO
M_EMACS.ICO
NANO.ICO
NANOPURP.ICO
NAVYCHES.ICO
NBAKUP.ICO
NC-30.ICO
NC.ICO
NC1-2.ICO
NC2-2.ICO
NC3-2.ICO
NC4-2.ICO
NCD-2.ICO
NDD.ICO
NEKO.ICO
NETW.ICO
NETWAR-2.ICO
NETWARE.ICO
NETWOR-2.ICO
NEWDOS-2.ICO
NEWPORT.ICO
NEWSMAST.ICO
NEWSPAPR.ICO
NI-2.ICO
NI1.ICO
NIGHT-2.ICO
NIGHT1-2.ICO
NIGHT2-2.ICO
NO.ICO
NOAPPL-2.ICO
NOID.ICO
NONETW.ICO
NOPARK.ICO
NORTBK1.ICO
NORTON(2.ICO
NORTON-2.ICO
NORTON10.ICO
NORTON12.ICO
NORTON13.ICO
NORTON14.ICO
NORTON15.ICO
NORTON16.ICO
NORTON17.ICO
NORTON19.ICO

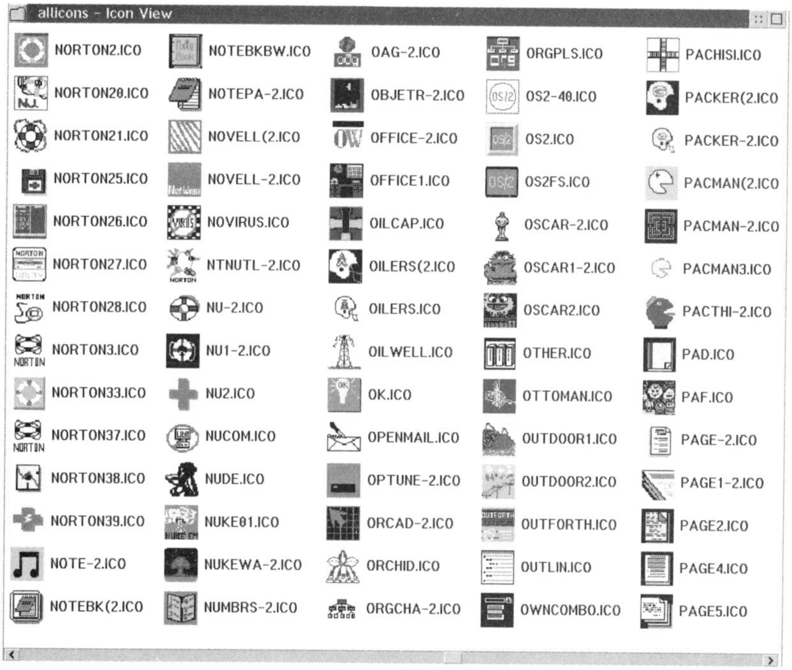
allicons - Icon View
NORTON2.ICO
NORTON20.ICO
NORTON21.ICO
NORTON25.ICO
NORTON26.ICO
NORTON27.ICO
NORTON28.ICO
NORTON3.ICO
NORTON33.ICO
NORTON37.ICO
NORTON38.ICO
NORTON39.ICO
NOTE-2.ICO
NOTEBK(2.ICO
NOTEBKBW.ICO
NOTEPA-2.ICO
NOVELL(2.ICO
NOVELL-2.ICO
NOVIRUS.ICO
NTNUTL-2.ICO
NU-2.ICO
NU1-2.ICO
NU2.ICO
NUCOM.ICO
NUDE.ICO
NUKE01.ICO
NUKEWA-2.ICO
NUMBRS-2.ICO
OAG-2.ICO
OBJETR-2.ICO
OFFICE-2.ICO
OFFICE1.ICO
OILCAP.ICO
OILERS(2.ICO
OILERS.ICO
OILWELL.ICO
OK.ICO
OPENMAIL.ICO
OPTUNE-2.ICO
ORCAD-2.ICO
ORCHID.ICO
ORGCHA-2.ICO
ORGPLS.ICO
OS2-40.ICO
OS2.ICO
OS2FS.ICO
OSCAR-2.ICO
OSCAR1-2.ICO
OSCAR2.ICO
OTHER.ICO
OTTOMAN.ICO
OUTDOOR1.ICO
OUTDOOR2.ICO
OUTFORTH.ICO
OUTLIN.ICO
OWNCOMBO.ICO
PACHISI.ICO
PACKER(2.ICO
PACKER-2.ICO
PACMAN(2.ICO
PACMAN-2.ICO
PACMAN3.ICO
PACTHI-2.ICO
PAD.ICO
PAF.ICO
PAGE-2.ICO
PAGE1-2.ICO
PAGE2.ICO
PAGE4.ICO
PAGE5.ICO

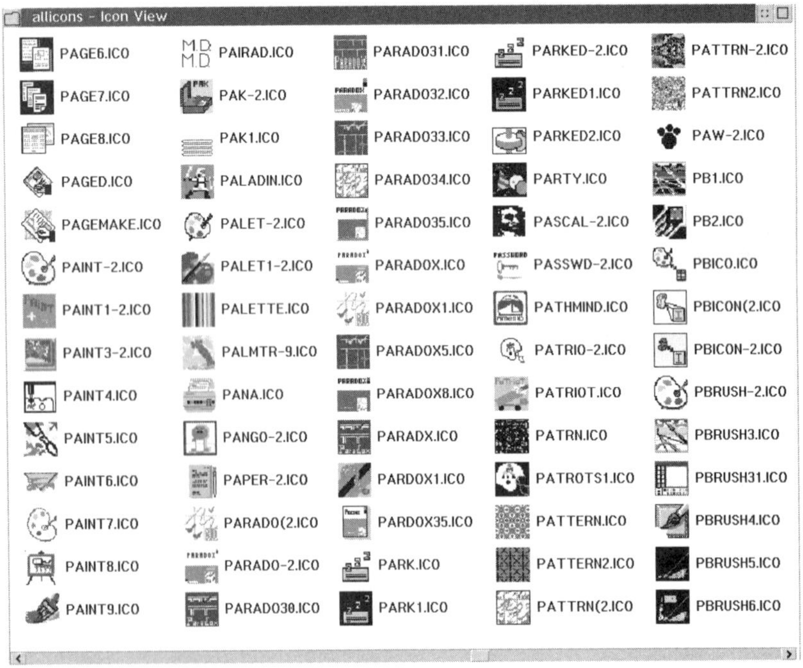
allicons - Icon View
PAGE6.ICO
PAGE7.ICO
PAGE8.ICO
PAGED.ICO
PAGEMAKE.ICO
PAINT-2.ICO
PAINT1-2.ICO
PAINT3-2.ICO
PAINT4.ICO
PAINT5.ICO
PAINT6.ICO
PAINT7.ICO
PAINT8.ICO
PAINT9.ICO
PAIRAD.ICO
PAK-2.ICO
PAK1.ICO
PALADIN.ICO
PALET-2.ICO
PALET1-2.ICO
PALETTE.ICO
PALMTR-9.ICO
PANA.ICO
PANGO-2.ICO
PAPER-2.ICO
PARADO(2.ICO
PARADO-2.ICO
PARADO30.ICO
PARADO31.ICO
PARADO32.ICO
PARADO33.ICO
PARADO34.ICO
PARADO35.ICO
PARADOX.ICO
PARADOX1.ICO
PARADOX5.ICO
PARADOX8.ICO
PARADX.ICO
PARDOX1.ICO
PARDOX35.ICO
PARK.ICO
PARK1.ICO
PARKED-2.ICO
PARKED1.ICO
PARKED2.ICO
PARTY.ICO
PASCAL-2.ICO
PASSWD-2.ICO
PATHMIND.ICO
PATRIO-2.ICO
PATRIOT.ICO
PATRN.ICO
PATROTS1.ICO
PATTERN.ICO
PATTERN2.ICO
PATTRN(2.ICO
PATTRN-2.ICO
PATTRN2.ICO
PAW-2.ICO
PB1.ICO
PB2.ICO
PBICO.ICO
PBICON(2.ICO
PBICON-2.ICO
PBRUSH-2.ICO
PBRUSH3.ICO
PBRUSH31.ICO
PBRUSH4.ICO
PBRUSH5.ICO
PBRUSH6.ICO

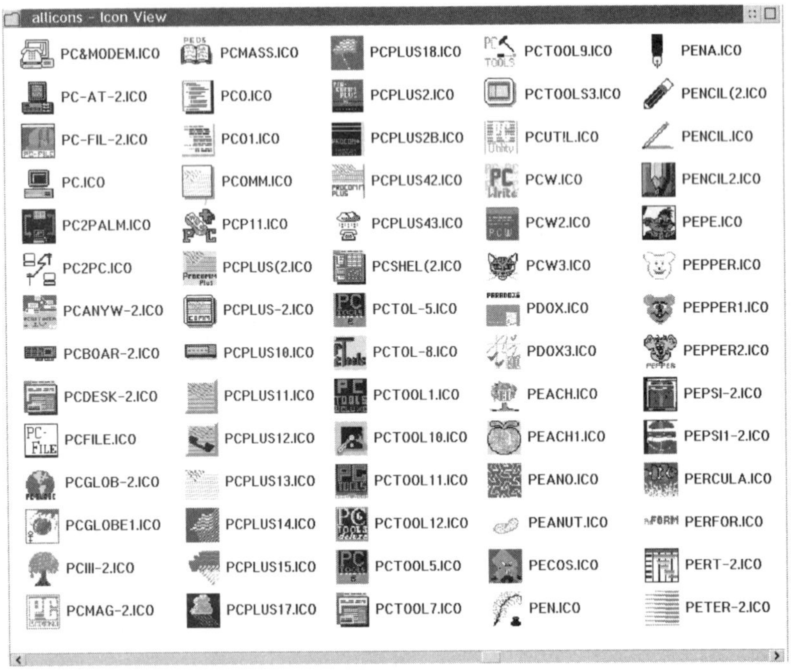
allicons - Icon View
PC&MODEM.ICO
PC-AT-2.ICO
PC-FIL-2.ICO
PC.ICO
PC2PALM.ICO
PC2PC.ICO
PCANYW-2.ICO
PCBOAR-2.ICO
PCDESK-2.ICO
PCFILE.ICO
PCGLOB-2.ICO
PCGLOBE1.ICO
PCIII-2.ICO
PCMAG-2.ICO
PCMASS.ICO
PCO.ICO
PCO1.ICO
PCOMM.ICO
PCP11.ICO
PCPLUS(2.ICO
PCPLUS-2.ICO
PCPLUS10.ICO
PCPLUS11.ICO
PCPLUS12.ICO
PCPLUS13.ICO
PCPLUS14.ICO
PCPLUS15.ICO
PCPLUS17.ICO
PCPLUS18.ICO
PCPLUS2.ICO
PCPLUS2B.ICO
PCPLUS42.ICO
PCPLUS43.ICO
PCSHEL(2.ICO
PCTOL-5.ICO
PCTOL-8.ICO
PCTOOL1.ICO
PCTOOL10.ICO
PCTOOL11.ICO
PCTOOL12.ICO
PCTOOL5.ICO
PCTOOL7.ICO
PCTOOL9.ICO
PCTOOLS3.ICO
PCUT!L.ICO
PCW.ICO
PCW2.ICO
PCW3.ICO
PDOX.ICO
PDOX3.ICO
PEACH.ICO
PEACH1.ICO
PEANO.ICO
PEANUT.ICO
PECOS.ICO
PEN.ICO
PENA.ICO
PENCIL(2.ICO
PENCIL.ICO
PENCIL2.ICO
PEPE.ICO
PEPPER.ICO
PEPPER1.ICO
PEPPER2.ICO
PEPSI-2.ICO
PEPSI1-2.ICO
PERCULA.ICO
PERFOR.ICO
PERT-2.ICO
PETER-2.ICO

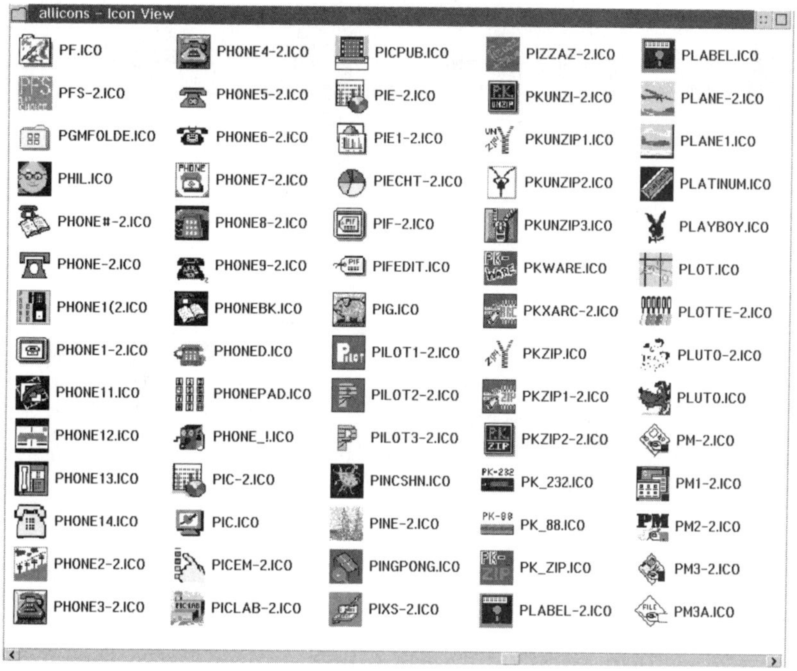
allicons - Icon View
PF.ICO
PFS-2.ICO
PGMFOLDE.ICO
PHIL.ICO
PHONE#-2.ICO
PHONE-2.ICO
PHONE1(2.ICO
PHONE1-2.ICO
PHONE11.ICO
PHONE12.ICO
PHONE13.ICO
PHONE14.ICO
PHONE2-2.ICO
PHONE3-2.ICO
PHONE4-2.ICO
PHONE5-2.ICO
PHONE6-2.ICO
PHONE7-2.ICO
PHONE8-2.ICO
PHONE9-2.ICO
PHONEBK.ICO
PHONED.ICO
PHONEPAD.ICO
PHONE_!.ICO
PIC-2.ICO
PIC.ICO
PICEM-2.ICO
PICLAB-2.ICO
PICPUB.ICO
PIE-2.ICO
PIE1-2.ICO
PIECHT-2.ICO
PIF-2.ICO
PIFEDIT.ICO
PIG.ICO
PILOT1-2.ICO
PILOT2-2.ICO
PILOT3-2.ICO
PINCSHN.ICO
PINE-2.ICO
PINGPONG.ICO
PIXS-2.ICO
PIZZAZ-2.ICO
PKUNZI-2.ICO
PKUNZIP1.ICO
PKUNZIP2.ICO
PKUNZIP3.ICO
PKWARE.ICO
PKXARC-2.ICO
PKZIP.ICO
PKZIP1-2.ICO
PKZIP2-2.ICO
PK_232.ICO
PK_88.ICO
PK_ZIP.ICO
PLABEL-2.ICO
PLABEL.ICO
PLANE-2.ICO
PLANE1.ICO
PLATINUM.ICO
PLAYBOY.ICO
PLOT.ICO
PLOTTE-2.ICO
PLUTO-2.ICO
PLUTO.ICO
PM-2.ICO
PM1-2.ICO
PM2-2.ICO
PM3-2.ICO
PM3A.ICO

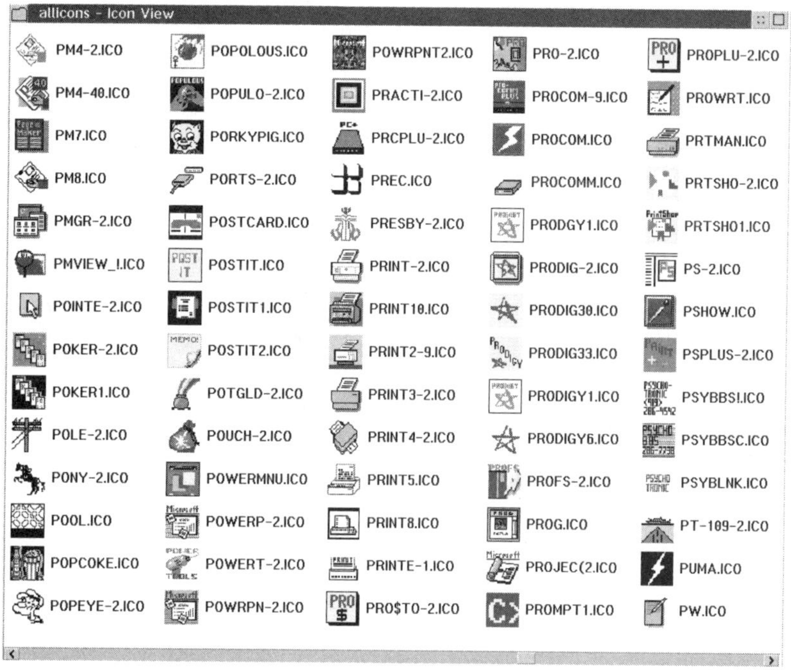
allicons - Icon View
PM4-2.ICO
PM4-40.ICO
PM7.ICO
PM8.ICO
PMGR-2.ICO
PMVIEW_!.ICO
POINTE-2.ICO
POKER-2.ICO
POKER1.ICO
POLE-2.ICO
PONY-2.ICO
POOL.ICO
POPCOKE.ICO
POPEYE-2.ICO
POPOLOUS.ICO
POPULO-2.ICO
PORKYPIG.ICO
PORTS-2.ICO
POSTCARD.ICO
POSTIT.ICO
POSTIT1.ICO
POSTIT2.ICO
POTGLD-2.ICO
POUCH-2.ICO
POWERMNU.ICO
POWERP-2.ICO
POWERT-2.ICO
POWRPN-2.ICO
POWRPNT2.ICO
PRACTI-2.ICO
PRCPLU-2.ICO
PREC.ICO
PRESBY-2.ICO
PRINT-2.ICO
PRINT10.ICO
PRINT2-9.ICO
PRINT3-2.ICO
PRINT4-2.ICO
PRINT5.ICO
PRINT8.ICO
PRINTE-1.ICO
PRO$TO-2.ICO
PRO-2.ICO
PROCOM-9.ICO
PROCOM.ICO
PROCOMM.ICO
PRODGY1.ICO
PRODIG-2.ICO
PRODIG30.ICO
PRODIG33.ICO
PRODIGY1.ICO
PRODIGY6.ICO
PROFS-2.ICO
PROG.ICO
PROJEC(2.ICO
PROMPT1.ICO
PROPLU-2.ICO
PROWRT.ICO
PRTMAN.ICO
PRTSHO-2.ICO
PRTSHO1.ICO
PS-2.ICO
PSHOW.ICO
PSPLUS-2.ICO
PSYBBSI.ICO
PSYBBSC.ICO
PSYBLNK.ICO
PT-109-2.ICO
PUMA.ICO
PW.ICO

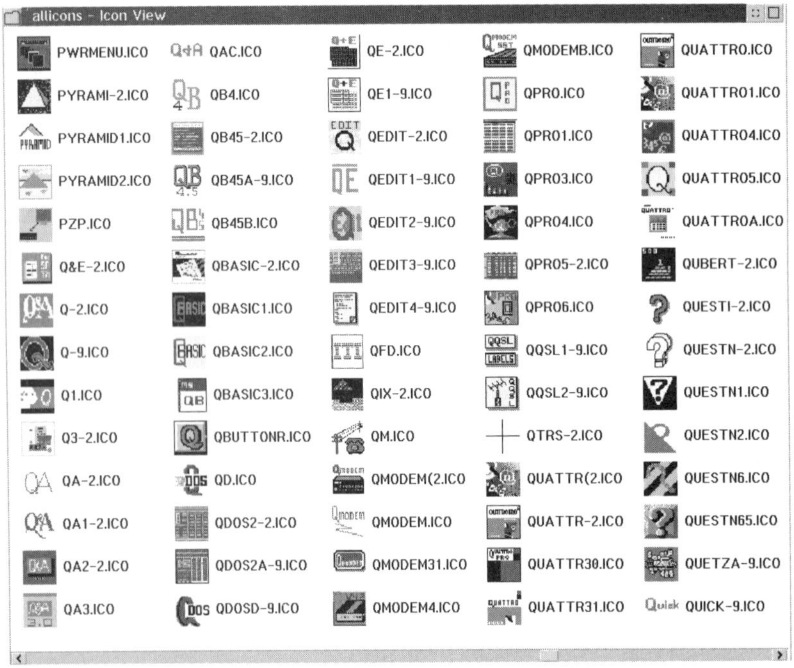
allicons - Icon View
PWRMENU.ICO
PYRAMI-2.ICO
PYRAMID1.ICO
PYRAMID2.ICO
PZP.ICO
Q&E-2.ICO
Q-2.ICO
Q-9.ICO
Q1.ICO
Q3-2.ICO
QA-2.ICO
QA1-2.ICO
QA2-2.ICO
QA3.ICO
QAC.ICO
QB4.ICO
QB45-2.ICO
QB45A-9.ICO
QB45B.ICO
QBASIC-2.ICO
QBASIC1.ICO
QBASIC2.ICO
QBASIC3.ICO
QBUTTONR.ICO
QD.ICO
QDOS2-2.ICO
QDOS2A-9.ICO
QDOSD-9.ICO
QE-2.ICO
QE1-9.ICO
QEDIT-2.ICO
QEDIT1-9.ICO
QEDIT2-9.ICO
QEDIT3-9.ICO
QEDIT4-9.ICO
QFD.ICO
QIX-2.ICO
QM.ICO
QMODEM(2.ICO
QMODEM.ICO
QMODEM31.ICO
QMODEM4.ICO
QMODEMB.ICO
QPRO.ICO
QPRO1.ICO
QPRO3.ICO
QPRO4.ICO
QPRO5-2.ICO
QPRO6.ICO
QQSL1-9.ICO
QQSL2-9.ICO
QTRS-2.ICO
QUATTR(2.ICO
QUATTR-2.ICO
QUATTR30.ICO
QUATTR31.ICO
QUATTRO.ICO
QUATTRO1.ICO
QUATTRO4.ICO
QUATTRO5.ICO
QUATTROA.ICO
QUBERT-2.ICO
QUESTI-2.ICO
QUESTN-2.ICO
QUESTN1.ICO
QUESTN2.ICO
QUESTN6.ICO
QUESTN65.ICO
QUETZA-9.ICO
QUICK-9.ICO

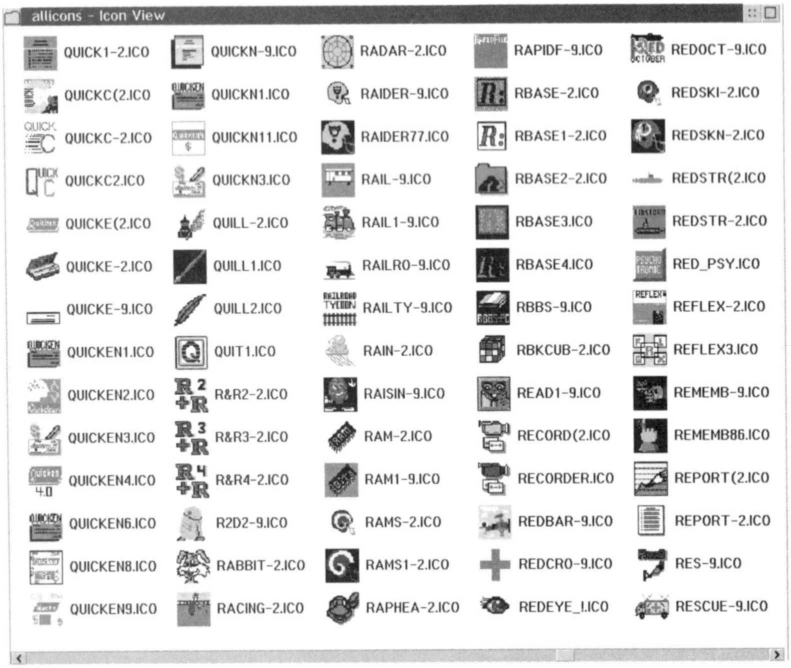
allicons - Icon View
QUICK1-2.ICO
QUICKC(2.ICO
QUICKC-2.ICO
QUICKC2.ICO
QUICKE(2.ICO
QUICKE-2.ICO
QUICKE-9.ICO
QUICKEN1.ICO
QUICKEN2.ICO
QUICKEN3.ICO
QUICKEN4.ICO
QUICKEN6.ICO
QUICKEN8.ICO
QUICKEN9.ICO
QUICKN-9.ICO
QUICKN1.ICO
QUICKN11.ICO
QUICKN3.ICO
QUILL-2.ICO
QUILL1.ICO
QUILL2.ICO
QUIT1.ICO
R&R2-2.ICO
R&R3-2.ICO
R&R4-2.ICO
R2D2-9.ICO
RABBIT-2.ICO
RACING-2.ICO
RADAR-2.ICO
RAIDER-9.ICO
RAIDER77.ICO
RAIL-9.ICO
RAIL1-9.ICO
RAILRO-9.ICO
RAILTY-9.ICO
RAIN-2.ICO
RAISIN-9.ICO
RAM-2.ICO
RAM1-9.ICO
RAMS-2.ICO
RAMS1-2.ICO
RAPHEA-2.ICO
RAPIDF-9.ICO
RBASE-2.ICO
RBASE1-2.ICO
RBASE2-2.ICO
RBASE3.ICO
RBASE4.ICO
RBBS-9.ICO
RBKCUB-2.ICO
READ1-9.ICO
RECORD(2.ICO
RECORDER.ICO
REDBAR-9.ICO
REDCRO-9.ICO
REDEYE_!.ICO
REDOCT-9.ICO
REDSKI-2.ICO
REDSKN-2.ICO
REDSTR(2.ICO
REDSTR-2.ICO
RED_PSY.ICO
REFLEX-2.ICO
REFLEX3.ICO
REMEMB-9.ICO
REMEMB86.ICO
REPORT(2.ICO
REPORT-2.ICO
RES-9.ICO
RESCUE-9.ICO

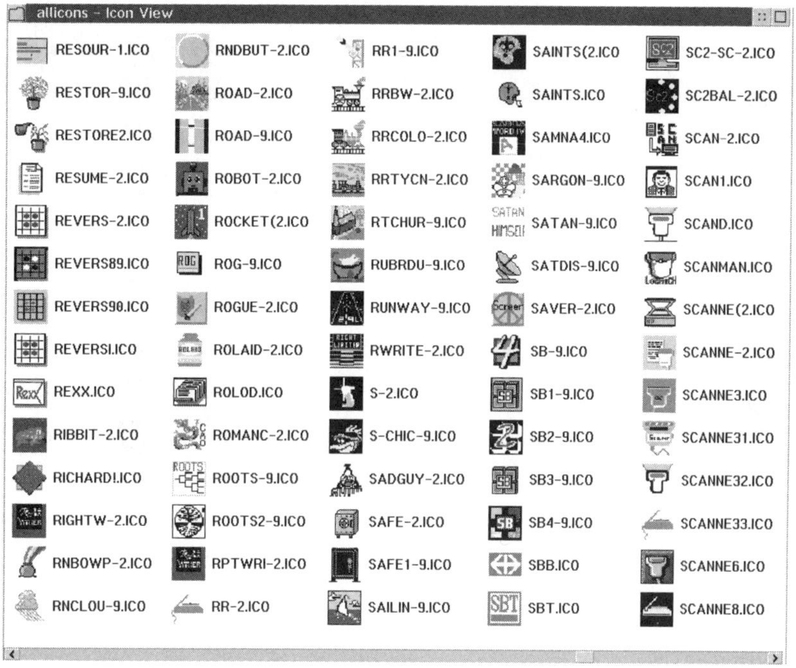
allicons - Icon View
RESOUR-1.ICO
RESTOR-9.ICO
RESTORE2.ICO
RESUME-2.ICO
REVERS-2.ICO
REVERS89.ICO
REVERS90.ICO
REVERSI.ICO
REXX.ICO
RIBBIT-2.ICO
RICHARDI.ICO
RIGHTW-2.ICO
RNBOWP-2.ICO
RNCLOU-9.ICO
RNDBUT-2.ICO
ROAD-2.ICO
ROAD-9.ICO
ROBOT-2.ICO
ROCKET(2.ICO
ROG-9.ICO
ROGUE-2.ICO
ROLAID-2.ICO
ROLOD.ICO
ROMANC-2.ICO
ROOTS-9.ICO
ROOTS2-9.ICO
RPTWRI-2.ICO
RR-2.ICO
RR1-9.ICO
RRBW-2.ICO
RRCOLO-2.ICO
RRTYCN-2.ICO
RTCHUR-9.ICO
RUBRDU-9.ICO
RUNWAY-9.ICO
RWRITE-2.ICO
S-2.ICO
S-CHIC-9.ICO
SADGUY-2.ICO
SAFE-2.ICO
SAFE1-9.ICO
SAILIN-9.ICO
SAINTS(2.ICO
SAINTS.ICO
SAMNA4.ICO
SARGON-9.ICO
SATAN-9.ICO
SATDIS-9.ICO
SAVER-2.ICO
SB-9.ICO
SB1-9.ICO
SB2-9.ICO
SB3-9.ICO
SB4-9.ICO
SBB.ICO
SBT.ICO
SC2-SC-2.ICO
SC2BAL-2.ICO
SCAN-2.ICO
SCAN1.ICO
SCAND.ICO
SCANMAN.ICO
SCANNE(2.ICO
SCANNE-2.ICO
SCANNE3.ICO
SCANNE31.ICO
SCANNE32.ICO
SCANNE33.ICO
SCANNE6.ICO
SCANNE8.ICO

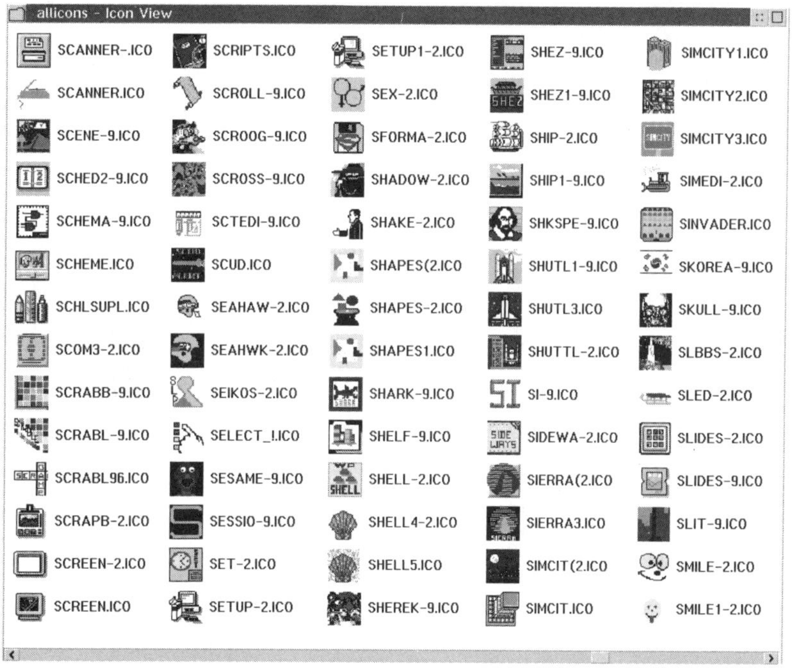
allicons - Icon View
SCANNER-.ICO
SCANNER.ICO
SCENE-9.ICO
SCHED2-9.ICO
SCHEMA-9.ICO
SCHEME.ICO
SCHLSUPL.ICO
SCOM3-2.ICO
SCRABB-9.ICO
SCRABL-9.ICO
SCRABL96.ICO
SCRAPB-2.ICO
SCREEN-2.ICO
SCREEN.ICO
SCRIPTS.ICO
SCROLL-9.ICO
SCROOG-9.ICO
SCROSS-9.ICO
SCTEDI-9.ICO
SCUD.ICO
SEAHAW-2.ICO
SEAHWK-2.ICO
SEIKOS-2.ICO
SELECT_!.ICO
SESAME-9.ICO
SESSIO-9.ICO
SET-2.ICO
SETUP-2.ICO
SETUP1-2.ICO
SEX-2.ICO
SFORMA-2.ICO
SHADOW-2.ICO
SHAKE-2.ICO
SHAPES(2.ICO
SHAPES-2.ICO
SHAPES1.ICO
SHARK-9.ICO
SHELF-9.ICO
SHELL-2.ICO
SHELL4-2.ICO
SHELL5.ICO
SHEREK-9.ICO
SHEZ-9.ICO
SHEZ1-9.ICO
SHIP-2.ICO
SHIP1-9.ICO
SHKSPE-9.ICO
SHUTL1-9.ICO
SHUTL3.ICO
SHUTTL-2.ICO
SI-9.ICO
SIDEWA-2.ICO
SIERRA(2.ICO
SIERRA3.ICO
SIMCIT(2.ICO
SIMCIT.ICO
SIMCITY1.ICO
SIMCITY2.ICO
SIMCITY3.ICO
SIMEDI-2.ICO
SINVADER.ICO
SKOREA-9.ICO
SKULL-9.ICO
SLBBS-2.ICO
SLED-2.ICO
SLIDES-2.ICO
SLIDES-9.ICO
SLIT-9.ICO
SMILE-2.ICO
SMILE1-2.ICO

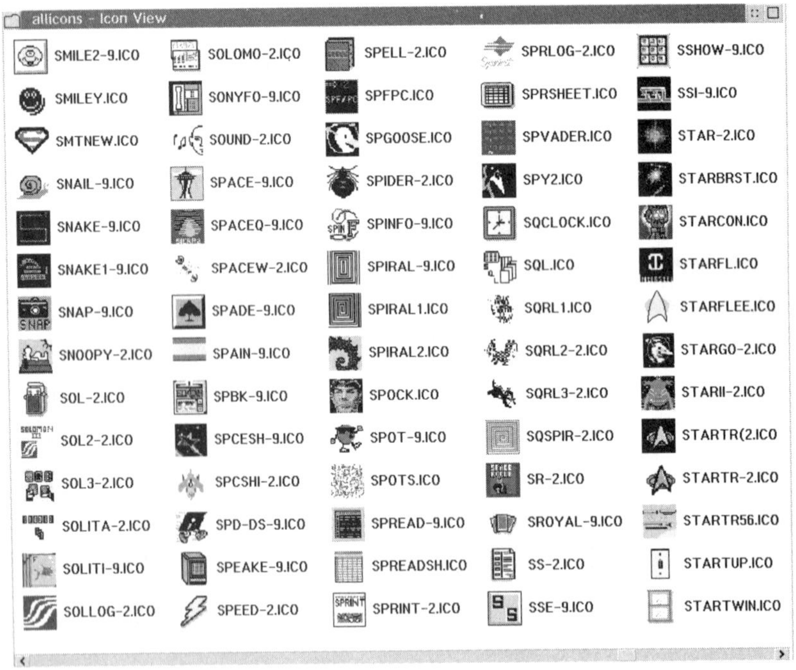
allicons - Icon View
SMILE2-9.ICO
SMILEY.ICO
SMTNEW.ICO
SNAIL-9.ICO
SNAKE-9.ICO
SNAKE1-9.ICO
SNAP-9.ICO
SNOOPY-2.ICO
SOL-2.ICO
SOL2-2.ICO
SOL3-2.ICO
SOLITA-2.ICO
SOLITI-9.ICO
SOLLOG-2.ICO
SOLOMO-2.ICO
SONYFO-9.ICO
SOUND-2.ICO
SPACE-9.ICO
SPACEQ-9.ICO
SPACEW-2.ICO
SPADE-9.ICO
SPAIN-9.ICO
SPBK-9.ICO
SPCESH-9.ICO
SPCSHI-2.ICO
SPD-DS-9.ICO
SPEAKE-9.ICO
SPEED-2.ICO
SPELL-2.ICO
SPFPC.ICO
SPGOOSE.ICO
SPIDER-2.ICO
SPINFO-9.ICO
SPIRAL-9.ICO
SPIRAL1.ICO
SPIRAL2.ICO
SPOCK.ICO
SPOT-9.ICO
SPOTS.ICO
SPREAD-9.ICO
SPREADSH.ICO
SPRINT-2.ICO
SPRLOG-2.ICO
SPRSHEET.ICO
SPVADER.ICO
SPY2.ICO
SQCLOCK.ICO
SQL.ICO
SQRL1.ICO
SQRL2-2.ICO
SQRL3-2.ICO
SQSPIR-2.ICO
SR-2.ICO
SROYAL-9.ICO
SS-2.ICO
SSE-9.ICO
SSHOW-9.ICO
SSI-9.ICO
STAR-2.ICO
STARBRST.ICO
STARCON.ICO
STARFL.ICO
STARFLEE.ICO
STARGO-2.ICO
STARII-2.ICO
STARTR(2.ICO
STARTR-2.ICO
STARTR56.ICO
STARTUP.ICO
STARTWIN.ICO

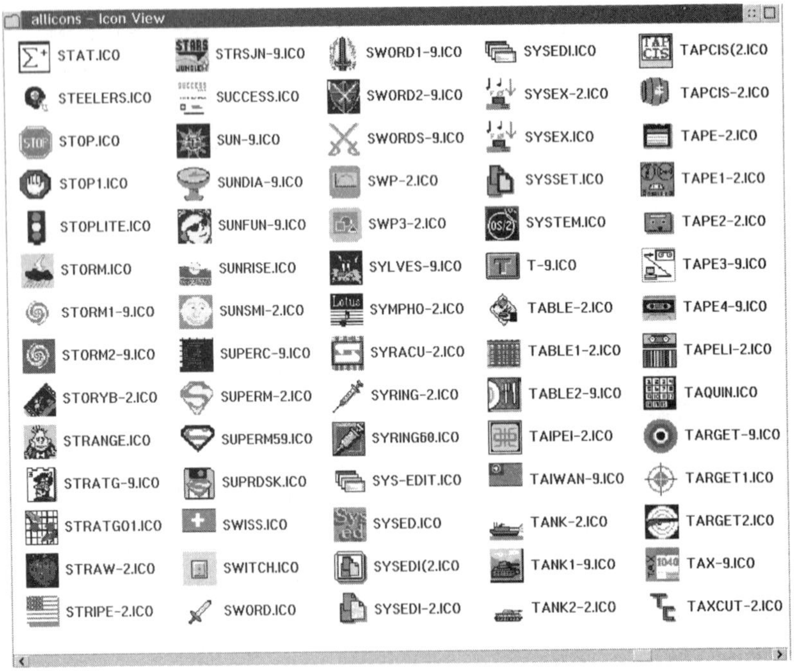
allicons - Icon View
STAT.ICO
STEELERS.ICO
STOP.ICO
STOP1.ICO
STOPLITE.ICO
STORM.ICO
STORM1-9.ICO
STORM2-9.ICO
STORYB-2.ICO
STRANGE.ICO
STRATG-9.ICO
STRATG01.ICO
STRAW-2.ICO
STRIPE-2.ICO
STRSJN-9.ICO
SUCCESS.ICO
SUN-9.ICO
SUNDIA-9.ICO
SUNFUN-9.ICO
SUNRISE.ICO
SUNSMI-2.ICO
SUPERC-9.ICO
SUPERM-2.ICO
SUPERM59.ICO
SUPRDSK.ICO
SWISS.ICO
SWITCH.ICO
SWORD.ICO
SWORD1-9.ICO
SWORD2-9.ICO
SWORDS-9.ICO
SWP-2.ICO
SWP3-2.ICO
SYLVES-9.ICO
SYMPHO-2.ICO
SYRACU-2.ICO
SYRING-2.ICO
SYRING60.ICO
SYS-EDIT.ICO
SYSED.ICO
SYSEDI(2.ICO
SYSEDI-2.ICO
SYSEDI.ICO
SYSEX-2.ICO
SYSEX.ICO
SYSSET.ICO
SYSTEM.ICO
T-9.ICO
TABLE-2.ICO
TABLE1-2.ICO
TABLE2-9.ICO
TAIPEI-2.ICO
TAIWAN-9.ICO
TANK-2.ICO
TANK1-9.ICO
TANK2-2.ICO
TAPCIS(2.ICO
TAPCIS-2.ICO
TAPE-2.ICO
TAPE1-2.ICO
TAPE2-2.ICO
TAPE3-9.ICO
TAPE4-9.ICO
TAPELI-2.ICO
TAQUIN.ICO
TARGET-9.ICO
TARGET1.ICO
TARGET2.ICO
TAX-9.ICO
TAXCUT-2.ICO

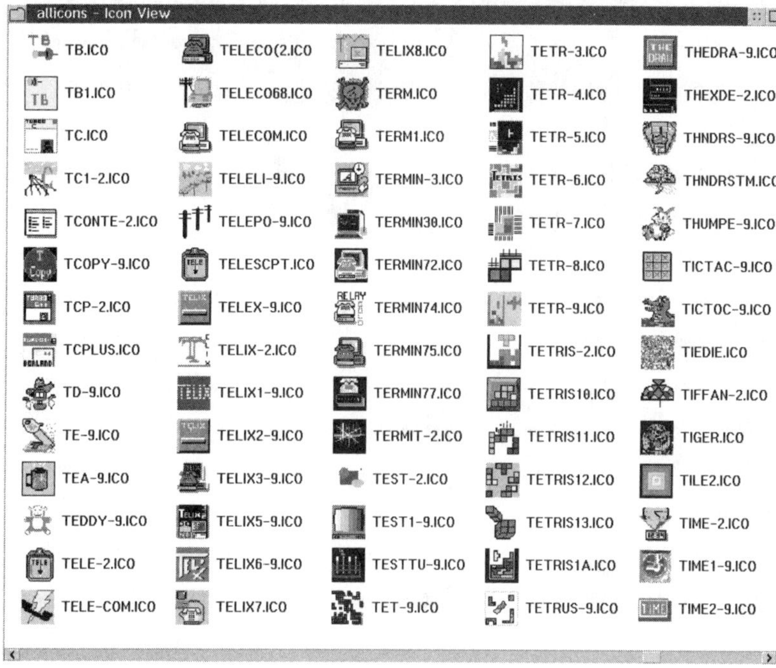
allicons - Icon View
TB.ICO
TELECO(2.ICO
TELIX8.ICO
TETR-3.ICO
THEDRA-9.ICO
TB1.ICO
TELEC068.ICO
TERM.ICO
TETR-4.ICO
THEXDE-2.ICO
TC.ICO
TELECOM.ICO
TERM1.ICO
TETR-5.ICO
THNDRS-9.ICO
TC1-2.ICO
TELELI-9.ICO
TERMIN-3.ICO
TETR-6.ICO
THNDRSTM.ICO
TCONTE-2.ICO
TELEPO-9.ICO
TERMIN30.ICO
TETR-7.ICO
THUMPE-9.ICO
TCOPY-9.ICO
TELESCPT.ICO
TERMIN72.ICO
TETR-8.ICO
TICTAC-9.ICO
TCP-2.ICO
TELEX-9.ICO
TERMIN74.ICO
TETR-9.ICO
TICTOC-9.ICO
TCPLUS.ICO
TELIX-2.ICO
TERMIN75.ICO
TETRIS-2.ICO
TIEDIE.ICO
TD-9.ICO
TELIX1-9.ICO
TERMIN77.ICO
TETRIS10.ICO
TIFFAN-2.ICO
TE-9.ICO
TELIX2-9.ICO
TERMIT-2.ICO
TETRIS11.ICO
TIGER.ICO
TEA-9.ICO
TELIX3-9.ICO
TEST-2.ICO
TETRIS12.ICO
TILE2.ICO
TEDDY-9.ICO
TELIX5-9.ICO
TEST1-9.ICO
TETRIS13.ICO
TIME-2.ICO
TELE-2.ICO
TELIX6-9.ICO
TESTTU-9.ICO
TETRIS1A.ICO
TIME1-9.ICO
TELE-COM.ICO
TELIX7.ICO
TET-9.ICO
TETRUS-9.ICO
TIME2-9.ICO

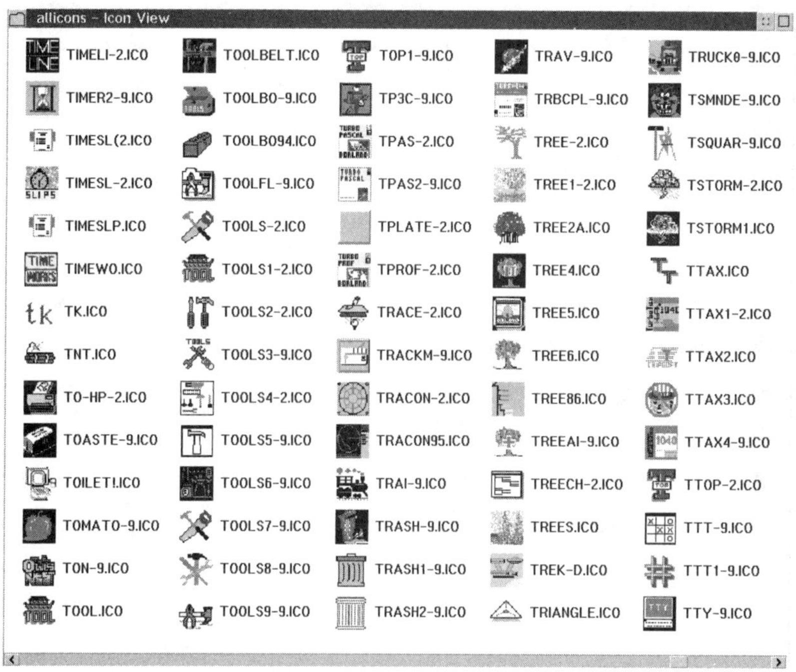
allicons - Icon View
TIMELI-2.ICO
TOOLBELT.ICO
TOP1-9.ICO
TRAV-9.ICO
TRUCK0-9.ICO
TIMER2-9.ICO
TOOLBO-9.ICO
TP3C-9.ICO
TRBCPL-9.ICO
TSMNDE-9.ICO
TIMESL(2.ICO
TOOLBO94.ICO
TPAS-2.ICO
TREE-2.ICO
TSQUAR-9.ICO
TIMESL-2.ICO
TOOLFL-9.ICO
TPAS2-9.ICO
TREE1-2.ICO
TSTORM-2.ICO
TIMESLP.ICO
TOOLS-2.ICO
TPLATE-2.ICO
TREE2A.ICO
TSTORM1.ICO
TIMEWO.ICO
TOOLS1-2.ICO
TPROF-2.ICO
TREE4.ICO
TTAX.ICO
TK.ICO
TOOLS2-2.ICO
TRACE-2.ICO
TREE5.ICO
TTAX1-2.ICO
TNT.ICO
TOOLS3-9.ICO
TRACKM-9.ICO
TREE6.ICO
TTAX2.ICO
TO-HP-2.ICO
TOOLS4-2.ICO
TRACON-2.ICO
TREE86.ICO
TTAX3.ICO
TOASTE-9.ICO
TOOLS5-9.ICO
TRACON95.ICO
TREEAI-9.ICO
TTAX4-9.ICO
TOILETI.ICO
TOOLS6-9.ICO
TRAI-9.ICO
TREECH-2.ICO
TTOP-2.ICO
TOMATO-9.ICO
TOOLS7-9.ICO
TRASH-9.ICO
TREES.ICO
TTT-9.ICO
TON-9.ICO
TOOLS8-9.ICO
TRASH1-9.ICO
TREK-D.ICO
TTT1-9.ICO
TOOL.ICO
TOOLS9-9.ICO
TRASH2-9.ICO
TRIANGLE.ICO
TTY-9.ICO

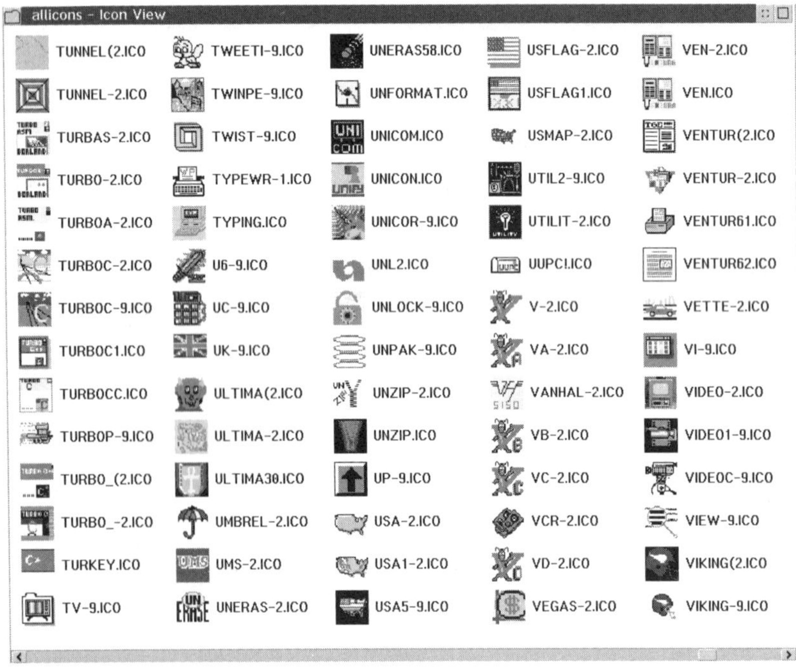
allicons - Icon View
TUNNEL(2.ICO
TUNNEL-2.ICO
TURBAS-2.ICO
TURBO-2.ICO
TURBOA-2.ICO
TURBOC-2.ICO
TURBOC-9.ICO
TURBOC1.ICO
TURBOCC.ICO
TURBOP-9.ICO
TURBO_(2.ICO
TURBO_-2.ICO
TURKEY.ICO
TV-9.ICO
TWEETI-9.ICO
TWINPE-9.ICO
TWIST-9.ICO
TYPEWR-1.ICO
TYPING.ICO
U6-9.ICO
UC-9.ICO
UK-9.ICO
ULTIMA(2.ICO
ULTIMA-2.ICO
ULTIMA30.ICO
UMBREL-2.ICO
UMS-2.ICO
UNERAS-2.ICO
UNERAS58.ICO
UNFORMAT.ICO
UNICOM.ICO
UNICON.ICO
UNICOR-9.ICO
UNL2.ICO
UNLOCK-9.ICO
UNPAK-9.ICO
UNZIP-2.ICO
UNZIP.ICO
UP-9.ICO
USA-2.ICO
USA1-2.ICO
USA5-9.ICO
USFLAG-2.ICO
USFLAG1.ICO
USMAP-2.ICO
UTIL2-9.ICO
UTILIT-2.ICO
UUPCI.ICO
V-2.ICO
VA-2.ICO
VANHAL-2.ICO
VB-2.ICO
VC-2.ICO
VCR-2.ICO
VD-2.ICO
VEGAS-2.ICO
VEN-2.ICO
VEN.ICO
VENTUR(2.ICO
VENTUR-2.ICO
VENTUR61.ICO
VENTUR62.ICO
VETTE-2.ICO
VI-9.ICO
VIDEO-2.ICO
VIDEO1-9.ICO
VIDEOC-9.ICO
VIEW-9.ICO
VIKING(2.ICO
VIKING-9.ICO

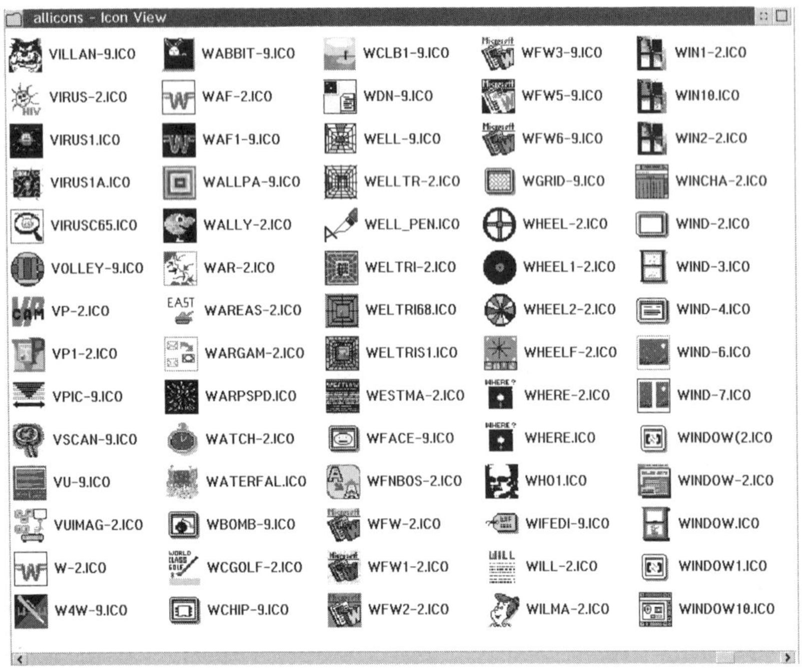
allicons - Icon View
VILLAN-9.ICO
VIRUS-2.ICO
VIRUS1.ICO
VIRUS1A.ICO
VIRUSC65.ICO
VOLLEY-9.ICO
VP-2.ICO
VP1-2.ICO
VPIC-9.ICO
VSCAN-9.ICO
VU-9.ICO
VUIMAG-2.ICO
W-2.ICO
W4W-9.ICO
WABBIT-9.ICO
WAF-2.ICO
WAF1-9.ICO
WALLPA-9.ICO
WALLY-2.ICO
WAR-2.ICO
WAREAS-2.ICO
WARGAM-2.ICO
WARPSPD.ICO
WATCH-2.ICO
WATERFAL.ICO
WBOMB-9.ICO
WCGOLF-2.ICO
WCHIP-9.ICO
WCLB1-9.ICO
WDN-9.ICO
WELL-9.ICO
WELLTR-2.ICO
WELL_PEN.ICO
WELTRI-2.ICO
WELTRI68.ICO
WELTRIS1.ICO
WESTMA-2.ICO
WFACE-9.ICO
WFNBOS-2.ICO
WFW-2.ICO
WFW1-2.ICO
WFW2-2.ICO
WFW3-9.ICO
WFW5-9.ICO
WFW6-9.ICO
WGRID-9.ICO
WHEEL-2.ICO
WHEEL1-2.ICO
WHEEL2-2.ICO
WHEELF-2.ICO
WHERE-2.ICO
WHERE.ICO
WHO1.ICO
WIFEDI-9.ICO
WILL-2.ICO
WILMA-2.ICO
WIN1-2.ICO
WIN10.ICO
WIN2-2.ICO
WINCHA-2.ICO
WIND-2.ICO
WIND-3.ICO
WIND-4.ICO
WIND-6.ICO
WIND-7.ICO
WINDOW(2.ICO
WINDOW-2.ICO
WINDOW.ICO
WINDOW1.ICO
WINDOW10.ICO

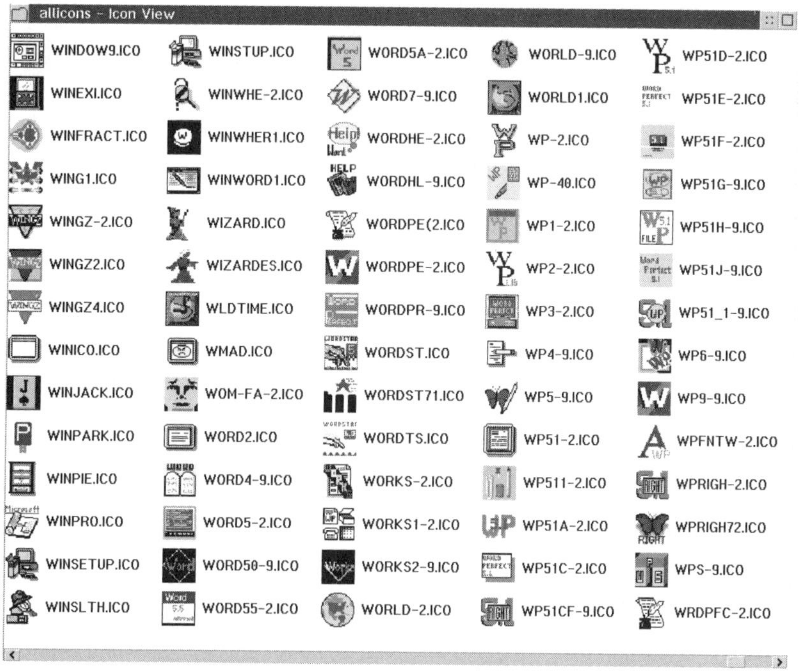
allicons - Icon View
WINDOW9.ICO
WINSTUP.ICO
WORD5A-2.ICO
WORLD-9.ICO
WP51D-2.ICO
WINEXI.ICO
WINWHE-2.ICO
WORD7-9.ICO
WORLD1.ICO
WP51E-2.ICO
WINFRACT.ICO
WINWHER1.ICO
WORDHE-2.ICO
WP-2.ICO
WP51F-2.ICO
WING1.ICO
WINWORD1.ICO
WORDHL-9.ICO
WP-40.ICO
WP51G-9.ICO
WINGZ-2.ICO
WIZARD.ICO
WORDPE(2.ICO
WP1-2.ICO
WP51H-9.ICO
WINGZ2.ICO
WIZARDES.ICO
WORDPE-2.ICO
WP2-2.ICO
WP51J-9.ICO
WINGZ4.ICO
WLDTIME.ICO
WORDPR-9.ICO
WP3-2.ICO
WP51_1-9.ICO
WINICO.ICO
WMAD.ICO
WORDST.ICO
WP4-9.ICO
WP6-9.ICO
WINJACK.ICO
WOM-FA-2.ICO
WORDST71.ICO
WP5-9.ICO
WP9-9.ICO
WINPARK.ICO
WORD2.ICO
WORDTS.ICO
WP51-2.ICO
WPFNTW-2.ICO
WINPIE.ICO
WORD4-9.ICO
WORKS-2.ICO
WP511-2.ICO
WPRIGH-2.ICO
WINPRO.ICO
WORD5-2.ICO
WORKS1-2.ICO
WP51A-2.ICO
WPRIGH72.ICO
WINSETUP.ICO
WORD50-9.ICO
WORKS2-9.ICO
WP51C-2.ICO
WPS-9.ICO
WINSLTH.ICO
WORD55-2.ICO
WORLD-2.ICO
WP51CF-9.ICO
WRDPFC-2.ICO

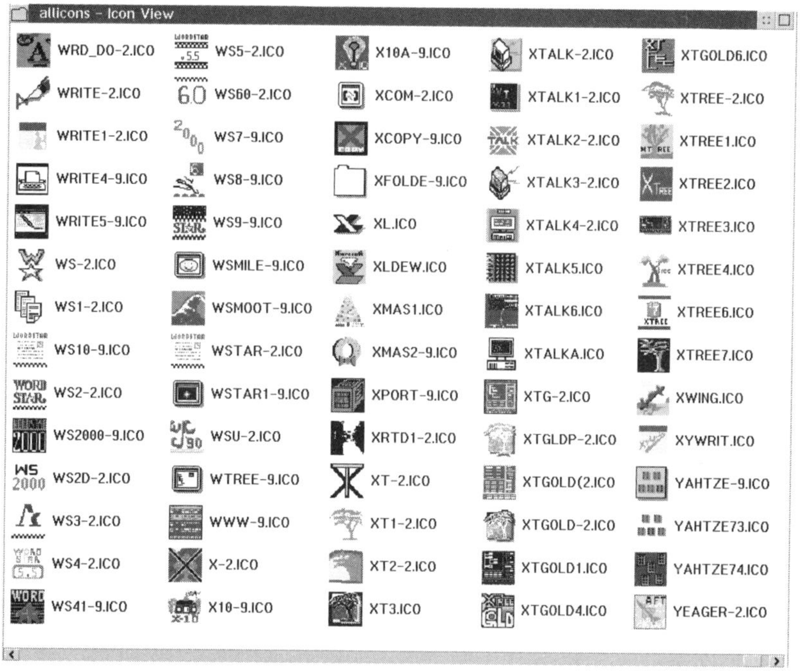
allicons - Icon View
WRD_DO-2.ICO
WS5-2.ICO
X10A-9.ICO
XTALK-2.ICO
XTGOLD6.ICO
WRITE-2.ICO
WS60-2.ICO
XCOM-2.ICO
XTALK1-2.ICO
XTREE-2.ICO
WRITE1-2.ICO
WS7-9.ICO
XCOPY-9.ICO
XTALK2-2.ICO
XTREE1.ICO
WRITE4-9.ICO
WS8-9.ICO
XFOLDE-9.ICO
XTALK3-2.ICO
XTREE2.ICO
WRITE5-9.ICO
WS9-9.ICO
XL.ICO
XTALK4-2.ICO
XTREE3.ICO
WS-2.ICO
WSMILE-9.ICO
XLDEW.ICO
XTALK5.ICO
XTREE4.ICO
WS1-2.ICO
WSMOOT-9.ICO
XMAS1.ICO
XTALK6.ICO
XTREE6.ICO
WS10-9.ICO
WSTAR-2.ICO
XMAS2-9.ICO
XTALKA.ICO
XTREE7.ICO
WS2-2.ICO
WSTAR1-9.ICO
XPORT-9.ICO
XTG-2.ICO
XWING.ICO
WS2000-9.ICO
WSU-2.ICO
XRTD1-2.ICO
XTGLDP-2.ICO
XYWRIT.ICO
WS2D-2.ICO
WTREE-9.ICO
XT-2.ICO
XTGOLD(2.ICO
YAHTZE-9.ICO
WS3-2.ICO
WWW-9.ICO
XT1-2.ICO
XTGOLD-2.ICO
YAHTZE73.ICO
WS4-2.ICO
X-2.ICO
XT2-2.ICO
XTGOLD1.ICO
YAHTZE74.ICO
WS41-9.ICO
X10-9.ICO
XT3.ICO
XTGOLD4.ICO
YEAGER-2.ICO

allicons - Icon View
YEAGER1.ICO
YEILD.ICO
YELBUD.ICO
YES
NO
YESNO-9.ICO
YOSEMI-9.ICO
WAY
YOURWA-2.ICO
ZGOLF-9.ICO
ZIP
ZIP-2.ICO
ZIP1-2.ICO
ZIP2-9.ICO
ZIPPER-2.ICO
ZM-2.ICO
ZM1-9.ICO
ZM2-9.ICO
ZORTECH
V2.0
ZORTEC-2.ICO
ZUG-2.ICO
ZUG1.ICO
ZUG2.ICO

D
Batch file icons

The two screen shots in this appendix show the icons for the batch files that come with this book. They are stored uncompressed in the \BAT subdirectory.

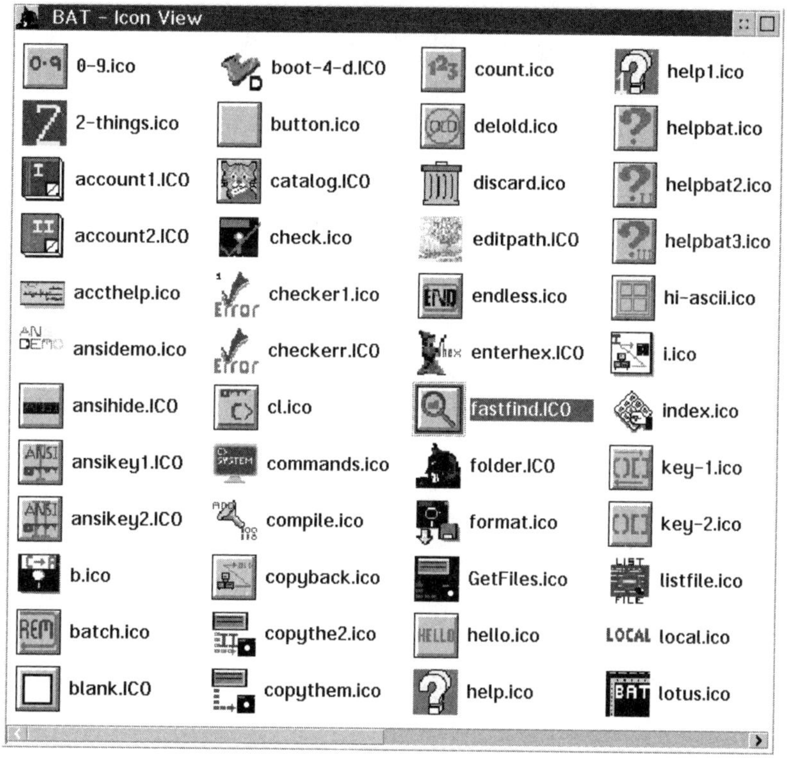

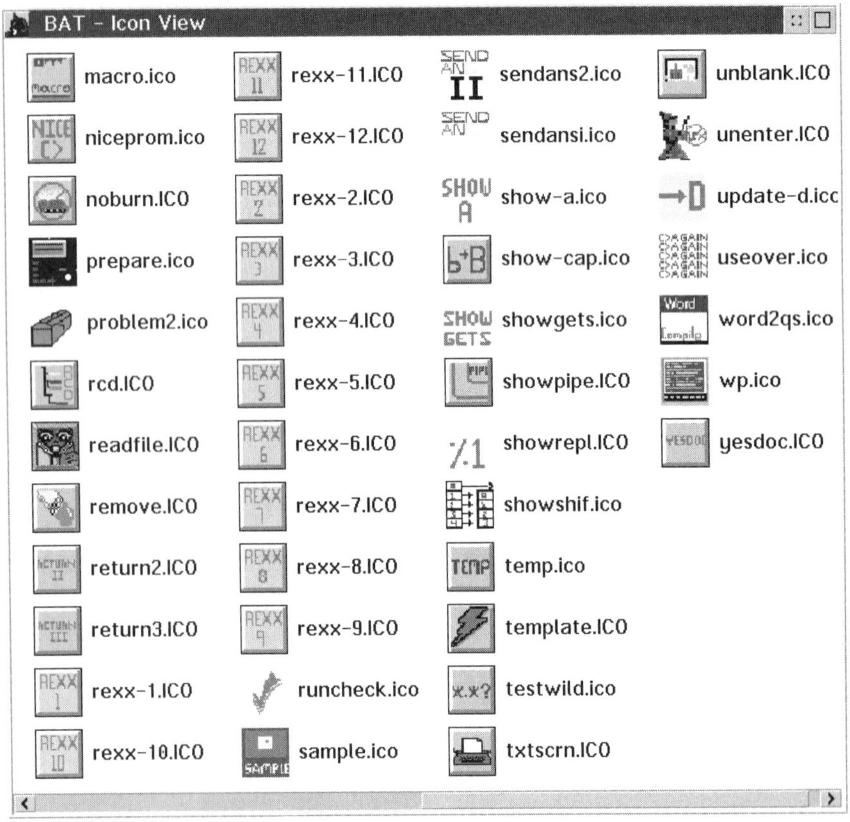
BAT - Icon View
macro.ico
niceprom.ico
noburn.ICO
prepare.ico
problem2.ico
rcd.ICO
readfile.ICO
remove.ICO
return2.ICO
return3.ICO
rexx-1.ICO
rexx-10.ICO
rexx-11.ICO
rexx-12.ICO
rexx-2.ICO
rexx-3.ICO
rexx-4.ICO
rexx-5.ICO
rexx-6.ICO
rexx-7.ICO
rexx-8.ICO
rexx-9.ICO
runcheck.ico
sample.ico
sendans2.ico
sendansi.ico
show-a.ico
show-cap.ico
showgets.ico
showpipe.ICO
showrepl.ICO
showshif.ico
temp.ico
template.ICO
testwild.ico
txtscrn.ICO
unblank.ICO
unenter.ICO
update-d.icc
useover.ico
word2qs.ico
wp.ico
yesdoc.ICO

E
Utility icons

The screen shot in this appendix show the icons for the utility programs that come with this book. They are stored uncompressed in the \UTILITY subdirectory.

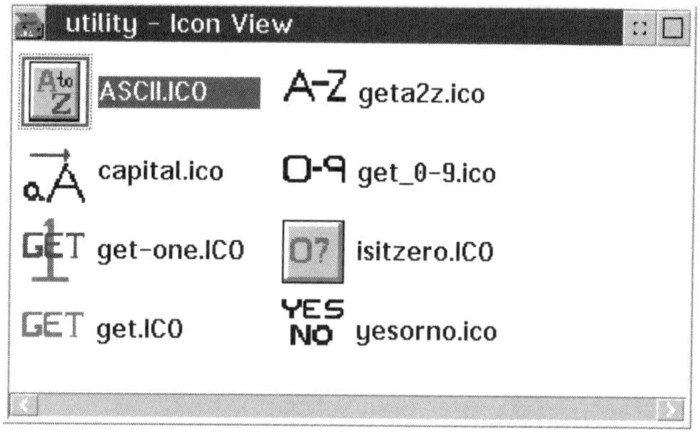

Index

Order Form for Readers Requiring a Single 5.25" Disk

This Windcrest/McGraw-Hill software product is also available on a 5.25"/1.2MB disk. If you need the software in 5.25" format, simply follow these instructions:

- Complete the order form below. Be sure to include the exact title of the Windcrest/McGraw-Hill book for which you are requesting a replacement disk.
- Make check or money order made payable to *Glossbrenner's Choice*. The cost is **$5.00** (**$8.00** for shipments outside the U.S.) to cover media, postage, and handling. Pennsylvania residents, please add 6% sales tax.
- Foreign orders: please send an international money order or a check drawn on a bank with a U.S. clearing branch. We cannot accept foreign checks.
- Mail order form and payment to:

  Glossbrenner's Choice
  Attn: Windcrest/McGraw-Hill Disk Replacement
  699 River Road
  Yardley, PA 19067-1965

Your disks will be shipped via First Class Mail. Please allow one to two weeks for delivery.

✂ ....

Windcrest/McGraw-Hill Disk Replacement

Please send me a replacement disk in 5.25"/1.2MB format for the following Windcrest/McGraw-Hill book:

Book Title ____

Name ____

Address ____

City/State/ZIP ____

DISK WARRANTY

This software is protected by both United States copyright law and international copyright treaty provision. You must treat this software just like a book, except that you may copy it into a computer in order to be used and you may make archival copies of the software for the sole purpose of backing up our software and protecting your investment from loss.

By saying "just like a book," McGraw-Hill means, for example, that this software may be used by any number of people and may be freely moved from one computer location to another, so long as there is no possibility of its being used at one location or on one computer while it also is being used at another. Just as a book cannot be read by two different people in two different places at the same time, neither can the software be used by two different people in two different places at the same time (unless, of course, McGraw-Hill's copyright is being violated).

LIMITED WARRANTY

Windcrest/McGraw-Hill takes great care to provide you with top-quality software, thoroughly checked to prevent virus infections. McGraw-Hill warrants the physical diskette(s) contained herein to be free of defects in materials and workmanship for a period of sixty days from the purchase date. If McGraw-Hill receives written notification within the warranty period of defects in materials or workmanship, and such notification is determined by McGraw-Hill to be correct, McGraw-Hill will replace the defective diskette(s). Send requests to:

Customer Service
Windcrest/McGraw-Hill
13311 Monterey Lane
Blue Ridge Summit, PA 17294-0850

The entire and exclusive liability and remedy for breach of this Limited Warranty shall be limited to replacement of defective diskette(s) and shall not include or extend to any claim for or right to cover any other damages, including but not limited to, loss of profit, data, or use of the software, or special, incidental, or consequential damages or other similar claims, even if McGraw-Hill has been specifically advised of the possibility of such damages. In no event will McGraw-Hill's liability for any damages to you or any other person ever exceed the lower of suggested list price or actual price paid for the license to use the software, regardless of any form of the claim.

MCGRAW-HILL, INC. SPECIFICALLY DISCLAIMS ALL OTHER WARRANTIES, EXPRESS OR IMPLIED, INCLUDING, BUT NOT LIMITED TO, ANY IMPLIED WARRANTY OF MERCHANTABILITY OR FITNESS FOR A PARTICULAR PURPOSE.

Specifically, McGraw-Hill makes no representation or warranty that the software is fit for any particular purpose and any implied warranty of merchantability is limited to the sixty-day duration of the Limited Warranty covering the physical diskette(s) only (and not the software) and is otherwise expressly and specifically disclaimed.

This limited warranty gives you specific legal rights; you may have others which may vary from state to state. Some states do not allow the exclusion of incidental or consequential damages, or the limitation on how long an implied warranty lasts, so some of the above may not apply to you.

IMPORTANT

Read the Disk Warranty terms on the previous page before opening the disk envelope. Opening the envelope constitutes acceptance of these terms and renders this entire book-disk package nonreturnable except for replacement in kind due to material defect.

If you need help with the enclosed disk . . .

This disk contains the batch file programs and icons presented in *OS/2 Batch Files To Go* (Windcrest book 4516), © 1994 by Windcrest, an imprint of McGraw-Hill, Inc.

The batch files and batch-file icons are contained in the \BAT subdirectory, the general-purpose icons in \ICON, and the utility icons in \UTILITY.

Please note that the icons contained in the \ICON subdirectory have been compressed with the LHA compression utility, which is contained in the \LHA subdirectory. Refer to appendix C for information on how to decompress these files.